Engaging
BOYS
in Treatment

D1072939

The Routledge Series on Counseling and Psychotherapy With Boys and Men

SERIES EDITOR

Mark S. Kiselica
The College of New Jersey

ADVISORY BOARD

Deryl Bailey
University of Georgia

Chris Blazina
Tennessee State University

J. Manuel Casas
University of California –
Santa Barbara

Matt Englar-Carlson
California State University –
Fullerton

Ann Fischer
Southern Illinois University –
Carbondale

David Lisak
University of Massachusetts – Boston

William M. Liu
University of Iowa

James O'Neil
University of Connecticut

Steve Wester
University of Wisconsin – Milwaukee

VOLUMES IN THIS SERIES

Volume 1:   *Counseling Troubled Boys: A Guidebook for Professionals*
Mark S. Kiselica, Matt Englar-Carlson, and Arthur M. Horne, editors

Volume 2:   *BAM! Boys Advocacy and Mentoring: A Leader's Guide to Facilitating Strengths-Based Groups for Boys – Helping Boys Make Better Contact by Making Better Contact With Them*
Peter Mortola, Howard Hiton, and Stephen Grant

Volume 3:   *Counseling Fathers*
Chen Z. Oren and Dora Chase Oren, editors

Volume 4:   *Counseling Boys and Men With ADHD*
George Kapalka

Volume 5:   *Culturally Responsive Counseling With Asian American Men*
William M. Liu, Derek Kenji Iwamoto, and Mark H. Chae, editors

Volume 6:   *Therapy with Young Men: 16–24 Year Olds in Treatment*
David A. Verhaagen

Volume 7:   *An International Psychology of Men: Theoretical Advances, Case Studies, and Clinical Innovations*
Chris Blazina and David S. Shen Miller, editors

Volume 8:   *Psychotherapy With Older Men*
Tammi Vacha-Haase, Stephen R. Wester, and Heidi Fowell Christianson

Engaging

BOYS

in Treatment

Creative
Approaches
to the
Therapy
Process

EDITED BY

CRAIG HAEN

Routledge
Taylor & Francis Group
New York   London

Routledge
Taylor & Francis Group
270 Madison Avenue
New York, NY 10016

Routledge
Taylor & Francis Group
27 Church Road
Hove, East Sussex BN3 2FA

© 2011 by Taylor and Francis Group, LLC
Routledge is an imprint of Taylor & Francis Group, an Informa business

Printed in the United States of America on acid-free paper
10 9 8 7 6 5 4 3 2 1

International Standard Book Number: 978-0-415-87405-2 (Hardback) 978-0-415-87406-9 (Paperback)

Library of Congress Cataloging-in-Publication Data

Haen, Craig.
    Engaging boys in treatment : creative approaches to the therapy process / Craig Haen.
        p. cm.
    Includes bibliographical references and index.
    ISBN 978-0-415-87405-2 (hardcover : alk. paper) -- ISBN 978-0-415-87406-9
(pbk. : alk. paper)
    1. Child psychotherapy. 2. Boys--Counseling of. I. Title.
    RJ504.H334 2010
    618.92'8914--dc22

2010037176

Visit the Taylor & Francis Web site at
http://www.taylorandfrancis.com

and the Routledge Web site at
http://www.routledgementalhealth.com

For Stephanie.
In the context of you, I've learned everything I
need to know about how to be a good man.

Contents

Series Editor's Foreword

From January 1980 to August 1981 I was employed as a mental health worker at the inpatient adolescent unit of Fair Oaks Hospital, a private psychiatric hospital located in Summit, New Jersey. Fresh out of college and a young man in my early 20s at the time, I was excited about being assigned to the adolescent unit because I was eager to gain experience working with teenagers diagnosed with psychiatric illnesses.

The team of professionals in our unit at Fair Oaks consisted of a psychiatrist, two clinical social workers, several psychiatric nurses, and eight mental health workers. Although my colleagues and I were dedicated to helping all of the boys and girls assigned to our care, the boys admitted to our hospital tended to pose more difficult challenges to our entire staff than the hospitalized girls did. These boys tended to be harder to reach than the girls on the unit. The boys were typically closed-up, defensive, disruptive, and hostile, posing numerous management problems for us on and off the unit. Their aggressive, defiant, and oppositional ways had the effect of making other people hate them, which made the task of treating them complicated and frustrating. In short, these troubled boys were their own worst enemies because they alienated the very people charged with helping them.

I saw it as a personal challenge to succeed with these boys—to find a way to connect with them so that they would trust me, accept my attempts to help them, and let me into their troubled hearts and minds. So, I reached out to every boy on our unit, no matter how uncooperative or rebellious he might be, in as many ways as I could, following my instincts and discovering a variety of strategies that worked and earned currency for me with these youngsters. I would hang out with them and talk with them about topics that were of interest to them. We would joke around and play sports together. I would bring in my guitar and sing songs to them and with them, particularly numbers that they found appealing. I invited them to play fun competitive games, such as taking a sponge ball and seeing who could hit a designated crack on the wall. We would shoot games of pool and play checkers, chess, or "hang man" together. We took turns drawing pictures and explaining what the pictures meant to us. We discussed our favorite cartoons, television shows, and movies, and our favorite actors, athletes, characters, and rock stars. We talked about girls and dating. I would tell them about the most exciting, happy, and scary moments in my life, and they would tell me about theirs. Amid these activities, they opened their psyches to me, sometimes in bits and pieces, and at other times in raging floods of self-disclosure, so that I got to know them as well as—if not more than—anyone knew them. And that awareness of their fears, joys, and sorrows earned for me the therapeutic currency that I had sought to acquire: I could get these boys to do what others could not get them to do, and they were helped significantly in the process.

Deeply inspired by these rewarding and successful experiences, I decided to dedicate my professional life to assisting troubled boys and their families when I left Fair Oaks to begin my graduate studies in psychology for the fall semester of 1981. So, over the course of the next 7 years, as I completed my master's degree in psychology at Bucknell University, my doctorate in counseling psychology at Penn State University, and my predoctoral internship at the University of Medicine and Dentistry of New Jersey, I read everything I could get my hands on about helping boys. Although the literature in counseling and clinical psychology of that period contained valuable information about the efficacy of different theoretical models with certain problems (e.g., aggression, hyperactivity, and substance abuse) that are common among boys, I was disappointed by the dearth of information about the clinical process with boys. At the time, there were no books explaining to clinicians in a systematic way how to work with boys in a creative and gender-sensitive manner as I had years earlier at Fair Oaks.

Addressing this glaring shortcoming of the literature was a major reason why I decided to start the Routledge Series on Counseling and Psychotherapy With Boys and Men. More than anything, I had hoped the series would attract scholars who not only had worked extensively with boys and men, but also had a keen understanding of what it means to be a male and what it takes to connect with boys and men in therapeutic contexts. Recognizing my vision for the series, Craig Haen, a gifted registered drama therapist, certified group psychotherapist, and clinical director of adolescent services for Kids in Crisis, in Greenwich, Connecticut, contacted me to discuss his vision for a potential book for my series that would be focused on creative approaches to treatment with boys. Each chapter would be written by an established author who is well respected in his or her chosen modality, or one who is new to publishing, but is currently engaged in groundbreaking work with boys.

I distinctly remember how I felt the day Craig and I discussed this idea over the phone. As I listened to Craig describe his plans for this project, I was taken back to my days at Fair Oaks, realizing this was the kind of book that would have been invaluable to me when I was a young mental health worker and would also be invaluable for any practitioner working with boys today and well in the future. Our respective visions for this project were in sync, and we agreed that Craig's book, *Engaging Boys in Treatment: Creative Approaches to the Therapy Process*, would be the next volume in this series.

In *Engaging Boys in Treatment*, Craig and his esteemed colleagues explain how to use physical play, animal-assisted therapy, computers and digital animation, superheroes in role play, metaphor and play therapy, and art therapy with all boys and how to tailor these tools and modalities to the needs of several special populations with boys. Cutting across all of these topics is information about the male socialization process and how masculinity issues must be incorporated into all therapeutic work with boys. Thus, this book contains a gold mine of ideas for enhancing the clinical process with boys in a male-sensitive way, and I welcome it to this series. Moreover, I am grateful to Craig and his colleagues for their many years of fine work with troubled boys, and for sharing their expertise with us through their impressive volume.

Mark S. Kiselica, Series Editor
The College of New Jersey
Ewing, New Jersey

About the Editor

Craig Haen, MA, RDT, CGP, LCAT, is a registered drama therapist and certified group psychotherapist. He is currently the assistant clinical director for Andrus Children's Center, in Yonkers, New York, and has a private practice working with children, adolescents, adults, and families in White Plains, New York. He serves as an adjunct faculty member at Manhattanville College, as well as on the advisory board for Creative Alternatives of New York. Craig has worked with boys and their families in shelters, community centers, hospitals, residential facilities, schools, and on Native American reservations, and was particularly active in the treatment of children, families, and service professionals in the New York area following the 9/11 terrorist attacks. He is a coeditor, with Anna Marie Weber, of *Clinical Applications of Drama Therapy in Child and Adolescent Treatment* (Brunner-Routledge, 2005) and is a doctoral student at Lesley University. He has presented trainings and published clinical papers internationally.

Contributors

Gregory Barker, PhD, received his doctorate in school/clinical child psychology from the University of Virginia in 1981. For over 25 years he has specialized in working with children and adolescents in residential, hospital, college counseling, and school settings. For 17 years, Gregory served as a consultant to the Bard College Counseling Center, and he is currently a school psychologist in the Rondout Valley public schools. He also has a private practice in Rhinebeck, New York, where he specializes in working with families and children.

Mark Beauregard, LCAT, RDT, is a drama therapist and creative arts therapist who has worked with children and adolescents in New York City in various mental health settings, from inpatient and outpatient psychiatry programs to school-based community programs. Mark researched the use of drama therapy with transgender and gender variant children and adolescents for his master's thesis at New York University and continues to present workshops on the importance of gender and sexual orientation sensitivity in psychotherapy.

John Bergman, MA, RDT/MT, is the founder/artistic director of Geese Theatre Company USA and has worked for 30 years in drama therapy and psychoeducational drama in New Zealand, Romania, Australia, England, and the United States. He has worked in all parts of criminal justice, particularly in corrections with prisoners, therapists, and correctional officers around issues of sexual offending, ethical behavior, and violence prevention. John was the clinical supervisor and program creator for AWARE, a therapeutic neurological program for adolescents in Melbourne, and is currently the senior clinician for Community Strategies Massachusetts, where he works to create therapeutic milieu programs and curricula that are brain/trauma/attachment based. He is a contributor to numerous books and the author of *Challenging Experience: An Experiential Approach to the Treatment of Serious Offenders* (Wood N' Barnes, 2003), which is currently in use in 15 countries.

Christine Bowers received her BA in psychology from California State Polytechnic University, Pomona. She has been interested in the human–animal bond ever since she was 11 years old, when a Saint Bernard visited her through a pet therapy program while she was hospitalized. She has also volunteered through various programs with her own therapy dogs for several years. She plans to pursue her master's in clinical psychology to obtain an MFT license in order to formally practice animal-assisted therapy.

Cassandra L. Brooks, MS, MA, communications specialist, is a project manager with a multicity research study of adolescent substance use behavior with the Department of Psychiatry at the University of Michigan. She was previously the project supervisor for the Fathers and Sons Project and program coordinator for the American Lung Association of Michigan. Her major interest is improving adolescent health choices through community-based interventions.

Cleopatra Howard Caldwell, PhD, social psychologist, is an associate professor of health behavior and health education at the School of Public Health. She is the associate director of the Program for Research on Black Americans, Institute for Social Research at the University of Michigan. Her research and publications focus on psychosocial and family factors as influences on the mental health and health risk behaviors for African American and Caribbean Black adolescents, intergenerational family relationships and early childbearing, discrimination, racial identity, adolescent well-being, research with Black churches, and intervention research using community-based participatory research approaches.

Kevin Creeden, MA, LMHC, is the director of assessment and research at the Whitney Academy in East Freetown, Massachusetts. He has over 30 years of clinical experience with children, adolescents, and their families. Kevin has worked extensively with physically and sexually aggressive youth. Over the past 15 years, his primary focus has been on issues of trauma and attachment difficulties, especially with regard to the neurological impact of trauma on behavior problems. Kevin trains and consults nationally and internationally to school systems as well as youth service and mental health agencies.

David A. Crenshaw, PhD, ABPP, RPT-S, is the director and founder of the Rhinebeck Child and Family Center, LLC. He is a past president of the New York Association for Play Therapy (2004–2008), board certified in clinical psychology by the American Board of Professional Psychology, a fellow in the Academy of Clinical Psychology, and a registered play therapist–supervisor by the American Association for Play Therapy. He is co-author with John B. Mordock of *A Handbook* *of Play Therapy With Aggressive Children* (Jason Aronson, 2007) and *Understanding and Treating the Aggression of Children: Fawns in Gorilla Suits* (Jason Aronson, 2007). He is the author of *Bereavement: Counseling the Grieving Throughout the Life Cycle* (Wipf and Stock Publishers, 2002), *Evocative Strategies in Child and Adolescent Psychotherapy* (Jason Aronson, 2007), and *Therapeutic Engagement of Children and Adolescents: Play, Symbol, Drawing and Storytelling Strategies* (Jason Aronson, 2008); and editor of *Child and Adolescent Psychotherapy: Wounded Spirits and Healing Paths* (Jason Aronson, 2010) and *Reverence in Healing: Honoring Strengths Without Trivializing Suffering* (Jason Aronson, 2010).

Jason Cruz, MA, ATR, earned his master's degree in expressive arts therapy from Lesley University, where he was selected by the faculty and student body to receive the Outstanding Achievement in Graduate Studies Award. Jason has presented lectures and workshops on arts education, young men's issues, learning differences, race, and culture at venues that include Harvard University, Endicott College, and the YMCA. Jason has worked at Raw Art Works (RAW) since 1996 and currently serves as clinical supervisor, leads three boys' groups, coleads a RAW Chiefs teen mentor program, and also leads a court-mandated program for juvenile offenders. Jason received the Isaac Monroe Award for Service to Youth and an outstanding service award from Help for Abused Women and Children (HAWC). Outside of RAW, Jason serves as a youth minister at St. Stephen's Episcopal Church and is co-founder of the Build a New America (BANA) Fellowship that addresses racial and social issues through action. He also has his own art and photography business, CRUZ ART.

Michael Currie, BSc (Hons), BMusPerf (Hons), PhD, MAPS, has offered innovative clinical treatments to adolescents and their families for over two decades. He spent 10 years of this time consulting to secondary schools and treating violent and aggressive boys on the verge of expulsion. His consultation included using a "boys group" approach and Latin American percussion to engage boys in treatment. He has written two books about this topic: *Doing Anger Differently: Helping Adolescent Boys* (2008) and *The Doing Anger Differently Manual: A School Group Program for Talking About Aggression* (2008), both available through Melbourne University Press. He is a training psychoanalyst and clinical member of the Freudian School of Melbourne. He conducts a psychoanalysis clinic privately and also publicly at the Centre for Psychotherapy. Michael is also a senior lecturer at the School of Psychology, University of Newcastle.

E. Hill De Loney, MA, psychologist, is the director of the Flint Odyssey House in Flint, Michigan. She was the community co-principal investigator of the Flint Fathers and Sons Project. She has extensive experience as a community-based participatory researcher, community organizer, and program developer, especially for youth programming. She is an expert in cultural competence in working with African American communities and families. She conducts cultural awareness trainings and workshops throughout the nation.

Avril Lindsay Dennis LCSW-R, ACSW, CGP, has been practicing as a social worker at the Children's Village for more than 15 years and is currently the program manager of the crisis residence. In her time at the Children's Village, she has specialized in the treatment of trauma and psychiatric illnesses of children and adolescents and explored creative ways to provide effective treatment. Since 2001, she has been involved in the East Coast Assistance Dogs program as a volunteer puppy raiser and trainer and co-chaired the inception of the Children's Village Animal-Assisted Therapy program. Avril is certified by ECAD as an AAT team with Jaguar, a yellow Labrador and Golden Retriever mix. She has presented on the uses of AAT throughout the New York area to residential treatment centers, hospitals, and conferences.

George Enfield, MHR, Med, PCC, is an independently licensed counselor in the State of Ohio where he currently works with preadolescent boys, infants, and toddlers. He has been working with children since 1993 and has a broad range of experience in individual and family counseling, in both inpatient and outpatient group settings. These experiences have taught him that boys provide both the language and desire to work on their own issues, and it is our job as clinicians to hear them and adapt what we know about counseling so that they are able to make the most of treatment.

Aubrey H. Fine, PhD, has been in the field of animal-assisted therapy for over 25 years and has been on the faculty of the California State Polytechnic University since 1981. His leadership among faculty and teaching excellence earned him the Wang Award in 2001, given to a distinguished professor within the California State University system, for exceptional commitment, dedication, and exemplary contributions within the areas of education and applied sciences. Aubrey is the editor of the most widely accepted book on the subject, *The Handbook on Animal-Assisted Therapy* (Academic Press, 2006), which is now in its second edition, and is the author of the book *Afternoons With Puppy* (Purdue University Press, 2007).

Erna Grönlund, BC-DMT, PhD, is professor emerita in dance education at the University of Dance in Stockholm, Sweden. She is founder of the Swedish Dance Therapy Association and she has developed and leads the Graduate Dance Therapy Program at the University of Dance in Sweden. She began her work with dance for physically handicapped children at a hospital in Stockholm. Since 1982, Erna has been working with children and adolescents with emotional disturbances. She has published many books and articles on dance therapy.

Steve Harvey, PhD, RPT/S, ADTR, is currently working as a consultant psychologist with the Child and Adolescent Mental Health Service in New Plymouth, New Zealand. Previously he worked as a child clinical psychologist in private practice in Colorado. Prior to becoming involved in the mental health profession, Steve was active in improvisational dramatic/dance performance and continues to practice physical storytelling. Besides being a clinical and educational psychologist, Steve is registered with the American Dance and Play Therapy Associations and has been an active contributor in the integration of all the expressive modalities in play therapy. Steve helped pioneer the field of family play therapy and has published many chapters on this topic in major play therapy texts as well as in publications by the American Psychological and American Psychiatric Associations. He has led workshops in family play therapy internationally for the last 20 years.

Serena Klempin, MSW, social worker, is a research associate at Columbia University School of Social Work. She has worked with the collaborative spin-off project between Columbia University and the University of Michigan based on the Fathers and Sons Program. The goal of this project is to replicate the intervention in four additional sites. She has substantial experience working with fatherhood service agencies in the New York area. Her research interest is in the area of fatherhood and sexual development among boys.

Andrew Malekoff, MSW, is executive director/CEO for North Shore Child and Family Guidance Center in Roslyn Heights, New York, and editor in chief of *Social Work With Groups*, a journal of community and clinical practice published by Taylor & Francis. He is the author of *Group Work With Adolescents* (The Guilford Press, 2007), now in its second edition.

Ronald B. Mincy, PhD, economist, is the Maurice V. Russell Professor of Social Policy and Social Work Practice, Columbia University School of Social Work, and director of the Center for Research on Fathers, Children and Family Well-Being. His research and publications focus on economic and social mobility, family support, income security policy, the U.S. labor market, and urban poverty. Prior to assuming his current position, Ronald was a senior program officer with the Ford Foundation, where his work focused on improving U.S. social welfare policies for low-income fathers, especially child support, and workforce development policies; he also served on the Clinton administration's Welfare Reform Task Force.

Darby Moore, LCAT, RDT-BCT, has worked with adolescents for 20 years as a primary therapist, creative arts therapist, and teacher. She received her MA from New York University and interned at St. Luke's Hospital Child and Adolescent Department, where she has worked for over a decade. She has also worked for the Department of Education as a substance abuse prevention and intervention specialist and with the Eastern Bronx Region Summer Program. She currently lives and works on the North Fork of Long Island.

Jane Rafferty, MA, sociologist, is a research area specialist with the Program for Research on Black Americans, Research Center for Group Dynamics, Institute for Social Research, University of Michigan. She specializes in analyzing data with complex survey designs, such as the National Survey of American Life. Jane is also the data analyst for the Michigan Center for Integrative Approaches for Health Disparities and the Flint Fathers and Sons Project at the School of Public Health.

Barbro Renck, RN, DrPH, is associate professor in Public Health Sciences at Karlstad University, Sweden. She is a psychiatric nurse and has worked for many years as a leader in psychiatric care. Her main research interests are issues of violence against women, especially those who have been sexually abused in childhood. Her psychiatric experiences are reflected in her research about dance/movement therapy for children and adolescents with emotional disturbances. She has published many articles and book chapters.

Laying the Ground

Boys and Therapy
The Need for Creative Reformulation

CRAIG HAEN

When Kyle was first referred to me, his mother warned me that it would be a difficult road working with her 10-year-old son. She reported that he had made mincemeat out of the previous three therapists, had nearly sabotaged a psychological evaluation, and was not at all pleased to be coming to see someone new. However, since I had a good track record of working with boys similar to Kyle, I wasn't deterred. In fact, when Kyle entered my office for the first time, it was with ease. I was quite pleased shortly after the session started to see him laughing, joking, tolerating my mentioning some of the difficulties he had been having at home, and eagerly taking out his cell phone to show me the photos he'd recently taken. All seemed positive as we began to establish an initial rapport.

However, a week later things shifted rapidly. As I attempted to move in the direction of even dipping our toes into discussing some of the reasons he had come into treatment—his tendency to have emotional outbursts in his therapeutic classroom, his rigid locking down whenever he didn't want to transition from an activity he loved, his inability to communicate his feelings to others, his tension-filled relationship with his father, and his excessive generalized fears about the world—Kyle withdrew. His responses to my exploratory questions barely constituted whole phrases, and my attempts to connect with him through a variety of tried-and-true, road-tested methods were met with minimal response. He did not like sports, had no interest in the superhero action figures in my office, could care less about drawing, had no desire to take a walk, thought board games were "stupid," did not want to show me his phone again, and could not formulate any suggestions of his own about how we might spend our time together.

I saw Kyle for a few months, determined to patiently await his evolution into being more open to me, and to therapy. At times I was able to maintain my steady resolve to meet him on his terms. In other moments, I impatiently wanted to provoke him into action. I invited his mother into a session to assist in the engagement process, I spoke with his teachers and father and sought their consultation, and I looked to colleagues for advice. Generally, though, I just sat spinning my wheels in mud.

At times, there were moments of hope—an occasional smile on Kyle's face in spite of himself, or a begrudging compliance to play or joke with me—but generally the sessions felt flat, uninteresting, and quite frustrating. I had successfully engaged so many other boys in my office, many more diagnostically challenging than Kyle. His parents were making progress in their sessions with me in better understanding their son and adapting new parenting strategies, so what was making working with *him* so difficult? I started to dread our individual sessions and would leave them with a strong somatic countertransferential response of my shins aching. As I reflected on this strange sensation, it occurred to me: I felt like this boy was kicking me in the shins every week! Internally, my want to hang in there and not be the fourth casualty in Kyle's therapy history wrestled with my desire to be practical and, in the name of progress and of releasing us all from this bind, refer him on to a colleague. It was around this time that Kyle started refusing to exit the car to come into the building where my office is located.

I made several attempts to invite him to join me, including talking with his disengaged visage through the closed window of the car (in the pouring rain!), sitting with his mother on the porch steps and conversing in the hopes that seeing us there might pique his curiosity, working with Mom on a behavioral plan of potential rewards for coming inside, and holding parenting sessions with her alone when he failed to join us. Kyle was making little progress at home and school. After a few weeks without his emerging from the car, it was time to admit defeat and refer him to a female colleague whom I hoped might have greater success than I had.

Readers may have felt a range of things while digesting the above anecdote from my practice, from bemused empathy and understanding, to a sense of camaraderie and recognition of their own past clinical "failures," to self-assurance as they generated clear ideas of where I went wrong or how they might have handled the case differently. Kyle's story provides an apt starting point for examining the treatment of boys because of this range of potential reactions. As Selekman (1997) noted, it is rare to hear stories of botched treatment at workshops or to read about therapeutic failures. We speak of our grand interventions, we write of our magical moments. But the truth is that therapy, particularly with children and adolescents, is rarely a tidy affair; nor does it often develop in a steady, sequenced fashion like the paced unfolding of a well-constructed play.

Treatment is frequently messy, characterized, in the words of Chaplin Kindler (2010), by "the unpredictable, nonlinear, often trial-and-error process of therapeutic interactions" (p. 257). At times it is mundane, and occasionally it falls flat on its face. Failures, though, are the bedrock on which our creativity is birthed. These moments

> can teach us to stop thinking that we are privileged experts, to bring back curiosity to help keep our minds dynamic, to ... be more therapeutically flexible, to avoid falling into the trap of one-size-fits-all therapy complacency, and to expand our horizons to learn about new therapy approaches and techniques that we can add to our therapeutic repertoire. (Selekman, 1997, p. 190)

As colleagues heard about my initial work on this book and the topic of engaging boys in treatment, it was often with a look of relief that they told me how challenging they found conducting therapy with boys at times, and how they worked hard but often felt as I had with Kyle—inept and defeated. They told me about times when the boys they had been seeing successfully for months abruptly withdrew from engagement and the therapy process, and they told me about the ones that got away, the boys they were never able to reach in order to begin a productive relationship. Occasionally, these colleagues also spoke to me about their success stories—the boys who connected to them and to the process, and those who made progress in spite of their initial hesitation. Sometimes these therapists talked with pride about the moments when they were able to step beyond their usual methods to design an intervention that helped them strike gold, clinically speaking.

While it is unrealistic to expect that one therapist will be effective with all clients, there was clearly a theme running through my colleagues' stories that validated the central premise of this book: boys and therapy make an odd and uneasy couple. Kiselica, Englar-Carlson, and Horne (2008a) support the idea that the traditional therapy environment and the ways in which many clinicians have been trained to relate to their clients are ill-suited to the relational, communicative, and affective styles of many boys. This poor fit can perpetuate treatment failure and lead to therapists making erroneous conclusions about boys, particularly that they are resistant, unemotional, and amotivated to change (Kiselica, 2005).

The concept of cultural competence has been given just due in the field of psychotherapy within the last decade, but often gender competence is overlooked (Sinclair & Taylor, 2004). Perhaps because most practitioners see gender from a binary standpoint of male and female, there doesn't appear to be much to integrate in terms of competency. If there are only two groups, how much could there be to learn? But if one takes into account the many other factors that serve to inform identity and that impact gender formation, including race, class, ethnicity, socioeconomic status, temperament, and culture (all undoubtedly not binary; Maccoby, 2004), then it seems that each client who crosses the threshold into the therapy office brings a unique set of needs and desires.

Keeney (2009) wrote, "If we believe each human being is unique, along with all the social interactions and contexts that hold the performance of everyday living, it follows that every clinical session should hold the possibility for conceiving a uniquely invented therapy" (p. 2). Indeed, being effective with boys in treatment requires our creativity, not just in how we approach the process, but also in how we take in and understand the client in front of us and how we formulate his difficulties. Keeney continued: "The creative therapist is ready to create, compose, construct, form, parent, give rise to, grow, bring forth, bring about, and bring into being an authentic, made-in-the-moment, one-of-a-kind session" (p. 2).

Phillips (2006), in defining creativity, wrestled with whether it involves the creation of something novel as described above (an original approach, an innovative theory) or whether it entails the discovery of something unique in what already exists (highlighting the overlooked aspects of an object of inquiry, questioning what was previously assumed to be fact). Like him, I believe that both results are essential components of the creative process. In this book, the chapters to follow will offer many approaches to treatment—novel in their existence beyond the overtrodden paths of mainstream therapy, inventive in their reformulation of clinical doctrine. I hope they will offer readers tools to utilize as they meet boys in their offices, schools, community centers, and hospital units and work to refashion the therapeutic encounter—in its initial fostering of engagement and relationship, in the formulation of problems and strengths, and in its sustainment through the moments of listlessness to the creation of something transformative.

As the contributors provide the novel approaches, I endeavor in this chapter to critically examine the existing clinical and research literature that describes the tendencies and preferences of boys. In doing so, I will advocate for expanding our existing notions of who boys are and, in turn, widening the lens through which we view our male clients. In the spirit of narrative therapy, I will hone in on the less explored parts of boys, the alternative or untold aspects of their stories. I have been preceded in this quest by many fine thinkers and practitioners in the field, and I will attempt to connect their ideas as they have influenced my own while offering a rationale for creative alterations to the therapy process that ultimately promote treatment efficacy.

UNDERSTANDING BOYS

How a boy knows himself to be a boy, or not, continues to matter. How he comes to that knowledge in a social world continues to matter. How that social knowledge is internalized and becomes psychological continues to matter. We would, however, do well to live with the certainty that someday, even today, we will be wrong.

—Ken Corbett (2009, p. 15)

Like many in the field interested in the needs of boys, I was deeply inspired by the outpouring of books that appeared in the clinical and mainstream literature in the late 1990s. These tomes (the most popular of which included Garbarino, 1999; Pollack, 1998; Kindlon & Thompson, 1999) were valuable in bringing attention to boys and in advancing thinking about them. I carried the ideas they presented about the crisis of masculinity with me into the world and into the therapy office, as well as citing them in my own writings. But over the next decade, dissonance began to gnaw at me.

Some of the detrimental components of male socialization these authors described—the abandonment of boys by society, the pressures placed on them to suppress emotions, and the oppressive dictates of the boy code—continued to resonate. But I also began to notice that their descriptions of boys did not always adequately capture my own experience growing up male and becoming a man in Western society. And I was starting to see more and more boys, both in a clinical context and out in the world at large, who didn't seem to be the emotionally vacuous, alexithymic, relationally inept, passive victims of socialization I was taught to expect. Indeed, traditional, hegemonic masculinity continues to exist as a detrimental force, but so many of the young people I work with don't seem to fit the bill like they used to. They are more able to talk about their feelings, they question some of the more curious messages about who men should be, and they seem more open and accepting of homosexuality. Are boys evolving, or did these texts not fully capture the diversity of male experience?

To answer these questions, I returned to the literature. Quickly, I started to appreciate how murky the business of wading through studies of gender can become. Clinical discussions were so easily entwined with politics, educational policy debates, and an ensuing competition over which gender was more truly in crisis, that it became difficult to separate the signal from the noise. As Roiphe (1994) wrote, "It often seems that when we stray into the world of sexual politics every gesture is exaggerated, every conflict magnified. Our conversations so easily turn into arguments, thoughts become polemics, pulses race, passions rise" (p. xiii).

The problem with the "boy crisis" is not that it's categorically untrue. When taken together, statistics about underachievement, suicide rates, violence and aggression, and substance use are certainly alarming. The trouble comes when the message that we must pay better attention to some of our boys and assist them in areas where they may struggle gets extended into the dictum that *all* boys are at risk for mental health problems, school failure, substance abuse, and the commission of violent acts and oppression. This monolithic, deficit-based view unjustly lumps boys into one category with little appreciation for diversity and individuality, or strengths and resilience (Kimmel, 2004; Kiselica et al., 2008a; Weaver-Hightower, 2008). Saval (2009) summed up this tendency toward hyperbole:

> Most available books about boys ... focus on our young men as a homogenous whole, a collective entity with no discernible varying characteristics. Boys are often thought of as unknowable enigmas who *all* seem to need help. Boys are in crisis. Boys have ADD. Boys are unemotional. Boys don't talk. Boys are on the verge of apocalyptic self-destruction. Over the course of the past decade, boys have been reduced to an anxiety-inducing headline. (pp. 2–3)

Bettis and Sternod (2009) pointed out that the notion of boys being in crisis is not a new phenomenon, but instead a historically cyclical one that also appeared over 100 years ago when similar concerns were expressed. Like Eliot (2009), I believe it's time for a truce in the gender crisis competition. Understanding one sex's needs should not come at the expense of ignoring the other's, nor should boys be viewed in a way that excludes the contributions and concerns of girls. She wrote:

> The problem with each crisis is that it has demonized the other sex, pitting boys and girls against each other, as if learning and achievement were zero-sum games. The truth, however, is that neither sex is in serious trouble ... the difference in achievement between the sexes remains much smaller than the gaps in achievement among different racial and economic groups, where we should no doubt be directing more of our energy. Nor have the gender gaps changed precipitously in the last two decades. In fact, both sexes are earning higher grades, graduating from high school at higher rates, and attending college in greater numbers than ever before. Neither sex is sinking into the abyss predicted by each wave of crisis books. (Eliot, 2009, p. 18)

This is not to say that the books that broached the discussion of the clinical needs of boys were without merit. Zeki (2009) describes how the field of neurobiology is presently excessively focused on determining the structure and function of the human brain, delineating what is common among people. He attributes this to a dearth in technological tools that allow scientists to reliably study variability—how and why brain function differs across individuals, or within an individual across cultures and circumstances. The current work on brain similarities provides a necessary precursor to better understanding individualism and variability. Similarly, the boy crisis literature initiated important discourse about how to best help boys that has paved the way for more precise clinical dialogues. This book is intended to further those conversations and, in so far as it is possible, move the discussion of boys away from the political arena and into the play rooms and therapy offices where treatment takes place.

BEYOND SIMILARITIES AND DIFFERENCES

> There is a secret about the scientific method which every scientist knows and takes as a matter of course, but which the layman does not know.... The secret is this: Science cannot utter a single word about an individual molecule, thing, or creature in so far as it is an individual but only in so far as it is like other individuals.
>
> —Walker Percy (1954/2000, p. 22)

While a well-known nursery rhyme from the early 19th century told us that boys were made of snips, snails, and puppy dogs' tails while girls were fashioned out of sugar, spice, and all things nice, science tells us that all humans are composed largely of the same materials. Males and females deviate by only one chromosome out of 46 pairs, making us 98% chromosomally similar (Synnott, 2009) and our genetic coding more than 99% identical (Brizendine, 2006). Theorists vary widely in how much they consider that small percentage of difference to matter, from those who feel that minor variations in construction add up to wide gulfs in application, behavior, and process (Brizendine, 2006, 2010; Sax, 2005, 2007), to others who believe that the results of gender difference studies have been irresponsibly inflated to promote an unrealistic picture of the real gaps between the sexes (Eliot, 2009, 2010).

Studies show relatively few differences in the attachment patterns of infant boys and girls, suggesting that both sexes have equivalent desires for the safety and dyadic regulation provided by relationships, and equal capacities to seek them out (Berzoff, 2008; Shilkret & Shilkret, 2008). Similarly, no large-scale differences in infant temperament, distress, or regulatory behaviors have been reliably identified between boys and girls (Buss, Brooker, & Leuty, 2008).

In the realm of psychological traits and value differences, there is relatively little predictable divergence between the sexes, except in the area of political polling (Rudman & Glick, 2008; Synnott, 2009). Similarly, differences in emotion, cognitive capacity, and interpersonal behavior are primarily small to moderate (Eliot, 2009). In fact, across domains, boys and girls, men and women, are far more similar than they are disparate, with greater variations being observed within the sexes than between them (Kiselica & Englar-Carlson, 2008; Pinker, 2008). Even linguist Deborah Tannen (1990), whose theories about the distinct ways men and women communicate have been widely read and cited, recently conceded:

> Men's and women's conversational styles are more alike than they may appear. Although these styles may seem opposite, they can be used for similar purposes. Boys and men are also concerned with connection, and girls and women with power, even as they may have different ways of pursuing these goals. (Tannen, 2010, p. 57)

In the area of neuroscience, there are fewer differences between boys' and girls' brains than one would think. Eliot (2009) wrote, "Certainly, there are some data showing subtle sex differences in children's sensory processing, memory and language circuits, frontal-lobe development, and overall neural speed and efficiency.... But overall, boys' and girls' brains are remarkably alike" (p. 5). Two reliable findings are that boys' brains, on average, are generally larger by about 10%, with greater cerebral and cerebellum volume than females' (Day, Chiu, & Hendren, 2005; Giedd, 2008; Nopoulos, Flaum, O'Leary, & Andreasen, 2000). At the same time, girls' brains move through the neuromaturation process—which involves pruning and myelination—earlier, reaching full maturity one to two years before boys' brains (Giedd, 2008; Johnson, Blum, & Giedd, 2009).

The discrepancy in brain size parallels the general difference in physical size and strength in males (such as greater upper arm strength) (Eliot, 2009; Rudman & Glick, 2008), while the variation in the trajectory of brain maturation is connected to the earlier pubertal timing of girls, which also occurs one to two years earlier than it does for boys (Day et al., 2005). While these distinctions may be indicative of the brains of boys and girls having "different areas of vulnerability, specialization, or abilities" (Day et al., 2005, p. 177), these conclusions have yet to be reliably supported by neuroscience research. Of greater concern may be the impact that the differing rates of brain development have on gender differences within specific age groups, which I will elaborate on later in the chapter.

The preliminary research on the differences in the brains of males and females has been met with excitement among gender theorists, and some have fashioned careers around identifying neural distinctions in the ways boys and girls learn, socialize, aggress, and emote based on existing data. However, the field of neuroscience, as Zeki (2009) described above, is still in its infancy. Scientists caution us against making sweeping generalizations about the impact of brain maturation and gender variations until further research can be conducted to better understand the results of initial inquiries in this growing field (Johnson et al., 2009).

It is worth making mention of the ideas of Baron-Cohen (2003), who hypothesized that there are indeed systematic differences between what he labels the female brain and the male brain. In his estimation, female brains are biased in their hardwiring toward empathy, while male brains are more selectively hardwired for the understanding and building of systems. He extended these ideas to explain why more males are diagnosed with autism, a condition marked by the absence of social interest and a sharp deficit in theory of mind. Baron-Cohen (2003) was careful to emphasize that "not all men have the male brain, and not all women have the female brain" (p. 8), even though he advocated that more men are systematizers and more women empathizers. The studies on which Baron-Cohen based his conclusions, particularly one that found that infant boys are more likely to stare at a mobile than a human face, have been subsequently criticized on methodological grounds and have yet to be successfully replicated (Eliot, 2009; Nash & Grossi, 2007).

When researchers speak of gender differences as patterns, often what is being compared are the differences between outliers—those who fall at the extreme ends of the continuum—as opposed to those overlapping within the middle ranges. By ignoring the overlap, we miss the ways in which some girls, for example, may exceed boys on measures of aggression or impulsivity, while some boys may have a greater capacity for empathy and verbalizing than girls. According to Pinker (2008), in many studies males tend to be more variable in their scores than women.

> Compared to women, there are more men who are extreme.... So there are more very stupid men and more very smart ones, more extremely lazy ones and more willing to kill themselves with work.... The bell curve simply looks different for males, with more men at the tail ends of the distribution, where their measured skills are either dismal, stellar, or a mix of the two. So, even though male and female averages are the same, there are more male outliers—and more "normal" women overall. Comparing men and women in the middle ranges one finds fewer sex differences, but at the extremes the picture looks—well—extreme. (pp. 13–14)

Similarly, many of the early "boy crisis" authors based their findings on boys they were seeing in clinics, as opposed to more normative, community samples. As such, the gender differences they spoke about may have been more pronounced than those that actually existed in the general population. By focusing solely on the differences between two groups, we miss the important subdomains of strength and unique capacities that each gender possesses (Eliot, 2009). The result is that clinicians can find themselves working, in the words of Corbett (2009), "more often with ideas about boys than with boys themselves" (p. 216).

Maccoby (2004), who has studied gender differences for the better part of four decades, recently opined, "We have spent a great deal of time and effort examining sex differences. Now I think we would benefit by focusing more on each sex in its own terms" (p. 15). This transition toward examining each gender beyond how it may differ from the other and better understanding the wide variety of within-sex differences allows us to move from a position of one-size-fits-all masculinity to one of appreciating the depth and breadth of boys. Corbett (2009) concurred: "Variance is read as disturbance or illness; rarely is variance recognized for the ways in which it speaks to the range of that which is normal, and never is it read for its potential, or relished for its ideality" (p. 97).

By attending to variability, we can appreciate the ways in which boys are, in some respects, not the same as they were 20 years ago. For example, in the area of romantic relationships, we now find many more adolescent boys who are not just looking to gratify lust or attain sexual conquests like belt notches, as the boy crisis literature suggested. We can identify many more boys today who are interested in the affiliative and intimate aspects of being in connection with another person (Tolman, Spencer, Harmon, Rosen-Reynoso, & Striepe, 2004). Likewise, Korobov and Thorne (2006) suggested that the intimacy practices of young adult males may be expanding in accordance with what they view as a cultural shift away from traditional gender roles.

It is a difficult balancing act to discuss boys as unique individuals while also placing them in the context of their gender. Doing so requires holding two dialectical notions in tandem while appreciating the tension between them. These two notions are that each boy is a unique individual, different from those around him, while also a member of his gendered group and subject to being a boy like other boys. Moving forward, I will attempt to hold both positions while discussing boys in their own right. I will refer to gender comparisons only in so far as they serve to refute those notions about boys that have become shibboleths.

EXPANDING NOTIONS ABOUT HOW
BOYS FORM IDENTITIES

I find the question of whether gender differences are biologically determined or socially constructed to be deeply disturbing. This way of posing the question implies that people, men and women alike, are either genetically determined or a product of socialization—that there is no voice—and without voice, there is no possibility for resistance, for creativity, or for a change whose wellsprings are psychological.

—Carol Gilligan (1993, p. xix)

Most scientists readily agree that human development involves a complex interplay between biological priming and its interaction with environment and experience. We generally no longer see human beings as solely the sum of their genetic wiring nor their upbringing. Why, then, in the field of gender does the debate between nature and nurture continue with such force? On one extreme end of the continuum reside those theorists who adhere to Freud's notion that anatomy is destiny, emphasizing the roles of body chemistry, genetics, and hormones (specifically testosterone) in shaping male behavior. On the far side sit the social constructionists, who believe that gender is entirely a product of human socialization and conditioning, and that, as such, the construct of masculinity necessarily varies based on the demands of culture and time period.

Neuroscience has helped to clarify the debate by demonstrating the ways that brains, in their essential neuroplasticity, or malleability, are powerfully shaped by the experience that comes from early nurturing and lifelong learning (Robertson & Shepard, 2008; Schwartz & Begley, 2002). A proponent of this theory, Eliot (2009) emphasized that "mental and emotional abilities are not fixed. Second: they are *not* strongly determined by gender. For most traits, there is … plenty of room for learning or plasticity to raise achievement in any child" (p. 301). The relationship of brains and behavior suggests holding a both/and position regarding gender differences—that who boys are is related to both biological factors and social learning, and the two serve to inform one another in dialogic ways.

As Gilligan asserted above, debating the primary factors that serve to inform gender can often mean losing sight of the active, agentic role that both boys and girls play in the gendering process (Chu, 2004; Sinclair & Taylor, 2004). As Aydt and Corsaro (2003) highlighted, "Children are not merely the passive recipients of adult culture, they interpret and reproduce gender roles in ways that are often surprising to us" (p. 1307). By viewing them as active players in the gendering process, we can move away from the idea of boys as victims of socialization and instead witness the ways in which they make choices about what lessons from society they will take in regarding who a boy or man should be (Way, 2004). Similarly, rather than viewing a specific gender norm or choice in and of itself as being connected to negative outcomes, we can better appreciate how adolescents in particular engage in a continual, evolving process of making choices about gender, each one having its own set of trade-offs (Oransky & Fisher, 2009; Rose & Rudolph, 2006). In Chu's (2004) words:

> As active participants in their identity development, boys are responsive in the sense that they have the capacity to internalize and resist masculine norms and ideals that manifest, for instance, through other people's expectations for and assumptions about them. However, boys are also creative in the sense that they construct their identities, or senses of self, in ways that reflect their individual experiences as well as their cognitive abilities. (p. 79)

Chu (2004) framed this process in terms of the Piagetian concepts of accommodation and assimilation, in which boys internalize some components of prescriptive stereotypes and societal messages about masculinity, while they resist other assumptions and therefore preserve aspects of self. She suggested that identity development involves a balancing of both processes. This balance is reflected in the ways boys and young men alternate between intimacy (relational) and distancing (traditional masculinity) scripts in their conversations with peers. In this way, they couch intimate disclosures, at times, in humor or balance discussions about vulnerability with self-deprecation, disclaimers, innuendo, or ironic commentary in which they distance from the "heat" of what they have just said (Korobov & Thorne, 2006). This communication style is often mistakenly viewed as being indicative of boys' fear of affect, rather than a more subtle process of identity formation related to the sometimes bifurcated sense of a public and private self that boys can evolve.

The Public and Private Selves

No topic in the clinical encounter has been met with a more energetic response in my work with adolescent boys than the discussion of the "two selves" they must balance. Like Tolman and colleagues (2004) and Chu (2004), I have been struck by how the boys I work with often seem to be acutely aware of who society, or at least the smaller circle of their family and peers, expects them to be. They can usually talk reflectively about masculine norms and messages about their gender, assessing the ways in which they may or may not believe in and live up to these stereotypes, or the ways in which they feel constrained by them. When I bring up the concept of having two guys inside of them, one who is perhaps more traditionally masculine and one who deviates from this role, many boys resonate with this concept. They acknowledge that they have one side of themselves they choose to show the world and another that is reserved for select people in their lives or that perhaps doesn't get expressed to others.

Walker (2004), in her study of British adolescents, described the formation of the two selves in the following way: "There was evidence that these two developmental processes felt very different, although they operated in parallel and the boundaries were fluid. Perhaps it is in the tension between the two, where the barriers come into being and crossovers occur, that attitudes and self-knowledge are formed" (p. 55). How these two selves manifest and relate is as much an individual process and balancing act as it a cultural one. For example, Anderson (2008) described the tension impoverished African American males experience between being "decent" and being "street." With family these boys may enact the former role, while with friends they take on the latter, learning to code switch between the two audiences.

While it is tempting to view this balancing act as evidence that boys are distressed or somehow lacking integration, it is important to remember that all teenagers go through a process of trying on various identities prior to consolidating these roles, or self states, into a cohesive whole (Haen & Weil, 2010). As such, the relegation of certain emotions and aspects of self to a more private self state is both adaptive and resilient as boys navigate situational expectations and the evolving relational demands of life. By welcoming the private self into the therapy space, we may be privileged to see the fears, doubts, questions, confusion, insecurity, pride, passion, love, and other human emotions that are as much a part of boys' lives as the anger we have come to expect.

BEYOND THE EMOTIONALLY STOIC MALE

It's an equally inaccurate myth that boys, in particular, do not talk.

—Ron Taffel (2005, p. 77)

John Wayne, Stiff Upper Lip, Lone Ranger, Marlboro Man, Boys Don't Cry, Man Up ... It is challenging to approach the topic of the emotionally stoic male without evoking these clichés that have been cited time and again in the literature as models for how boys are socialized to respond. Some would argue that it is because of their evocative capacity to capture societal conceptions of traditional men that we return to these phrases, metaphors, and images. But few boys resonate with frontier myths today, and it is perhaps time to question, in addition to whether these clichés hold relevance anymore, whether the idea that boys are strong, unemotional, and somehow stunted in their ability to perceive and express affect continues to be pertinent.

While there does appear to be some difference in the verbal abilities of males and females, on average (Pinker, 2008), the extent of these differences is debatable, particularly those statistics relating to girls possessing and using a more widely varied vocabulary than boys (Eliot, 2009). A sole focus on the disparities means that we miss the subdomains of strength that also may exist. As we more closely examine gender differences in language, we find, for example, that there are no significant distinctions between boys and girls in receptive vocabulary or word knowledge (Eliot, 2009).

As verbal expression moves into the realm of affect, some authors have advanced the theory of "normative male alexithymia." This idea is the curious speculation, first proposed by Levant (2001), that due to societal pressure to suppress emotions, males are somehow impaired in their abilities to identify and describe affect. Levant sees the problem as being so widespread as to be "normative." Like the notion of males being normatively traumatized due to premature abandonment by their mothers (which is discussed in greater detail in Chapter 7), the theory of male alexithymia serves to pathologize boys and skew expectations in working with them. Despite there being no evidence to suggest that the average boy is alexithymic (Kiselica, 2005), this concept persists in clinical literature.

In Wexler's (2009) recent book on therapy with men, this concept is reified even while the author clarifies that male alexithymia doesn't "reach the level of clinically significant proportions like bona fide alexithymia" and concedes that "we don't yet have any solid data on exactly how many men meet the threshold for this description" (p. 14). To advocate that a concept is significant to the treatment of males while at the same time stating that there are no data for its existence, and that it is a subclinical phenomenon at best, is inherently contradictory and therefore makes the term *normative* an embellishment.

Multiple practitioners who have put boys' voices at the center of their work and fostered the conditions in which they might express themselves have refuted the idea that boys are inarticulate emotional dummies (Chu, 2004; Kiselica, Englar-Carlson, Horne, & Fisher, 2008b; Way, 2004). As Saval emphasized, "Boys cry. Boys emote. Some don't, of course, but some girls don't either. Some boys talk *more* than girls.... Boys, if they *are* in crisis, are in as much a state of crisis as the rest of us" (2009, p. 3).

This is not to say that boys always express their feelings easily. Certainly, many therapists see boys who have a shaky handle on their affective experience or who habitually suppress emotional expression. Some of this may be a consequence of their age or experience, some of it can be attributed to the emotional openness (or lack thereof) of their families, and some of it connects to the division of public and private that was discussed earlier. Studies of boys and men exposed to distressing situations have shown that, although they may not react externally, their internal, physiological reactions are heightened, often more than females in the same experimental conditions (Eliot, 2009; Mortola, Hiton, & Grant, 2008).

The suppression of affect is a concerning trend that can be linked to a number of potential mental health risks. However, suppression also has a notably adaptive, healthy aspect. There are many situations in which showing the full extent of one's emotions can be detrimental. For example, some of the very anxious and traumatized boys I treat are able to successfully mask their anxiety during the school day, despite it being triggered, to minimize the negative impact on peer relationships and academic performance.

Research on female friendships points to a more pronounced trend among girls toward ruminating with peers about worries and problems (Rose & Rudolph, 2006). Rumination about negative experiences has been found to exacerbate internalizing symptoms, trauma, and depression in some people (Buss et al., 2008; Ehring, Silke, & Anke, 2008; Hankin, 2008). These results suggest that the expression of emotions is not always warranted, contrary to a general bias of clinicians, and that, while there are times in which greater expression should be encouraged for males, not all expression is equivalently positive.

BEYOND THE WHITE, MIDDLE-CLASS MALE

Failure to see race while looking at gender will cause us to miss the real story.

—**Michael Kimmel and Matthew Mahler (2003, p. 145)**

One of the most pronounced criticisms of the boy crisis literature is that it tended to focus primarily on the experiences of White, middle-class boys to the exclusion of boys who fall outside of this group—those whose ethnic, cultural, socioeconomic, and sexual orientation experiences are more varied (Kidd, 2004; Kimmel, 2004; Weaver-Hightower, 2008). Similarly, by generalizing the findings from a sampling that is not representative of the greater demographic landscape, we can miss varying hues of experience. In addition to capturing diversity, focusing on ethnic and sexual minorities, for example, can help us to better understand how "experiences with societal oppression and marginalization can impact how gender norms are defined, adopted, and enacted" (Oransky & Fisher, 2009).

As an example, research with African American boys highlights several interesting narratives. The first is that African American boys may have slightly more intimate, trusting friendships, particularly in middle school, than their White male peers (Way, 2004). In studies of sex differences in friendship support, no significant gender distinctions are made between the relationships of African American boys and girls, or between those of Asian American boys and girls (Chu & Way, 2009). Among African American and Latino boys, family tends to be an important factor in their friendships, more so than it might be in White boys' relationships. These boys often refer to their friends with terms like *brother* and *blood* (Haen, 2007), and knowing their friends' families and feeling part of them can be meaningfully linked to feelings of closeness (Way & Pahl, 1999).

Similarly, literature on the gender development of sexual minority boys has been lacking, as has reliable information for clinicians and parents. Riggs (2008) noted the absence of discussions about homosexuality in mainstream parenting and developmental books about boys. In many of these texts, there is a presumption, and sometimes a promotion of the idea, that boys will grow up to be straight. Similarly, Paechter (2007) identified the assumption of heterosexuality that exists in the same-sex groups boys form in the early school years. However, as all boys grow up hearing derogatory terms about homosexuality used to insult their masculinity, the experiences of gay, bisexual, transgendered, and questioning boys can inform us uniquely about gender development, especially as it relates to confronting societal and internalized homophobia, developing gay sexual identity, and initiating the coming-out process (Kiselica, Mulé, & Haldeman, 2008c; Nealy, 2008).

BEYOND THE ALPHA MALE: BOYS IN GROUPS

Unfortunately, many in our culture believe that there is an entire subset
of boys building bombs and cooking up Molotov cocktails in their base-
ments while plotting the destruction of the world.

—Malina Saval (2009, p. 12)

Like many in America, I was glued to my television set on April 20,
1999, the day that Dylan Klebold and Eric Harris staged an all-out
assault with homemade bombs and guns, terrorizing the school community of Columbine, Colorado. As is natural after tragedy, Americans
searched for answers about the causes of this unprecedented school
massacre, attributing the actions of the two teenagers to everything
from video games and hard-core music to Satanism, the glorification
of guns, and the Goth subculture. But the explanation that the media
locked onto, and that most resonated with the public, was a story of
bullying that cast Klebold and Harris in the role of outsiders tormented
by the hypermasculine jock culture of their school because they were
different.

This story of two boys who were continually taunted by dominant
males and lashed out in order to prove their masculinity and express
their hurt no doubt captivated therapists who worked with boys. It provided a visceral example of all that was wrong with traditional masculinity. The only problem with this story is that it wasn't true. Cullen
(2009), who spent the bulk of a decade researching the tragedy, recently
dismantled the ideas of Klebold and Harris as the ultimate victims. He
exposed how their images were distorted to fit a more compelling narrative than the one that actually existed—that of an antisocial misfit and a
depressed boy who sought notoriety through massive destruction.

In the years following Columbine, attention to male violence was
pervasive. Discussions about boy's aggression, risk taking, and dominance became so ubiquitous that I found myself having to reassure the
parents of many of the boys I was treating that their sons were not going
to similarly "snap" one day. Underlying these fears were widely held
notions about male competition, autonomy, and aggression.

Starting in infancy, boys are noted, on average, to venture farther
away from parents in their initial exploration of the environment
(Buss et al., 2008). When they become school age, they appear to
play farther away from grown-ups on the playground while engaged in
group games with same-sex peers (Boyle, Marshall, & Robeson, 2003).
Within the context of these male groups, they are noted, like primates,
to establish hierarchies marked by the most dominant, competitive
alpha males at the top and the less aggressive males at the bottom.
The boys are seen organizing group games, rough housing, playing out
scenarios of danger and fantasy violence, and generally engaging more
aggressively with their peers (Baron-Cohen, 2003; Maccoby, 1990).

If we were to draw conclusions about boys based on these studies, we might say that they demonstrate a love of power, violence, autonomy, and control, and fear the dependence and affiliation linked with relationships.

However, if we are to truly appreciate any group of people, we must dig deeply into their behaviors in relationship with others, lest we study them in a vacuum. This means going further inside boys' peer groups to comprehend not only the observable behaviors, but also the resulting impact on boys' senses of self. Gender expression, like culture, is not a fixed entity that is consistent across situations, but is fluid (Corbett, 2009; Diamond, 2009) and best understood within the context of the social circumstances in which it occurs, bearing in mind the social goals toward which the expression is directed (Maccoby, 2002; McNelles & Connolly, 1999). In other words, gender roles are enacted in relationship to others and may shift and change based on whom the boy is interacting with. Maccoby (1990), for example, emphasized that boys' behavior changes based on the number of same-gendered peers present.

Because of its shifting nature, gender expression, particularly in adolescence, can be likened to a theatrical performance or the playing of a game in which roles are taken on and enacted, discarded, or incorporated as boys move through varying social situations (Chase, 2008; Haen & Weil, 2010). In this way, I agree with other theorists who assert that gender is not a singular entity, or informed by a singular ideal as the boy code would suggest, but is marked by multiplicity—multiple meanings, multiple expressions—among boys (Corbett, 2009; Kimmel & Mahler, 2003).

Turning back to the subject of male autonomy, there is some evidence to suggest that baby boys may actually cry and fuss more than girls (Eliot, 2010; Mortola et al., 2008). While they may venture farther away from parents, perhaps because of this physical distance, boys may be more likely to seek parental proximity when afraid (Buss et al., 2008). Interestingly, mothers may be less accurate in predicting fear behaviors in sons than daughters (Buss et al., 2008) and may direct their sons to suppress their fears more often (Casey & Fuller, 1994). These findings suggest some ingrained stereotypical thinking about boys: that they are generally expected to display more bravery than girls. If this tendency is accurate (research is preliminary), it has important ramifications in terms of boys' ability to have their frightened affect validated and soothed by their caregivers.

Maccoby (2004) speculated that the greater competition of boys in free-play scenarios may be a function of the large groups in which they play. Contrary to the extant *Lord of the Flies* image of these groups, Maccoby (2002, 2004) described them as coalitions that form around one another and serve to support boys in conflicts with other boys, as well as closing their ranks to shield their members from adult gaze and intervention. In this sense, boys' groups may be more cohesive and

inclusive than those of girls and involve larger friendship networks*
(Benenson et al., 2009; Pinker, 2008).

While these groups have an impact on shaping boys' gendered behavior, they also can be powerful sources of support. Boys seem to express more positive affect in their groups and to engage in more cooperative, group-oriented problem solving (Xie & Shi, 2009). Maccoby (2004) wrote, "I want to suggest that boys' groups empower them, through their joint endeavors, in ways that girls' responsiveness to each other does not" (p. 14). As such, she reflected that boys' needs for autonomy have been greatly overemphasized, pointing out that they do seek independence from adults "but seldom from each other" (p. 10).

While dominance hierarchies are more easily observed by adults in boys' groups, they do exist in female peer groups as well. And though subcliques are rare, they may be more present in girls' friendship groups (Xie & Shi, 2009). Similarly, Hawley, Little, and Card (2008) found that boys and girls were both among the most dominant members of social groups, using a combination of aggression and pro-social strategies to maintain their dominance. Contrary to previous literature that suggested that girls are looked at disfavorably for engaging in aggressive behavior, these researchers found that aggressive females were viewed somewhat more favorably by peers than their dominant male counterparts.

Consistent with the themes of this chapter, Xie and Shi (2009) concluded:

> Dominant boys and girls in their peer networks are more similar than different in their use of prosocial and coercive strategies and of winning positive peer regard. Boys' and girls' networks are stratified by similar status levels, and the peer dynamics within each gender strongly resemble one another in terms of inclusion and exclusion. (p. 160)

Male Violence and Aggression

Lewis (1998) wrote, "There is, of course, a normal genetic condition, characteristic of about 50 percent of the human population, that is associated with violent crime: the XY syndrome, or being male" (p. 287). While it is certainly true that the majority of violent crimes continue to be committed by males, a closer look reveals fewer gender disparities in less extreme uses of violence. Maccoby (2004) clarified that when we examine rates of aggression in children, which she emphasized are rare for both sexes, we must make "a distinction between children who show a persistent pathway of antisocial behavior from preschool years into adulthood, and children for whom antisocial behavior emerges during

---

* There is debate about whether boys' peer networks are indeed larger than those of girls, with studies reporting varying results (Xie & Shi, 2009). Rose (2007) concluded that the criterion by which friendships were defined seemed to be the prime differential between these studies. The concept of defining friendships will be examined more clearly in the next section.

adolescence and has a fairly brief time-course" (p. 11). The children who show antisocial tendencies throughout life are a relatively small group, and it is in this group that boys exceed girls 10:1. "Among the late-onset group, the sexes are much more similar—boys outnumber the girls by a ratio of only 1.5 to 1" (p. 11).

In more recent years, the topic of relational or social aggression has shed new light on discussions of violence in young people; however, contrary to the commonly held view that relational aggression is the female form of aggression due to girls using it more often than boys (Straus, 2007), recent studies show equivalent uses of this form of aggression in both sexes (Card, Stucky, Sawalani, & Little, 2008; Lilienfeld & Arkowitz, 2010). Research also shows no significant sex differences in the threshold for anger, meaning that boys and girls may both feel anger equivalently but respond to it differently (Campbell, 2006).

Maccoby (2004) pointed out that while it is true that boys have more intergroup conflict and display aggression more frequently than their female counterparts, many of the studies that provide this data were conducted with children ages 3 to 7. In this age group, aggression and conflict is heightened due to slower development of impulse control among boys (Else-Quest, Hyde, Goldsmith, & Van Hulle, 2006). This lag in developing internal controls, as well as distinctions in verbal abilities, may be due to differing rates of neurological development for boys and girls (Giedd, 2010). While there is not yet sufficient evidence to support this correlation (Eliot, 2009), it may be an important feature of future research, moving comparisons of the sexes away from generalized conclusions based on one age group and toward consideration of the differential timetables around skill acquisition.

Finally, as boys move into adolescence and adulthood, they are more frequently the perpetrators *and* the victims of violence (excluding sexual assault; Morash, 2005). There is one notable exception, however. In the area of domestic, or intimate partner, violence, women are found to aggress just as often as men (Lilienfeld & Arkowitz, 2010; Maccoby, 2004). Because of their difference in size and strength, though, the violence enacted by women tends to cause less harm and injury.

The literature also suggests, as Baron-Cohen (2003) did, that females tend to have more empathy than males. However, studies that concluded a gender difference in empathy based on self-report measures have been found to cue test subjects to the fact that empathy was being evaluated. In these situations, females become more focused on appearing empathic (Szalavitz & Perry, 2010). In a meta-analysis of facial expression processing, which has been linked to empathy, there is a small advantage for infant girls in this domain, and the gap seems to grow with age (McClure, 2000), suggesting that experience shapes this skill (Eliot, 2010). In adults, facial expression processing favors women by "about four tenths of a standard deviation, meaning that the average woman is more accurate than just 66% of men" (Eliot, 2010, p. 27) in this empathy-related task. The generally accepted idea that males are

far less empathic, something many male therapists might take exception to, has been widely inflated.

EXPANDING NOTIONS ABOUT BOYS IN RELATIONSHIP

> Recognizing the power of relationships and relational cues is essential to
> effective therapeutic work and, indeed, to effective parenting, caregiv-
> ing, teaching and just about any other human endeavor.
>
> **—Bruce Perry and Maia Szalavitz (2005, p. 67)**

Girls are typically understood, as they have been described in the
feminist literature, to be more oriented to relationships and social concerns, while boys are depicted as being more selectively consumed with
competition and establishing independence, a trend that is said to continue into adulthood as men vie for success in the occupational realm
(Gilligan, 1993). The boy crisis literature echoed this impression by
describing boys as struggling to form meaningful relationships characterized by emotional reciprocity and commitment, hampered by their
need for solitude. Studies that examined social relationships pointed
to boys being less intimate with their friends and tending to compete
with them (Belle, 1989). Way (2004) advocated against the tendency to
focus on gender differences rather than how boys uniquely experience
their friendships. "This skews the findings so that the only elements of
boys' friendships that are understood are those that appear to be distinct from girls' friendships" (p. 170).

The criterion used to interpret gender differences in relationships is
important as well. There has been a propensity to evaluate boys' relational styles by female standards, a pattern that can distort the conclusions and lead to pathologizing boys' styles of connecting to others
(Kiselica et al., 2008b). Chu and Way (2009) wrote:

> Just as feminist researchers revealed the inadequacy of simply impos-
> ing on girls developmental models that were based on boys' experiences,
> it may be similarly problematic to evaluate boys' relationships solely in
> terms of behavior such as voice or self-disclosure, which may be more
> common or central to girls' experiences. (p. 53)

By moving away from behavioral markers and instead evaluating the
quality of boys' friendships based on a felt sense of security or closeness,
another narrative emerges (Chu & Way, 2009; McNelles & Connolly, 1999).
When intimacy is defined affectively, distinctions between boys' and girls'
friendships are reduced, such that there is no difference in either gender's
ability to sustain connectedness with friends. McNelles and Connolly
(1999) emphasized that the pathways to achieving connectedness may be
different between boys and girls, with boys tending more toward "activity-
centered intimacy" (p. 156) rather than the verbal sharing of feelings.

These authors offered a few additional conclusions that are often overlooked by others who cite their study. The first is that, although the different forms of intimate behaviors showed gender-specific patterns, both boys and girls were noted to self-disclose and attain connection through shared activity so that "preferences for particular behavioral pathways do not preclude the use of others" (McNelles & Connolly, 1999, pp. 156–157). In addition, they found that, in looking longitudinally across a three-year period, the closest friends of *both* sexes in the study were more likely to turn toward activity-centered intimacy than were the other dyads. While surprised by this finding, the authors speculated, "It may be that it is among the close friend dyads that there is sufficient familiarity to engage in the somewhat 'immature' and 'silly' behaviors that form the basis of activity-centered intimacy" (p. 157).

Levy (2005) proposed a more nuanced view of male relationships. He distinguished between friendships, which he characterized as being marked by intimacy and emotional closeness, and comradeships, which might be best thought of as the connection between two buddies who spend time together but have no deep commitment to one another. In his study with middle-aged men, he linked comradeship to men who subscribe more to traditional masculinity.

Unlike Levy, I don't view the two types of relationships as mutually exclusive. I have known healthy boys who have only one close relationship and unhealthy boys who have many close friends. Chu and Way (2009) found that "boys could feel close in a relationship without necessarily talking and, conversely, they could talk in a relationship without feeling close" (p. 55). In fact, a balance of both friends and buddies, those with whom one can share personal feelings and those who are best for just hanging out, is both natural and desirable. Having a wide array of friends who serve different purposes maximizes the number of choices available to boys, giving them a range of opportunities to fulfill varying needs (Greif, 2009).

In fact, it is this very flexibility in interpersonal relationships that may serve as a strength for males. According to Saval (2009), "Loyalty ... is one of the most undersold qualities of boys" (p. 10). In Way's (2004) research, this loyalty connected to a tendency of boys to mistrust others in late adolescence due to experiences of betrayal in relationships. But other researchers posit that males may have longer-lasting same-sex friendships across the life span (Benenson et al., 2009) and may recover more quickly from fights than girls (Maccoby, 2004). In their research with college-age males, Benenson and colleagues (2009) found young men to show greater tolerance toward their male roommates despite differing social styles, interests, values, and habits, and to be less likely than females to let violations of friendship norms negatively impact the relationship.

Multiple authors (Chu & Way, 2009; Saval, 2009; Way & Pahl, 1999) have highlighted the capacity of boys to both express and experience closeness in their relationships, to know their friends well, to place trust in them, to sensitively respond to them, and to feel connected.

Many of those boys lacking close relationships expressed loneliness and a desire for connection with someone who knows and understands them (Tolman et al., 2004; Way, 2004). Some boys find this in other males, while other boys find it in friendships with girls (Chase, 2008).

Regardless of the source, contrary to popular belief, relationships are important to boys, just as they are to all human beings. The way boys define themselves is intimately tied to their relationships with others. Chu (2004) viewed friendships, and the resulting sense of validation, as fundamental to boys' development of resilience and mitigating factors in how they choose to either take in or resist ideas about traditional masculinity.

Two future horizons of research into male friendships that might help to tell more of the story of boys' relational styles involve further examination of both cross-gender friendships and antipathetic relationships, or those in which two boys mutually dislike one another (Card, 2010). While observational studies of grade schoolers on playgrounds largely support the idea that boys mainly play in same-gendered groups, children are noted to engage in cross-gender play about 9% of the time (Eliot, 2009). Rose (2007) found that more children reported having cross-gender friendships when the definitions of friendship were loosened. It may be that while cross-gender play exists more in neighborhoods and homes, it doesn't manifest with the same frequency in school because of pressures children place on one another to segregate.

REMAKING THE THERAPY PROCESS: CREATIVE APPROACHES

No matter what therapeutic orientation one practices, it must breathe and circulate creativity in order for sessions to come alive.

—Bradford Keeney (2009, p. 2)

Therapeutic efficacy is about creating the conditions that allow clients the space for emotional expression and containment, insight, cognitive restructuring, and neural growth and connectivity. As clinicians facing a boy coming into our office, we wrestle with the question of how to replicate the contexts from his life that facilitate access to the private, and often guarded, self (Kiselica & Englar-Carlson, 2008). In reflecting on the change process in treatment as captured by a variety of colleagues' vignettes, Terr (2008) noted "how playful, creative, and elastic good child/adolescent psychotherapy is" (p. 266). Central to each of these vignettes, identified by the contributing therapist as a turning point in his or her treatment of a young person, were the elements of metaphor, humor, surprise, counterintuitive response, and relationship, as well as the small moments in which the young person felt seen or understood.

Being open to creating these contexts often means, as far as boys are concerned, that we have to break the rules of therapy as they have been taught to us and instead be open to the creation of new possibilities. Margulies (1984) referred to this as suspending our preconceptions "in the service of discovery" (p. 1029), while Selekman (1997) urged us to "become better improvisers, be more critical of our own therapeutic assumption, and interventions, and be more therapeutically flexible" (p. 29). Both descriptions could just as easily characterize the creative process itself.

While it is tempting to relegate the concept of creativity in treatment to the domain of the creative arts therapies (and certainly this book contains several approaches emanating from this branch of psychotherapy), all treatment modalities lend themselves to creative applications. Indeed, it was from moments of inspiration and discovery that each of these modalities first originated. It is also a commonly held belief that creative treatment, in its flexibility and spontaneity, is in direct opposition to an evidence-based practice stance because it involves going "off book," so to speak. But without adaptation to meet the unique interactional beats of the therapeutic encounter, even the most efficacious of models may fail. Duncan and Miller (2006) supported this idea:

> Specific treatments are not unique—but clients are. From this perspective, manuals fall flat. Experienced therapists know that the work requires the tailoring of any approach to a particular client's unique circumstances. The nuances and creativity of an actual encounter flow from the moment-to-moment interaction of the participants—from the client, relational, and therapist idiographic mix, not from step A to step B on page 39. (p. 148)

Many therapists who have attended trainings I have led share their fears that they are not innately inventive enough to foster the kinds of "Aha!" moments that they perceive as necessary to create change. Preliminary studies investigating the neural patterns of creative thought suggest that creativity takes a slower, more meandering pathway than intelligence in the efficient processing machine that is the human brain (Jung et al., 2009), and that creative processing is less linear and more holistic (Grabner, Fink, & Neubauer, 2007). While no direct inferences can be made from these findings, they do have metaphoric value in thinking about creativity in treatment as a process of not just spontaneity, but also of moving forward while not always knowing where things are headed in order to co-compose the process with boys (Keeney, 2009).

Similarly, Selekman (1997) emphasized the importance of taking the time to accurately hone in on and define the problems to be addressed. He stressed that this exploratory work of being collaboratively present with a client and generating curiosity about his thoughts and feelings is a key component of utilizing creativity in treatment. Creativity without context is merely a party trick. Wilson (2007) concurred: "Novelty for its own sake is self-indulgence, but a search for enhanced performance as a practitioner requires the courage to challenge our preferred orientation to stop us from settling for a comfortable set of methods and practices which lack novelty and improvisation" (p. 26).

Welcoming the Boy's Whole Self

At the heart of this chapter is the idea that responsible treatment of boys entails seeing all parts of who they are, not just the edited-for-television parts or those that distill nicely into an alarming headline. As I have endeavored to show, the concerning aspects of boys have been given their fair share of airtime, while boys' strengths and healthy traits often get pushed to the edge of the picture. Kimmel (2004) wrote:

> Starting from the premise that there is something wrong with these boys—either inherent or acquired— ... offers a skewed perspective that may help us to understand boys' problems but not boys' strengths, including the ways in which boys resist succumbing to negative stereotypes and actively seek out ways to thrive in the midst of great challenges. (p. 2)

Part of moving from a deficit-based to a strengths-focused perspective involves listening for the hero stories from boys' lives outside of session, not the moments of machismo and false bravado, but the times when they have exercised genuine heroism in overcoming challenges, taking effective action, and showing empathy and vulnerability (Duncan, Miller, & Sparks, 2007; Kiselica et al., 2008b).

An exclusive focus on strengths, however, can lead to an idealization of clients and unwittingly promote the message that they cannot "disappoint" us or that we can't tolerate their more vulnerable and shameful aspects (Wilson, 2007). Instead, we have to strive to see boys three-dimensionally, in all their messy imperfectness. This includes welcoming the rambunctious, mischievous, irreverent parts of them that may not be ideally suited to the solemnity of many a therapist's office: their humorous selves, their embodied selves, their curiosity, their sexuality, their clumsiness. In identifying some of these overlooked parts, Corbett (2009) mused, "Too often a kind of dulled and false Eddie Haskell sociality is substituted for candor. No one talks about *South Park*. No one buys 50 Cent on the sly. No one dances on the goal line. No one is named McLovin. No one cuts a fart in chapel ..." (p. 215). Boys need just as much as any of our clients to be seen, heard, and validated, and to know that we are open to all they are and have to offer.

Expanding Methods of Contact

As Mortola and colleagues (2008) pointed out, male toddlers are robustly engaged in the world around them at the same time as they are connected to their thoughts, feelings, and experiences. They take in the environment by being in "full contact" with it, "literally poking it, touching it, and climbing all over it" (p. 1). As with all children, this immediacy of engagement tempers as they get older. But it is still accessible within the right contexts and circumstances. These authors suggested that "if we want to help boys make better contact, we have to learn to make better contact with them" (p. 12).

Kiselica (2005) has made numerous recommendations for adapting the traditional therapy environment, which is often incompatible with boys, to offer multiple ways of connecting. Among his suggestions are therapists moving the work out of their offices to sites where boys are more naturally at ease, including the basketball court, their homes, a diner, a park, or walking the streets. He advised thinking beyond the traditional, weekly 50-minute hour to consider drop-in sessions and contracting or extending the session length and frequency to meet each boy's needs. In a school or residential setting, this could mean meeting multiple times for very short conversations throughout the week. In a private practice setting, this could mean embracing email and text messages as the main mode of contact between appointments. Kiselica (2005) recommended conducting issue-based discussions that target those things that the boy finds most prescient, often practical matters. This requires maintaining a careful balance between working on these needs and incorporating the overarching treatment goals that others in the boy's life demand. The goals identified by others, often related to behavioral change, may not be what the boy is motivated to work on.

Kiselica (2005) also suggested strategies such as offering food, using judicious self-disclosure, and throwing a ball or engaging in physical activity while fostering dialogue. Central to many of the approaches offered in this book is the belief that activity is a vital component of successful treatment with boys. Many authors (Haen, 2007; Kiselica, 2005; Kiselica et al., 2008b; Mortola et al., 2008; Pollack, 2010; Wexler, 2009) have discussed the action orientation of males as displayed in the ways they problem-solve, express empathy, show nurturance, and connect with others. Engaging in activity has the effect of lessening the intimacy of the therapeutic relationship and easing the awkwardness, which can help boys to feel safe to let down their guard. "Action," wrote Wilson (2007), "cuts through over-intellectualizing—when too many words obscure meaning—and provides a language when people don't yet have the words to express themselves" (p. 65).

Action in treatment can range from the presence of small toys that allow boys to fidget with their hands, as I have scattered about the desk in the office of the crisis shelter where I do part of my work, to incorporating structured physical challenges, as Mortola and colleagues (2008) have in their group model for working with boys. Engaging boys in activities and fostering their instrumental strengths can also aid in the process of skill building (Haen, 2007). These cherished activities, if they take root, may help the boy to construct what Kimmel and Mahler

(2003) referred to as "a pocket of resistance" (p. 145) in the face of stress and pressure. On a deeper level, there may be other, more direct treatment effects connected to the use of action.

Neuroscience researcher Panksepp (2009) is a proponent of the importance of play for building brain structures related to impulse control, as well as strengthening "positive social affect circuits" (p. 22) that may buffer against depression. He wrote:

> Play may be the most underutilized emotional force that could have remarkable benefits in psychotherapy, especially with children. There are, of course, many play therapies, but most of them … have no resemblance to the bodily vigor, spontaneity, and creativeness of "real" physical play.… Psychiatric distress can be conceptualized as overturned tables that need to be set right again, and there is unlikely to be any stronger emotional aid than that contained in the joyous potentials of play. (p. 21)

Humor and silliness have a particular place in therapy with boys (Kiselica et al., 2008b). Just as McNelles and Connolly (1999) noted the important role of joking around in the formation of activity-centered intimacy, shared laughter between therapist and patient can strengthen attachment in the relationship and serve as a form of affect regulation and attunement (Nelson, 2008). By being able to laugh, and especially by being able to laugh at ourselves, we model flexibility and self-esteem for boys in a real-world kind of way.

Expanding the Use of the Therapist's Self

Kiselica (2005) suggested that sitting side by side may be a more effective posture in the therapy space when working with boys. While his suggestion is a tactical one, it also hints at a psychological position that is beneficial to boys. Male therapists, in particular, may find themselves fulfilling a number of related roles, including coach, mentor, father figure, and big brother. While the focus of a discussion may remain the same, each of these roles requires a slightly different use of the therapist's self. Being able to flexibly shift between them as necessary is one of the important arts of good clinical work.

For example, with at-risk teenagers in a crisis shelter, I have found that a more direct, fatherlike relationship is often effective, as it speaks to their own yearning for a father figure. This can include pulling their aggression toward me so that it can be worked through in the transference and gently confronting rigid modes of seeing the world. With this population, self-disclosure of the therapist's own resolved struggles with issues of loss, anger, and aggression can be facilitative of role modeling and expanding the "stuckness" that can at times pervade these boys' lives (Reese, Horne, Bell, & Wingfield, 2008).

By consciously shifting our presence, we can help boys pivot away from moments of connection that feel too intimate, as is often the case with the traditional therapy stance. Many of the boys who come to see me after having failed in treatment with another therapist will mock the therapeutic voice of their past clinician. Similarly, in moments when I have become more affectively expressive than my clients can tolerate, they will often let me know in their own humorous ways, as did a 13-year-old client when he broke an intense moment of sadness in the session by pointedly asking, "Why are you talking to me like I'm slow?"

However, therapists should not avoid using affective language or establishing connection in the treatment relationship for fear that boys cannot tolerate this approach. Instead, we should assist boys in balancing and buffering, distancing from intimacy when they need to, just as they tend to shift back and forth between the public and private self in their dialogues. Spencer's (2007) research on male mentoring relationships found that the successful adult mentors established a connection that allowed for emotional expression and closeness, but in some cases they also distanced themselves linguistically at times when this connection might feel excessively intimate. In the more conscious balancing act of the clinician, at times of intolerable discussion, affect can be shifted to cognition, words to action, and direct attention to a more removed presence.

Sometimes, when boys at the crisis shelter are in my office and I feel I am getting nowhere with them, I shift my attention to the computer, telling them I have a lot of work to do but they are welcome to stay in the office. Often, they remain planted in their chair, and gradually they open up about painful feelings, comforted that I am not zeroing in on them while they do so. Similarly, when working on a psychiatric unit, I used to marvel at the way many of the boys would begin to disclose their trauma histories while riding with me in the hospital van on the way to a field trip or appointment.

Incorporating Storytelling and Ritual

The use of narrative is a powerful tool in therapeutic practice with boys, perhaps because it links back to a long-standing male tradition. In Gersie's (1997) book, a male client explains it in this fashion:

> In my day we had bull sessions. It occurs to me now that the stories were an important part of male bonding. We called them war stories. We realized that these war stories were not objective accounts of events. They were the sort of accounts that men who shared a war might later tell. We were young. None of us had seen war. But we told accounts of experiences which emphasized the thrills. It wasn't the story that mattered, it was the rhythm of life. It articulated communality. (p. 27)

The engagement of stories with boys can happen in a number of ways. With younger ones, I may use puppets to act out a fictional story that hews very closely to issues I know are going on in their own lives. With latency age boys, I may tell them a pointed story about another guy I know whose experiences resemble their own. DeGangi and Nemiroff (2009) used fictional letters from kids seeking advice as a framework for exploring issues of self-esteem, identity, social and family relationships, and emotional regulation with 10- and 11-year-olds in a boys' group. Mortola and colleagues (2008) wrote about the use of strategic story-telling by group leaders, in which disclosing carefully chosen moments from their own lives served as a catalyst for boys in discussing develop-ment and gender.

Just as storytelling harkens back to an ancient tradition, the use of ritual can assist in connecting boys to the therapy process in a mean-ingful way. Rituals can be used to mark transitions, celebrate accom-plishments, recognize milestones, and highlight therapeutic progress (Cervantes & Englar-Carlson, 2008). They can also become a frame-work for treatment, helping boys to navigate the shift from the outside world into the therapeutic space, or supporting affect regulation at the end of a session.

A 10-year-old client of mine begins each session with an elaborate handshake, adding one additional step to the already complex series of movements each time he sees me. A five-year-old boy spent many weeks entering the room and announcing it was "time to feed the frog." He would name all the happenings of the previous week that he did not like, asking me to write them on small pieces of paper that he then threw away in my garbage can designed like a frog. He was delighted when I would respond by making the chewing and "ribbit-ing" sounds of the frog. Teenagers in a previous boys group would end each session by engaging in the "Ziggy, zoggy, ziggy, zoggy. Oi! Oi! Oi!" chant that was used to end each episode of late-night television's *The Man Show*.

Building Reflective Capacities, Mindfulness, and Self-Regulation

As was previously discussed, boys tend to lag in their development of inhibitory controls. When this delay is pronounced, it feeds directly into the kind of impulsivity that characterizes those diagnosed with atten-tion deficit hyperactivity disorder. Few branches of psychotherapy have grown in recent years like the use of mindfulness practices in treatment. In fact, the presence of the creative therapist described here, as one who remains open to possibility and moment-to-moment experience without the imposition of preconceived ideas or judgment, is similar to Siegel's (2010) recent description of the mindful therapist.

We would do well in our work to teach boys to attend to their own experience, both physiological and affective. Helping them to become reflectively curious about the thoughts, intentions, and feelings of others, and better able to regulate their own impulses and emotions, may prove to be some of the more significant contributions we can make to their long-term adjustment, identity formation, and neural growth. These skills can be practiced in a number of ways, from structured games, to role play, to the simple practice of breathing and pausing to notice what is happening internally. Progress can be noted in a boy's ability to step away from the heat of the moment to reflect on the experience, and an eventual ongoing internal dialogue between his experiencing and reflective selves.

Welcoming Others

Just as boys cannot be viewed in a vacuum, our treatment efforts should not occur in one. Studies demonstrate that a sense of connectedness to family and to school are some of the most robust protective factors against distress, depression, suicidality, substance abuse, and engagement in violent behaviors, particularly for adolescents (Resnick et al., 1997; Resnick, Harris, & Blum, 2008). Contrary to what we have been taught to believe, boys do experience trust and intimacy in their relationships with their parents (Jeffries, 2004). For boys, fathers can play an especially important role, with their support buffering young men against aggression, academic failure, and potentially mediating the negative correlation between substance abuse and suicidal ideation (Parke & Brott, 1999; Tarver, Wong, Neighbors, & Zimmerman, 2004).

In the United States, it is estimated that one in three male children live without their birth father (Tyre, 2008). In African American families, the number of households in which women were the primary caregivers doubled between 1970 and 1990 (Perry, 2008), and absent fathers are now considered the rule rather than the exception. However, while these boys are almost always considered fatherless in the literature, nonresidential fathers can and often do play a role in their sons' lives (Perry, 2008).

In tandem with the trend toward absenteeism is a contrasting societal increase in stay-at-home fathers, males who are not the family's primary breadwinners but remain at home as the caretaker. This number has grown to almost 160,000, nearly triple what it was 10 years ago (Legato, 2008). Fathers now comprise about 18% of stay-at-home parents in the United States (Synnott, 2009). In light of the recent economic collapse, family structure may be continuing to change along with parenting responsibilities.

It behooves us in our treatment of boys to foster these connections with family and significant others. For minority boys, in particular, the extended network of relatives, pastors, mentors, and adult males may be significant (Boyd-Franklin, 2008). Though it is difficult, I work hard to encourage divorced and separated fathers, working parents, and extended family members to feel that they have a significant role in a boy's treatment and that they will not be judged when they come to session, even if their participation needs to be by telephone. When this is not possible, for logistical or other reasons, I work with the boys to actively plan who in their life might provide support and how they may begin conversations with these people about difficult subjects. We have no better way to combat the image of boys as solo warriors and lone wolves than to bridge and support their connections to relationships and community.

CLOSING THOUGHTS

Epic Fail: A mistake of such monumental proportions that it requires its own term in order to successfully point out the unfathomable shortcomings of an individual or group.

—*Urban Dictionary*

A 13-year-old patient whom I have been treating for several years has recently insisted that we spend part of each session throwing a baseball. This burgeoning young man was a socially awkward, quirky boy when he first came to see me. He loved art but was entirely uncomfortable playing sports with peers on his elementary school playground, something he wanted to be able to do. Starting with some games of Nerf™ basketball, I began, a year into our work together, to encourage him to become more expressive and accepting of his physical self. Shortly thereafter, he embarked on playing ball again with the boys at school and experienced some success and camaraderie. This change gradually blossomed into a fervent passion for Sports Center, baseball cards, and inventing the "perfect pitch."

When middle school came around, my patient flourished in a way he hadn't before, developing a small group of buddies who shared his new interests. Now, at his urging, we throw the ball in sessions. My decided lack of athletic prowess often results in me dropping the ball, to which my patient will smile and utter, "Epic." In those moments, I sometimes flash back to my own failed childhood attempts at sports. These failures ultimately forced me to look a little harder to find the strengths in myself and to better define who I was—to become creative.

Bromfield (2005) wrote, "Doing therapy defines imperfection" (p. 175). In our efforts to understand, respond to, and strengthen the boys who come to see us, we often proceed imperfectly, frequently fumble, and sometimes fail. Epically. In those moments, it is tempting to return to our maps and our guidebooks to figure out why we got lost in the first place. But getting lost is where the journey becomes generative. In conducting therapy with boys, we must be willing to blaze new trails or notice something unseen in the landscape. We have to be open to venturing into uncharted territory and appreciating what we might discover. In doing so, we may find ourselves in a place beyond rhetoric, politics, and stereotypes where we can appreciate the boys who come to see us, and they can thrive. Epically.

REFERENCES

Anderson, E. (2008). Against the wall: Poor, young, black, and male. In Author (Ed.), *Against the wall: Poor, young, black, and male* (pp. 3–27). Philadelphia, PA: University of Pennsylvania Press.

Aydt, H., & Corsaro, W. A. (2003). Differences in children's construction of gender across culture. *American Behavioral Scientist, 46*(10), 1306–1325.

Baron-Cohen, S. (2003). *The essential difference: Male and female brains and the truth about autism.* New York: Basic Books.

Belle, D. (1989). Gender differences in children's social networks and social supports. In Author (Ed.), *Children's social networks and social supports* (pp. 173–188). Oxford, UK: Wiley.

Benenson, J. F., Markovits, H., Fitzgerald, C., Geoffroy, D., Flemming, J., Kahlenberg, S. M., & Wrangham, R. W. (2009). Males' greater tolerance of same-sex peers. *Psychological Science, 20*(2), 184–190.

Berzoff, J. (2008). Psychodynamic theory and gender. In J. Berzoff, L. M. Flanagan, & P. Hertz (Eds.), *Inside out and outside in: Psychodynamic clinical theory and psychopathology in contemporary multicultural contexts* (2nd ed., pp. 229–244). Lanham, MD: Jason Aronson.

Bettis, P., & Sternod, B. (2009). Anakin Skywalker, *Star Wars* and the trouble with boys. *THYMOS: Journal of Boyhood Studies, 3*(1), 21–38.

Boyd-Franklin, N. (2008). Working with African Americans and trauma: Lessons for clinicians from Hurricane Katrina. In M. McGoldrick & K. V. Hardy (Eds.), *Re-visioning family therapy: Race, culture, and gender in clinical practice* (2nd ed., pp. 344–355). New York: Guilford.

Boyle, D. E., Marshall, N. L., & Robeson, W. W. (2003). Gender at play: Fourth-grade girls and boys on the playground. *American Behavioral Scientist, 46*(10), 1326–1345.

Brizendine, L. (2006). *The female brain.* New York: Morgan Road Books.

Brizendine, L. (2010). *The male brain.* New York: Broadway Books.

Bromfield, R. (2005). *Teens in therapy: Making it their own.* New York: Norton.

Buss, K. A., Brooker, R. J., & Leuty, M. (2008). Girls most of the time, boys some of the time: Gender differences in toddlers' use of maternal proximity and comfort seeking. *Infancy, 13*(1), 1–29.

Campbell, A. (2006). Sex differences in direct aggression: What are the psychological mediators? *Aggression and Violent Behavior, 11*(3), 237–264.

Card, N. A. (2010). Antipathetic relationships in child and adolescent development: A meta-analytic review and recommendations for an emerging area of study. *Developmental Psychology, 46*(2), 516–529.

Card, N. A., Stucky, B. D., Sawalani, G. M., & Little, T. D. (2008). Direct and indirect aggression during childhood and adolescence: A meta-analytic review of gender differences, intercorrelations, and relations to maladjustment. *Child Development, 79*(5), 1185–1229.

Casey, R. J., & Fuller, L. J. (1994). Maternal regulation of children's emotions. *Journal of Nonverbal Behavior, 18*(1), 57–89.

Cervantes, J. M., & Englar-Carlson, M. (2008). Surviving in a sea with few lifeboats: Counseling boys from impoverished families. In M. S. Kiselica, M. Englar-Carlson, & A. M. Horne (Eds.), *Counseling troubled boys: A guidebook for professionals* (pp. 69–96). New York: Routledge.

Chaplin Kindler, R. (2010). Theater and therapy: How improvisation informs the analytic hour. *Psychoanalytic Inquiry, 30*(3), 254–266.

Chase, S. A. (2008). *Perfectly prep: Gender extremes at a New England prep school.* New York: Oxford University Press.

Chu, J. Y. (2004). A relational perspective on adolescent boys' identity development. In N. Way & J. Y. Chu (Eds.), *Adolescent boys: Exploring diverse cultures of boyhood* (pp. 78–104). New York: New York University Press.

Chu, J. Y., & Way, N. (2009). Presence in relationship: A new construct for understanding adolescent friendships and psychological health. *THYMOS: Journal of Boyhood Studies, 3*(1), 50–73.

Corbett, K. (2009). *Boyhoods: Rethinking masculinities.* New Haven, CT: Yale University Press.

Cullen, D. (2009). *Columbine.* New York: Twelve.

Day, J., Chiu, S., & Hendren, R. L. (2005). Structure and function of the adolescent brain: Findings from neuroimaging studies. *Adolescent Psychiatry, 29,* 175–216.

DeGangi, G. A., & Nemiroff, M. A. (2009). *Kids' Club letters: Narrative tools for stimulating process and dialogue in therapy groups for children and adolescents.* New York: Routledge.

Diamond, M. J. (2009). Masculinity and its discontents: Making room for the "mother" inside the male—An essential achievement for healthy male gender identity. In B. Reis & R. Grossmark (Eds.), *Heterosexual masculinities: Contemporary perspectives from psychoanalytic gender theory* (pp. 23–53). New York: Routledge.

Duncan, B. L., & Miller, S. D. (2006). Treatment manuals do not improve outcomes. In J. C. Norcross, L. E. Beutler, & R. F. Levant (Eds.), *Evidence-based practices in mental health: Debate and dialogue on the fundamental questions* (pp. 140–149). Washington, DC: American Psychological Association.

Duncan, B. L., Miller, S. D., & Sparks, J. (2007). Common factors and the uncommon heroism of youth. *Psychotherapy in Australia, 13*(2), 34–43.

Ehring, T., Silke, F., & Anke, E. (2008). The role of rumination and reduced concreteness in the maintenance of posttraumatic stress disorder and depression following trauma. *Cognitive Therapy and Research, 32*(4), 488–506.

Eliot, L. (2009). *Pink brain, blue brain: How small differences grow into troublesome gaps—and what we can do about it.* New York: Houghton Mifflin Harcourt.

Eliot, L. (2010, May/June). The truth about boys and girls. *Scientific American Mind, 21*(2), 22–29.

Else-Quest, N. M., Hyde, J. S., Goldsmith, H. H., & Van Hulle, C. A. (2006). Gender differences in temperament: A meta-analysis. *Psychological Bulletin, 132*(1), 33–72.

Garbarino, J. (1999). *Lost boys: Why our sons turn violent and how we can save them.* New York: Free Press.

Gersie, A. (1997). *Reflections on therapeutic storymaking: The use of stories in groups.* London, UK: Jessica Kingsley.

Giedd, J. N. (2008). The teen brain: Insights from neuroimaging. *Journal of Adolescent Health, 42*(4), 335–343.

Giedd, J. N. (2010). The teen brain: Primed to learn, primed to take risks. In D. Gordon (Ed.), *Cerebrum 2010: Emerging ideas in brain science* (pp. 62–70). New York: Dana Press.

Gilligan, C. (1993). *In a different voice: Psychological theory and women's development* (2nd ed.). Cambridge, MA: Harvard University Press.

Grabner, R. H., Fink, A., & Neubauer, A. C. (2007). Brain correlates of self-rated originality of ideas: Evidence from event-related power and phase-locking changes in the EEG. *Behavioral Neuroscience, 121*(1), 224–230.

Greif, G. L. (2009). *Buddy system: Understanding male friendships.* New York: Oxford University Press.

Haen, C. (2007). "Make me wanna holler": Dramatic encounters with boys from the inner city. In V. A. Camilleri (Ed.), *Healing the inner city child: Creative arts therapies with at-risk youth* (pp. 212–228). London, UK: Jessica Kingsley.

Haen, C., & Weil, M. (2010). Group therapy on the edge: Adolescence, creativity, and groupwork. *Group, 34*(1), 37–52.

Hankin, B. (2008). Rumination and depression in adolescence: Investigating symptom specificity in a multiwave prospective study. *Journal of Clinical Child and Adolescent Psychology, 37*(4), 701–713.

Hawley, P. H., Little, T. D., & Card, N. A. (2008). The myth of the alpha male: A new look at dominance-related beliefs and behaviors among adolescent males and females. *International Journal of Behavioral Development, 32*(1), 76–88.

Jeffries, E. D. (2004). Experiences of trust with parents: A qualitative investigation of African American, Latino, and Asian American boys from low-income families. In N. Way & J. Y. Chu (Eds.), *Adolescent boys: Exploring diverse cultures of boyhood* (pp. 107–128). New York: New York University Press.

Johnson, S. B., Blum, R. W., & Giedd, J. N. (2009). Adolescent maturity and the brain: The promise and pitfalls of neuroscience research in adolescent health policy. *Journal of Adolescent Health, 45*(3), 216–221.

Jung, R. E., Gasparovic, C., Chavez, R. S., Flores, R. A., Smith, S. M., Caprihan, A., & Yeo, R. A. (2009). Biochemical support for the "threshold" theory of creativity: A magnetic resonance spectroscopy study. *The Journal of Neuroscience, 29*(16), 5319–5325.

Keeney, B. (2009). *The creative therapist: The art of awakening a session.* New York: Taylor & Francis Group.

Kidd, K. B. (2004). *Making American boys: Boyology and the feral tale.* Minneapolis, MN: University of Minnesota Press.

Kimmel, M. (2004). Foreword. In N. Way & J. Y. Chu (Eds.), *Adolescent boys: Exploring diverse cultures of boyhood* (pp. xi–xiii). New York: New York University Press.

Kimmel, M., & Mahler, M. (2003). Adolescent masculinity, homophobia, and violence: Random school shootings, 1982–2001. *American Behavioral Scientist,*
46(10), 1439–1458.

Kindlon, D., & Thompson, M. (1999). *Raising Cain: Protecting the emotional life of*
boys. New York: Ballantine Books.

Kiselica, M. S. (2005). A male-friendly therapeutic process with school-age boys.
In G. E. Good & G. R. Brooks (Eds.), *The new handbook of psychotherapy and*
counseling with men: A comprehensive guide to settings, problems, and treatment
approaches (rev. & abridged ed., pp. 17–28). San Francisco, CA: Jossey-Bass.

Kiselica, M. S., & Englar-Carlson, M. (2008). Establishing rapport with boys in
individual counseling and psychotherapy: A male-friendly perspective. In
M. S. Kiselica, M. Englar-Carlson, & A. M. Horne (Eds.), *Counseling troubled*
boys: A guidebook for professionals (pp. 49–65). New York: Routledge.

Kiselica, M. S., Englar-Carlson, M., & Horne, A. M. (2008a). Preface: The strug-
gles and strengths of boys and how we can help them. In Authors (Eds.),
Counseling troubled boys: A guidebook for professionals (pp. xi–xxiii). New
York: Routledge.

Kiselica, M. S., Englar-Carlson, M., Horne, A. M., & Fisher, M. (2008b). A positive psychology perspective on helping boys. In M. S. Kiselica, M. Englar-
Carlson, & A. M. Horne (Eds.), *Counseling troubled boys: A guidebook for*
professionals (pp. 31–48). New York: Routledge.

Kiselica, M. S., Mulé, M., & Haldeman, D. C. (2008c). Finding inner peace in a
homophobic world: Counseling gay boys and boys who are questioning
their sexual identity. In M. S. Kiselica, M. Englar-Carlson, & A. M. Horne
(Eds.), *Counseling troubled boys: A guidebook for professionals* (pp. 31–48).
New York: Routledge.

Korobov, N., & Thorne, A. (2006). Intimacy and distancing: Young men's conversations about romantic relationships. *Journal of Adolescent Research, 21*(1),
27–55.

Legato, M. (2008). *Why men die first: How to lengthen your lifespan.* New York:
Palgrave Macmillan.

Levant, R. F. (2001). Desperately seeking language: Understanding, assessing and
treating normative male alexithymia. In G. R. Brooks & G. Good (Eds.), *The*
new handbook of counseling and psychotherapy for men (Vol. 1, pp. 355–368).
San Francisco, CA: Jossey-Bass.

Levy, D. P. (2005). Hegemonic complicity, friendship, and comradeship: Validation
and causal processes among White, middle-class, middle-aged men. *Journal*
of Men's Studies, 13(2), 199–224.

Lewis, D. O. (1998). *Guilty by reason of insanity: A psychiatrist explores the minds*
of killers. New York: Ballantine Publishing Group.

Lilienfeld, S. O., & Arkowitz, H. (2010, May/June). Are men the more belligerent
sex? *Scientific American Mind, 21*(2), 64–65.

Maccoby, E. E. (1990). Gender and relationships: A developmental account.
American Psychologist, 45(4), 513–520.

Maccoby, E. E. (2002). Gender and group process: A developmental perspective.
Current Directions in Psychological Science, 11(2), 54–58.

Maccoby, E. E. (2004). Aggression in the context of gender development. In M.
Putallaz & K. L. Bierman (Eds.), *Aggression, antisocial behavior, and violence*
among girls: A developmental perspective (pp. 3–22). New York: Guilford.

Margulies, A. (1984). Toward empathy: The uses of wonder. *American Journal of Psychiatry, 141*(9), 1025–1033.

McClure, E. B. (2000). A meta-analytic review of sex differences in facial expression processing and their development in infants, children, and adolescents. *Psychological Bulletin, 126,* 424–453.

McNelles, L. R., & Connolly, J. A. (1999). Intimacy between adolescent friends: Age and gender differences in intimate affect and intimate behaviors. *Journal of Research on Adolescence, 9*(2), 143–159.

Morash, M. (2005). *Understanding gender, crime, and justice.* Thousand Oaks, CA: Sage.

Mortola, P., Hiton, H., & Grant, S. (2008). *BAM! Boys advocacy and mentoring: A leader's guide to strengths-based groups for boys.* New York: Routledge.

Nash, A., & Grossi, G. (2007). Picking Barbie's™ brain: Inherent sex differences in scientific ability? *Journal of Interdisciplinary Feminist Thought, 2*(1), 5.

Nealy, E. C. (2008). Working with LGBT families. In M. McGoldrick & K. V. Hardy (Eds.), *Re-visioning family therapy: Race, culture, and gender in clinical practice* (2nd ed., pp. 289–299). New York: Guilford.

Nelson, J. K. (2008). Laugh and the world laughs with you: An attachment perspective on the meaning of laughter in psychotherapy. *Clinical Social Work Journal, 36*(1), 41–49.

Nopoulos, P., Flaum, M., O'Leary, D., & Andreasen, N. C. (2000). Sexual dimorphism in the human brain: Evaluation of tissue volume, tissue composition and surface anatomy using magnetic resonance imaging. *Psychiatry Research: Neuroimaging, 98*(1), 1–13.

Oransky, M., & Fisher, C. (2009). The development and validation of the Meanings of Adolescent Masculinity Scale. *Psychology of Men & Masculinity, 10*(1), 57–72.

Paechter, C. (2007). *Being boys, being girls: Learning masculinities and femininities.* New York: Open University Press.

Panksepp, J. (2009). Brain emotional systems and qualities of mental life: From animal models of affect to implications for psychotherapeutics. In D. Fosha, D. J. Siegel, & M. F. Solomon (Eds.), *The healing power of emotion: Affective neuroscience, development and clinical practice* (pp. 1–26). New York: Norton.

Parke, R. D., & Brott, A. A. (1999). *Throwaway dads: The myths and barriers that keep men from being the fathers they want to be.* Boston, MA: Houghton Mifflin.

Percy, W. (2000). *The message in the bottle: How queer man is, how queer language is, and what one has to do with the other.* New York: Picador. (Original work published 1954)

Perry, B. D., & Szalavitz, M. (2005). *The boy who was raised as a dog and other stories from a child psychiatrist's notebook: What traumatized children can teach us about loss, love, and healing.* New York: Basic Books.

Perry, I. (2008). "Tell us how it feels to be a problem": Hip hop longings and poor young black men. In E. Anderson (Ed.), *Against the wall: Poor, young, black, and male* (pp. 165–177). Philadelphia, PA: University of Pennsylvania Press.

Phillips, A. (2006). On not making it up: The varieties of creative experience. In A. Phillips, *Side effects* (pp. 75–100). New York: HarperCollins.

Pinker, S. (2008). *The sexual paradox: Men, women, and the real gender gap.* New York: Scribner.

Pollack, W. S. (1998). *Real boys: Rescuing our sons from the myths of boyhood.* New York: Random House.

Pollack, W. S. (2010). Gender issues: Modern models of young male resilient mental health. In J. E. Grant & M. N. Potenza (Eds.), *Young adult mental health* (pp. 96–109). New York: Oxford University Press.

Reese, L. E., Horne, A. M., Bell, C. D., & Wingfield, J. H. (2008). Counseling aggressive boys and angry males. In M. S. Kiselica, M. Englar-Carlson, & A. M. Horne (Eds.), *Counseling troubled boys: A guidebook for professionals* (pp. 191–217). New York: Routledge.

Resnick, M. D., Bearman, P. S., Blum, R. W., Bauman, K. E., Harris, K. M., Jones, J., ... Udry, J. R. (1997). Protecting adolescents from harm. *JAMA, 278*(10), 823–832.

Resnick, M. D., Harris, L. J., & Blum, R. W. (2008). The impact of caring and connectedness on adolescent health and well-being. *Journal of Paediatrics and Child Health, 29*(s1), s3–s9.

Riggs, D. W. (2008). All the boys are straight: Heteronormativity in contemporary books on fathering and raising boys. *THYMOS: Journal of Boyhood Studies, 2*(2), 186–202.

Robertson, J. M., & Shepard, D. S. (2008). The psychological development of boys. In M. S. Kiselica, M. Englar-Carlson, & A. M. Horne (Eds.), *Counseling troubled boys: A guidebook for professionals* (pp. 3–29). New York: Routledge.

Roiphe, K. (1994). *The morning after: Sex, fear, and feminism.* Boston, MA: Little, Brown and Company.

Rose, A. J. (2007). Structure, content, and socioemotional correlates of girls' and boys' friendships: Recent advances and future directions. *Merrill-Palmer Quarterly, 53*(3), 489–506.

Rose, A. J., & Rudolph, K. D. (2006). A review of sex differences in peer relationship processes: Potential trade-offs for the emotion and behavioral development of girls and boys. *Psychological Bulletin, 132*(1), 98–131.

Rudman, L. A., & Glick, P. (2008). *The social psychology of gender: How power and intimacy shape gender relations.* New York: Guilford.

Saval, M. (2009). *The secret lives of boys: Inside the raw emotional world of male teens.* New York: Basic Books.

Sax, L. (2005). *Why gender matters: What parents and teachers need to know about the emerging science of sex differences.* New York: Doubleday.

Sax, L. (2007). *Boys adrift: The five factors driving the growing epidemic of unmotivated boys and underachieving young men.* New York: Basic Books.

Schwartz, J. M., & Begley, S. (2002). *The mind and the brain: Neuroplasticity and the power of mental force.* New York: HarperCollins.

Selekman, M. D. (1997). *Solution-focused therapy with children: Harnessing family strengths for systemic change.* New York: Guilford.

Shilkret, R., & Shilkret, C. (2008). Attachment theory. In J. Berzoff, L. M. Flanagan, & P. Hertz (Eds.), *Inside out and outside in: Psychodynamic clinical theory and psychopathology in contemporary multicultural contexts* (2nd ed., pp. 189–203). Lanham, MD: Jason Aronson.

Siegel, D. J. (2010). *The mindful therapist: A clinician's guide to mindsight and neural integration.* New York: Norton.

Sinclair, S. L., & Taylor, B. A. (2004). Unpacking the tough guise: Toward a discursive approach for working with men in family therapy. *Contemporary Family Therapy, 26*(4), 389–408.

Spencer, R. (2007). "I just feel safe with him": Emotional closeness in male youth mentoring relationships. *Psychology of Men & Masculinity, 8*(3), 185–198.

Straus, M. B. (2007). *Adolescent girls in crisis: Intervention and hope.* New York: Norton.

Synnott, A. (2009). *Re-thinking men: Heroes, villains and victims.* Burlington, VT: Ashgate.

Szalavitz, M., & Perry, B. D. (2010). *Born for love: Why empathy is essential—and endangered.* New York: HarperCollins.

Taffel, R. (2005). *Breaking through to teens: A new psychotherapy for the new adolescence.* New York: Guilford.

Tannen, D. (1990). *You just don't understand: Women and men in conversation.* New York: HarperCollins.

Tannen, D. (2010, May/June). He said, she said. *Scientific American Mind, 21*(2), 22–29.

Tarver, D. B., Wong, N. T., Neighbors, H. W., & Zimmerman, M. A. (2004). The role of father support in the prediction of suicidal ideation among black adolescent males. In N. Way & J. Y. Chu (Eds.), *Adolescent boys: Exploring diverse cultures of boyhood* (pp. 144–163). New York: New York University Press.

Terr, L. (2008). *Magical moments of change: How psychotherapy turns kids around.* New York: Norton.

Tolman, D. L., Spencer, R., Harmon, T., Rosen-Reynoso, M., & Striepe, M. (2004). Getting close, staying cool: Early adolescent boys' experiences with romantic relationships. In N. Way & J. Y. Chu (Eds.), *Adolescent boys: Exploring diverse cultures of boyhood* (pp. 235–255). New York: New York University Press.

Tyre, P. (2008). *The trouble with boys: A surprising report card on our sons, their problems at school, and what parents and educators must do.* New York: Crown Publishers.

Walker, B. M. (2004). Frames of self: Capturing working-class British boys' identities through photographs. In N. Way & J. Y. Chu (Eds.), *Adolescent boys: Exploring diverse cultures of boyhood* (pp. 31–58). New York: New York University Press.

Way, N. (2004). Intimacy, desire, and distrust in the friendships of adolescent boys. In N. Way & J. Y. Chu (Eds.), *Adolescent boys: Exploring diverse cultures of boyhood* (pp. 167–196). New York: New York University Press.

Way, N., & Pahl, K. (1999). Friendship patterns among urban adolescent boys: A qualitative account. In M. Kopala & L. A. Suzuki (Eds.), *Using qualitative methods in psychology* (pp. 145–161). Thousand Oaks, CA: SAGE.

Weaver-Hightower, M. B. (2008). Inventing the "all-American boy": A case study of the capture of boys' issues by conservative groups. *Men & Masculinities, 10*(3), 267–295.

Wexler, D. B. (2009). *Men in therapy: New approaches for effective treatment.* New York: Norton.

Wilson, J. (2007). *The performance of practice: Enhancing the repertoire of therapy with children and families*. London, UK: Karnac.

Xie, H., & Shi, B. (2009). Gender similarities and differences in preadolescent peer groups. *Merrill-Palmer Quarterly, 55*(2), 157–183.

Zeki, S. (2009). *Splendors and miseries of the brain: Love, creativity, and the quest for human happiness*. Chichester, West Sussex, UK: Wiley-Blackwell.

2

Honoring Masculine Strivings in Individual Psychotherapy With Boys

GREGORY BARKER AND DAVID A. CRENSHAW

We reject gender stereotypes. Boys are not Martians and girls are not extraterrestrials from Venus. Though John Gray's popular bestselling book *Men Are From Mars, Women Are From Venus* (2004) contained many useful insights, we contend that narrow cultural roles result in the dysfunctional socialization affecting far too many adolescents in Western cultures. We take particular exception to the wholesale rejection of masculine traits that may prove either beneficially adaptive or dysfunctional, depending on one's situation.

We support research that identifies human traits such as courage and personal sacrifice (Kiselica, Englar-Carlson, & Horne, 2008) to be positive masculine strivings in some circumstances, while other human traits exhibited by males may be dysfunctional, depending on the relational context. Research has identified a list of negative strivings, among them emotional constriction, homophobia, hypercompetitiveness, and hyperfocus on success (Kiselica et al., 2008; Levant, 1995; O'Neil, 2006). Those four behaviors frequently preclude any possibility of satisfying closeness in relationships for males. We believe that any discussion of those traits should identify the behavior not merely as masculine, but as human traits that appear in both men and women with the understanding that those behaviors may be adaptations to certain circumstances (Silverstein & Rashbaum, 1995).

POTENTIAL INVISIBLE WOUNDS OF BOYS

The tendency for authorities to label some boys as disruptive troublemakers can begin early in life. Garbarino (2008) reported the startling fact that more children are expelled from kindergarten than from high school; most are males who are regarded as too aggressive or impulsive to be around others. We have seen referrals in our private practices of five- and six-year-old boys who, even with their high energy levels and sometimes impulsive behavior, appeared to us to be perfectly normal. These young boys were at risk for being removed from their school programs. The struggle to attain adequate impulse and affect regulation can still be developing in kindergarten and first grade without the need for *Diagnostic and Statistical Manual of Mental Disorders*, Fourth Edition (DSM-IV) classifications. The timetables for this and other developmental achievements can vary widely for individual children, and usually difficulties in these areas can be treated effectively without the need for expulsion. Boys ages 5 through 12 are twice as likely to be regarded as hyperactive or as aggressive than girls of the same age (Spinks, Nagle, Macpherson, Bain, & McClure, 2008). The "zero-tolerance" approach to violence of all kinds has pervaded our educational systems, both public and private. Though understandable in light of the rare but highly publicized and tragic incidents of school shootings, we must guard against the danger of developing zero tolerance for young boys who have not fully mastered the crucial developmental task of self-regulation.

Social toxicity psychologically wounds all children, but stressors such as poverty or exposure to violence may manifest differently in boys and girls. A study of 1,200 low-income, African American early adolescents found that girls reported more symptoms (largely internalizing symptoms), while boys reported more stress resulting from exposure to violence and sexual stressors. Boys in gangs reported additional stress from these exposures (Carlson & Grant, 2008). Frequently, emotional wounding in children takes the form of some kind of devaluation (Crenshaw, 2008b; Crenshaw & Garbarino, 2007; Crenshaw & Hardy, 2005, 2007; Garbarino & Crenshaw, 2008; Hardy & Crenshaw, 2008; Hardy & Laszloffy, 2005). Devaluation occurs when children are made to feel "less than" others because of race, gender, sexual orientation, poverty, or ethnic, national, or regional background. Although the trauma is expressed differently, we should never assume the wounding causes less suffering because a child is male or female. In general, there is a tendency to discount invisible (emotional) wounds of children in Western culture because they can't be seen or quantified. Yet these invisible wounds can be far more painful for children than their physical wounds.

The Dilemma of Males Cut Off From Affect

Silverstein and Rashbaum (1995) argued the position that mothers are conditioned in Western culture to push their sons away for fear of feminizing them. The earlier this happens, the greater the loss, as a child's primary attachment in the early period of life is most often with his or her mother. There are exceptions, as the father or sometimes the grandparents may be the child's primary attachment figure. The rupture in the mother–son relationship can be painful to the male child and, in the view of Silverstein and Rashbaum, contributes to the often described cutoff affect in males. Yet this rupture can, in keeping with the diversity of male development described by Haen in Chapter 1, also serve as a possible springboard for positive masculine identification and strivings.

STRENGTHS AND ADAPTIVE QUALITIES OF MASCULINE STRIVINGS

Traits expressed in the form of aggressive pursuit of goals or willingness to take courageous stands for what one believes should be celebrated and honored. Also, male daring and risk taking when the context calls for it, as well as male self-reliance and humanitarianism, should be accepted (Kiselica et al., 2008). However, the tendency to dominate by aggression or to exert coercive power over others may be said to succeed if one's goal is to prevail over others, but at the cost of precluding intimacy. The need to belong and to be accepted by one's peers is among the most compelling of all human needs, so for a culture to reward traits of dominance that impede expressions of intimacy is a disastrous price for its members to pay. Silverstein and Rashbaum (1995) observed that we train our young men for combat at age 18 and send them off to war to potentially die in battle, but we also complain when they are not able to express tender, warm feelings—the very feelings that would make a warrior feel too vulnerable.

THERAPEUTIC TASKS WITHIN A RELATIONAL THERAPY FRAMEWORK

Tasks of Engagement

Engagement in therapy is a particularly challenging task once boys enter the preadolescent period. When boys are eight years or younger, they often enjoy gaining the attention of a therapist. They lack the self-consciousness, embarrassment, and sense of shame that inhibits preadolescent and teenage boys upon entering a therapist's office. We often observe, however, that preadolescent boys and teens often protest or devalue therapy up to the office door and then milk it for all they can get once inside. This is typically a face-saving tactic on the part of boys who were taught not to show vulnerability, and if these strategies are honored, they need not interfere with engagement. Our clinical experience has taught us to respect and honor whatever defenses the boys employ, and to assume their tactics are necessary and serve a useful function. By honoring their defenses, we find that they need them less or can employ them more discriminately and flexibly.

Working With Resistance

We give little credence to the traditional concept of "resistance." Our combined 70 years of clinical experience of treating boys in psychotherapy suggests that, as much as boys try to avoid our exploration of the painful and sensitive areas of their hearts and lives, they often harbor a secret wish to unburden themselves and to tell their story. What we used to consider resistance in our male clients, and female as well, we now realize was our lack of the requisite skills earlier in our careers to make it sufficiently comfortable and natural for our young clients to talk. We fully adhere to the philosophy of Ross Greene (1998) that children will do well if they can; our job is to find out what blocks their path. The strategies detailed in the next section are intended to give sufficient structure and to provide the tools that will enable our clients to share with us what is blocking their path.

Expressing a Full Range of Affect

Due to the way boys are socialized in Western culture, the constraints on expressing emotions that are "unmanly" lead in some males (but certainly not all, as stressed by Haen in the first chapter of this book) to a constricted range of affect expression. We know that young males experience tender feelings, fear, sadness, and other emotions that imply vulnerability, but they sometimes cannot give voice to them. Such constriction of emotional expression stunts the healthy growth of some males in our culture and inhibits their potential for fulfilling intimacy. The task of psychotherapy for such boys is to expand the range of acceptable emotional expression in male children and adolescents. This therapy goal overlaps with the following issue of coping with vulnerability.

Managing the Exposure to Vulnerability

It takes courage to reveal one's weakness and vulnerability, yet those experiences are part and parcel of being human. If one is denied the right to feel weak or to acknowledge vulnerability, he is denied a basic sense of his humanity. Films rarely depict male actors as sensitive, vulnerable, and capable of a full range of human feelings, yet there are more examples today than in the past. The "Marlboro Man"—macho, tough, and unfeeling—was the ideal male image for many boys growing up in the authors' generation. While still limited, today there are more varied male role models for contemporary youths to emulate. Counselors can reframe candid efforts to express weakness, fear, doubt, sadness, or tears as acts of courage and strength.

Combating Shame

Since negative messages about self in childhood are encoded with intensity (James, 1989), therapists need to match the underlying emotional intensity if they are to refute shameful messages. For example, boys whose fathers are incarcerated may feel their fate is sealed and assume that jail is their destination as well. It is essential for the therapist to dispute and challenge such beliefs, not only with emotional conviction, but also to delineate specifically how a child who is kind to animals and who helps younger children is not destined for a jail cell. It is important to recognize that a boy's fatalistic beliefs may be based on a close, loyal identification with his father. The boy's natural desire for a bond with his father can be acknowledged as positive and a healthy drive while disputing the conclusion that incarceration is an inevitable outcome.

Discerning When Male Strivings Are to Be Valued and When Not

In our view, the goal of therapy with boys is to identify that traits that have been traditionally labeled as "male" traits (the aggressive pursuit of goals; the capacity to fight and even die for a cause or to defend one's dignity; physical strength, particularly upper body strength; and courage) are to be valued, even when they might be ill-suited to a boy's circumstances. Adolescent males need to be taught explicitly that one can be strong and courageous, yet still express tender emotions when the situation calls for such feelings. They need to be told repeatedly that being fully human is an act of courage, and that even the bravest fighting men are capable of acknowledging fear.

Supporting Boys in Making Healthy Choices When Faced With High-Risk Peer Influences

There is perhaps no more critical choice that adolescents face than the selection of friends. The choice of friends is influenced by a wide range of factors beyond the scope of this chapter. But one key factor that leads to choosing delinquent peers as friends is a shared lack of social and academic success. Young males who feel deprived of both social and academic standing and thereby feel devalued and marginalized in school search for acceptance by seeking out peers who also feel they don't belong or by joining gangs (Garbarino, 1999; Hardy & Laszloffy, 2005). We use cognitive techniques to help boys to make healthy judgments regarding their peer relational world. These techniques include asking boys to reflect on signals they might look for to determine if a particular choice of peers is a positive one and those that would indicate their choice was a poor one.

SPECIFIC THERAPEUTIC STRATEGIES

Creating Portals of Entry

For many boys we've seen in therapy, stories of sports heroes and metaphors have proved a useful way of creating a portal of entry that is face-saving (Crenshaw & Barker, 2008). Pictures of sports heroes hung on the walls in the office have consistently drawn the attention of male clients of all ages, as well as a lesser number of female clients. The pictures were carefully selected to honor sports figures who are known not only for their athletic abilities but also for their charisma in projecting a model of positive masculinity. For example, Cal Ripken Jr. and Derek Jeter are superstars who established early in their careers a high standard of conduct, both on and off the field.

The pictures can be springboards for dialogue with young males about men they admire and whom they wish to emulate, as well as men in their own lives who have exerted a profound influence. The therapist also could pursue other persons (not necessarily males) who have been what the late Dr. Julius Segal (1988) called "charismatic adults," people in the lives of young people from whom they gather strength.

Another tool (Crenshaw, 2008a) utilized by the authors to create portals of entry with children is the Heartfelt Feelings Coloring Cards Strategy (HFCCS). The HFCCS consists of several applications, but the Relational Series, in which the child draws an image of a person within the heart according to various directives from the clinical manual of the HFCCS, is designed to explore the key attachments and relational world of the client. A boy can be instructed to draw a picture of someone who has been a "charismatic adult" for him, someone from whom he has been able to gather strength. It is important to insist that the client draw the person in the heart even if they do a stick figure, rather than just write the name of the person, because our consistent clinical experience has been that images are more powerful than words.

In using this tool, we are continually amazed at the creative expressiveness of our clients. It is not unusual, for example, for a boy to draw not only a picture of a person in the heart, but also symbols that depict the connections between the boy and his role model. One child drew his father as his charismatic adult, but also drew a bike, a fishing pole, and a hunting rifle, all symbols of loved and shared activities that forged the bond between them. On the inside of the card (designed like greeting cards), the child writes a note to his charismatic adult or alternatively tells the story of why he picked this particular person.

Use of Therapeutic Drawings and Stories

The use of drawings and storytelling enjoys a long tradition in child therapy and counseling (for a review of the literature on these tools, see Crenshaw, 2006). Projective drawing and storytelling strategies (Crenshaw, 2006, 2008a) have been used to address a range of therapeutic goals, such as constructive anger expression and modulation, development of empathy, recovering from loss and trauma, dealing with social rejection, honoring strengths, facilitating hope, and preparing for termination. One three-step strategy consists of the therapist telling a story, the child doing a drawing in response to the therapist's story, and finally the child telling a story that addresses some missing piece, unresolved conflict, or decision that needs to be made, as embedded in the original story (for examples of such strategies, see Crenshaw, 2006, 2008a). One story that is particularly well suited to the strengths-based philosophy of this chapter is "The Ballistic Stallion" (Crenshaw, 2008a). The story of courage and determination is told through the metaphor of a wild stallion that no one had been able to ride until the owner's 12-year-old daughter, through sheer determination and careful consideration of what had gone wrong in the past, finally succeeded in riding the stallion. The story can become a jumping off point to honor the strengths and courage of children by asking the boy to tell a story about a time when he also triumphed over some challenge or adversity.

Creative Characters Technique

Robert Brooks (1981, 2009) developed the creative characters technique as a storytelling technique rooted in the strengths-based perspective. As the story evolves, Brooks introduces various characters that are played out in storytelling drama that accentuates the strengths of children. In one clinical example of this technique, Brooks (2009) introduced the role of an animal trainer to work with a scared elephant in a circus in order to help a boy who was afraid of failing to access his strength and personal courage.

Discrimination Exercises: Role Playing and Behavioral Rehearsal

Role playing and behavioral rehearsal are frequently used tools in child therapy and counseling. Asking boys to demonstrate and rehearse positive masculinity in a variety of social situations can help expand the range of options available to them. One of the most important of all pro-social skills can be practiced in role play: the capacity for empathy. Specific role-playing exercises for expanding skills in empathy and appropriate assertion can readily be designed by the therapist (for examples, see Crenshaw, 2006). Role playing and behavioral rehearsal can take place in individual work, but can be especially helpful in group counseling sessions. It can add a measure of humor, as well as reducing performance anxiety, to ask participants to do it the "worst way" possible first before attempting to do it in the way they view as best.

Evocative Video Clips

Hardy and Laszloffy (2005) described the use of evocative video clips in groups with adolescents as a way of creating a meaningful stimulus to group discussion. This approach has been used in individual therapy to illustrate positive demonstrations of masculine strivings to create meaningful discussion. Some examples of film clips utilized include *Stand by Me* (1986), *Ordinary People* (1980), and *This Boy's Life* (2003).

Focusing On and Honoring Strengths

Opportunities arise frequently in the course of therapy to focus attention on the positive polarities of traits viewed as typical of males, such as courage in taking a stand or strength and determination in defending or advancing a just cause. However, therapists must be equally vigilant and responsive to behavioral patterns not traditionally associated with maleness. Kindness, tenderness, gentleness, and bravery in acknowledging weakness are examples of the latter.

Rubin (2006) highlights strengths by asking boys to create their own superhero. The boys decide what special powers their superhero is endowed with, along with any vulnerabilities. The follow-up includes asking the child how this created superhero reminds the youngster of his own special talents and strengths. In addition, strengths can be identified that help boys cope with specific vulnerabilities.

Another application of the HFCCS is called "everyday heroes." The child is asked to draw in the heart shape on the front of the greeting card a picture of someone in his or her everyday life whom he or she admires. On the inside of the card, the clients write a note to or tell a story about their everyday hero. The procedure is repeated until they've honored all their everyday heroes. It is important in this technique to emphasize that these heroes are not people who make the news, sports heroes, or rock stars, but members of their family, friends, teachers, coaches, or other people they've met along the way who in some quiet, unsung way have been heroic. The next step is to ask the boy if there is some way that he has been an everyday hero to someone. Perhaps he protected a smaller child from a bully, or did something emotionally courageous, such as admitting he was wrong in front of his peers. He is then invited to draw an image of self in the heart and to write the story of his heroic feat on the inside of the card. Some young clients will prefer to tell the story and, in that case, the therapist will transcribe the story on the inside of the card.

Expanding the Range of Emotional Expression in Boys

The determined pursuit of affect in child therapy is one of the ways that therapists prove their mettle. The late Walter Bonime (1989), who provided psychoanalytic supervision to the second author, emphasized that feelings are analogous to a chord in music as compared to a single note. Children in general, but boys especially, are inclined to strike a single note when it comes to discussing feelings in therapy. The richness in the child's affective life requires elucidation from the therapist. The multiple variations in tone and intensity, the mixed, conflicting, and ambivalent feelings that are hard to talk about and describe, reveal the personality of the child in its most vivid way since emotions and their many variations are what give color and meaning to life.

The HFCCS is made up of two main components, the expressive and the relational cards. The expressive cards give children who generally have trouble identifying, labeling, and expressing more than a limited range of feelings a set of tools for expanding emotional expression. The expressive cards are utilized in a psychoeducational approach to teach a language of feelings. Boys are instructed to color in the heart on the front of the greeting card with the color chosen for a given feeling. The clinical manual for the HFCCS lists 40 emotions, ranging from very simple ones like sad and glad to more complex ones like perplexed or perturbed for older boys. On the inside of the card, clients are asked to describe a time when their heart was filled with that particular emotion. This process offers practice in providing a context for each of the emotions selected. This tool can be used with young boys to expand their constricted range of a feelings vocabulary.

Engaging the Father in the Therapeutic Process

Many young men spend an inordinate portion of their lives in search of their fathers. A father who is absent, either emotionally or physically, from a son's life can have a profound impact on his growth and sense of self. Boys are often raised in father-absent homes due to the high divorce rate, the tendency of courts to award child custody to mothers, and the pronounced social pathology of fathers abandoning their children. As a result, boys will often feel confused about what it means to be a man as they struggle to fit in without the steady guidance of their fathers (Perrin, Baker, Romelus, Jones, & Heesacker, 2009).

All too often, the adolescent boy's initial sessions in counseling are absent the father. Frequently, the mother initiates the referral due to her son's acting out or behavioral concerns. The father cannot make the first meeting because "he is too busy at work" or simply does not approve of therapy for his son. Such was the case when Carlos's mother called and made contact with me (GB) for our intake session.

The session was comprised mostly of mother's complaints about Carlos's impact on the family. Everything had been going reasonably well until the past year. Carlos was a good athlete and had participated on a number of teams while in middle school. But, during the ninth grade, he began hanging out with the wrong type of kids. Many of them just wanted to skateboard, play Xbox®, and smoke marijuana. On several occasions, Carlos's mother suspected him of smoking but she could never be sure. Then she received a call from the assistant principal at the high school informing her that Carlos had been caught with a small amount of marijuana while in gym class. He had neglected to bring a change of clothes for gym and was caught exchanging "weed" with a friend while they sat in the stands as the other boys played basketball.

Carlos's mother, Angelina, burst into tears as she described the multitudinous and occasionally vicious arguments that had erupted in the last six months with her husband. She complained that her husband was in "denial" about their oldest son's problems. Her husband was frustrated and described her as being a "drama queen." Basically, he perceived Carlos as being a good boy who was simply going through a "stage that all boys go through." In his opinion, his wife needed to lighten up. All the while, school referrals mounted for Carlos's oppositional and disrespectful behavior at school. Angelina felt overwhelmed by her responsibilities at work and home, so she called a friend whom she knew had taken her teenage son to me several years previously. Despite the overt protests of her son and the subtle protests of her husband, Carlos's mother set up an appointment with me.

Carlos's relationship with his father had been fractured for years. His father, Jordan, worked for a large computer company that required most of his time be spent either in the office or traveling. As his only son grew, Jordan believed that he had to make a choice between his job and his family. He simply could not keep up with both. As had been the case with his own father, Jordan relinquished his relationship with his son in favor of the daily and nightly rigors of his job. Somebody had to keep the family above water financially, he thought, and surely his wife's modest salary as a schoolteacher would not keep them afloat.

I further questioned, without expecting an answer, whether his father would be comfortable with me talking to his son. Most fathers don't want somebody else doing the speaking for them. I suggested that I call Jordan and invite him to my office so we could get to the bottom of this whole thing and get this counseling business over with as quickly as possible. I ventured that I preferred to avoid a series of long, drawn-out meetings that might last over a course of months or, even worse, years.

It has been our experience that the absent father will subtly (or not so subtly) discourage his son from talking to another man about the family's problems. Without the father's approval, the son might continue to present his resistant front of disrespect and opposition to counseling. It is critical for a father to provide his son with an opportunity to recognize his part in solving the family dilemma.

Now that we had heard his mother's side of the story, I suggested to Carlos that he should encourage his father to accept my invitation and attend the next session to offer his perception about the family situation. Despite his father's likely reluctance, Carlos should "continue to take charge" of the situation and help his father find time to meet and get things out on the table.

Crossing the Bridge Into Manhood

When Carlos's father entered the office with his son for the second session, I complimented Carlos on facilitating the meeting with the three of us. I informed Jordan that his son had been orchestrating this meeting for the past several months, in view of the host of acting-out behaviors that he had been exhibiting at both home and school. I reiterated that I perceived Carlos to be a "take charge" individual who must have been modeling the behavior of one or both of his parents. I noted that Carlos is clearly at a pivotal point in his development and that his behavior was not necessarily "bad," but misguided. He simply was looking for guidance at this juncture in his life. This take-charge and assertive characteristic had the potential to lead both Carlos and his parents out of their current predicament.

Before either Jordan or Carlos had much time to comment on my observations, I asked each for their patience in listening to my following proposal. First, it is important to realize that Carlos was facing a normal developmental crossroads in his life. In today's world, there never seems to be any time to honor the respective roles that each of us possesses in our families. In primitive cultures, there were rituals that were initiated to cope with what our current American culture has diagnosed as "oppositional" or "pathological" behavior. Carlos's behavior warranted neither a psychiatric diagnosis nor the simple dismissal that his behavior reflected that "boys will be boys." His acting out was much more complex and deeply ingrained than it might appear on the surface. Perhaps we had overlooked some of the rituals that should guide his behavior. Carlos was at a transition point, and his needs might have been overlooked as he strived to become a man.

I persisted in describing to Carlos and his father how primitive cultures frequently possessed deep human wisdom and enacted rituals to assist their members in moving from one stage of life to another, including birth, marriage, and death. Distinct rites of passage guided tribal members from childhood to adulthood. Margaret Mead addressed this issue in *Coming of Age in Samoa* (1973), when she expressed the idea that all children, regardless of their ethnic milieu, come to a moment during their teenage years when they begin to look beyond themselves and become aware of the rest of society. This is a time of awakening when the adolescent begins to celebrate his or her gifts and looks for ways to fit into the community. At this point in development, the boy is a child no longer, nor is he yet a man. In some cultures, certain rites were established just for males to lead them to become the accomplished elders of the tribe who would someday impart their wisdom to another generation.

Each rite of passage follows a prescribed series of events. Inevitably, there is an informational period punctuated with rituals that require a boy to accomplish something noteworthy to mark his transition. In the case of girls and women, there is a physiological transition point that boys and men do not experience. A girl's first menstruation marks her entry into womanhood, and menopause marks her passage into a more mature stage of life. Women learn naturally about the seasons of life, but men experience no clear demarcation between childhood and adulthood. To compensate, distinct rituals are created in primitive cultures for boys to experience the changes in life.

In some tribes, the father and elders of the community set aside a time to lead the boy into manhood. For the most part, the rearing of children is relegated to the women in the community. Then, in early adolescence, a boy indicates he is ready to move to the next stage in his life. Elders in the community note his intention and make preparations for the boys of the tribe to become initiated into adulthood. On one specific night in the spring, male elders go from one home to the next to select boys for initiation. The mother anticipates this ritual for her son and argues and fights with the elders. The mother dramatically contends that her adolescent boy is not ready to become a man. Often the elders pull the reluctant and sobbing boy from his home against the mother's wishes. This marks the beginning of his role as a man in the village.

There is much commotion and screaming as the mothers follow their sons and elders down the pathways of the village. Eventually, they reach the shore and a bridge leading to an island where more of the elders await the boys for the rites of passage. The mothers make one last effort to convince the elders that their sons are not ready for the passage across the bridge, but their efforts ultimately fail and they all return to the village. In actuality, the mothers and elders had been play-acting for this rite. The mothers then return to one of the female elders' homes to drink tea and compliment each other on their Academy Award-winning performances. "I put up quite a fuss. I am sure that my son really believed that I wanted him to stay and remain a little boy."

Only the father can help the boy get across the bridge. In our culture, the forbidden acts of consuming alcohol/drugs, engaging in sex, and driving a car are seen as gateways into manhood, so few boys in our society have the opportunity for their fathers to guide them to manhood. In our modern and "sophisticated" culture, this most important life passage is treated more as an extended period of "illness." Boys will protest that they need their independence while they continue to behave in ways that guarantee their protracted dependence. This adolescent period is endured with much complaining on both sides until it mercifully passes with time. By contrast, once a tribal boy crosses the bridge, his elders engage him in a series of rituals and he subsequently assumes the responsibilities accompanying manhood. When he returns to the village after the weekend sojourn, the boy is no longer considered by the members of his village to be a child. It is now time for him to be a responsible and contributing adult.

During the course of therapy, it becomes the father's job to help his son reach manhood, no matter how much he might kick and scream while being led across to the "island." I suggested that Jordan take charge of a specific activity that would begin his son's initiation into manhood. At this point, I wanted to empower Jordan with taking a more active role in guiding his son through this difficult life transition. Jordan suggested that they spend a weekend "away from everything" while camping in the mountains. They had not been away together since Carlos's days as a Cub Scout. Carlos started to protest that his father would not follow through and that a business meeting would interfere with their plans. I suggested that Carlos was cleverly challenging his father to take charge of the situation by denying his own ability to begin the process of initiation. However, Carlos should know that his father doesn't need the impetus to initiate the rituals, since this is actually a natural process that his father will undertake.

After the first camping weekend, Jordan and Carlos admitted that they had a good time, but no magical transformation had taken place. Carlos continued to argue with his mother and received another discipline referral at school for talking back to a teacher in the cafeteria. As an elder in his family's "tribe," I encouraged Jordan in the subsequent meetings to counsel his son about his responsibilities to school and family. Furthermore, I recommended to Jordan that he set up a "boys' night out" in which he and Carlos could watch a selection of movies with themes regarding masculine rites of passage. To start, I suggested that they view a personal favorite of mine, *Ordinary People*. Following the movie, father and son were to give a critique of the primary character's role in striving to establish his manhood.

It was important that Carlos recognize that all future advice delivered by his father would take into consideration that he is now a young adult who is receptive to change. It was Carlos's responsibility to take charge of setting up the weekly luncheon meetings at a restaurant in town so that they could share some of this time for "counsel." As a young adult, it was imperative that Carlos set the time and place for the Saturday meetings to discuss his concerns with his father/elder. Within two months, Jordan and Carlos decided that they no longer needed to attend therapy sessions with me as their Saturday meetings served the same purpose. Tensions in Carlos, Jordan, and Angelina's home declined considerably. Throughout this period of ritual, the entire family demonstrated a creative means of promoting their own resilience and their ability to transcend old, unconstructive patterns of interaction.

CASE STUDIES

The Genetic Cards Stacked Against Him:
Brian Determines His Own Course

After he was suspended from school for fighting for the third time during his sophomore year, school officials and his probation officer mandated counseling for Brian. At the first session, Brian walked into my office (GB) and manically began talking nonstop about how he was going to a skateboard park after school. Brian exhibited patches of dark hair from where he had awkwardly attempted to shave his own head the night before in order to impress his 13-year-old girlfriend. In all his 16 years, Brian contended he had never felt better and really did not need any counseling.

That day, Brian was optimistic about the upcoming weekend and the events that were to follow—at least, those that he hoped would follow. Brian's father had no idea that Brian was staying with friends for the weekend, nor did he ask when Brian left in the morning for school with his pack stuffed full of clothes. For that matter, Brian had not asked his friend if he could spend the night. But he hoped the family would let him stay there permanently if he behaved well at their home.

A week later, at the second session, an inevitable swing of darkness and depression left Brian feeling destitute and hopeless. On those dark days, he could barely lift his head from his desk in school. Frustrated by his own sense of hopelessness, Brian would refuse to complete any work in his behavior management special education classroom. He would mock his teachers, argue with authorities, set records for detention and suspension, and return home to fight with his clinically depressed father.

Brian had lost touch with his mother seven years earlier, even though she lived only 15 miles away. Brian's mother lived in a trailer park with her parents while receiving money from Social Security for an emotional disability. She met Brian's father when she was 14 years old and residing in the intensive care ward of a psychiatric center after experiencing psychotic episodes. Brian's chronically depressed father was 15 when he was admitted to the unit following the most alarming of three suicide attempts. Brian was conceived on the evening shift when the counselors were on a cigarette break.

Like his parents, Brian had a history of psychiatric hospitalizations following acts of violence at home. Brian had been diagnosed as having a bipolar disorder in conjunction with an oppositional defiant disorder that often culminated in his being prescribed antipsychotic medications such as Abilify, Risperdal, Lamictal, or Seroquel. He would be released somewhat sedated, often refusing to take the medication subsequently. On the days when he was agitated, Brian would assume an "I don't care" stance, refusing to listen to the interventions of teachers and school counselors. Anything adults suggested was responded to with consistent agitation and a repetitive mantra of "I don't care" or "Fine, leave me alone." Brian was further frustrated with his academics due to a reading disability and a visual processing disorder. Brian's experience at school left him feeling helpless and hopeless. His acting out only led to a greater sense of failure and a loss of dignity.

Brian's father had a familiar, but somewhat tragic story. He had a history marked by fractional involvement with his own alcoholic father. At times, Brian was sent to live with his paternal grandparents as a respite when his father became frustrated and couldn't "take it anymore." Brian's father had been attending mental health sessions at the community mental health clinic following a Child Protective Services report that had been brought against him for being physically abusive with two of his three children. Brian was the oldest of the siblings and received the brunt of his father's fury, particularly when the father was in a bad mood or had been drinking too much.

Brian described his teachers and administrators as a bunch of people who didn't care about him and believed that he was a "bad kid." We discussed his perception of himself and how that differed from the perceptions of others, particularly the adults in his life. Since he viewed them as disrespecting him, he was not going to give them any respect back. In fact, Brian would launch preemptive strikes before his teachers could criticize him. He was not going to back down to anybody. He proudly recounted how he had told an assistant principal to get out of his life and how he didn't know "who he was dealing with." That threat earned him three days of suspension and having to be home with his father. His father was frustrated that Brian had interrupted his time alone to drink. As a result, Brian and his father clashed for three days and he returned to school more frustrated and angry than ever.

Brian and I discussed the power he had over people by "not backing down to anybody." Often, he could control adults with his negative comments and verbal diatribes. When they would ask him to stop what he was doing, his behavior escalated. Instead of pumping the emotional brakes, Brian would push down on the accelerator and take the adults for a freewheeling ride that he controlled.

From a systemic perspective, it was evident that a "problem cycle" (Eron & Lund, 1996) was being maintained without an adequate solution being provided. For example, when Brian became agitated during a depressed mood swing, he would act badly. The school, or his father, would attempt to punish him by putting restrictions on his behavior. Suspensions, groundings, and withdrawal of contact with friends only caused Brian to become more defiant and oppositional. In turn, the school authorities, or his father, would increase the punishment in order "to fit the crime." As there were more repetitions of this cycle, Brian's problematic behaviors would intensify and grow, ultimately leading to more hospitalizations. This problem-maintaining cycle needed to be shifted to a solution-based cycle.

I remarked what a powerful role Brian had in taking people "along for the ride." Was he ever afraid of crashing? He said that he didn't care. If he crashed, at least the teacher/administrator was going to get injured or go down with him as well. I questioned whether the adults really might have had a hand on the wheel, kind of like the driver's education teachers who have a separate brake in their cars. That is, who really is driving? I remarked how people around Brian often misinterpreted his significant determination and drive as a negative attribute.

Was it possible Brian could use his strength and determination to drive that car in another direction without the administrator possibly controlling the wheel? Brian was a very determined individual who liked to set his own course without anyone else intervening. We concluded that others had misconstrued Brian's strong will as oppositional or stubborn behavior. About that time, Brian began to stand on his own two feet without anyone propping him up. He began to request assistance from others on his own terms and when he was ready. It takes strength and determination to ask for help from others. (Brian relayed a story illustrating how his mother never followed through on the recommendations of the caseworker from the Department of Social Services. Further, Brian described disappointingly how his father started to attend AA meetings but stopped going when his sponsor recommended that he attend more meetings each week.)

I agreed with his assessment. Brian came from a family of strong personalities who were determined to not let anybody push them around. However, who was really driving their "car"? It seemed as if Brian needed to veer off course and take his own route. I pointed out that Brian was very sensitive to the plight of his parents and redefined his anger as a form of compassion for their mistakes. Perhaps it was time for Brian to let his natural abilities show through and to be unashamed to go in a different direction than his parents had selected. Perhaps it was time for Brian to drive to a different destination and away from the location that some of his administrators had preset on his car's navigation system. "They think I will probably drop out of high school and maybe only get my GED. Nobody in my family has ever gone to college and they think I am going to be just like my dad, who was in special education at the same school."

We tried to discuss different scenarios that might ensue should he take another highway. Would others be surprised? Would his father or mother be discouraged that he veered off in another direction? Would he be seduced into returning to the old road in order to make them more comfortable? Or could he utilize his determination to set his own course?

We then decided that it might be helpful for him to develop a plan or road map that could put his determination to good use. I professed that I was pretty talented at creating maps for myself but I could never make Brian's for him. However, I would be glad to review his map at the next session. I suggested that he write down his plans in the form of a road map with short-term stops that he might have to take along the way before he reached his ultimate destination. Of course, it would be necessary for him to decide on his own destination without the input or ideas of others who might be trying to influence him. Nobody could set those goals for him since so many in his life had such disparate and mistaken perceptions of who he really was as a person.

Over the course of several months, we devised a map that would reflect Brian's determination and natural ability to fend for himself. During the course of treatment, we employed the therapeutic strategies of role playing and behavioral rehearsal. I would take on the persona of a teacher at school who was upset with Brian's behavior in the cafeteria and he would develop creative ways to avoid causing a conflict. Brian's strategies became more diverse and unique as he sometimes took on the role of the teacher and instructed me on ways that I could have better handled the potential conflict.

In order to keep himself on this personal route, Brian agreed to attend school every day so he could receive enough credits to begin a vocational program in large engine repair during his senior year. He concluded that maintaining a regimen of exercise and forsaking cigarettes and alcohol would make him feel more alert. Further, Brian believed that he would consult a psychiatrist at the mental health clinic for regular follow-up on his medication. He was determined not to "fall off the wagon" with the medication, as had been the case with his parents.

By his senior year, Brian had moved out of his father's home to live with a friend's family. He had been admitted to the vocational program and anticipated receiving a degree in June. Brian had resiliently determined his own course.

Finding Strength Through Silence: Roberto Elects to Be Mute

Roberto could not recall anything about his parents. For that matter, it was difficult to know what Roberto could recall. He had not talked in the past two years. For some reason, after having seen a combination of six psychologists and psychiatrists over the course of his two-year silence, Roberto refused to talk or answer any questions. Roberto was now 14 years old and becoming more difficult for his caretakers to handle.

Roberto was adopted shortly after birth by a young professional couple who hoped to begin their own family. Little was known about his natural parents at the time of Roberto's adoption, only that they were teenagers who were unable to care for a child. Roberto's mother was of Peruvian descent and his father was African American.

Roberto was a handsome boy with dark hair and light brown skin. He had been an agitated and difficult baby from the outset of his adoption. Roberto was born prematurely and his doctors identified in him characteristics of a child experiencing withdrawal from drugs. In other words, Roberto appeared to be a "crack baby." He exhibited colic and rarely slept through the night during his first year with his adoptive parents. He cried constantly and was difficult to satiate. The young couple began to have second thoughts as to what they had undertaken around the time of Roberto's first birthday. The pressure was intense as both parents tried to maintain their work schedules. However, daycare was difficult to maintain due to Roberto's constantly demanding temperament. Prior to Roberto's second birthday, with great reluctance, the couple returned to the agency and gave up rights to their adopted son.

At this early point in his life, Roberto stepped into the revolving door of multiple foster home placements. Actually, there were 12 in all. Nobody was clear as to why Roberto had been sent to so many homes. Some of the foster homes were therapeutic in nature, meaning the parents were trained to provide for the needs of psychiatrically impaired children. However, his last several placements were through a church organization and he was under the supervision of the church elders.

During the past two years, Roberto had fallen silent. He refused to talk at either home or school. Allegations of sexual abuse had been filed after Roberto alleged that one of his caretakers had touched him during his sleep. Child Protective Services had made a cursory investigation; however, this was the third time that Roberto had made such allegations. It was generally concluded that Roberto was "crying wolf," simply drawing attention to himself because he was a lonely, angry, and desperate child.

When I (GB) was introduced to Roberto, he had just returned from a four-week stay in a psychiatric center following a host of evaluations and observations. Nobody had been able to penetrate his formidable defenses. Professionals had labeled Roberto with a number of "disorders," such as selective mutism, a reactive attachment disorder, an oppositional defiant disorder, and a borderline personality disorder. Experienced therapists were frustrated in their efforts to draw Roberto out of his world of silence.

Roberto's new adoptive parents wanted Roberto to attend therapy in order to relate to somebody, since he had cut himself off from his teachers and adults in general. Roberto would interact with other students in school; however, he would not talk. He was assessed as possessing superior cognitive ability when he was in the second grade. Despite his refusal to talk, Roberto was passing all his courses in school.

As would be expected, Roberto entered hesitatingly when his adoptive mother brought him to my office. I made it clear to Roberto and his mother that I had no goals in therapy and that I was very reluctant to take this particular case in the first place. When all the other therapists had failed to break through, what chance had I in getting Roberto to speak? In fact, since I am a competitive individual and someone who does not like to lose, I suggested that we might want to set up new parameters for the therapy. Maybe, with his mother's permission, we could just "hang out" and not do anything. I emphasized that my day is stressful enough as it is, and I would welcome an hour when I would not have to talk as well. Seeing Roberto once a week would be like a "little vacation" for me whereby I did not have to diagnose and treat a client. In fact, there was no paradoxical intention in my description of my therapeutic approach. I truly believed that Roberto was an intelligent individual who had undergone multiple traumas in his life. He had the power to choose to talk whenever and with whomever he wanted.

Roberto wore a Mets baseball cap to our first meeting. His mother stated that Roberto loved the Mets and they had gone as a family to a game at Shea Stadium the previous week. This was Roberto's first professional baseball game and he bought every Mets souvenir he could get his hands on. I asked if he had any baseball cards and suggested that maybe we could trade cards instead of doing any therapy during our meetings. Further, I admitted to being a diehard Dodgers fan, and maybe I could trade some of my "worthless" Mets cards for some Dodgers cards. Roberto nodded in agreement that he would prefer trading cards to playing the games he had with the previous therapists.

Our early sessions had the outcomes that I had predicted. Basically, we traded cards and Roberto would write me abbreviated notes when he had a particularly pertinent issue he wanted to convey to me. Gradually, I accumulated a wealth of Dodgers cards and had collected most of the members of the previous year's team. I reassured Roberto that I respected his choice to remain silent in our meetings. Although he was having a positive experience with his new adoptive family, I suggested that he proceed with caution before speaking to them about what had transpired in his other foster settings.

I reinforced the notion that his choice of remaining silent was the best choice he could make at this point. By remaining silent, people around him were beginning to listen to his story for the first time. He was not ill. In fact, he was not really experiencing what the psychiatrists in the hospitals diagnosed as selective mutism. He did not fear speaking, nor was he shy or fearful of social embarrassment. What was being interpreted as an attempt at social isolation was actually a flight into health and expression. I impressed upon Roberto that I viewed his silence as an adaptation to his difficult life. He had made a "Darwinian" adaptation to cope with adversity and struggle. In fact, Roberto's silence was the ultimate act of expression.

During the course of our therapy, Robert chose to begin to talk with a custodian at the school whom he helped in an after-school program. Eventually, he let his special education teacher and a few selected friends into his talking world. By the next academic year, Roberto entered into all regular education classes and began speaking regularly. During this whole time, Roberto and I remained true to our pact to refrain from speaking during our sessions. At our last session, Roberto wrote a long note of thanks for our time together.

Roberto had chosen to be "sick" in order to get well. Roberto's strength came in the form of his most effective means of self-protection. He chose to have others perceive him as "sick" in order to save and protect himself from the pain of physical and sexual abuse that had transpired over the past eight years of his life. It was not until he stopped talking that he was removed from one of his previously abusive foster homes. Roberto demonstrated his resilience through silence. With time, once he was ready, another form of speaking evolved.

Five years later, on a warm summer evening, my car was idling with the windows down at a stoplight in the city. A group of young people were at the corner waiting to cross the street. One of the boys looked like Roberto, but I couldn't be sure. I had not seen him since our last session. As they began to cross the street in front of my car, one of the young men pulled away from the pack and approached the passenger seat window. It was Roberto. Roberto stuck his head in the window of my car and said two very poignant words: "Dodgers suck!"

Roberto is now a sportswriter for a local newspaper.

CONCLUSION

The stories of these three young men indicate the capacity for resilience and personal power demonstrated during the course of therapy. Carlos, Brian, and Roberto struggled to avoid the pitfalls of pathology scattered along their roads to manhood. Each young man found hope to alter his life during this period of stress and confusion. As therapists, it becomes our role to provide a palette with which a boy may begin to paint a self-portrait that accentuates his power and strengths. With these strengths discovered, no longer will the boy be lured back into a customary cycle of self-destructive pathology.

No strategic, solution-focused, or paradoxical interventions will ever be effective unless the therapist truly believes in the boy's ability to cope with his personal roadblocks. Only then can the adolescent male be armed with means for transforming pathology into strength. Once this transformation takes place, we come to realize that men really are not from Mars. Rather, men are from Earth and capable of utilizing their innate strengths to overcome personal struggles.

REFERENCES

Bonime, W. (1989). *Collaborative psychoanalysis: Anxiety, depression, dreams and personality change*. Madison, NJ: Fairleigh Dickinson Press.

Brooks, R. (1981). Creative characters: A technique in child therapy. *Psychotherapy: Theory, Research and Practice, 18*(1), 131–139.

Brooks, R. (2009). The power of mindsets: A personal journey to nurture dignity, hope, and resilience in children. In D. A. Crenshaw (Ed.), *Resilience in healing: Honoring strengths without trivializing suffering* (pp. 19–40). Lanham, MD: Jason Aronson.

Carlson, G. A., & Grant, K. E. (2008). The roles of stress and coping in explaining gender differences in risk for psychopathology among African American urban adolescents. *The Journal of Early Adolescence, 28*(3), 375–404.

Crenshaw, D. A. (2006). *Evocative strategies in child and adolescent psychotherapy.* Lanham, MD: Jason Aronson.

Crenshaw, D. A. (2008a). *Therapeutic engagement of children and adolescents.* Lanham, MD: Jason Aronson.

Crenshaw, D. A. (Ed.). (2008b). *Child and adolescent psychotherapy: Wounded spirits and healing paths.* Lanham, MD: Lexington Books.

Crenshaw, D. A., & Barker, G. (2008). Sports metaphors and stories in counseling with children. In L. Rubin (Ed.), *Popular culture in counseling, psychotherapy, and play-based interventions* (pp. 297–309). New York: Springer.

Crenshaw, D. A., & Garbarino, J. (2007). The hidden dimensions: Profound sorrow and buried potential in violent youth. *Journal of Humanistic Psychology, 47*(2), 160–174.

Crenshaw, D. A., & Hardy, K. V. (2005). Understanding and treating the aggression of traumatized children in out-of-home care. In N. Boyd Webb (Ed.), *Working with traumatized youth in child welfare* (pp. 171–195). New York: Guilford.

Crenshaw, D. A., & Hardy, K. V. (2007). The crucial role of empathy in breaking the silence of traumatized children in play therapy. *International Journal of Play Therapy, 16*(2) 160–175.

Eron, J., & Lund, T. (1996). *Narrative solutions in brief therapy.* New York: Guilford.

Garbarino, J. (1999). *Lost boys: Why our sons turn violent and how we can save them.* New York: Anchor Books.

Garbarino, J. (2008). *Children and the dark side of human experience: Confronting global realities and rethinking child development.* New York: Springer.

Garbarino, J., & Crenshaw, D. A. (2008). Seeking a shelter for the soul: Healing the wounds of spiritually empty youth. In D. A. Crenshaw (Ed.), *Child and adolescent psychotherapy: Wounded spirits and healing paths* (pp. 49–62). Lanham, MD: Jason Aronson.

Gray, J. (2004). *Men are from Mars, women are from Venus: The classic guide to understanding the opposite sex.* New York: HarperCollins.

Greene, R. (1998). *The explosive child: A new approach for understanding and parenting easily frustrated, "chronically inflexible" children.* New York: HarperCollins.

Hardy, K. V., & Crenshaw, D. A. (2008). Healing the wounds to the soul camouflaged by rage. In D. A. Crenshaw (Ed.), *Child and adolescent psychotherapy: Wounded spirits and healing paths* (pp. 15–30). Lanham, MD: Jason Aronson.

Hardy, K. V., & Laszloffy, T. (2005). *Teens who hurt: Clinical interventions to break the cycle of adolescent violence.* New York: Guilford.

James, B. (1989). *Treating traumatized children: New insights and creative interventions.* Lexington, MA: Lexington Books.

Kiselica, M. S., Englar-Carlson, M., & Horne, A. M. (Eds). (2008). *Counseling troubled boys: A guidebook for professionals.* New York: Routledge.

Levant, R. F. (1995). Toward the reconstruction of masculinity. In W. S. Pollack & R. F. Levant (Eds.), *A new psychology of men* (pp. 229–251). New York: Basic Books.

Mead, M. (1973). *Coming of age in Samoa: A psychological study of primitive youth for western civilization.* New York: American Museum of Natural History.

O'Neil, J. (2006). Helping Jack heal his emotional wounds: The gender role conflict diagnostic schema. In M. Englar-Carlson & M. S. Stevens (Eds.), *In the room with men: A casebook of therapeutic change* (pp. 259–284). Washington, DC: American Psychological Association.

Ordinary people. (1980). Paramount Pictures Home Entertainment, Hollywood, CA.

Perrin, P. B., Baker, J. O., Romelus, A. M., Jones, K. D., & Heesacker, M. (2009). Development, validation, and confirmatory factor analysis of the Father Hunger Scale. *Psychology of Men & Masculinity, 10*(4), 314–327.

Real, T. (1997). *I don't want to talk about it. Overcoming the secret legacy of male depression.* New York: Scribner.

Segal, J. (1988). Teachers have enormous power in affecting a child's self-esteem. *Brown University Child Behavior and Development Newsletter, 10,* 1–3.

Silverstein, O., & Rashbaum, B. (1995). *The courage to raise good men.* New York: Penguin Books.

Spinks, A. B., Nagle, C., Macpherson, A. K., Bain, C., & McClure, R. J. (2008). Host factors and childhood injury: The influence of hyperactivity and aggression. *Journal of Developmental & Behavioral Pediatrics, 29*(2), 117–123.

Stand by me. (1986). Columbia Pictures Industries, Hollywood, CA.

This boy's life. (2003). Warner Brothers Home Entertainment, an AOL Time Warner Company, Burbank, CA.

3

Strengths-Based Group Work With Boys

ANDREW MALEKOFF

INTRODUCTION

Hitting the Wall

Schoolyards, playing fields, gymnasiums, vacant lots, street corners, makeshift clubhouses, and stoops were but a few of the special places of my boyhood. These were the platforms upon which the richest of memories, sweet and sour, were built. In later years, it has been the countless hours of group work with boys that have been most evocative of those special places and times. The associated images and scenarios provide me, at each memorable stop, with a visceral reminder of my earliest struggles to belong, to feel special, and to be valued.

I can vividly recall the yearlong struggle, at age 12, in trying to scale the grammar school roof—a rite of passage. There was the repeated disappointment in falling short and the intermittent beat of humiliating taunts by the older boys. However, what sticks with me even more is the image of dangling arms from above, my friends reaching out for my outstretched hand: a majestically simple gesture that captured the mutuality upon which our time together would be permanently rooted (Malekoff, 1984).

Twin Anchors and Boys Helping Boys

Whenever I am with a group of boys, in the midst of the swirl of noise and activity, I hear two unspoken questions that emerge from the deepest part of their souls: "Am I ever gonna fit in?" and "Am I ever gonna be any good at anything?" "Am I ever gonna fit in?" suggests the need for attachment and belonging, so critical to human growth and development. "Am I ever gonna be any good at anything?" touches on the desire for a sense of competence and the wish to feel confident and trusted by others. When combined, these two questions represent a need for growth-oriented group experiences.

William Pollack (1998), in *Real Boys: Rescuing Our Sons From the Myths of Boyhood*, wrote about "boys helping out boys" (p. 182) and the importance of them having peers on which to lean. In *Season of Life*, journalist David Marx (2004) developed this theme from an unusual vantage point that is most often associated with what many think of as modern-day gladiator culture—football.

"Building Men for Others"

Marx wrote about a season that he spent with a private high school football team in Maryland led by two unconventional coaches (group leaders), Joe Ehrmann and Biff Poggi. The coaches' mission with the boys on their team was "to build men for others" by helping the boys develop empathic and nurturing relationships and helping them to commit themselves to causes greater than themselves. Their core lesson was that success was measured by what kind of friends, brothers, husbands, and fathers the boys would become, versus surrendering to attributes of "false masculinity" comprised exclusively of athletic prowess, sexual conquest, and economic success. Developing empathic relationships and reaching beyond oneself for the greater good of all are integral to strengths-based group work with boys.

Working with boys in groups to help them learn to develop empathic and caring relationships is a counterforce to boys modeling themselves, exclusively, on the reclusive, antisocial macho man that Clint Eastwood epitomized on screen in the "spaghetti Western" and "Dirty Harry" flicks in the early years of his acting career. Or, after the iconic "Marlboro Man," a metaphor for a rugged individual who is strong, smokes cigarettes, and goes it alone, quietly rejecting any semblance of "no man is an island" sentimentality.

This chapter offers illustrations of boys leaning on one another and finding value in mutual aid. This is not to decry the need for boys developing a sense of self-sufficiency; rather, the goal is for them to find a comfortable balance between going it alone and standing tall, as opposed to depending on and caring for others. As a longtime group worker with boys (and girls), my twin anchors are belonging and competence. Far from weighing me down, they help to ground me when, sometimes in the midst of chaos, flight seems so inviting. Likewise, curative and dynamic factors in group psychotherapy and group work are critical for grounding practitioners working with boys in groups.

CURATIVE AND DYNAMIC FACTORS

To serve as a guide, Northen and Kurland (2001) and Yalom and Leszcz (2005) have identified some of the curative and dynamic factors in group work and group psychotherapy, respectively. These include *mutual support, universalization, instillation of hope, altruism, acquisition of knowledge and skills, group control, catharsis, corrective emotional experiences,* and *reality testing.* The following is a summary of these forces as they apply to work with boys.

Mutual Support

As young people redefine their relationship within the family, they need to learn about and experience the capacity for mutuality outside the family. Boys can learn what they have to offer, and how to offer it, in a cohesive group. This intermediary space can become a stepping stone to greater intimacy.

Universalization

Gaining a collective sense of common ground, that is, "we're all in the same boat," can serve as a counterforce to the isolation and frustration of feeling unheard and misunderstood. For adolescents who are moving away from the family and taking tentative steps toward the peer group, there is a susceptibility to periods of intense isolation that one may experience as being unique to oneself. The group experience helps to universalize this and other normative, transitional experiences, providing the young person with a sense of community and affinity with others who are encountering many of the same feelings.

Instillation of Hope

Lending a vision is a core group work skill that, along with universalization, can help the young person who feels "stuck" in predicaments and crises, real and existential, to emerge from the morass with a sense of hope that things can get better.

Altruism

The opportunity to give as well as to receive is crucial for the young person who is looking to loosen ties of dependency as he moves to adolescence. But this move is reciprocal rather than linear. Giving to others, receiving from others, giving to others, receiving from others ... this interplay is the essence of mutual aid—a process that enables the young person to make the transition from dependence to independence to interdependence.

Acquisition of Knowledge and Skills

Group work can provide members with opportunities to address openly both tame and taboo subjects. Misinformation and myths can be challenged. For preadolescent boys, issues of sexuality, alcohol and other drug use, cultural diversity, and interrelated problems and needs can be confronted in a safe environment in group.

Group Control

Young group members must adhere to certain norms and expectations that help the group as a whole to reach its goals. Boys who are members of groups must endure frustration, accept fair guidelines and limits, moderate their resistance to authority, and contain their inappropriate behavior. Waiting to take turns, sharing center stage, and allowing others to contribute is the mark of a good group.

Catharsis

Giving expression to one's ideas, feelings, experiences, hopes, and dreams in an accepting environment can reduce anxiety and energize group members to work together to reach valued goals. One group of adolescent boys shared its frustration about violence after a widely publicized murder rocked the community. Rather than assume a position of helplessness, they joined the March for Unity and organized its largest youth contingent, transforming feelings of despair and resignation into hope and possibility.

Corrective Emotional Experiences

The group can offer the members an opportunity to reexperience dysfunctional patterns and relationships, and to work through these dynamics in a safe and supportive environment. For instance, for the young person(s) growing up in a capricious home or community environment characterized by unpredictability, the caring structure and consistency of a good group can lead to a corrective experience. For the boy who has developed a behavioral pattern that invites rejection, the group becomes an arena in which the same behavior is repeated and addressed with the goal of behavioral and affective change. It is the enactment of dysfunctional and then corrective behaviors in the group—the doing and the positive reinforcement of the doing—that is a most powerful contributor to a corrective emotional experience and consequent behavioral-cognitive-affective change.

Reality Testing

Distortions in perception can be safely presented and challenged in the group. Some young group members might find it difficult to hear an adult; however, the voice of a contemporary, especially a group of them, may be hard to escape. For example, a valued method in the treatment of chemical dependency is group work. The combination of confrontation and support provided by a group of peers "in the same boat" helps to challenge denial, minimization, and distortions of reality. In an era when adolescents are exposed to and involved with risky behaviors that can be life threatening (i.e., carrying weapons, unprotected sex, drug abuse), good reality testing can make a significant difference in the trajectory of one's life.

STRENGTHS-BASED GROUP WORK

In this chapter, I present a model for strengths-based group work (Malekoff, 2001, 2007) well grounded in these curative and dynamic factors, with a special focus on working with boys ages 5 through 21. Seven principles will be presented and illustrated, combining concepts and practice:

1. Form groups based on members' felt needs and wants, not diagnoses.
2. Structure groups to welcome the whole person, not just the troubled parts.
3. Decentralize authority and turn control over to group members.
4. Integrate verbal and nonverbal activities.
5. Develop alliances with other relevant people in group members' lives.
6. Maintain a dual focus on individual change and social reform.
7. Understand and respect group development as the key to promoting change.

Paths to Strengths-Based Group Work in Which Caring, Care-taking, and Context Count

The strengths perspective presented herein is supported by research in the areas of developmental resilience, health and wellness, story and narrative, and solution-focused approaches (Saleebey, 1996, 2001, 2002). Readers might do well to consider Dennis Saleebey's exposition on principles of the strengths-based perspective (2002): "Every individual, group, family, and community has its strengths ... every environment is full of resources; and caring, care-taking, and context count" (pp. 13–18). This focus is particularly meaningful in work with boys who, in the context of their lives, may not have been exposed to male models of caring and care-taking. A good mutual aid group can address that gap in their experience.

Youth Development: Building Blocks for Strengths-Based Group Work

An important arena of strengths-based research is in the youth development field where the identification of personal and social assets (i.e., strengths) that facilitate positive youth development (Benson, 1997; Eccles & Gootman, 2002) is paramount. A review of over 800 studies provided a scientific foundation for the 40 developmental assets identified by the Search Institute (Scales & Leffert, 1999). As both a theoretical and research framework, the assets are categorized as external (e.g., factors in the environment that promote health and strengths) or internal (e.g., factors in the individual, such as competencies and prosocial values that represent strengths). The assets have relevance to group workers helping boys from a strengths-based perspective. They offer direction for identifying boys' needs, setting group goals, building stable alliances with parents and other relevant adults, promoting creative activities, and developing leadership skills.

One cautionary note: Please consider that in changing times different theoretical approaches gain favor as an accommodation to the social, political, and economic realities of the day. Group workers who treat boys and decide to adapt various approaches (evidence-based or curriculum-driven and manualized models, for example) can integrate them with the strengths-based principles described herein. The challenge for group workers subscribing to strengths-based principles in their work with boys is to find paths for integration across disciplines and models, whether evidence based or eclectic, that address some of the unique needs of boys.

NEEDS OF BOYS

Boys to Men

If we hope to raise our boys to become stable, secure, successful, happy, principled, courageous, and inspired men with meaningful relationships in their lives, we must be prepared to attend to their unique needs. Boys emulate what they observe. If what they see is emotional distance, extreme competition, guardedness, and coldness between men, they are prone to copy that behavior. Kindlon and Thompson (2000) remind us that boys need to be encouraged to initiate friendships, maintain them, and experience and resolve the conflicts that arise in male friendship. Group work is an ideal arena for learning, *in vivo*, how to build relationships, negotiate differences, and resolve conflicts.

Many authors have written eloquently about the unique needs of boys and have placed particular emphasis on boys' emotional lives (Biddulph, 2008; Dabs & Dabs, 2000; Gurian, 2000, 2005, 2006; Marx, 2004; Pollack, 1998). Boys need permission to have an internal world of feelings, peer and adult support to help them to express a full range of emotions, and models of manhood that exemplify emotional attachment. Boys also need to see that physical toughness and stoicism, as stand-alone attributes, are narrow indicators of male strength. They need to see that emotional courage is as genuine an item as physical courage, and that empathy is a source of strength and a foundation for lasting relationships.

Boys Will Be Boys

The road for group workers dealing with boys is clogged with those who insist that the only worthwhile group is one that speaks politely and insightfully. Arch enemies of the noise police, group workers helping with boys tend to be viewed as amateurs dabbling where deeper, more learned, and more individualized work is necessary. Our work often looks as if it just crawled out of bed. Whatever it means to be politically correct in the human services, we are not. At our best what we are is a legion of Detective Columbos—rumpled and befuddled, yet dogged and full of savvy (Malekoff, 2008).

Boys need to know that the grown-ups that work with them in groups can not only tolerate the often fluctuating change-on-a-dime energy, but can fully embrace, enjoy, and celebrate it as well. Strengths-based group work is a powerful path for addressing these and other critical needs in boys' lives. Following is a more detailed description of the seven strengths-based principles and how they are brought to life to meet some of these essential needs.

SEVEN PRINCIPLES FOR STRENGTHS-BASED GROUP WORK WITH BOYS

This seven-principle framework for strengths-based group work with boys evolved from the author's group work practice experience since the early 1970s. Included are brief definitions of the seven principles and practice illustrations that bring the concepts to life. The illustrations are a combination of practice summaries, brief vignettes, poetry, and longer narratives. Readers should note that although examples are chosen to illustrate specific principles, the principles overlap and are interrelated.

Principle 1: Form Groups Based on Need and Not Diagnosis

Groups must not be formed on the basis of a diagnosis or label. Groups should instead be formed on the basis of particular needs that the group is being created to address. Felt needs are different from ascribed labels. Understanding need is where we begin in group work.

As the following example will illustrate, *need* refers to individual desires, interests, and areas of concern that are both *unique* to individuals in the target population (e.g., children with disabilities, youths that are subjected to bias) and *universal* to individuals in the target population (i.e., normative developmental tasks and the need to negotiate difficult environments).

What's in a Name? Terrorist!

In an intergenerational group that I led that was aimed at helping immigrant youths to address issues of bias, Ibrahim, a 13-year-old middle school student, explained with a quivering voice and tears filling his eyes how frustrating it was to be taunted by peers who had dubbed him "terrorist" ever since the 9/11 terrorist attack on America. The group listened intently to Ibrahim. They praised him for his painful disclosure, which he said he rarely discussed with anyone. His admission spurred reflection from others who also had experienced the sting of ethnic bias and had carried on in stoic silence—until now, that is.

In time, and after more sharing of similar hurts by other group members—adults and youths alike—I turned back to Ibrahim to ask him, "What was it like for you to speak so openly and honestly before a group of boys and adults about such a painful matter in your life?" He said that he had never talked about this publicly before and that "it felt good, it felt okay saying it here." In time, Ibrahim received a good deal of positive reinforcement and support from other participants, young and old, for being so forthright and open, and for articulating his experiences and expressing his emotions so clearly. When I bumped into Ibrahim at the buffet lunch of Subway® hero sandwiches, salads, soda, and chips, he was chatting with a few people who were standing in line. When they told him that they liked what he had to say in the group, he lit up and said, "I never knew that I could talk so good." He was beaming and beginning to recognize the freedom of stepping beyond hurt and shame, as well as the power and pride in finding his own voice.

With a boy like Ibrahim having the experience of openly sharing his emotional bruises versus simply swallowing hard in stoic silence, we get a perfect example of the value of stepping beyond labels and into need in strengths-based group work with boys. The experience allowed Ibrahim, and then others in turn, to unburden themselves and feel the strength in speaking up and speaking out—to see that releasing emotion can help to heal and can be a powerful tool to move others.

Alexithymia is an interesting word with Greek roots that refers to the *inability to put emotions into words* (Pollack & Levant, 1998). The fact that alexithymia is most common in males suggests that male gender role socialization is a process by which boys are often taught to curb the expression of vulnerable and caring emotions and to be unflinching and stoic in the face of passion, joy, or grief (Marx, 2004). Good group work experiences, as described above, offer an antidote to alexithymia and an invitation to express vulnerable and caring feelings, without perceiving them as a sign of weakness or as incompatible with masculine identity.

Principle 2: Structure Groups to Invite the Whole Person

Group workers must learn to structure groups to invite the whole person to participate and not just the troubled, hurt, and broken parts.

Moving beyond diagnoses and labels requires the willingness of group workers to reach outside of the deficit-thinking box in order to embrace the capacities, the competencies instead of pathologies (Corey, 2008), of their group members and to promote empathic connections. As Corey (2008) wrote, "I agree with the postmodern approaches, which are grounded on the assumption that people have both external and internal resources to draw upon when constructing solutions to their problems" (p. 6). Although this is critical for all group members regardless of age or gender, for boys whose emotions need thawing, a good group experience can go a long way in melting the ice around their (and their loved one's) hearts, as the following example illustrates.

Building Memories and Empathic Connections

My earliest experience as a group worker occurred when I joined Volunteers in Service to America (VISTA) in the early 1970s. At that time, I lived in a low-income, Mexican American community in mid-Nebraska (Malekoff, 2001). The first group that I formed, with no formal experience or academic preparation, was composed of adolescent boys and girls ranging in age from 13 to 18. I got to know them and their families by eating dinner in their homes, joining them at the Friday night dances at the Latin Club, and playing basketball and softball with the men and boys. I was even recruited to coach a women's softball team.

Living in the indigenous community was the VISTA tradition and an expectation for its volunteers. Living side by side with my neighbors, many of us became good friends. My commitment was to stay for one year. I stayed for three and lived in the same place throughout, to the puzzlement of "gringo" outsiders. I learned firsthand about the stress that many of the young people faced, including poverty, alcoholism, and domestic violence. However, I learned far more about the considerable strengths and talents that, with a little encouragement, they could bring to the world.

By launching a group that encouraged them to explore their own needs, desires, and interests, the group members intuitively gravitated to activities that tapped their strengths and were grounded in their ethnic identities. What evolved in time was a cultural dance group that carried the message of Mexican American pride. The group performed dances and read poetry across the state of Nebraska, with its various pockets of Mexican American families that lived in such places as urban Omaha to the east and rural Scottsbluff to the west. The inaugural dance and poetry performance was held before a large hometown crowd in a local community center. The event was remarkable and offered an unexpected payoff for Felipe, the most charismatic and talented dancer in the group.

Rehearsals were filled with a mix of excitement and anxiety. Everything almost fell apart when two of the members, Felipe and Regina, who were "an item," got into a huge conflict and stormed off during a rehearsal, vowing to quit the group just one day before the big night. Through an impromptu combination of compelling leadership and "highly honed beginning social work skills"—outreach (tracking them down like a dog in the street all the way to their homes), conflict resolution ("C'mon guys, can't we please work this out?"), and cheerleading (pleading with them to return for the final rehearsal)—I finally convinced them to rejoin the group.

A major component of the preparation and development of the group was to engage adults in the community to help (see principle 5, below). Neighborhood women—moms, grandmas, aunts, and others—sewed dresses for the girls and matching outfits for the boys. Neighborhood men, dads and others, offered their sombreros to the boys. The event was a great success.

A few days after their moving performance, which led to a full-page spread of photos in the local newspaper, Felipe approached me. We chatted about the performance. I asked Felipe how his family enjoyed the night. Felipe's dad was a "tough guy" in town with a checkered past and a criminal record. Felipe told me that after the performance his dad, who let him borrow his sombrero, told his son, "Felipe, I'm proud of you." With tears in his eyes, Felipe said to me, "That's the first time I can remember my dad saying that to me." The dance group focused on what Felipe *had to offer*, enabling his dad to experience his son's competence and to see him being admired, praised, and applauded in a public setting. Empathic connections like these, spurred on by good group experiences, can help boys to gain a sense of what their place in the world and as men might be.

Principle 3: Decentralize Authority and Turn Control Over to Group Members

Group workers must understand that losing control is not what you want to get away from, it's what you want to get to. What this means is that when control is turned over to the group and when the group worker gives up his or her centrality in the group, mutual aid can follow and members can find expression for what they have to offer. Encouraging "what they have to offer"—that's the kind of group work we need to practice, that's what real empowerment is all about.

When I offer group work training I often ask participants to share their greatest fear about working with groups. "Losing control" always tops the list. There is an expression in the field that sums up the idea of turning over control to the group: "If *you* are working too hard, then there is something wrong." However you phrase it, the unspoken imperative behind this phrase and the importance of decentralizing authority, is to let the group members share the workload.

The More You Try to Control the Group, the Less in Control You Are

Practitioners who work with boys in groups, in my experience, suffer most from feeling the need to "control" their groups, particularly when boys are being boys. And, I do not mean this in a pathological or destructive way. The following original poem, based on my experience of years of boys' groups, best captures this sentiment and a feel for the boys' groups in action.

> Playing, planning, confronting, creating,
> fighting, protecting, joking, berating;
> Burping, sleeping, farting, snacking,
> cooperating, disrupting, insulting, attacking;
> Listening, ignoring, teasing, supporting,
> resolving, deciding, defying, conforming;
> Pondering, clowning, denying, admitting,
> talking, laughing, standing, sitting;
> Yelling, crying, touching, hugging,
> opening, closing, coming, going;
> Dancing, singing, grabbing, poking,
> Mimic-ing, acting, threatening, stroking;
> Revealing, hiding,
> prying, confiding,
> Stretching, crawling,
> jumping, falling;
> Taking, giving,
> thanking
> and
> living.
>
> —Andrew Malekoff

Turning over control to the group members is not simply about tolerating the noise and movement in boys' groups, but accepting and celebrating it. A group work paradox that I have come to embrace is: The more you try to control the group, the less in control you are. Face it, group work with boys often feels like a roller coaster ride, harrowing yet fun, with unexpected twists and turns, ascents and declines. Sometimes you experience anxious anticipation and vertigo-inducing surround sound; other times, however, it is not so exciting: more like a crawling commute in rush-hour traffic, enervating, meandering, puzzling, endless. Group work with boys is a half-eaten slice of pizza, a shirt hanging out, a chair leaning back, a runny nose, mismatched socks, and a dripping ice cream cone. At times it is like a sunset. Group work with boys is a beautiful thing (Malekoff, 2007, 2008).

Boys need parents, teachers, coaches, clergy, counselors, and other adults in their lives who recognize and accept their high activity level, and who give them safe places in which to express it (Kolodny, 1984). What boys need in groups are group workers who understand that group work with them is rarely neat. It is more abstract than still life, more jazz than classical (Malekoff, 2008). Group workers worth their salt invite their young group members to be co-creators in a context of decentralized authority. This is a radical concept for many grown-ups, although not a new one.

"Chaos theory holds that within simple, seemingly orderly systems there are pockets of wild disorder and within disorderly, seemingly chaotic systems there are precise pockets of order" (Pozatek, 1994, p. 397). A boys group that looks messy on the surface is not necessarily a mess, and what appears as a calm, cool, and collected group of buttoned-down professional adults (let's say at a faculty meeting) is not quite as neat as it looks when one peeks beneath the surface and finds hidden agendas, underground politics, and simmering resentments. Where might we find more chaos, among the messy boys or slick suits?

Planning a Meal Together

Beyond the "real feel" of a rough-and-ready boys group, turning over control in no way suggests supporting a group with no purpose, norms, or structure. Turning over control refers more to the importance of group workers allowing group members to "own the group." For example, in one group of early adolescent boys with developmental disabilities, the group members decided that they would join in preparing a meal for a succeeding group meeting. They planned well—who would *make what, buy what,* and *bring what* to the "dinner party." On the evening of the event, one of the boys showed up empty-handed despite an interim reminder. Rather than jump in quickly to address this boy's lapse, the group worker sat back and let the group take over, offering just a little constructive redirecting (after they cursed him out) to enhance their effectiveness. And work it out they did. They let the offender have it, but good, in a manner that no adult could, and that would all but ensure he wouldn't forget what to bring next time.

Sex Education: Fact and Fiction

One group of teenage boys struggling with getting accurate information about risky sexual behavior and its consequences rejected the group worker's earnest attempts to clarify and provide accurate information about safe sex. He backed off and suggested that they call a national hotline concerned with the spread of sexually transmitted diseases. The boys took over by dialing and asking questions of a disembodied voice from an unknown place, while the group worker sat back and observed. He concealed a smile as the boys' spokesperson disguised his voice so as not to be identified. The group worker looked on bemused, enjoying the boys' conversation with the national expert. Putting one's ego outside the door is critical for group workers working with boys.

If you don't have to know and control everything, then you can invite others to participate in sharing the power and authority. This is a difficult lesson for adult group workers who help children and teens in groups. It is up to you whether you share the burden or carry it alone. It is much more fun when you choose the former. Try it, you'll like it. I promise.

Principle 4: Integrate Verbal and Nonverbal Activities

Group work requires the integration of verbal and nonverbal activities. Group work practitioners must, once and for all, learn to relax and abandon the bizarre belief that the only successful group is one that consists of people who sit still and speak politely and insightfully.

In addition to a wealth of structured resource material available (e.g., games, exercises, and curricula), there are activities that emerge spontaneously out of good group experiences. These are the creative applications that can be cultivated and brought to life in the group, contributing to a growing sense of "groupness" and a rich history of experience together.

Ping-Pong Feelings

Following is an illustration of a group led by a female social worker with a group of boys that suffered a devastating loss. The setting for the group is a local elementary school. The service was funded by Project Liberty, a Federal Emergency Management Agency (FEMA) program, in the immediate aftermath of 9/11. The group worker is a social worker attached to the FEMA-funded local mental health agency.

A group of rambunctious eight- and nine-year-old boys was formed in a local elementary school. Their fathers were killed in the September 11, 2001, terrorist attack on the World Trade Center. Nothing seemed to work to encourage them to talk. I racked my brain and then decided to try something different. I told each of them to wear t-shirts under shirts, "We're going to try something fun and new." "What?" they asked. "Wait until next week and you'll see," I said. I brought in a large bowl to be filled with water and several wiffle ping-pong balls, with the name of a different feeling (e.g., *angry, sad, frustrated,* and so on) taped to each ball. The balls were then wrapped in a clear plastic covering to keep them dry and reveal the name of the feeling. I directed each of the group members to take turns, using only one hand to pick up a ball, and then hold it down in the bowl filled with water and to say something about the feeling related to a day of the week. For example, *anger:* "On Sunday I got angry when my favorite football team lost," or *nervous:* "I got nervous on Monday when I had to go to back to school."

I purposely did not start them off talking about the loss, as that would have been too threatening. First, I wanted them to understand feelings, to label them. After each ball was chosen and held down in the water, I asked them to take a second, third, and fourth ball, and so on, never letting go of any of the balls they chose. As they held down several balls in one hand, the water started to spill over the side, or they might lose their grip of one or more of the balls and they would then pop up to the surface. One member threw up his hands and said, "Okay, okay, I get, I get it already, we can't keep down all our feelings at once or they will pop up or spill over." "What does that mean," I asked them, "feelings popping up and spilling over?" And the once silent members answered almost in unison: "It means we can't control it, can't keep it in anymore, it can pop up in bad ways ... you cannot hold down what you cannot control."

This little game seemed to open them up and they were off and running, or should I say talking? Now that their feelings were out, we could move to the task of how to reduce stress. (Toni Kolb Papetti, personal communication, 2005)

This creative, tactile exercise offered a group of boys that had shut down their feelings an avenue to openly express their emotions and grieve for their dads. Nonverbal methods, when thoughtfully conceived and implemented, can make all the difference in getting a group unstuck and moving in a beneficial direction. In this case, the boys learned the indelible lesson, without being lectured on it, that holding feelings down only increases the hurt of frozen emotion. Another boys' group learned a different kind of lesson by being given an opportunity to exercise their competence by painting the group worker's office.

The Paint Job

This practice illustration demonstrates an unusual path to changing the self-image and self-esteem of members of a young adolescent boys' group known mostly for their deficits (Malekoff, 1984). The boys' experiences outside of the group proved inadequate for developing feelings of trustworthiness, reliability, and competence. Through the group experience, a spontaneous decision, thoughtful plan, and well-implemented activity developed, all of which contributed to the emergence of a series of newly reflected images, accentuating the members' growing capabilities.

Five 9- and 10-year-old boys had become members of a weekly group at a community mental health center after being referred to the guidance center by school personnel for problems defined as immaturity, poor social judgment, and low self-esteem. Socially, all were said to have been scapegoated to varying degrees. They were described as academic under-achievers and as overly dependent on adult supervision to complete assignments.

By the time the boys were together for about three months, it had been established that the room was not bugged, that hands needn't be raised to talk, and that no member could strike another in anger. Following a bittersweet moment of mutual discovery in which the five boys each revealed a personally detested schoolyard nickname representing physical, intellectual, or temperamental Achilles' heels, one of the boys, Vincent, shared that he felt "untrusted" by his parents. When encouraged to elaborate, he explained that his parents had refused to let him contribute to a recent household paint job. After some discussion, it became clear that these boys experienced little autonomy in the presence of their parents, or any other adults for that matter.

As this information emerged, the worker realized that his room was in dire need of a paint job. Over the years young "decorators," including these boys, had adorned the office walls with reclining chair backrest compressions, assorted handprints, multicolored soda pop blotches, and the dried remnants of not-quite-scraped-off-the-wall chewing gum. Since the agency administration had ignored all prior requests for a fresh coat of paint, the worker seized the opportunity to solicit the group members to do the job. There was spontaneous unanimity in their decision to perform the task. As a result, discussion was slowly transformed into an activity that was intended to support the group's sense of competency and autonomy.

The painting of the office required several steps: (1) making a list of supplies and tasks (planning), (2) studying a paint color chart (decision making), (3) organizing a trip to the hardware store to price and purchase materials (environmental competence), (4) learning the functions of the equipment (skill development), (5) committing time to a weekend day to do the job (time investment), and (6) deciding on the workday plan—break time, lunch time, and salary (negotiating).

The job itself, which lasted six hours, was completed with great care. An older adolescent, a participant in the agency's vocational training program, agreed to serve as job foreman. This pleased the younger boys and provided them with a role model not too far beyond their reach. The worker, who was present during the job, intervened minimally and primarily to "inspect" the work in progress and to praise the boys' effort and skill.

In addition to the job and life skills indicated above, patience, judgment, problem solving, and cooperation were highlighted as the work proceeded. The aftermath provided an opportunity for review (work inspection) and the chance to show off their good work to their parents and to center staff (public affirmation). As the weeks unfolded, the boys basked in the glow of their cleanly painted meeting place.

The paint job demonstrates tapping in to what the boys have to offer as a means to promote a sense of competence and belonging, build ego strengths, and enhance the self-esteem of a group of young adolescent boys. The worker served as a catalyst, mediator, and resource to the boys until they gradually came to rely on one another to complete their tasks. The project also stimulated the boys' capacity to enjoy one another and increased their openness and ability to use adult assistance to complete a task. As each group member's mastery of this new situation grew, so grew the competence of the group and the members' sense of pride in one another, as well as their parents' pride in what they had accomplished.

Just ahead is a discussion of the importance of including relevant others, such as parents' participation, when working with boys in groups. The paint job offers a good illustration of a nonintrusive approach to including parents, offering them an opportunity to celebrate their sons. Try to imagine for a moment what this boys' group might have looked like if, instead of the activity described, the worker had insisted on the exclusive use of discussion to probe what it is like to not feel trusted by one's parents.

Principle 5: Develop Alliances With Other Relevant People in Group Members' Lives

Group workers involved with youth must understand that anxious and angry parents, teachers, and school administrators are not our enemies and that we must collaborate and form stable alliances with them if we are to be successful with children. We must learn to embrace their frustrations and anxieties rather than becoming defensive and rejecting. Alliances are needed with relevant others who are deeply invested in the plight of our group members.

Following are two illustrations. The first highlights the need to engage school personnel in the development of an elementary school-based group for boys with serious emotional disturbances. The second explores the obstacles that a group worker faces when approaching an immigrant family in an attempt to recruit their son for a group to address the needs of isolated boys. Both examples emphasize the need to carefully tune in during the engagement/recruitment phase of the group.

Engaging School Personnel and the Primacy of Purpose and Negotiating Values

Offering a group work service for a classroom group for 5-, 6-, and 7-year-old boys in a special education school setting presents group workers with a unique set of challenges. As a group worker, I knew that I needed to contract with the classroom teachers, integrate group purpose with academic and behavioral goals, and support the pro-social values promoted daily in the classroom. I thought that a poetry club (Malekoff, 2002) could build spirit, tap students' creativity, provide an alternative and fun means of expression, and cultivate an appreciation for poetry that could extend beyond the life of the group itself.

In a pregroup planning meeting the teachers expressed ambivalence about whether the group would work. Would it disrupt the daily routine? Would it interfere with the academic goals they felt great pressure to achieve? Did the younger students have the intellectual capacity to deal with poetry? All good questions. I knew that I needed the teachers as allies and partners in order to make a poetry club work.

I asked the teachers to provide a list of academic goals for each student so that academic needs could be included in determining a mission for the group, formulating a group purpose. It was important that the group not be perceived by the teachers as a burden, but instead as a means of assisting them in accomplishing their aims. The teachers provided a list of academic goals representing the grade level of students in their classes. A sample of the stated goals was: comprehends a story; listens to and enjoys stories; recalls important facts and ideas; reads orally with phrasing and expression, pacing and volume, and expresses personal opinions about readings. It is so important to work collaboratively with teachers and respect the goals they wish to accomplish and standards they aim to maintain if one expects to be a welcomed guest in their classrooms. When reviewed with the teachers, it became clear that academic goals were compatible with defining a group purpose and group goals.

The purpose and goals of the group were conceived as follows:

> The poetry club is a weekly group that is about learning to work together, share, have fun, and build confidence through the self-expression of poetry. The goals of the poetry club are related to academic goals, including following directions, participating in discussions, and reading aloud fluently and accurately. The poetry club members will learn to help one another, applaud one another, and appreciate one another.

Once we surmounted the hurdle of acceptance by the teachers, there were other issues that needed tending in order to maintain an alliance with them. At times the boys were rambunctious and, in some instances, went beyond what observing classroom teachers found tolerable. In one instance, a teacher pulled one of the boys aside and admonished him. Later, I asked to meet with her. She explained that what she was trying to teach in the classroom, behaviorally, seemed at odds with the looseness of the poetry club. I assured her that I respected and agreed with the pro-social values she was teaching in the classroom. I added that I wanted to work with her to make sure that my "looseness" wouldn't compromise the classroom values.

The behavior itself wasn't the issue. The reprimand was really meant for me. She needed to trust that I respected her authority and would not undermine classroom standards. Only working together in this way, avoiding a defensive posture, would bring the mutual respect that would make the poetry club a success inside and outside the group meetings. Beginning with the careful negotiation with elementary school teachers to gain sanction for a group idea that was at first greeted with ambivalent feelings, to coming to an understanding about values and standards for classroom behavior, the poetry club exemplifies the importance of establishing and maintaining alliances with relevant others.

Engaging Immigrant Parents: Obstacles and Opportunities

The following reflection on forming a boys group dates back to the 1940s and illustrates the importance of tuning in carefully during the pregroup engagement process. In this case the group worker is recruiting a boy from an immigrant family (Kolodny, 1997). Although the illustration dates back over half a century, the practice issues are as fresh and pertinent today as then.

> The practice of my agency was to draw together a group of "more socially capable" kids in a neighborhood around one or more youngsters who were less capable because of emotional disturbance or physical handicap. I had taken particular pride in my preliminary work in forming one such boys' group. The child's mother had been referred by a physician in a poor neighborhood and she spoke very little English. She had been a Displaced Person in Germany along with her husband, was Russian-speaking originally, and was most anxious about her socially isolated 9-year-old-son. I struggled manfully to recover the shreds of German and Russian I had studied in college and, to my surprise, I succeeded in conducting a successful interview. The mother was pleased and relieved and I was delighted with myself. With her permission, I conferred with the boy's grade school teacher who made some fine suggestions for other group members. As was our practice, I wrote explanatory letters to the parents of the boys suggested, after the teacher called and explained to them that I would be contacting them. I then visited each of them. One family of Ukrainian Displaced Persons greeted me with particular graciousness. They spoke English haltingly but intelligibly. Emboldened by my success in my interview with the original referred child's mother, however, I asked if they spoke Russian as well. They said they did, and I launched into a disquisition in broken Russian as to what the group was to be about, filling in the blanks with broken German. They smiled and accepted politely what I had to say and proceeded to ask a couple of questions in English. They then whispered together and said that, if I didn't mind, their child would not be joining the group. I was startled, but then quickly began to put a number of things together. These were Eastern Europeans. They had lived under the Soviets. They had come to America a few years before, right after the war. This was the early Cold War period. They have now been approached by this social worker, whatever this is, who then invites their son to join a group of

youngsters. He speaks (sort of) Russian. Is he trying to recruit for the Komsomol, the Young Communists? (Or is he an agent provocateur sent by Immigration?) I finally blurted out, "Vwi doomayete shot ya Kommunist?" "You think I'm a Communist?" Quickly the wife protested that this was not the case. "Um Gottes Willen, nyet!" "For God Sakes, No!" she said in mixed German/Russian. Her blush and embarrassed smile, however, indicated that I was probably right. I had tried to make these parents feel comfortable and to appear non-threatening and accepting, but I had achieved the opposite effect. I left them without getting them to change their minds. It was only through hard work by the principal and the teacher who had suggested their youngster that they agreed them to let him join the group two weeks later. (Kolodny, 1997, p. 2)

Sometimes connecting with adults takes a different turn, such as when one's rights and dignity are at stake. Developing groups that promote the dual focus of individual change and social reform opens up the possibility that boys can not only change themselves, but can also change the world around them by taking on causes that are bigger than themselves.

Principle 6: Maintain a Dual Focus of Individual Change and Social Reform

Group workers must help group members see the potential of changing not only themselves but also their surroundings, so that they may become active participants in community affairs, so that they might make a difference and might change the world one day where others have failed. A good group can be a great start for this kind of consciousness development and action.

Group workers must stay tuned in to the "near things of individual need and the far things of social reform" (Schwartz, 1986, p.12). This dual vision was first conceptualized by one of the earliest group work researchers, Wilbur Newstetter (1935). Encouraging boys to identify important issues that affect their lives and to assert themselves by taking steps to make a difference and take on causes bigger than themselves helps in the development of competency and in learning to negotiate difficult environments.

One group that stands out that tackled a cause close to home was a group of boys that shaved their heads in solidarity with a classmate and friend who was losing his hair as a consequence of being treated for cancer. Another is a group of older teenaged boys, all gay, that created a traveling exhibit of life-size high school lockers that they sprayed with antigay graffiti to raise consciousness about gay bashing in local high schools and to encourage gay-straight alliances.

These are two examples that highlight the themes identified earlier of boys having opportunities to develop empathic and caring relationships and to take on causes greater than oneself—you might say, on the road to "building men for others" (Marx, 2004). Forthcoming is another example that is not as dramatic as shaved heads and shocking lockers, but shows that causes don't have to be dramatic to be meaningful or to build solidarity and help boys to find their voices. This group of high school boys, all tagged with serious emotional disturbances, fought an unconventional battle for dignity and respect (Malekoff, 1999).

Pink Soap and Stall Doors

"Who the f--- ... wants to take a dump with no privacy?" asked an exasperated Patrick, who flailed his arms wildly in frustration. The other members of Young Men's Club, sitting shoulder to shoulder around the perimeter of the group room, nodded affirmatively. Patrick hoisted his electric guitar, plugged in the amp, and furiously pawed the strings, generating explosions of discordant sound that seemed to cry out, "Will somebody listen to us?"

Being heard and really listened to was a rare experience for the dozen boys in the Young Men's Club. Some saw them as castaways, shipped out to Manasora, an alternative school, after their local schools threw in the towel. They ranged in age from 15 to 19, representing many ethnic groups and shades of color. Each had done at least one tour of duty in an inpatient psychiatric setting. They knew about life on the edge and what being misunderstood, rejected, and isolated was all about. They were familiar with the eerie and disconcerting sensations associated with feeling alone among others. But not in this crowd, this group. Not now. They felt connected to one another. On this day, they were angry and united—outraged.

Marshall jumped up, "Do you think they have any idea how humiliating it is to go to the bathroom with no doors on the stalls? There's no privacy; it's embarrassing. It's like they don't trust us; they're treating us like little boys...." In the midst of Marshall's searching for yet richer hues with which to paint his portrait of frustration, Bernard filled the gap, adding, "It's disrespectful, that's what it is, it's disrespectful."

Then Matthew, getting back to basics, pointed out, "Man, it's a lot of pressure when you gotta go bad and you know you can't [in this school]."

Patrick leaped in between the intermittent guitar bursts with his own throaty plea, "It says 'Boys' Room' on the bathroom door! We're men! Dammit! What kind of shit is this anyway?"

Felix asked the others if it was true that boys urinated into the soap dispenser. Ronnie said that he saw someone do it but no one could really tell until it was too late because the soap is yellow. This time, with his music and words in synch, Patrick sang out, "We have to get them to put pink soap in the dispensers! Then we'll know if anyone pisses in there. Then we'll know."

Molly, the group worker, listening intently, suggested that they make a list of concerns. Always-dependable Matthew, sitting in the swivel chair behind Molly's desk, grabbed a pen and started to organize a list as the others voiced their concerns in rapid-fire succession.

Improvements for the Bathroom

Soap—pink, not yellow
Toilet paper—three-ply
Doors with locks on the stalls
Only boys in boys' bathroom
No faculty—especially teachers
Toilet cleaner—2,000 flushes with no bleach
Functioning sinks
Roach spray
Roach traps
Softer paper towels
Newer paper towel dispensers

As the director of program development, I traveled from the agency's central office to the high school and sister middle and elementary schools in round-robin fashion throughout the week. Most of my responsibilities were supervisory and administrative. I tried to make connections with all the young people in the program, keeping track of the group's progress. I was excited to learn about the tentative steps that had taken to advocate for better bathroom conditions.

One day, weeks after the boys started to make noise about bathroom conditions, I came to the high school after the dismissal hour and headed down a long vacant hallway to attend an administrative meeting. As I proceeded, something told me to turn around. I did. I took a few steps back down the hall. I pushed open the boys' room door and peered in, pleasantly surprised to find pink soap in the dispensers and doors on the stalls.

Participating in a change effort that includes identifying a problem, exploring it in some depth, seeking solutions, and implementing and evaluating them is an important learning experience for young group members trying to make sense of the world and a good practical lesson about the problem-solving process and the importance of understanding, respecting, and valuing group development as a key to promoting change.

Principle 7: Understanding Group Development as a Key to Promoting Change

Each good group has a life of its own, each one with its own unique personality—what group workers refer to as a culture. All those working with groups must learn to value the developmental life of a group. Because if people can understand this, when those that inhabit the world outside of our groups question the value of our efforts, amidst the noise and movement and excitement of typical kids groups, and when they raise an eyebrow or toss puzzled and disapproving looks our way and ask us, "What is going on in there?!?" we'll have more confidence to move ahead and to hang in there and not bail out as too many adults already have.

A vital tenet of group work practice is that "the worker must actively understand, value, and respect the group process itself as the powerful change dynamic that it is" (Middleman & Wood, 1990, pp. 10–11) over time and in each meeting. This demands that the practitioner have a good knowledge base, reinforced by practice experience, of group developmental theory.

Three distinguished developmental models, Schwartz's interactional model (Berman-Rossi, 1994), the Boston model (Bartolomeo, 2009; Garland, Jones, & Kolodny, 1973), and the relational model (Schiller, 2007, 2009), are good starting points. The interactional model emphasizes the reciprocal relationship between the individual and group, and the group and the social environment (i.e., the significance of interacting systems seeking common ground and reaching out to one another for their mutual benefit and the common good). This model stresses the functions of identifying and challenging obstacles in interacting systems; sharing information, ideas, facts, and values for problem resolution; identifying the requirements (and limitations) of all parties involved in order to effect change; and lending a vision to maintain commitment and inspire hope.

The Boston model was first presented in an article entitled "A Model for Stages of Development in Social Work With Groups," the seminal work of three practitioners/scholars—Garland, Jones, and Kolodny (1973). The method was formulated through observation in clinical practice settings and review of records of young adolescent groups. The model consists of five stages of group development: *preaffiliation, power and control, intimacy, differentiation,* and *separation.* The authors postulate that *closeness* is the central theme running through all five stages: From the moment that a number of individuals consent to be together in one spot, through the period during which they make their first tentative efforts to acquaint themselves with and find satisfaction in one another, on through the time when they share the intense feelings they have toward one another, until the dissolution of their common bond, they must struggle with how near they will come to one another emotionally.

The relational model is a variation of the Boston model and was originally developed to elucidate and emphasize normative pathways through which women's groups develop. However key elements of the relational model, *establishing a relational base and developing mutuality and interpersonal empathy,* are critical to developing boys' groups that value these themes in their members' development.

Some group leaders have an intuitive sense of group development and its phases. For example, in the ending transition of a group, it is vital that we help boys to look back at their time in the group to evaluate it. It is equally important that we help them to openly express what being together has meant to them and what they, the group members, mean to one another. By "openly express," I am referring to using activities that enable a full range of expression, not just "adult-like conversation."

"Won't You Play a Simple Melody...?"

In one mixed preadolescent group, the members spontaneously decided to sing songs as part of their ending time together. Most chose contemporary songs with themes that had to do with saying goodbye and that they bravely performed despite varying talent levels. Some chose silly songs that brought lots of laughter to the group. These included parodies by "Weird Al" Yankovic, the most famous contemporary performer of the genre. I made no attempt to offer a clinical interpretation about any of their song choices. What the members had created was a sort of spirited ending ritual that I did not want to step on, control, or contaminate.

For me, the most moving "performance," that seemed at the time to come out of nowhere, was by 10-year-old Ronnie (pseudonym) who witnessed his mother's murder. He sang an old-time song that I was not familiar with and that struck a different chord than the other songs. I do not know the name or original performer of Ronnie's song. As I listened I imagined that it was a song that his mother had sung to him and that maybe her mother had sung to her. As he started to sing, the other members grew quiet and gave Ronnie the space that he needed. He choked on the word *mother* the first time, but continued through until the end, with his sweet smile and soulful eyes.

> Won't you play a simple melody, like my mother used to play for me, one with good ol' fashion harmony, like my mother played for me?

Following is the author's original poetry that offers readers another view of phases of group development.

THE GROUP HAS A LIFE

A group
begins
by
building
trust,
chipping away
at the
surface crust.
Once the
uneasy
feeling is
lost,
a
battle rages
for who's
the boss;
Kings and
Queens

of what's
okay
and who
shall
have the
final say.
Once that's clear
a moment
of calm,
is quickly
followed
by the
slapping of
palms.
A clan
like feeling
fills
the air,

the
sharing
of
joy,
hope,
and
despair.
Family
dramas
are replayed
so new
directions
can be
made.
Then in
awhile
each
one

stands out,
confident
of his
own
special
clout.
By then
the group
has
discovered
its
pace,
a
secret gathering
in a
special place.
Nothing
like it
has occurred
before,
a bond
that exists
beyond
the door.
And
finally

it's time
to say
goodbye,
a
giggle,
a
tear,
a
hug,
a
sigh.
Hard to
accept,
easy to
deny,
the
group
is
gone
yet
forever
alive.
So you've
asked me
"what is
going

on in
there?"
I hope
that my
story has
helped
make it
clear.
Maybe
now
it is
easier
to see,
that a
group
has a
life,
just
like
you
and
like
me.

—Andrew Malekoff

An understanding that the group has a *life of its own* enables group workers to gently invite trust in the beginning of a group, aid group members in establishing norms, support the intimacy that shared activity and action can bring, invite free expression as the members' individual gifts spring forth, and help the group to say goodbye in a meaningful way in the end.

CONCLUSION

Too much of what passes as group work today is nothing more than manualized, pseudo-group work with little interaction among group members, no mutual aid, cookbook agendas, and canned exercises. Too often the emphasis is on controlling boys, getting them to sit still, shoving education down their throats, and stamping out creativity. The seven principles for strengths-based practice demystify group work with boys so that it can be more easily understood, flexibly approached, and purposefully practiced.

Group workers should always remember that boys need to be seen as whole people who need support and encouragement to give and receive a helping hand, experience and express a full range of emotions, develop meaningful relationships, and reach out to the wider world (extending the bonds of belonging to seek and engage in large and small causes greater than themselves). The principles of strengths-based group work offer a foundation for group workers to help boys to step off the narrow path of false masculinity and to take a step forward in expressing a full range of emotions and developing caring, empathic relationships grounded in mutual support and respect.

REFERENCES

Bartolomeo, F. (2009). Boston model. In A. Gitterman & R. Salmon (Eds.), *Encyclopedia of social work with groups* (pp. 103–106). New York: Routledge.

Benson, P. (1997). *All kids are our kids: What communities must do to raise caring and responsible children and adolescents.* San Francisco, CA: Jossey-Bass.

Berman-Rossi, T. (Ed.). (1994). *Social work: The collected writings of William Schwartz.* Itasca, IL: Peacock.

Biddulph, S. (2008). *Raising boys: Why boys are different—and how to help them become happy and well-balanced men.* Berkeley, CA: Celestial Arts.

Corey, G. (2008). *Theory and practice of group counseling* (8th ed.). Belmont, CA: Brooks/Cole.

Dabs, J. M., & Dabs, M. G. (2000). *Heroes, rogues, and lovers: Testosterone and behavior.* New York: McGraw-Hill.

Eccles, J., & Gootman, J. (Eds.). (2002). *Community programs to promote youth development.* Washington, DC: National Academy Press.

Garland, J., Jones, H., & Kolodny, R. (1973). A model for stages of development in social work with groups. In S. Bernstein (Ed.), *Explorations in group work* (pp. 17–71). Boston, MA: Milford House.

Gurian, M. (2000). *The good son: Shaping the moral development of our boys and young men.* New York: Jeremy P. Tarcher/Putnam.

Gurian, M. (2005). *The minds of boys: Saving our sons from falling behind in school and life.* San Francisco, CA: Jossey-Bass.

Gurian, M. (2006). *The wonder of boys* (10th anniv. ed.). New York: Jeremy P. Tarcher/Putnam.

Kindlon, D., & Thompson, M. (2000). *Raising Cain: Protecting the emotional life of boys.* New York: Ballantine.

Kolodny, R. (1984). "Get'cha after school": The professional avoidance of boyhood realities. *Social Work With Groups, 7*(4), 21–38.

Kolodny, R. (1997). Unforeseen events and unintended consequences. In A. Malekoff (Ed.), *HUH?!? A newsletter about working with children and youth in groups* (Spring, 2). Roslyn Heights, NY: North Shore Child and Family Guidance Center.

Malekoff, A. (1984). Socializing pre-adolescents into the group culture. *Social Work With Groups, 7*(4), 7–19.

Malekoff, A. (1999). Pink soap and stall doors. *Families in Society, 80*(3), 219–220.

Malekoff, A. (2001). The power of group work with kids: A practitioner's reflection on strengths-based practice. *Families in Society, 82*(3), 243–249.

Malekoff, A. (2002). "What could happen and what couldn't happen": A poetry club for kids. *Families in Society, 83*(1), 29–34.

Malekoff, A. (2007). *Group work with adolescents: Principles and practice* (2nd ed.). New York: Guilford.

Malekoff, A. (2008). Why we get no respect: Existential dilemmas for group workers who work with kids' groups. In C. Cohen, M. Phillips, & M. Hanson (Eds.), *Think group: Strength and diversity in social work with groups* (pp. 121–132). New York: Routledge.

Marx, J. (2004). *Season of life: A football star, a boy, a journey to manhood.* New York: Simon and Schuster.

Middleman, R., & Wood, G. G. (1990). From social group work to social work with groups. *Social Work With Groups, 13*(3), 3–20.

Newstetter, W. (1935). What is social group work? In *Proceedings of the National Conference of Social Work* (pp. 291–299). Chicago, IL: University of Chicago Press.

Northen, H., & Kurland, R. (2001). *Social work with groups* (3rd ed.). New York: Columbia University Press.

Pollack, W. (1998). *Real boys: Rescuing our sons from the myths of boyhood.* New York: Random House.

Pollack, W., & Levant, R. (1998). *New psychotherapy for men.* Hoboken, NJ: Wiley.

Pozatek, E. (1994). The problem of certainty: Clinical social work in the postmodern era. *Social Work, 39*(4), 396–404.

Saleebey, D. (1996). The strengths perspective in practice: Extensions and cautions. *Social Work, 41*(3), 296–305.

Saleebey, D. (2001). Practicing the strengths perspective: Everyday tools and resources. *Families in Society, 82*(3), 221–222.

Saleebey, D. (2002). *The strengths perspective in social work practice.* Boston, MA: Allyn and Bacon.

Scales, P., & Leffert, N. (1999). *Developmental assets: A synthesis of the scientific research on adolescent development.* Minneapolis, MN: Search Institute.

Schiller, L. (2007). Not for women only: Applying the relational model of group development with vulnerable populations, *Social Work With Groups, 30*(1), 11–26.

Schiller, L. (2009). Boston model. In A. Gitterman & R. Salmon (Eds.), *Encyclopedia of social work with groups* (pp. 106–108). New York: Routledge.

Schwartz, W. (1986). The groupwork tradition and social work practice. In A. Gitterman & L. Shulman (Eds.), The legacy of William Schwartz: Group practice as shared interaction [special issue]. *Social Work with Groups, 8*(4), 7–27.

Yalom, I. D., & Leszcz, M. (2005). *Theory and practice of group psychotherapy* (5th ed.). New York: Basic Books.

Creative Approaches

Physical Play With Boys of All Ages

STEVE HARVEY

A 12-year-old boy, Alex, was in therapy to help him return to school. He had recently moved to a new city after his parents had separated. His father remained living in the family's original home, which was quite a distance from his new residence. After the initial week following the family relocation, Alex had refused to go to school, and all attempts by the school and family to correct the situation had failed to make a difference. The school psychologist had even resorted to coming to pick him up in the morning. After arriving at school, Alex usually left after a short time and found his way into his family's locked home. Alex had four siblings, two older brothers and one younger sister, who were all reasonably adjusted to their new community and active in school and various age-related activities (e.g., sports, clubs, and so on). They were all actively involved in trying to convince their brother to comply, as he was clearly causing his mother a great deal of distress since she was often called away from her new job to attend to him. Alex was also becoming aggressive at home.

The intake interviews suggested that Alex had no developmental, social, or family problems prior to his school refusal. His problems appeared to be an adjustment to the breakup of his family and the subsequent move. During Alex's individual sessions, his therapist had attempted to discuss his anger about moving and being forced to leave his father, and then connect these feelings to his current behavior. In family-oriented meetings, the therapist suggested various consequences and plans using reinforcement for making small steps toward a return to school and being more respectful at home. When these efforts appeared to make no progress, as Alex refused to engage in any meaningful way, the therapist called a large family session to include the mother, her parents, the siblings, and the father by phone to encourage joint action on the family's part. However, Alex again refused to engage or even speak. He then became so disruptive that he was asked to leave and go with another male therapist, Scott, who had joined the intervention to assist with the large family session. As Alex left, the family therapists who were staying with the other family members made it clear to everyone, including Alex, that the session would proceed. They continued to develop strategies for getting Alex to return to school and to begin treating other family members with more respect, whether or not he was going to participate. Alex was asked to return once he and Scott thought he could participate in a more meaningful manner.

Throughout these attempts by professionals and family, Alex clearly was stuck in a noncompliant role of troublemaker. He was viewed by his family and professionals alike in a negative way for his seeming refusal to participate in the usual efforts to help him. With this unspoken thought in mind, the intervention planned by the family therapists and agreed to by the family was simply to not include Alex and his noncompliance in their efforts to influence his behaviors.

While the family continued their discussions about their frustrations and then what they might all do as a collective to help, Alex and Scott went into the play room. Scott asked Alex to pick those things that interested him to take into a much larger open room away from where the others were talking. Alex chose a few long elastic ropes, a large life-sized stuffed bear, and several large pillows. When Alex and Scott entered the bigger room, Scott suggested that they could create something with the props they had with them. These directions had no direct link to the problems or what had just occurred. Alex's emotional state dramatically changed, and he immediately began to shift the few chairs around the room and fashion the elastic ropes to become part of a huge slingshot that he and Scott could use to fling the bear across the room. The game progressed in such a way that Scott and Alex developed a competition to see who could sling his bear the longest distance and who could come closest to hitting the pillows on the other side of the room. Alex became very engaged in this game and tried his best to "outsling" Scott for the next 20 minutes.

When one of the family therapists came to the room to see if Alex would return to the family session, he found Alex and Scott totally engaged and laughing. Clearly the two were having a great deal of fun and Alex was in a very different mood than when he had left the session and the rest of the family earlier. Both were highly engaged in their physical game play together. Before returning to his family, Alex essentially agreed to a simple outline of a return to school and a few basic rules around aggression at home on the condition that he could return and use the large props to do physical play as his "therapy." Alex and Scott went back to the family session with this agreement.

Alex returned for a few more sessions with Scott and the props. They again constructed the "flying bears" game and had various competitions between them. Scott made comments (in addition to those required to ensure the rules) in which he connected the bears with Alex's move, going to school, getting out of the house, and so on. Once he and Alex established the flying bears game as a playful metaphor, they could begin to discuss Alex's feelings, behaviors, and the several things that had occurred since his family's breakup. Many of these discussions occurred as Alex associated parts of the game with the events of his life. Such associations were nonlinear in that Alex could address his feelings as he saw the relevance while simultaneously continuing the competition of trying to have his bear thrown farther than Scott's. The activity developed in such a way that it constituted physical game play with competition that led to fun and a positive emotional state, juxtaposed with a discussion about Alex's life. Alex began to be interested in continuing sessions with Scott. He also started going to school on a mostly regular basis and his behaviors at home improved.

The above case illustrates the negative experiences boys can have with mental health interventions that are meant to help them. Alex was angry and had the perception of being outnumbered and having no power or say in what was being done on his behalf. He clearly did not want to be part of these efforts, and his family and professionals had a similar resistance. In short, no one really wanted to be together, and so the therapeutic efforts were aimed at attempting to reframe this essentially negative experience of being at the clinic.

The inclusion of the physically oriented play gave Alex a chance to be something other than a mere troublemaker surrounded by angry family members. As he turned the elastic ropes and chairs of the empty therapy room into a large slingshot and developed a competitive game in which he believed himself to have a good chance at winning, Alex could begin to experience himself on a more equal footing with Scott and could allow himself to become involved in the activity. When he later began to discuss his situation, he could control the pace of thinking and verbalization in ways that were more familiar to him. He could also begin to trust Scott and the experience of being in therapy more than he was able to when he was required to sit and answer questions he thought showed him in a negative way. He also could begin to trust that his own expression of physical play could be about his experience rather than the meaning others verbally provided him.

This chapter will present how physically oriented play experiences can be incorporated into mental health intervention with boys to help increase their active participation. Developmental adaptations for boys from infancy through adolescence will be presented. Of special importance, the engagement of fathers in their son's play, when possible, will be discussed. Physical play is related to the natural rough and tumble play intrinsic to boys' experience growing up, especially with their fathers and brothers. Unfortunately, such full-body, physically interactive play is often overlooked in approaches to psychotherapy, including play therapy, with boys and their families. This chapter is meant to address this oversight. Some of the few approaches that use physical action will be presented as a way to describe elements that contribute to a positive outcome in interventions with boys.

BACKGROUND FOR THE USE OF PHYSICAL PLAY

Rough and Tumble Play

Rough-and-tumble play refers to physically vigorous play interactions such as chasing, jumping, play fighting, pushing, wrestling, grabbing the body of other players, banging body to body with another player, using full-body motions, crashing into objects, kicking and throwing objects, and using a loud and roaring voice. Such play actions are often accompanied by positive emotions toward others, and are highly social and structured by complex sets of unspoken expectations. Play actions include reciprocal role taking, role reversal, spontaneous expression of feelings, and encoding and decoding of social/emotional signals. These actions are clearly differentiated from true aggression by the players through metacommunication, such as the players showing a play face, the intrinsic enjoyment of the players, and the end result of social inclusion and friendships generated from play episodes rather than separation produced by real aggression (Pellegrini, 1988).

Jarvis (2007) reported that rough and tumble play is distinctively different from aggression in several ways, including its performance, intensity, and the narrative themes that develop from such activity, with physical play making a strong contribution to social development. When children are able to determine that similar behaviors such as fighting action are different in play, they are learning how physical action can be a metaphorical expression that is mutually co-created by the players in a spontaneous manner. By play fighting together, children can experience themselves as sharing and also expressing a mutual positive social experience.

Such play has been observed frequently among young animals (Harlow, 1962) and similarly across human cultures (Blurton Jones, 1967). Importantly, children can easily and instantly recognize rough and tumble activity as play with far greater accuracy than adults, even without needing language cues (Jarvis, 2007). According to Pellegrini and Smith (1998), researchers conclude that rough and tumble play has a more significant role in the development of males than females. This gender difference has been explained as being related to male hormones (Hines, Golombok, Rust, Johnson, & Golding, 2002) as well as to the style of play their families use in interactions with them (Lindsey & Mize, 2001). Whatever the cause, boys engage in far more physical play interactions and with greater intensity than girls do. Boys also appear to benefit socially and emotionally from such physical action.

Freeman and Brown (2001) reported that, despite the positive aspects associated with rough and tumble play, such activity is often discouraged by adults who fail to see the potential for social/emotional development, and instead see such physical interaction as contributing to true aggression and bullying. Pellegrini and Smith (1998) pointed out how physical play has traditionally been understood as less important than pretend play, as it appears to contribute less to cognitive development. This position may have contributed to the relatively minor role physically oriented activity has occupied within play therapy and other, more traditional mental health approaches.

However, as the above authors (Freeman & Brown, 2001; Jarvis, 2007; Pellegrini & Smith, 1998) and several others have pointed out, rough and tumble play does especially contribute to social improvements among boys. Of primary importance, boys appear to genuinely experience pleasure from physical play, and they show high amounts of intrinsic motivation to participate, even when such activity is not approved of by adults. In situations in which physical play is limited in some way, boys appear to continue to engage in it in disguised ways (Freeman & Brown, 2001).

In addition to the pleasure derived from physical play, boys seem to differentiate such interaction as play and not actual aggression. This recognition of rough and tumble action as representing a co-created social state provides a useful way for boys to enhance their social development through ongoing play as a spontaneous, metaphor-making activity. In this way, physical play provides an important type of experiential learning for boys.

Pellegrini (1988) and Jarvis (2006) pointed out that participants become aware of each other's emotional expressions and how to take on and exchange roles through such play. Freeman and Brown's (2001) observations suggest that play fighting, especially among older latency-aged boys, facilitates the expression of caring and can help to develop and maintain friendships. Pellegrini (1988) concluded that rough and tumble play also assists boys in developing and understanding social dominance and control of aggressive impulses, even in social interactions outside of the play. Jarvis (2007) observed that young boys are able to develop story narratives to derive meaning from their physical play interactions. Typical narrative themes involve power, independence, and direct confrontation. Such themes are different from the themes of inclusion and caring more often seen in the narrative or pretend play of young girls. This author suggests that the natural spontaneous physical play among boys and between the genders forms the basis for important and complex social/emotional learning.

MacDonald and Park (1986) reported that fathers engage in physically interactive play more with their young children, and especially with their sons, than mothers do. Lindsey and Mize (2001) observed this same gender-related difference with slightly older children as well. These authors concluded that boys appear to prefer play interaction that is more physical and assertive, while girls prefer pretend play with cooperative themes derived from their play experiences with their mothers and fathers. Boys especially prefer physical play with either parent, but their pleasure seems more intense during their play with their fathers (Ross & Taylor, 1989). As a result, it seems that there is a special place for fathers in their son's development, that of the preferred playmate (Lamb, 1996).

Such work points to several benefits that come from naturally occurring physical play particularly relevant for boys. Though much has been written about the application of play expression in mental health interventions, such expression refers to pretend rather than physical play, despite the experiential nature of social metaphor making afforded by mutually improvised physical play. However, some mental health approaches do make use of physical action that has similarities to physical play as presented above. Applications for boys include dance therapy (see Chapter 10) and developmental transformations (James, Forrester, & Kim, 2005). The main theoretical ideas of each will be presented here as background. The aspects of physical interaction and expression from dynamic play therapy (Harvey, 1994, 1995, 2003, 2006, 2008, 2009) will also be addressed. Dynamic play therapy is an approach developed by the author that makes direct use of physical action throughout all aspects of interventions with children.

USE OF PHYSICAL ACTION IN INTERVENTION

Dance Therapy

Dance therapy emerged in the 1940s and 1950s primarily as pioneers from creative dance began to apply improvisational movement to groups of people who had identifiable psychiatric difficulties. Perhaps one of the most important of these early innovators was Marion Chace (Chaiklin, 1975). Ms. Chace began using movement with psychiatric patients at St. Elizabeth's Hospital in Washington, D.C. Her basic assumption was that every person had a desire to communicate, and that dance fulfilled this need. Basic components of her work included body action, symbolism, therapeutic movement relationship, and rhythmic activity. In this work, the dance therapist begins initially by following the movement patterns in a group setting using the natural movement gestures and postural changes of each individual as he or she responds to others. Such interactions involve the therapist in a movement relationship with a patient as a way of fostering deep emotional acceptance and communication.

Such movements are then guided into more organized "dances" in which the whole group participates, especially through the use of common rhythmic movement. Verbal imagery provided by the group members helps to define emotional themes relevant to the participants. In this approach, the therapist maintains a role of observer/participant by carefully watching and attuning to the movement of the patients while joining these movements so that relationships can be established on a body level. The therapist then uses the movement deviations and variations produced as cues to transform and change the activity into an emergent flow connecting the movement of one person to another from one gesture to the next. As the group proceeds, the therapist identifies and verbalizes basic themes that have emotional relevance, particularly through the use of verbal imagery.

Dance therapy has also been applied to work with children. Adler (1968) and Kalish-Weiss (1974) described using their own movement to establish a relationship with autistic children. Leventhal (1974) reported using more structured movement to help children with hyper-activity and learning disabilities begin to organize their actions and apply thinking to control their bodies, as well as their behavior in general. Harvey (1994, 1995) adapted these movement approaches to children in family therapy. Such work involves using children's spontaneous movement as well as simple props such as parachutes and scarves to help organize movement interactions into dances that facilitate attach-ment communication.

Dance therapy emphasizes the communicative value of mutual phys-ical action by helping clients develop their interactive movement as an expression of inner subjective experience. In this way, dance therapy is closely related to the rough and tumble play of childhood. However, childhood physical play and dance therapy tend to emphasize slightly different aspects of movement interactions. While many dance therapy sessions do generate positive feelings at times and dances can be orga-nized around aggressive themes, the main therapeutic effort has the goal of using movement to develop empathic communication. On the other hand, children engage in rough and tumble play primarily for the intrinsic pleasure it gives them, and the communicative value emerges as an outcome. Rough and tumble play tends to emphasize aggression and competition among the players more than the movement episodes developed in dance therapy.

Developmental Transformations

Johnson (2009) extended the concept of Chacian dance therapy by adding the use of dramatic play through improvised character, story, and enactments of conflict to basic movement interactions in the drama therapy method of developmental transformations. In this style, expres-sive action is organized in a developmental continuum from purely physical action, to sounds, to imagery, to personified roles, and then into enactment of scenes and increased verbalization. Expressions early in the sessions demand less complexity in task, interpersonal relatedness, and emotional expressiveness but progressively increase in emotional, personal, and expressive demands. In developmental transformations, therapeutic activity begins with playful body interaction between client and the therapist, especially action that has joint rhythmic activity, and moves ahead through the use of a flow of movement and imagery.

In this activity, the therapist is a participant and maintains an empathic mirroring of the participant movement, mood, and affective tone. Developmental transformation achieves more dramatic enactment than is used by the dance therapist through the active use of the "play space," in which both therapist and participant become aware and agree that the interaction, imagery, and role enactment are indeed play. Symbolism becomes emphasized in the play space to differentiate roles, plot, a story line, and enactments of conflicts once players are moving together in playful ways. Dramatic enactments are improvised freely by the therapist and participant as the therapist follows the client's lead. The resulting episodes become improvised play between the therapist and client though dramatic role and story that is usually quite physical and has metaphorical significance as an expression of the client's inner experience.

Both developmental transformations and dance therapy utilize the communicative value intrinsic to movement interaction. However developmental transformations tends to emphasize dramatic roles and story as part of this communication. Additionally, in developmental transformations, the mutual agreement of the players to shift from normal functioning to a play reality within the play space is an important aspect in the co-creation of metaphors. This shift is very much like that which occurs among children who engage in rough and tumble play when they join in play fighting. In both developmental transformations and rough and tumble play, participants mutually engage in behavior that means something different than it seems. Aggressive action paradoxically becomes a way to develop and express positive feelings in spontaneously improvised mutual play. In this way, dance therapy and developmental transformations make use of the elements of nonverbal communication and the ability to spontaneously creatively imagine with others physically to build on the naturally occurring activities inherent in rough and tumble play to produce social/emotional change. Dynamic play therapy is a style of interactive intervention that combines all these elements to create an interactive, game-like, physical form of imagination to address the kind of problems that boys typically present with, including the lack of motivation to engage verbally with adults.

DYNAMIC PLAY THERAPY

Dynamic play therapy (Harvey, 2003, 2006, 2008) is an interactive intervention in which creative arts therapy modalities are used in an integrated way to address basic interpersonal, emotional conflict with the goal of using mutually developed expressions to generate corrective experiences. Central to this intervention style is the belief that the experience of shared, spontaneous, or "naturally creative" play produces intimacy, trust, and mutual, reciprocal positive feelings that are necessary for the formation of basic, secure attachment, the intimacy of friendships, and the development of a hopefulness that future relationships can be emotionally fulfilling. In addition, the play episodes that result from such interaction have value in terms of helping children develop intrinsic motivation to trust others, as well as an ability to engage in the problem solving of their conflicts. Russ (1998) noted that emotional expressiveness in play is related to creativity and positive, overall adjustment. In dynamic play therapy, children are helped to expand their emotional expression, leading to increased creativity, motivation to relate, and improvement in important socialization with significant others. Guided use of the metaphors generated in a child's interactive play can also help to develop more adaptive self-regulation skills in social situations, as well as some motivation to begin to solve their problems.

This chapter will address the component of physical play used in dynamic play therapy and present an adaption for use with boys and their fathers. Improvisations developed from such physical play look and feel much like the rough and tumble play with which boys easily engage. However, these play episodes are creatively extended by the therapist in terms of both process and content to address the problems that have led the boys to seek therapy.

The episodes of physical play are facilitated by the therapist as a planned part of the intervention. Initial sessions include conversations among parents and the boys about the situations that have brought the boys to treatment. In follow-up sessions, appointments begin with conversations tracking identified problem behaviors during the time between sessions. These conversations can occur with the boys alone or with family members. In general, younger boys are seen with their parent(s), while boys approximately 8 years and older are more often seen individually by the therapist.

Following the conversation about the problem behaviors, the therapist then sets up and coaches the boys in an episode of physical interaction (with the parents, if present, or with the therapist if the boy is seen by himself). These interactions are related to the problem behaviors discussed but have the potential to become playful extensions of the verbal presentations as the interactions largely consist of physical improvisation. For example, a boy and his father might be coached to engage in a long tug-of-war game using elastic ropes if the problems include opposition at home. At times, other siblings can be included, particularly brothers, when home interactions are part of the presenting situation (e.g., physical fights between brothers at home). Following the physical action, the boy and parent are given some kind of play activity to complete before the next session. Some concepts from dynamic play therapy follow that illustrate how the physical activities are constructed.

100   *Engaging Boys in Treatment*

Attuned Play

Attuned play is essential for the physical action to develop the benefit of emotional communication and joint creative problem solving. In attuned play, the players perform essentially the same actions in relatively close proximity and use similarly expressive nonverbal rhythms. If a young boy begins to run along a circular path, the adult (or other partner) follows along in a similar way at approximately the same speed and with the same intention. Often as play becomes more complicated and dramatic, the players take on different roles that require different actions. In attuned play, the players have the same focus on performing a common activity. For example, if the players are performing a race, both are trying to win according to the same set of rules and the physical action expresses this.

The goal of attuned play is for the players to develop a flow in which one play action leads to the next, with each player contributing something independently to the overall development of the action. If the play episode stops because one of the players stops contributing in some way, the therapist begins to intervene to help coach the improvisation to restart. Alex and Scott developed attunement in their play naturally as they both took roles in developing and then keeping a common focus on using the elastic ropes to "fly" the bear toward the pillows. Had either of these two players not agreed on the target or method of flying the bear, the activity would have quickly become unattuned and ceased.

Form and Energy

In successful interactive play improvisation, there is a balance of form or structure of the expression and the energy, or the felt emotional experience. If there is too much form, the expression becomes devoid of meaning, spontaneity, and interest for the players. If there is too much energy, the expression becomes unfocused and loses its communicative value. Throughout all the coaching strategies, the therapist aims to direct the physical play to have both form and energy together.

If a play episode is becoming overly structured through one player's direction or rules, the therapist makes suggestions to add more energy. This is done in several ways: asking the players to expand their current expressions, adding more physical activity to the play, or adding interactive challenges to the play by introducing competitive elements. If the play has too much energy, the therapist can direct the players to add more structure. This can be accomplished by introducing rules, planning, repeating actions in a similar manner, switching media (especially to art), or initiating conversation to add a more reflective emphasis to the expression.

For example, a simple game of chase can be given more structure in the event that the players lose their mutual focus and begin running through the room without awareness of each other's intentions by adding rules to change the activity into a game of tag. If the players appear to be losing energy (typically seen as a decline in the interest to continue), challenge might be added by creating the rule that the person who tags his partner can also make a new demand of that person, such as requiring that the other player move slowly, or on one foot, and so on. In this way, the therapist can coach a simple activity to become more engaging by adding something new to the improvised play action. Alex and Scott's play naturally developed a good balance of form (the way to fly the bear and rules related to the competition of getting the bear close to the target pillows) and energy (as each player spontaneously experienced interest in creating the game).

Use of Directive Versus Nondirective Activity

Often, to help boys and the adult (either therapist or parent) develop the initial play together, the therapist needs to set up a basic, physical, game-like interaction. This game is meant to be a starting point from which the players can begin to improvise together. However, some boys may need these kinds of structures for several sessions, as they may be unable to play interactively in an attuned way, especially with their fathers. These structures need to be organized around a simple physical interaction in which each player can have a role. Examples include activities such as chase, races across the room, follow the leader, tug-of-war using the elastic ropes, wrestling with the large stuffed animals, playing catch, and playing baseball with a balloon. It is expected that each of these beginning games will evolve to match each individual case situation through play improvisations. Applications of game structures for different ages will be presented.

Alex did not need a physical game set up for him as he was able to use the play material to begin and to creatively develop the activity spontaneously. Scott merely needed to use Alex's ideas to help him extend the play in a natural manner. Some boys are able to develop activities in this way. In this case, the therapist takes a more nondirective approach and becomes more of a participant than a coach.

Use of Verbalization

Not only does the therapist need to use verbal comment to present and set up the activities, but verbalization helps connect the play with the mental health situation the boy and his parent(s) identify. During the initial part of the session, the therapist informs the boy and family that physical play will be part of the intervention. This is usually accomplished most easily by showing the boy the play materials and letting him and his parent(s) know that activity will be an important part of the intervention.

During the session, the therapist verbally intervenes throughout the play, labeling players' feeling states, naming themes that repeat, and linking the play action to real-life problems. For example, opposition can be labeled within a game of tug-of-war and then linked to conflicts at home. Another example of speaking within the play is when the therapist takes a role in the action and makes comments that link play action to mental health concerns. An illustration of speaking within the role is when the therapist becomes a sports announcer during a play wrestling match. Often the therapist is able to describe the boy's character's dilemmas (this is usually a wrestler), emotional reactions, and possible solutions within the drama of the play fight in ways that link the wrestling match to the boy's life struggles. Such comments are meant to simultaneously refer to the moment-to-moment improvisation as well as the life difficulty. This technique of speaking during the play action to address the boy's real-life concerns occurred when Scott was able to help Alex use the slinging of the large bear across the room to discuss his own move from home and then his leaving school. The slinging actions that occurred in the improvisation were similar to and suggested the problematic action in Alex's life metaphorically. Scott was able to make use of this similarity.

Play Room

The most advantageous play room for dynamic play is one in which a variety of physically expressive and imaginative activities are encouraged. It is best if such play is conducted in a relatively large, open space where players can use whole body movements. There should be potential for activities such as chase games, tugs-of-war, and hide-and-seek. Stuffed animals of varying sizes help suggest imagined dramatic play scenarios that are appealing to boys, especially wrestling and fighting scenes such as shown in the World Wrestling Federation. Large, soft pillows can be used to make physical play safe and can be incorporated in making houses or imagined walls and places to hide. Colorful scarves and elastic ropes are easily employed in simple physical play and as props for large dramatic activity. The scarves can be very useful in having "scarf fights" in which players can throw this lightweight material at each other with no actual potential for harm. Large-sized newsprint paper and varying types of markers, crayons, pencils, and clay should also be available.

In general, the play material is relatively nonspecific and designed to help the players use their physical and dramatic imagination to turn these materials into what their play demands in the moment, and then to easily transform it into something else a few moments later. A large pillow might be used by a father and preschooler as a safe place to fall into together as an ending of a chase game, only to be used a few minutes later as the wall of an imaginary house filled with stuffed animals that represent both parents and children. It is very helpful to have a video camera and monitor in the room so that action episodes can be videotaped and reviewed shortly after the performance.

Scott purposefully had Alex select some play props to move into an unused large room so that they could utilize the open space to develop large-scale physical activity. The use of relatively nonspecific play material such as the pillows facilitated Alex accessing his imagination to develop the activity, and the elastic ropes further suggested physical action. In this way, the room setup itself encouraged Alex to engage in action that had the qualities of rough and tumble play.

The chapter will next review activities that are adapted for different ages: infants and toddlers, preschoolers, younger school-aged boys, older school-aged and middle school boys, and adolescents. Some general trends include the use of parent–child interactive play, the use of rules to organize the play action, and linking play action to problem behavior. The word *parent* in this chapter essentially refers to the father. However, it is sometimes difficult to engage fathers, so the adult play partner will be referred to generically.

Physical interactions between parent and son are mainly used for younger children, from infants to preschool aged, and the therapist is primarily a coach facilitating such play action as a "master player." In general, as boys become school aged, more time is devoted to play interactions with the therapist to be used for later sessions with the parent. Physical play with adolescents is almost exclusively conducted between the therapist and the boys. In general, the interactions with very young children are set up to utilize more spontaneous actions, with parents coached to follow the child's initiation. With school-aged boys, the therapist is more likely to introduce rules and competitive, game-like structures to organize the episodes. Activities used in sessions with adolescents are mutually designed by the therapist and the young person and incorporate discussions to address the problems.

In work with younger children, the therapist does not use comments to link play directly with real-life problems, but instead uses the action as a way for parents to better understand their son and enhance the relationship. Linking comments are used with school-aged children, initially connecting the problems observed in the immediate parent–child interactions to the play actions, then eventually using reports of problems at home to inform the design of physical activities. Full discussions of emotional, family, and social experiences are used with adolescents to mutually develop the action so that the metaphorical aspect of the play is clear to the young person.

Infants, Toddlers, and Preschoolers (0–4 Years)

The most typical problems encountered by mental health professionals working with very young children involve anxiety related to trauma, parenting difficulties, and separations. Such problems are seen in attachment-related interaction between the infant and his caretaker. In sessions, interactive physical play between the parent(s) and very young boys occurs fluidly as part of discussions with the parents. Sometimes more attention is devoted to the conversation, while at other times the parent-infant interactive play is the focus. The goal of these conversations is for the parents to develop the ability to understand their infant's needs, intentions, and emotional states by observing his interactions with them.

One technique is to have the parent speak for the boy as he is engaged in interactive play. When the parent and infant are involved in physical interactions, the central therapeutic goal is to assist the parent in responding to the young child's physical communication, especially noticing and responding to invitations to interact playfully, as well as signals that indicate when to stop and wait. When the child is very young (under six months), the main physical cues include eye contact and facial expressions such as smiling. Parental touch is another avenue to help develop an understanding of an infant's physical expression, especially for fathers. The inclusion of another professional trained in infant massage can be useful when a father is not as capable of sensitive physical play with his very young son. (See Harvey, 2008, for a case example of using massage to develop more normal physical play with an infant.)

As children become older and develop the physical ability to move by crawling and, later, walking and running, less time is spent in direct conversation with the parent while the boy is in the room, as toddlers often will be moving through the space. This action easily leads to interactive physical activities, such as having the parent chase the boy and use the pillows to develop hide-and-seek games as part of the chase. The following activities are suggested structured activities to be used for this age group.

Games With Infants

Such games include parent and child face-to-face play, games of peek-a-boo with eye contact, using transparent scarves to cover the parent's face while encouraging the child to pull the scarves away, using touch to a limb to develop movements that are initiated by the child, having the parent hold the child and move in different rhythms to find the child's favorite, and rolling and crawling interactions (e.g., rolling or crawling toward and away from the child) as the infant is developing these abilities. Music and props (large pillows and colorful scarves) can be used to enhance each activity.

Running and Falling Games With Toddlers

Such games include parents encouraging toddlers to run though the space with the adult following close behind, and using piles of soft pillows to fall into. The pillows can be spaced throughout the room. Different rhythms and types of falls can be used. The pillows can also be used to develop a pile to crawl over or through to extend chasing activities.

Swing Your Child Into the Pillows

The parent is asked to swing the child into a pile of pillows. To accomplish this activity with a sense of shared pleasure, the parent will have to match his rhythm to his child's physical tension and excitement. This activity is a good way to encourage nonverbal attunement. As the parent and child learn to enjoy this activity, the parent can be asked to increase the intensity of the swinging so that the child experiences maximal excitement, and then to use a slower swing to calm him down. A good way to end sessions is to have both the parent and another adult (therapist or other caregiver) rock the child slowly in a stretchy blanket several times.

Pillow Houses

The pillows can be used to build a house around children in the toddler years and older. This activity can then be extended by having the adults reach though the gaps in the pillows to attempt to catch the child, having the parent join the child in the house, and having the child break out by pushing the pillows down. The action of making the house and having it broken down can be repeated several times.

Hide-and-Seek

Versions of this game can be played with all children in this age range by matching the demands of the game to the skill and developmental level of the child(ren) involved. Both parent and child can take the role of the hider or seeker. With younger toddlers, the parent is asked to use the transparent scarves and a hiding place in full view of the child to help with the finding (the big moment of the episode). As children get older and more able to tolerate separation, the pillows can be used to make hiding places that are more elaborated, and the adults can have less direct involvement in the setup of the hiding aspect to increase the tension leading up to the "finding." The complexity of the game can be increased until the caretaker can leave the room briefly as part of the game while the child is helped to hide by the other adult (therapist or other parent).

Activities With Younger School-Aged Boys (5–7 Years)

The central idea for developing physical play with boys in this age range is to extend the complexity of the activity to correlate with the boy's increasing physical, imaginative, and interactive abilities. Problems that can be addressed with physical play at this age typically continue to be related to anxiety, such as with nightmares, separation issues, poor peer relationships, and the more significant anxiety problems that develop from trauma and family separation. The development of opposition can also be addressed successfully using physical play as part of larger mental health interventions.

In these activities, the parent is still included in the physical interaction, and activities begin to incorporate more structure to organize and extend the play action. Often, such structure is related to improvised stories and plots that emerge from the physical action due to the natural development of imaginative play that emerges in this age group. The therapist continues to make comments that link the play to the boy's emotional state to foster the parent's understanding of his son through the metaphor. Creative problem solving can be introduced within the play performance beginning at this age as well.

Various Physical Stories Using Large Stuffed Animals

Dramatic stories using large stuffed animals can be introduced at this age. Semistructured stories include asking the boy and parent to develop a narrative about a family using the large bears and the large pillows to make a home.

Monster

In this structure, the boy is asked to select one of the stuffed animals as a monster, and the boy and his parent are asked to build a safe house with the large pillows and any other materials they wish to include. The central focus of this game is that the parent and boy must work together to actively keep the monster from entering their home, while the therapist maneuvers the monster toward them. The therapist offers several potential physical actions, such as throwing props at the monster or yelling at it to "Go away!" This activity often leads to the boy wrestling with the monster while his father cheers him on (Harvey, 2001a).

WWF (World Wrestling Federation)

In this structure, the therapist helps the parent and boy use the pillows to make a wresting ring in which they can be safe physically, and the boy chooses his opponents from among the available stuffed animals. The therapist initially takes the role of the "sports announcer." After the announcer assists the boy in introducing his character and naming his opponent, the boy begins to wrestle while the announcer calls the action. As mentioned above, these comments emphasize the boy's strengths, emotions, and dilemmas that occur within the action. These comments are related to both the developments in the drama and the difficulties the boy has presented with. The therapist then helps the parent join in the action by casting him as a fellow wrestler who can come to the boy's aid or as a second announcer (which facilitates the parent's empathic verbalization by using the game action as a cue to identify feelings and encourage problem solving).

Tug-of-War

This activity is particularly effective in addressing a boy's problems with oppositionality. The activity is quite simple; the parent and boy are given a long elastic rope and the instructions to play tug-of-war. The therapist can then link this action to conflicts the boy has had previously, and use the action to cast the parent as more of an ally.

Sneak

This activity is particularly effective for boys who are overly impulsive as well as oppositional. The parent is asked to stand at one end of the room and initially look away. The boy is given the instruction to move without being seen, while the parent can look at any time. If the boy is seen moving, he must go back to his initial starting spot. If the boy can touch the parent, he then receives a point. Of course, the boy soon learns that he must control his action to be able to anticipate his parent's turning to look at him. The parent, for his part, must also not spend all his time looking or his son will simply want to stop playing. The therapist can use the game performance to discuss possible changes in parent–child interaction and then generalize these to the home environment.

Case Example

Carlos was a six-year-old who was brought to treatment by his father, Tony, due to his almost complete inability to spend time out of the family home. Going to school was very hard for him, and he was unable to attend typical childhood events without a parent right next to him. After the intake and some evaluative play interactions, Carlos and Tony were led to the play props and asked to play however they wished. Tony was instructed to allow his son to develop the action. Carlos immediately began wrestling with one to the bears while Tony explained that WWF was his son's favorite TV show. After the therapist helped make a safe mat using the pillows, Carlos engaged in vigorous wrestling while the therapist began to announce the match, describing the boy's strengths and his various challenges as he took on several opponents.

Carlos seemed somehow to always lose and played as if he was dying during each match. The therapist cast Tony as the medic who kept reviving him and then as Carlos's partner who could help defeat the other wrestlers. The therapist used this action to describe Carlos's dangerous emotional struggle and Tony's ability to provide help. After some sessions, Carlos was able to let Tony help him defeat his adversaries. The therapist was able to link the play action to Carlos's emotional difficulties and his father's ability to participate in providing emotional support. These comments helped this father and son successfully address their separation issues. While the play was left open in this case, Carlos's choice fit nicely into one of the above structures.

Play With Older School-Aged Boys (8–12 Years)

Physical activity is perhaps most useful in engaging boys of this age group. Often the mental health concerns involve opposition, anger, and a lack of interest in participating in treatment. Boys with these kinds of difficulties tend to show a disinterest in discussing their feelings or behavior, and their parent usually can only report a list of problems. As a result, physical activity is often one of the few ways to engage such boys. Activities usually are conducted with the therapist and developed into more set structures that parents are then invited to join. When the therapist is able to help develop the final structures of the action, he can help create roles within the game that are challenging (to ensure that there is motivation to continue) yet fair to the adult. There is more of a reliance on rules to organize these activities, and the therapist is able to verbally link improvisations to real problems, especially during the inactions. Home activities can extend the in-office games to help the physical action become more meaningful.

The game structures for this age group are mostly designed as a competition between the players to shift the expression of anger and opposition into a more playful physical context. The games mentioned above are also made more complex to engage older children. For example, a tug-of-war can be set up using more than one rope so that the players must decide which rope to pull and when to win. The monster game can be extended by having the player who is being chased by the monster give commands for how the monster should move when he attempts to pursue his victim (e.g., the monster might be told to move with his eyes closed). These additions make the game of the monster chase far more complex and interesting.

Other games of competitive opposition include the following.

Mr. Opposite Man

In this activity, one player tells the other how to move while the other attempts to do the opposite. For example, if the therapist commands the boy to move fast, the boy needs to respond by moving slowly. Roles are then reversed. The boy is then encouraged to make the commands more complex while the responding player likewise tries to produce more subtle opposite responses. After some practice, the parent is brought in and is asked to join the competition. The therapist then becomes the judge and gives a point to Mr. Opposite Man if he can produce the opposite response quickly or to the commanding player if Mr. Opposite Man fails. If disagreements in the scoring arise, part of the game is to verbally resolve them before moving on. The game can be extended to the home environment by using the name Mr. Opposite Man when opposition is noticed in the home. The enactment of home activities is then incorporated into the game in later sessions.

Slow-Motion Races

In this activity, the players are asked to race from one point to another in the room as different rules are added, such as moving slowly (the slowest person wins). Other commands can include moving backward, on the floor, and in various combinations, such as moving on the floor slowly. Again, the boy can practice with the therapist before the parent is invited in and the boy competes with him. When this happens, the therapist again becomes the judge of the racing. When disagreements occur, the parent, boy, and therapist must stop the action to work out new rules needed.

Screaming Without Making Noise

This is a competition between therapist (followed again by the parent) and the boy to see who can scream the "loudest" without making a sound. Usually the therapist is subsequently the judge of who performs the "best" scream between parent and child, rating the physical expressions (face and full body) while adding penalties to the player who makes noise through a lack of control.

Volcano

In this action, the boy is buried by the large pillows while lying on his back and is asked to kick the pillows off. The therapist (and later parent) then throws the pillows back on while the boy tries to keep the pillows off him through kicking and pushing. Sometimes it is helpful to set up "innings" by stopping the action every minute and awarding points. The boy earns a point if he is able to have kicked the pillows off at the end of an inning, while the parent earns the point if pillows cover the boy. This activity is particularly effective for anger by organizing a parent–child interaction in which physical activity is encouraged within a competitive game context. For this problem, the boy is asked to draw a volcano to take home, and he or the parent use the picture to label the angry episodes at home as a "volcano" (Harvey, 2001b).

Games With Balloons

Players engage in games such as baseball or volleyball with balloons and scores are kept. The parent plays with the boy in these games, as no practice is usually needed. When disagreements develop as to how the game is played or scored, it is again important to stop and determine a fair outcome to any disagreement. If these episodes can be videotaped, they can be reviewed to objectively work out the dilemma. The connection of the actions of these activities to home-related problems is usually very clear.

Case Example

Two brothers (Dan, age 8, and Tim, age 10) were referred due to their aggression toward each other and in the classroom. Their mother, Jan, had been extensively physically abused by the boys' father, as had both boys. Sam, Jan's new partner, reported at intake that both Dan and Tim had been quite resistant to him since he entered the home, and he was at a loss as to how to help them. The boys were also both resistant to previous attempts by school or agency counselors to engage them. Jan and Sam were seen separately to address parenting issues, while Tim and Dan were seen together and became engaged quite easily in physical play with each other. The primary goal was to help the boys begin to express themselves and to contain their aggression, especially toward each other. Once this was accomplished, the parents became involved in the activities to improve family interaction so that reasonable limits could be developed.

The boys found this very entertaining and were eager to return. Jan attended the beginning of the next few sessions to report on the boys' interaction at home as aggressive conflicts continued. The therapist introduced a series of slow-motion races complete with extensive discussions about the rules around what was considered a "win." When arguing ensued, the therapist gave the boys the option to use racing to settle their disputes.

Once they were able to accept a way to determine a winner with some sense of fairness and humor, the boys invited Sam into the session to play a few innings of volcano. The two boys challenged the therapist and their stepfather. The boys were then asked to make a joint picture of a volcano that was to be used in the home. They then engaged in full family discussions and were able to make progress on reducing the boys' aggressive outbursts and increasing the parents' ability to understand the boys' feelings. In the last session, the boys decided to use the pillows to create a wall they labeled "Problems" that they could high-jump over. In their usual manner, they tried to outdo each other by adding various enhancements to their jumps, such as flipping. However, they were able to collaborate in the end by even giving each other boosts to get over the wall of problems.

Adaptations for Adolescents

Physical play is used quite differently with adolescents. Play episodes are jointly planned by the young person and therapist together to address specific issues in a very conscious manner. There is usually little parent participation. Physical play is used flexibly to help address emotional conflicts that have been difficult to resolve with other verbal avenues. The setup and linking of the play is developed for each situation and is usually an adjunctive part of a larger intervention.

Some part of the physical activity can be used to enhance the therapeutic alliance. Often therapists who work with adolescents engage in more neutral game activities, such as playing one-on-one basketball or taking a walk before sessions as a part of building a more trusting relationship, as boys are often not likely to trust an adult-initiated activity without first experiencing some kind of mutual experience. Other action episodes are developed after a therapeutic alliance is built up, when both the therapist and boy can trust each other to use the physical experience in a helpful manner and talk through emotional material related to the activity fully.

The following case presentation will illustrate how physical play can be adapted for this age group. Devon (14) and his older brother Ben (16) were referred for individual and family therapy after Ben had attempted to hang himself. One of the presenting problems in the family was that these two brothers were aggressive toward their mother and often physically fought each other at home. The parents had separated due to the father's severe physical violence toward the mother. The boys' own violence seemed to escalate after visits with their father. Despite several sessions in which the boys were both able to talk about their conflicts constructively, the sibling aggression was hard for them to stop.

Both boys agreed to try to use physical play to reduce their aggression after several sessions on their own and with their mother. The therapist helped them plan sessions in which they had play fights using rules for physical and emotional safety. They split the room and agreed not to cross the middle dividing line into the other's space. The therapist was careful to function as a referee to ensure that neither boy violated any of the predetermined rules of safety. The sessions were videotaped and reviewed both in the office and in the room. The fights were also conducted at slow, medium, and normal speeds with at least 5 feet separating the boys. Each boy was able to choreograph his body being hit or kicked and use the pillows to fall into. As they became more practiced at the play fighting, they began to choreograph various scenes that were videotaped for later viewing. The boys were then able to add dialogue to their movies while they watched. They showed their mother their videos when they were ready.

The resulting play episodes resembled rough and tumble play, and both brothers showed enjoyment in their use of physical imagination and creative action. The play enhanced their connection with each other and helped maximize the effectiveness of verbal intervention that occurred later. If the play had lost this positive feeling or if the boys' actions were to actually show the potential for becoming harmful, the therapist would have stopped the action and addressed the break verbally. However, this was not needed in this case. Such preparation was used to keep this kind of physicality within a range of emotional expression that was therapeutic.

SUMMARY

Physically oriented play can be used to help boys become engaged in mental health interventions. Such play is related to the rough and tumble play often observed as boys playing with each other in more natural settings like the playground. This style of play has not been utilized in more traditional therapeutic approaches. This chapter reviewed how physically interactive play can be used both in directed action and as free improvisation to help boys become more engaged and focused. The central outcomes of such play are to develop more communication, improve intrinsic motivation to participate, and develop problem solving using physical imagination. Such episodes lead boys to an experiential understanding of wrestling with their problems, in physical as well as psychological ways.

REFERENCES

Adler, J. (1968). The study of an autistic child. In *Proceedings of the American Dance Therapy Association, Third Annual Conference* (pp. 42–48). Madison, WI.

Blurton Jones, N. G. (1967). An ethological study of some aspects of social behaviour of children in nursery school. In D. Morris (Ed.), *Private ethnology* (pp. 347–368). London, UK: Weidenfield and Nicholson.

Chaiklin, H. (Ed.). (1975). *Marian Chace: Her papers*. Columbia, MD: American Dance Therapy Association.

Freeman, N., & Brown, M. (2001). Reconceptualising rough and tumble play: Ban the banning. *Advances in Early Education and Day Care, 13*, 219–234.

Harlow, H. (1962). The heterosexual affective system in monkeys. *American Psychologist, 17*(1), 1–9.

Harvey, S. A. (1994). Dynamic play therapy: An integrated expressive arts approach to family treatment of infants and toddlers. *Zero to Three, 15*(1), 11–17.

Harvey, S. A. (1995). Sandra: The case of an adopted, sexually abused child. In F. Levy (Ed.), *Dance and other expressive arts therapies: When words are not enough* (pp. 167–180). New York: Routledge.

Harvey, S. A. (2001a). Monster. In H. G. Kaduson & C. E. Schaefer (Eds.), *101 more favorite play therapy techniques* (pp. 183–187). Lanham, MD: Jason Aronson.

Harvey, S. A. (2001b). Volcano. In H. G. Kaduson & C. E. Schaefer (Eds.), *101 more favorite play therapy techniques* (pp. 188–192). Lanham, MD: Jason Aronson.

Harvey, S. A. (2003). Dynamic family play with an adoptive family struggling with issues of grief, loss, and adjustment. In D. J. Wiener & L. K. Oxford (Eds.), *Action therapy with families and groups* (pp. 19–43). Washington, DC: American Psychological Association.

Harvey, S. A. (2006). Dynamic play therapy. In C. E. Schaefer & H. G. Kaduson (Eds.), *Contemporary play therapy: Theory, research, and practice* (pp. 55–81). New York: Guilford.

Harvey, S. A. (2008). Dynamic play with very young children. In C. E. Schaefer, S. Kelly-Zion, J. McCormick, & A. Ohnogi (Eds.), *Play therapy for very young children* (pp. 3–23). Lanham, MD: Jason Aronson.

Harvey, S. A. (2009). Family problem solving: Using expressive activities. In A. Drewes (Ed.), *Blending play therapy with cognitive behavioral therapy: Evidence-based and other effective treatments and techniques* (pp. 449–471). Hoboken, NJ: John Wiley.

Hines, M., Golombok, S., Rust, J., Johnson, K. J., & Golding, J. (2002). Testosterone during pregnancy and gender role behavior of preschool children: A longitudinal, population study. *Child Development, 73*(6), 1678–1687.

James, M., Forrester, A. M., & Kim, K. C. (2005). Developmental transformations in the treatment of sexually abused children. In A. M. Weber & C. Haen (Eds.), *Clinical applications of drama therapy in child and adolescent treatment* (pp. 67–86). New York: Brunner-Routledge.

Jarvis, P. (2006). "Rough and tumble" play: Lessons in life. *Evolutionary psychology, 4*, 330–346.

Jarvis, P. (2007). Monsters, magic and Mr. Psycho: A biocultural approach to rough and tumble play in the early years of primary school. *Early Years, 27*(2), 171–188.

Johnson, D. R. (2009). Developmental transformations: Towards the body as presence. In D. R. Johnson & R. Emunah (Eds.), *Current approaches in drama therapy* (2nd ed., pp. 89–116). Springfield, IL: Charles C. Thomas.

Kalish-Weiss, B. (1974). Working with an autistic child. In K. Mason (Ed.), *Focus on dance VII: Dance therapy* (pp. 38–40). Reston, VA: The American Alliance for Health Physical Education, Recreation, and Dance.

Lamb, M. E. (1996). *The role of the father in child development.* Hoboken, NJ: Wiley.

Leventhal, M. B. (1974). Movement therapy with minimal brain dysfunction children. In K. Mason (Ed.), *Focus on dance VII: Dance therapy* (pp. 42–48). Reston, VA: The American Alliance for Health Physical Education, Recreation, and Dance.

Lindsey, E. W., & Mize, J. (2001). Contextual differences in parent-child play: Implications for children's gender role development. *Sex Roles, 44*(3–4), 155–176.

MacDonald, K. B., & Parke, R. D. (1986). Parent-child physical play: The effects of sex and age of children. *Sex Roles, 15*(7–8), 367–378.

Pellegrini, A. D. (1988). Elementary-school children's rough-and-tumble play and social competence. *Developmental Psychology, 24*(6), 802–806.

Pellegrini, A. D., & Smith, P. K. (1998). Physical activity play: The nature and function of a neglected aspect of play. *Child Development, 69*(3), 609–610.

Ross, H., & Taylor, H. (1989). Do boys prefer daddy or his physical style of play? *Sex Roles, 20*(1–2), 23–33.

Russ, S. W. (Ed.). (1998). *Affect, creative experience, and psychological adjustment.* Philadelphia, PA: Brunner/Mazel.

Incorporating Animal-Assisted Interventions in Therapy With Boys at Risk

AUBREY H. FINE, AVRIL LINDSAY DENNIS, AND CHRISTINE BOWERS

Harvey was removed from his parents' custody and spent most of his developing years in the Child Welfare System of New York State. He spent time at various residential facilities and was bounced in and out of foster care. After being expelled from eight schools by the age of 9, Harvey was sent to the residential program Green Chimneys. He described himself at that time as short-tempered and disruptive. Once he arrived at Green Chimneys, Harvey refused to talk to anyone, especially the staff and therapists. However, Green Chimneys had one attraction that seemed to be the most enticing to Harvey, the animals. He soon realized that the only way to gain access to these animals was by interacting with the staff, to ask for help and permission. "That started a kind of chain reaction. The more I communicated with the staff, the more time I could spend with the animals. Although the therapists did help me, I got more comfort from the interaction with the animals, and, on some level, I felt we had something in common. It was important to recognize that animals have feelings and that they were at Green Chimneys for the same reason I was, to get better." From his experience in working with Laddie and a few of the other animals at Green Chimneys, Harvey now thinks about a positive future. His relationships with animals opened up new doors for him. They supported him to realize that he was a worthwhile person that could be loved. (Fine & Eisen, 2008, pp. 113–114)

UNDERSTANDING THE HUMAN–ANIMAL BOND

The unique bond between humans and animals, and its powerful impact on human well-being, has been documented for hundreds of years (Serpell, 2006). Many theories have been proposed to explain why people adore being around animals. One widely accepted hypothesis stems from attachment theory. Bowlby (1969, 1980) formulated that the biological function of attachment is that of protection. It seems logical that this theory, which has often been attributed to explaining parent–child relationships, would also apply to our understanding of the human–animal connection. Barba (1995) suggested that the roles humans play in relation to their pets often parallel the roles played in relationships with humans, especially the dyad of child and parent. In a similar fashion that young children rely on their parents, scholars believe that pets must depend on their human companions for continual care. It is quite simple to observe this phenomenon in our homes, where many people find themselves caring for and doting upon animals. Often, pet owners treat their animals, especially those with infantile features, as their own babies (Fine, 2008). In fact, it isn't uncommon to find pets sleeping in our bedrooms, going on family vacations, and even having events celebrated in their honor.

Pet owners commonly view their relationships with animals in humanistic terms. Many seem to develop anthropomorphic attitudes toward their pets, projecting onto the animals their own human feelings, motives, and qualities, and often perceiving pets as substitutes for other people. McNicholas and Collis (2006) view our relationships with animals in the context of social supports. They noted in their research that it often appears easier for humans to bond with animals than with other humans. Unlike most humans, pets are typically indifferent to their human companions' material possessions, status, well-being, and social skills. It is possible that pets can provide an escape from the strains of human interaction.

THE ROLES ANIMALS HAVE IN
THE LIVES OF CHILDREN

The literature is filled with data that suggest and support that animals can promote human physical and emotional wellness simply by being part of our lives. Companion animals have supported humans in many ways and have generated numerous psychosocial benefits (Hart, 2006; McNicholas & Collis, 2006). Evidence suggests that pets tend to protect their human companions against stress, act as a social catalyst for human interaction, provide social support, and aid in initiating and sustaining conversations (Hunt, Hart, & Gomulkiewicz, 1992; Messant, 1984). In regard to children, pets have been found to play various roles including friend, confidante, or even family member (Lookabaugh Triebencher, 2000). In reviewing the literature, there does not appear to be strong evidence documenting any significant differences between the way boys and girls positively relate and respond to pet companions (G. Melson, personal communication, August 12, 2009). This conclusion is supported by a study conducted by Kotrschal and Ortbauer (2003) that found no gender differences in ways children interacted with a dog in a classroom. They did find, however, that behavior changes in the presence of the dog were more pronounced for boys than for girls. Yet, the literature is filled with research that does perhaps illustrate one major distinction between genders—as it pertains to animal cruelty and abuse. The literature appears to suggest that, with boys, interactions with animals facilitates decreased levels of anger and, as a result, decreased violence or aggression. Decreased violence has been suggested to have a correlation to increased empathy (Lindsay, 2007). The combination of decreased aggression and increased empathy helps to combat patterns of animal cruelty and abuse in boys.

Both boys and girls often describe companion animals as siblings and cast them in a sibling role, according to a study conducted by Bryant (1986). The language used by the children to describe interactions and time spent with the pet was very similar to that used to describe interactions and time spent with peers and siblings (Melson, 2001). Only children or youngest siblings often assigned the pet the role of a younger sibling. These children spent significantly more time interacting with and caring for the pet than children who had younger siblings (Melson, 2001). The child took on the role of the leader and teacher of the pet, just as if it were a younger sibling.

Children often engage their pets as confidantes, beginning at a very early age and continuing into adolescence and adulthood. Many young children sincerely feel that their pet understands them and actually communicates back to them. As they grow older, children realize their pet is a being capable of feeling and communicating, even if these exchanges are nonverbal (Myers, 1998). Children confide many different feelings to their pets, ranging from anger and sadness to happiness. They recognize that the animal is able to handle full disclosure while remaining an uncritical and accepting audience capable of listening intently and keeping a secret. Additionally, it has been shown that children who are significantly involved with their pets show more empathy and are more skilled at predicting the feelings of others in certain situations (Bailey, 1987; Bryant, 1986; Melson & Fine, 2006; Melson, Peet, & Sparks, 1992).

Beyond playing the role of younger sibling or secret keeper, pets serve as a constant friend and social support for children. In one study, children ranked their dogs among those included in their "top five important relationships," while others labeled their pets as "my best friend" and expressed that their pet would be there "no matter what" (Furman, 1989). The idea that a pet will always be there is a comforting one to a child, especially a child who may be going through difficult transitions, such as starting at a new school, moving to a new neighborhood, or coping with some kind of change in the family structure. It has been found that many children will seek out their pet when they feel sad or upset because the pet is always available and doesn't demand reciprocity for its support (Collis & McNicholas, 1998).

Another important benefit pets may afford children is being an emotional buffer to help cope with a stressful environment or relational difficulties. According to Strand (2004), children who have pets in their homes often turn to them for comfort during high-stress situations, such as parental discord. Children who are able to use their pet interaction as a "buffer" or a self-calming technique may exhibit fewer behavioral problems because they have an outlet to help them regulate reactions to environmental stressors. Additionally, the pet provides the constant nurturing and acceptance needed to facilitate healthy coping skills, even in difficult times (Strand, 2004).

Pets also provide an excellent learning tool. They are used in homes to teach responsibility and nurturing. Martindale (2001) suggested that it is in this area that we may see a unique benefit of companion animals for boys. Pets are often the only source for nurturing others available to boys in which they are not accused of diminished masculinity because they are performing a caring behavior. Taking care of a pet is free of gender stereotypes. It is just as appropriate, both among children and adults, for a male to care for a pet as a female. When children ages 4 to 7 were asked who would be most appropriate to care for a baby or small child, pictures of "mommies" (adult females) were the resounding answer. Pictures of adult females were also chosen as appropriate caregivers for the elderly. When it came to who should care for animals, however, pictures of both males and females were chosen almost equally (Melson & Fogel, 1989).

Additionally, a family pet provides ample opportunity for a child to experience the calming effects of touch, which is thought to be important at all stages of development (Bowlby, 1980). This could be particularity important for boys, who may not be treated as affectionately or taught to be as affectionate as girls. This is extended one step further when addressing boys at risk. For boys who are being raised by a single parent, or a parent who is not available regularly, perhaps because she is working two or maybe three jobs, or young boys who are removed from their home situation due to trauma and abuse histories or because they exhibit delinquent behaviors, touch from these animals may have increased importance due to the limited amount of human touch available.

When addressing the link between animals and boys, the majority of the literature focuses on the negative associations, namely, the link between animal abuse as a child and how it relates to violence as an adult. Several studies, such as those conducted by Bell (2001), Patterson-Kane and Piper (2009), and Ascione and Shapiro (2009), have illustrated that children who abuse animals are prone to crime and domestic violence. Attention has also been given to the correlation between child abuse and animal abuse.

For some time, researchers have focused on the association between violence toward animals and violence toward humans. Ascione (1997) suggested that the development of empathy might play a role in this behavior. Furthermore, low levels of empathy correlate with high levels of aggressive behavior. As it relates to the difference between boys and girls, studies have shown that girls show more empathy for others than boys (Hastings, Zahn-Waxler, Robinson, Usher, & Bridges, 2000). Thompson and Gullone (2003) administered the Children's Treatment of Animals Questionnaire (CTAQ) to 25 boys and 36 girls to try to determine if there were significant gender differences in regard to their attitudes and behavior toward animals. They found that boys scored significantly lower on their measures of empathy, as expected, but the CTAQ did not suggest any significant difference between boys and girls and their ideas regarding humane behavior toward animals. These findings suggested that humane behavior and cruelty toward animals could be independent from, rather than opposite of, each other.

Whether or not one focuses on the positives or the negatives, there is no denying that companion animals play a large role in the everyday lives of children. In regard to pro-social behaviors, pets seem to positively affect both boys and girls equally. When looking at animal cruelty and abuse, the negative relationship between boys and animals is more pronounced. Nevertheless, it is obvious that companion animals are influential beings when it comes to children and how they relate to their environment.

ANIMAL-ASSISTED INTERVENTIONS

LaJoie (2003) suggested that over 12 different terms are in existence today to describe therapy that incorporates animals into the treatment process. Terms such as *pet therapy, animal-facilitated counseling, pet-mediated therapy, and pet psychotherapy* have commonly been used interchangeably. Nevertheless, the two most widely utilized terms are *animal-assisted therapy* and *animal-assisted activities*. Both terms could be classified under the rubric of animal-assisted interventions.

The Delta Society's *Standards of Practice for Animal Assisted Activities and Therapy* (1996) defined animal-assisted therapy (AAT) as an intervention with specified goals and objectives delivered by a health or human service professional with expertise in using an animal as an integral part of treatment. Whether provided in a group or individual setting, the Delta Society reported that AAT promotes improvement in physical, social, emotional, and cognitive functioning. For example, to help a client deal with issues of touch, a therapist may use the holding of a rabbit as a strategy to open up a discussion about that topic with the child. The animals used in AAT range from goldfish in aquariums to horses in fields, and many others in between.

In contrast, animal-assisted activities (AAAs) occur when specially trained professionals, paraprofessionals, or volunteers accompanied by animals interact with people in a variety of environments (Delta Society, 1996). In AAA, the same activity can be repeated with many different people or groups of people; the interventions are not part of a specific treatment plan and are not designed to address a specific emotional or medical condition, and detailed documentation does not occur. The familiar sight of volunteers taking their pets to visit patients at an assisted living facility meets the criteria for AAAs.

ANIMAL-ASSISTED INTERVENTIONS WITH YOUTH

Animal-assisted interventions (AAIs) can be applied in numerous settings with therapists who utilize diverse theoretical orientations. However, there needs to be a plan on how the AAI can be best incorporated. Fine (2006) advised that clinicians consider using a simple problem-solving approach as they begin to conceptualize how they would apply AAI with their patients. The questions that therapists should consider are the following:

1. *What benefits can AAI provide this client?* This rhetorical question needs to be considered clearly. How can animals in a clinical environment or a specific situation complement the ongoing therapy and make a difference?
2. *How can AAI strategies be incorporated within the planned intervention?* The clinician needs to consider how AAI fits into the overall treatment objectives, goals, and programs. This integration of AAI into the overall context of therapy is extremely vital. Unfortunately, some professionals neglect to problem-solve how to integrate AAI into the overall treatment, and the overall efficacy of the intervention is weakened. Fine (2006) believes that without making the necessary plans for integration, the generalization and transfer of the behaviors being focused upon is limited.
3. *How will I need to adapt my therapeutic approach to incorporate AAI?* This suggestion needs to be strongly considered. The interactions between the therapist and the animal should be fluid and seamless. Therefore, the clinicians must feel comfortable with how animals will work alongside them to make an impact on the treatment.

The following section will act as a brief description of the general strategies that should be considered when incorporating AAI. This introduction will be followed by more in-depth ideas of how to apply strategies with youth and, more specifically, boys.

Strategy 1: Animals Acting as a Social Lubricant

Fine (2006) stressed that animals can act as a social lubricant in a variety of settings. They can effectively ease the stress of the initial phase of therapy, act as a link in conversation between therapist and client, and help establish trust and rapport between patient and clinician. The mere presence of an animal can also give clients a sense of comfort, which further promotes rapport in the therapeutic relationship. A calm animal may also act as a signal of a safe environment. Since clients often view animals as an extension of the therapist, an animal may ease tension and serve as an icebreaker when greeting clients with warmth and enthusiasm.

Fawcett and Gullone (2001) suggested that youth with conduct disorders, who often attribute negative thoughts and feelings to those around them, could begin to form a positive bond with a therapist in the presence of a therapy animal. It is suggested that the therapist becomes a benign presence because of the animal. This is especially true when dealing with boys who, either by nature or nurture, have a predisposed sense of *machismo*, making them traditionally more guarded against assistance and less open to traditional therapeutic intervention. However, when the animal is used alongside a therapist, boys seek out excuses to spend time with the therapist. The presence of the animal, in turn, enables the therapist to interact more frequently with a client, increasing the chance of a strong client-therapist bond. Chandler (2001) and Fine (2006) surmised that the animal helps create a trusting environment by decreasing anxiety and tension during the session, especially when addressing some of the more challenging issues faced in the therapeutic process.

The following is a brief example of how any well-trained therapy dog could act as a social catalyst for therapeutic rapport to enhance the therapeutic regime. Fine and Eisen (2008) discussed the case of Charles, who was diagnosed as having attention deficit hyperactivity disorder (ADHD). Charles lacked impulse control and had limited ability to focus on tasks. In an interview, his mother confided that although Charles could be gentle, more often than not he was in constant motion, moving from toy to toy or place to place, leaving a mess in his wake. In one instance early in Charles's therapy, Fine recalls observing Charles sitting in the waiting room and interacting with a therapy dog named Puppy. These early interactions appeared to be an incentive to Charles for attending therapy.

> Charles lies on the floor playing with the train set in the waiting room. Puppy is laying on the floor too, in the middle of the train set, the tracks making a circle around her. Every two or three minutes Charles talks to Puppy. "I'm moving the bridge now, Puppy." She responds with an enthusiastic, but gentle, wave of her plumy tail. Charles' voice begins to build in volume and excitement. He walks around the tracks holding the train in the air and making louder and louder choo-choo sounds. Suddenly,

he stops in mid-choo, kneels in front of Puppy, and he throws his arms around her neck, knocking his glasses half off his face. Unable to contain himself, Charles sings, "I love you/You love me...." As Charles continues singing, his face radiates with happiness. Puppy stands up and gives his cheek a large swipe with her tongue. At this, Charles whoops in surprise and then dissolves into giggles, burying his face in the dog's fur, content and comfortable in Puppy's company. (Fein & Eisen, 2008, p. 3)

When working with young children, an animal may provide a sense of nonjudgmental love, fulfilling the most basic of developmental needs. According to Melson (2001), children may be able to experience a unique parenting role through a close emotional and tactile relationship with an animal companion. On the other hand, adolescents may feel less defensive when they are able to receive comfort from or project emotions onto an animal present in the therapeutic setting. They may also be able to identify with some of the animal's characteristics, such as playfulness, outgoing or shy behaviors, or devotion to others.

At the Children's Village (CV), an all-male child welfare residential program located in Dobbs Ferry, New York, an animal-assisted therapy group program seemed to have a strong effect on all the boys who participated. From 2004 to 2005, a study of group therapy at CV followed two groups of boys who were receiving group therapy three times weekly. During one of the weekly sessions, the therapy dog was present; the other two sessions used different modalities, including psychoeducational and didactic approaches. By far, the best attendance in a group therapy session, in which fewer boys left during the process, was when the therapy dog was present (Lindsay, 2004).

The boys in these groups also showed fewer outbursts, fewer disagreements or fights, and more cooperation. The boys didn't want to yell for fear of upsetting the dog. They wanted her to like them and come to them. The only way they could entice her to come to them was by having a calm demeanor, not by calling or pulling on her. They each learned from the others, and began to read body language and imagine the situation from the dog's point of view. There appeared to be a group sense of empathy for keeping the dog safe and secure. Prior to the start of the group session, the boys would work together to make sure there was nothing on the floor that she could get to that could endanger her. The boys also found something in common with the staff who liked the dog. That identification consequently led to enjoying a positive relationship with an adult, and being surprised by having things in common.

Devon stared at the wall, refusing to move to attend the group. This had been the usual sequence of events for him. Today, though, the staff tried something different. "Sky [one of the therapy dogs] is going to group today too," one of the staff softly said to Devon. He accused her of lying to him. But then he saw Sky walk past and into the room with the therapist. He'd never seen her in group before. His eyes lit up as he asked the staff, "Do you like Sky too?"

A conversation between youth and staff followed that ended with Devon in group that day, and each day forward. Sky had been the link to the group for him, as well as a link to a relationship with the staff with whom he usually argued about going to group.

Strategy 2: A Catalyst for Emotion

For many clients, the mere presence of an animal in a therapeutic set-ting can stir emotions and help a client express feelings and thoughts (Fine, 2006). Simply interacting with an animal in a therapeutic setting can lighten the mood. Animals also can display emotions and interact with the client in manners that may not be professionally appropriate for therapists. For example, the animal might climb into a client's lap or sit calmly while the client pets it. Holding or petting an animal may soothe clients and help them feel contained while exploring difficult emotions in treatment that might be overwhelming without this valu-able therapeutic touch. The animal may console, for example, by plac-ing a paw on a client's lap in a time of need. However, the therapist must be aware of occasions in which the client uses the animal to hide or screen from discussing difficult issues.

An animal's presence in the therapeutic setting can also lead to spon-taneous situations that help the client work through difficult emotions he or she may be experiencing. A terrific example of spontaneous inter-action with a boy and an animal occurred several years ago at CV just before Christmas. Outlined below is a brief excerpt from one of the ses-sions with an eight-year-old who rarely spoke of his feelings to anyone.

> That afternoon he tried to engage a therapy dog named Jaguar. She was tired, and not much into playing at that moment, so he lay on the floor nose to nose with her and began consoling her, seeming to have figured she was sad. "You must be feeling sad that you won't get to see your fam-ily at Christmas," he began, continuing the one-way conversation with her for about 20 minutes. "But the social workers and other people here love you, and they'll make it fun for you. You'll see."

His openness in expressing his feelings about the dog seemed to dem-onstrate how this little boy worked out his own disappointment that he would not be going home for Christmas.

Key to examples like this spontaneous interaction are the behind-the-scenes training of staff and therapists. It is important that all be educated at the beginning of the process of such a program about the benefits it could provide. Otherwise, the risk is that the animal is seen at times as a reward for negative behavior. Parameters should be clear, especially about the use of an animal when intervening in the crisis phase of a situation. Interaction with the animal should be set up as a routine part of the day or program.

Strategy 3: Animals as Teachers

Teaching animals and supporting their growth can also have therapeutic benefits for the clients. Arluke (2007) took a strong look at AAI programs, which were established in five settings treating teens at risk. Of the five programs he reviewed, he observed and studied two that were service dog programs, two that were obedience dog programs, and one that was a farm animal program that also offered gardening. The major goal of all the programs was to give the youth an opportunity to act as mentors and teachers for animals that needed their support.

One example of such a program exists at CV, which became a training site for Educated Canines Assisting with Disabilities (ECAD) in 1999, an organization that raises, trains, and places dogs with individuals who have various disabilities that cause loss of independence. Puppies in the program spend the week in school with the boys learning how to be service dogs and their weekends in the homes of local residents learning manners and socialization. Many of the first puppy raisers were in fact employees of CV. With the introduction of puppies into the offices of therapists who were also puppy raisers, an interesting phenomenon began to unfold.

Boys at the residential program were scheduling their therapy sessions for the days when the puppies were present. The dog was a natural pull to the therapist's office, leading in turn to a pull to therapy. Boys who had gone out of their way to avoid therapy, by either not showing up or not having much to say or do in the session, started coming to session. The boys actually wanted to be there. They also wanted to talk, and had many questions about the dogs: where they lived, what they did, who took care of them, as well as describing how they thought the dogs felt about their situation, even noting socialization patterns and family ties.

Although Arluke (2007) concluded that the findings gathered from most of these projects listed numerous positive anecdotal comments, there wasn't any clear scientific evidence that they were effective in reaching the outlined goal of the program. Nevertheless, Arluke (2007) speculated and generated several ideas of why he believed these interventions had a meaningful effect on the clients. These suggestions can be found in Table 5.1.

Fine (2007) pointed out that if the impact of the therapeutic intervention is to have overall efficacy, attention must be given to generalization and transfer of the behavior taught. Stokes and Osnes (1986), in their benchmark paper on the generalization of social skills, discussed numerous variables that need to be considered. They suggested that when the goals and procedures of training are more widespread, the outcomes could also be widespread. They advised that the more similar the training setting is to the natural environment in which the child lives, the more likely the training will elicit the wanted response in both settings. Fine and Kotkin (2003) also suggested that if there are peers

TABLE 5.1   Arluke's (2007) Suggestions for Why AAI Works With Youth

1. Buying into programs	Youth are curious and excited about working with the animals and are thus "hooked" on the idea of AAT.
2. Forming close relationships	Youth form close relationships with the animals and thus the therapists.
3. Feeling unjudged	Youth feel more secure in the nonbiased presence of the animals, and thus the therapists.
4. Empowering participants	Youth feel empowered through the training of the animals and the support from the staff.
5. Taking perspectives	The animals allowed the youth to experience situations based on how others are feeling.
6. Allowing frustration	Training animals is not easy, and thus the youth have to learn how to be patient and accept failures.

from the child's life that are included in the actual treatment program or are aware of the goals, the social behaviors that are being taught are more likely to transfer into their daily lives. This transfer will occur because the exposure will help increase the likelihood the child will utilize the learned responses in his or her natural environment with the peers present. AAI cannot be utilized in isolation. The interventions must incorporate relevant people in the therapeutic process so that they understand the value of the AAI and can apply the outcomes of the interventions in the child's daily life.

Finally, there have been numerous researchers and clinicians who have studied and written about how animals can be used as teachers with diverse groups of children. Katcher and Wilkins (2000) wrote about the use of therapeutic farms for children with ADHD, and have found positive results. Baról (2006) and Gee, Sherlock, Bennett, and Harris (2009) have used animals as a catalyst for teaching children (preschoolers and children with autism) developmental skills such as counting, cutting, expressing themselves, and problem solving.

Strategy 4: Adjuncts to Clinicians and Animals Changing the Therapeutic Environment

Having an animal in therapy may prove a catalyst for discussion, especially when clients share commonalities with animals. Some patients may see similarities between their own emotions and the perceived emotions expressed by an animal, such as shyness or fear. For example, children who have been abused or neglected may feel comfortable relating to an animal that was also abused or abandoned, and this may lead to them sharing about their own abuse or the abuse of a family member or pet they have witnessed.

> Oscar, a 13-year-old boy, came into the short-term, subacute setting after exhibiting aggression toward a younger sibling in his foster home. Having been removed from his mother two years prior due to allegations of excessive corporal punishment, he was reported to be doing poorly in school and had been in several foster homes where he was seen as poorly related or disengaged. Oscar would come to therapy and report that everything was "alright." He took little ownership for why he was placed in the program and saw no connections between his behaviors and those of his mother toward him. Oscar wasn't particularly impressed with the therapy dog, but would acknowledge her when he entered the therapist's office. Occasionally, he would make comments about her not really doing anything (during the workday), and say she was sad. Over time, the dog would move toward Oscar once he had settled into a seat in the room, until, without fail, she would sit in front of him, between him and the therapist, so that Oscar could scratch her neck. He would sit and almost absentmindedly scratch the dog's neck. On the days that she was more up front about it and stayed there until he did so, Oscar was much more prone to opening up about his life. He would ask questions about why the kids were not mean to her, paralleling his feelings about being picked on by his peers. This would later evolve into his exploring his difficulty with his mother's rejection since he had come into foster care. He wanted to know if the therapy dog knew her mother, and if she got to see her siblings. While the therapy dog had no known history of abuse, Oscar still was more apt to discuss this in relation to the dog and what they had in common. Oscar would use her literally as a shield from the therapist, or a safety net to interact. As long as she was sitting between him and the therapist, he could ask such questions.

Research suggests that the incorporation of metaphoric themes throughout the course of therapy may also enhance the therapeutic outcome (Angus, 1996; Barker, 1996). Both the client and the clinician can apply metaphors as a method of discovering and understanding the client's concerns. The imagery generated from the metaphors can be used to help the client uncover how he or she is coping or feeling (Fine, 2006). For example, while in a therapy session observing horses on a ranch, a 15-year-old client with depression drew insight about his emotions with a metaphor that the first author applied from a verse from Cole Porter's song "Don't Fence Me In" ("I want to ride to the ridge where the west commences, and gaze at the moon until I lose my senses. I can't look at hobbles and I can't stand fences. Don't fence me in"). Fine utilized the verse to capture the young man's perceived emotions and then assisted the client in expressing his feelings of internal captivity and discouragement.

The utilization of animals in the metaphoric sense is endless. Bringing in ties to real-life experiences and expanding these into an activity offers multiple options for engaging boys. Social networking is a seemingly favorite pastime of adolescents today. But where do they learn about informational boundaries and such? Group therapy projects such as providing a worksheet and pictures of the dog present, and then having the members create a social networking page for the animal, can communicate volumes about the boys and what they want people to know or think about them. By projecting their ideas onto the dog, they feel safer to share. Is the animal happy? Sad? What would she change if given the choice? Another group cohesion activity is one of creating a story, leaving out adjectives, then allowing the group to fill in the blanks one by one to create a whole story together. Boys then find a way to work with staff and each other to create one common goal.

TRAINING AND ANIMAL WELFARE

Mallon, Ross, and Ross (2006) and Fine and Stein (2003) provided several guidelines for developing and designing AAT programs. They concur in urging clinicians to obtain appropriate AAT training. The Delta Society's Pet Partner Program strongly advocates that clinicians must have training in techniques of AAT and AAI. Therapists should also contact their insurance carrier to notify them that AAI is being practiced, to assess coverage and address any questions the carrier may have. Requirements and coverage vary among insurers, and some may require a special binder for practicing AAI.

Early in the implementation of CV's AAT program, the cofounders realized that if the program was to succeed, the staff had to have a full understanding of and investment in the program. The introduction of an animal to an existing program, orientation, and a review of the literature and history of findings will help ensure understanding. This can be done as an overview while teaching staff what to watch for in the animal-child interactions. It is frequently helpful to have an expert in the field, or an organization that specializes in animal-assisted therapies, provide an in-service on the history and benefits. Time and attention should also be given to discussing the staff's reservations, anxieties, and fears about having the animals present. When this is done in advance, problems can be avoided and the staff becomes more engaged in the treatment. Once an animal is introduced as part of the milieu, helping staff watch for and allow spontaneous interactions will be key. Providing opportunities to review any interactions during supervision will fine-tune the staff's ability to spot such opportunities and maximize their efficacy.

Fine, Serpell, and Hines (2001) discussed ethical questions about the use of animals as therapeutic aides that arise out of tension between interests. While the therapeutic advantages of AAI to humans may be obvious, the benefits to the animals utilized in therapy are by no means always self-evident. Ultimately, as clinicians, the safety of one's patient should be the highest priority. Nevertheless, therapists must also safeguard the animals' integrity and welfare. Serpell, Coppinger, and Fine

(2006) developed a list of several guidelines that clinicians must consider if they are incorporating AAI. The following are a few ideas:

1. All animals must be kept free from abuse, discomfort, and distress.
2. Proper health care for the animal must be provided at all times. Animals must receive proper husbandry and have a proper diet.
3. All animals should have a quiet place where they can have time away from their work activities.
4. Interactions with clients must be structured to maintain the animal's capacity to serve as a useful therapeutic agent.
5. Situations of abuse or stress for a therapy animal should never be allowed. In the event that a client intentionally or unintentionally subjects a therapy animal to abuse, the animal's needs must be considered and the interaction must be discontinued.
6. As an animal ages, his or her schedule for therapeutic involvement will have to be curtailed. Accommodations and plans must be considered. The transition into retirement may be emotionally difficult for the animal as well as the therapist and clients familiar with the animal. Attention must also be given to this dimension.

Looking at the uses of animal-assisted therapy, one must also take into consideration several human factors. While the results of AAT are overwhelmingly positive, one must remember that not all humans like animals; in fact, some are very afraid. In order to have any therapeutic process be successful, input from those around or involved in peripheral ways must be obtained. Comfort levels must be respected. Likewise, children often have fears due to past experiences, lack of exposure, or learned behaviors. Along the same line is concern over allergies. Depending on the animal and the person, allergies can range from mild to severe, and at times life threatening. Careful assessment of and respect for allergies needs to be given. It is not uncommon for a fearful person to claim allergies as the reason to have the animal kept away; an astute clinician will identify that there is more to the story, yet honor the request either way.

Understanding and accepting animal behavior takes years of practice and cohabitation. Introducing an animal as a therapeutic partner needs to be closely monitored. All animals have their own personality, so it is key to understand their behavior and accurately read body language and warning signs. An animal's hygiene when participating in any therapeutic activities is key. Frequent baths, daily brushing, and clipped nails are all beneficial. The *Los Angeles Times* recently published an article reporting that studies have shown that animals participating in therapies can carry bacteria and infections that can be spread to places such as hospitals or group care settings. Consequently, special considerations need to be made to prevent potential contamination.

There are currently no national standards for training in and implementation of AAT. Current AAT practitioners understand the need for a group of experts to develop standards and guidelines for practice. Until then, the therapeutic animal partners are relying solely on their human counterparts to protect them against things such as being overworked, abused, and mistreated.

SUMMARY

When initiating psychotherapy for children, especially with boys, many different techniques, therapeutic orientations, and modalities can be used. The challenge as a therapist is to identify the correct approach that will make a difference in a boy's life. Animal-assisted interventions represent an outstanding adjunctive therapy, especially with boys who have a genuine love and appreciation for animals. The bond between humans and animals has been well documented, and the field of AAI is continually gaining credibility.

All children can pose challenges in psychotherapy, especially those with more significant psychopathology. It is evident that there are differences in best practice approaches when treating boys versus girls. Kiselica (2003) pointed out that there appear to be several male-friendly approaches that foster relationships and therapeutic outcomes. AAI could be considered in this vein and may offer therapists a unique alternative to complement the overall treatment of boys.

As has been discussed throughout this chapter, animals in the lives of boys can and do play many roles. These roles include surrogate siblings, confidantes, social supports, emotional buffers, and even teachers. The value of these interactions is viewed most in traditional homes, but it is now more common to see animals in residential group living settings as pets or therapy animals. It is clearly evident in the literature that most animals appear nonjudgmental in their interactions with boys. Animals do not seem particular about age, skin color, weight, or disability. They respond to kindness and appear more accepting of differences than most human counterparts. Traditionally, an animal trained to be a therapy animal has a gentle temperament, which assists a therapist in reaching out to a child.

AAI can offer an effective alternative to traditional therapy if the relationship between the animal and the therapist is balanced and extremely comfortable so they can work in tandem. The process may be arduous, and planning and adapting must occur. Therapists would do well to realize that not all animals are equipped to partner with a human in the therapy process. Careful attention should be given to the selection process in choosing the right animal for a therapist and therapy setting. Additionally, the efforts of AAI must be totally integrated into the overall treatment goals of the child. Working in isolation will decrease chances for optimal success. Most would agree that the ultimate test for AAI will be to facilitate long-lasting changes in a child's behaviors.

Professionals seeking to add animal-assisted interventions to their repertoire are encouraged to spend some time researching the area and possibly observing a colleague who utilizes AAI. If there appears to be a healthy interest, reading and attending continuing education courses would help develop the appropriate skills necessary. Partnering and becoming certified by any of the AAI organizations, such as the Delta Society or Therapy Dogs International, would be an extremely desirable step. Therapists should be aware of animal welfare issues and develop safeguards to ensure a good quality of life, health, and safety for the animal. Cautions need to also be considered for the clients as well, such as their possible fears, negative histories, and potential health-related concerns.

Martin Buber (1923/1970, p. 144), the famous philosopher, once stated, "An animal's eyes have the power to speak a great language." It is this gentle nonverbal communication that allows animals to make a major impact in the lives of many, including boys who are at risk or in need. Although not a panacea, AAI could provide a healthy addition to a dynamic therapeutic regime.

REFERENCES

Argus, L. (1996). An intensive analysis of metaphor themes in psychotherapy. In J. Mio & A. Katz (Eds.), *Metaphor: Implications of applications* (pp. 73–85). Mahwah, NJ: Lawrence Erlbaum Associates.

Arluke, A. (2007). *Animal assisted activities for at-risk and incarcerated children and young adults: An introductory ethnography of five programs.* Unpublished paper presented at the National Technology Assessment Workshop on Animal Assisted Programs for Youth at Risk, Baltimore, MD.

Ascione, F. R. (1997). Humane education research: Evaluating efforts to encourage children's kindness and caring toward animals. *Genetic, Social, and General Psychology Monographs, 123*(1), 57–77.

Ascione, F. R., & Shapiro, K. (2009). People and animals, kindness and cruelty: Research directions and policy implications. *Journal of Social Issues, 65*(3), 569–587.

Bailey, C. (1987). *Exposure of preschool children to companion animals: Impact on role-taking skills.* Unpublished doctoral dissertation, Oregon State University, Corvallis.

Barba, B. E. (1995). A critical review of research on the human/companion animal relationship: 1988 to 1993. *Anthrozoös, 8*, 9–15.

Barker, P. (1996). *Psychotherapeutic metaphors: A guide to theory and practice.* New York: Brunner/Mazel.

Baról, J. (2006). *The effects of animal assisted therapy on a child with autism.* Unpublished doctoral dissertation, New Mexico Highlands University, Las Vegas.

Bell, L. (2001). Abusing children—Abusing animals. *Journal of Social Work, 1*(2), 223–234.

Bowlby, J. (1969). Disruption of affectional bonds and its effects on behavior. *Canada's Mental Health Supplement, 69*, 1–17.

Bowlby, J. (1980). *Attachment and loss.* New York: Basic Books.

Bryant, B. K. (1986). The relevance of pets and neighborhood animals to the social-emotional functioning and development of school-age children. Final report to the Delta Society, Renton, WA.

Buber, M. (1970). *I and thou* (W. Kaufmann, Trans.). New York: Touchstone. (Original work published 1923)

Chandler, C. (2001, October). Animal assisted therapy in counseling and school settings. ERIC Clearinghouse on Counseling and Student Services, Greensboro, NC. Retrieved August 10, 2009, from http://www.ericdigests.org/2002-3/animal.htm

Collis, G., & McNicholas, J. (1998). A theoretical basis for health benefits of pet ownership: Attachment versus psychological support. In C. C. Wilson & D. C. Turner (Eds.), *Companion animals in human health* (pp. 105–122). Thousand Oaks, CA: Sage.

The Delta Society. (1996). *Standards of practice in animal assisted activities and therapy.* Bellevue, WA: Author.

Fawcett, N. R., & Gullone, E. (2001). Cute and cuddly and a whole lot more? A call for empirical investigation into the therapeutic benefits of human-animal interaction for children. *Behavior Change, 18*(2), 124–133.

Fine, A. H. (2006). Animals and therapists: Incorporating animals in outpatient psychotherapy. In A. Fine (Ed.), *Handbook on animal assisted therapy* (2nd ed., pp. 179–211). San Diego, CA: Academic Press.

Fine, A. H. (2007, September 27–29). *More than puppy love: The role of animal assisted interventions.* Presented at the 2007 National Meeting of the American Humane Association, Alexandria, VA.

Fine, A. H. (2008, September 30–October 2). *Understanding the application of animal assisted interventions.* Presented at the National Institute of Child and Human Development Meeting on the Impact of Animals in Human Health, Bethesda, MD.

Fine, A. H., & Eisen, C. (2008). *Afternoons with Puppy: Inspirations from a therapist and his therapy animals.* West Lafayette, IN: Purdue University Press.

Fine, A. H., & Kotkin, R. (2003). Social skills and children with attention deficit hyperactivity disorder and learning disabilities. In A. Fine & R. Kotkin (Eds.), *Therapist's guide to learning and attention disorders* (pp. 295–332). San Diego, CA: Elsevier Science.

Fine, A. H., Serpell, J., & Hines, L. (2001, September 14). *The welfare of assistance and therapy animals: An ethical commentary.* Presented at the International Conference on the Human Animal Bond, Rio, Brazil.

Fine, A. H., & Stein, L. (2003, October 25). *Animal assisted therapy and clinical practice.* Presented at the Psycho-legal Associates CEU Meeting, Pasadena, CA.

Furman, W. (1989). The development of children's social networks. In D. Belle (Ed.), *Children's social networks and social supports* (pp. 151–172). New York: Wiley.

Gee, N. R., Sherlock, T. R., Bennett, E. A., & Harris, S. L. (2009). Preschoolers' adherence to instructions as a function of presence of a dog and motor skills task. *Anthrozoös, 22*(3), 267–276.

Hart, L. (2006). Community context and psychosocial benefits of animal companionship. In A. Fine (Ed.), *Handbook on animal assisted therapy* (2nd ed., pp. 73–94). San Diego, CA: Academic Press.

Hastings, P. D., Zahn-Waxler, C., Robinson, J., Usher, B., & Bridges, D. (2000). The development of concern for others in children with behavior problems. *Developmental Psychology*, *36*(5), 531–546.

Hunt, S., Hart, L., & Gomulkiewicz, R. (1992). Role of small animals in social interaction between strangers. *Journal of Social Psychology*, *133*(2), 245–256.

Katcher, A. H., & Wilkins, G. (2000). The centaur's lessons: Therapeutic education through care of animals and nature study. In A. Fine (Ed.), *Handbook on animal assisted therapy* (1st ed., pp. 153–178). San Diego, CA: Academic Press.

Kiselica, M. S. (2003). Transforming psychotherapy in order to succeed with adolescent boys: Male-friendly practices. *Journal of Clinical Psychology*, *59*(11), 1225–1236.

Kotrschal, K., & Ortbauer, B. (2003). Behavioral effects of the presence of a dog in a classroom. *Anthrozoös*, *16*(2), 147–159.

LaJoie, K. R. (2003). *An evaluation of the effectiveness of using animals in therapy.* Unpublished doctoral dissertation, Spalding University, Louisville, KY.

Lindsay, A. (2004, February). *Animals as group therapist.* Unpublished paper presented at the American Group Psychotherapy Association Annual Conference, New York, NY.

Lindsay, A. (2007, December 6–7). *Staff perspectives on AAT.* Unpublished paper presented at the National Technology Assessment Workshop on Animal Assisted Programs for Youth at Risk, Baltimore, MD.

Lookabaugh Triebencher, S. (2000). The companion animal within the family: The manner in which animals enhance life within the home. In A. Fine (Ed.), *Handbook on animal assisted therapy* (1st ed., pp. 357–374). San Diego, CA: Academic Press.

Mallon, G., Ross, S., & Ross, L. (2006). Designing and implementing animal assisted therapy programs in health and mental health organizations. In A. Fine (Ed.), *Handbook on animal assisted therapy* (2nd ed., pp. 115–127). San Diego, CA: Academic Press.

Martindale, D. (2001). Breeding contentment. *Psychology Today*, *34*(6), 20.

McNicholas, J., & Collis, G. (2006). Animals as supports: Insights for understanding animal assisted therapy. In A. Fine (Ed.), *Handbook on animal assisted therapy* (2nd ed., pp. 49–71). San Diego, CA: Academic Press.

Melson, G. (2001). *Why the wild things are: Animals in the lives of children.* Cambridge, MA: Harvard University Press.

Melson, G., & Fine, A. H. (2006). Animals in the lives of children. In A. Fine (Ed.), *Handbook on animal assisted therapy* (2nd ed., pp. 207–226). San Diego, CA: Academic Press.

Melson, G., & Fogel, A. (1989). Children's idea about animal young and their care: A reassessment of gender difference in the development of nurturance. *Anthrozoös*, *2*(4), 265–273.

Melson, G., Peet, S., & Sparks, C. (1992). Children's attachment to their pets: Links to socioemotional development. *Children's Environmental Quarterly*, *8*(2), 55–65.

Messant, P. (1984). Correlates and effects of pet ownership. In E. Anderson, B. Hart, & L. Hart (Eds.), *The pet connection: Its influence on our health and quality of life* (pp. 331–340). Minneapolis, MN: University of Minnesota.

Myers, G. (1998). *Children and animals: Social development and our connections to other species.* Boulder, CO: Westview Press.

Patterson-Kane, E. G., & Piper, H. (2009) Animal abuse as a sentinel for human violence. *Journal of Social Issues, 65*(3), 589–614.

Serpell, J. (2006). Animal assisted interventions in historical perspective. In A. Fine (Ed.), *Handbook on animal assisted therapy* (2nd ed., pp. 3–20). San Diego, CA: Academic Press.

Serpell, J., Coppinger, R., & Fine, A. H. (2006). The welfare of assistance and therapy animals: An ethical comment. In A. Fine (Ed.), *Handbook on animal assisted therapy* (2nd ed., pp. 415–430). San Diego, CA: Academic Press.

Stokes, T., & Osnes, P. (1986). Programming the generalization of children's social behavior. In P. S. Strain, M. J. Guralnick, & H. H. Walker (Eds.), *Children's behavior: Development, assessment and modification* (pp. 407–443). Orlando, FL: Academic Press.

Strand, E. B. (2004). Interparental conflict and youth maladjustment: The buffering effect of pets. *Stress, Trauma, and Crisis, 7*(3), 151–168.

Thompson, K. L., & Gullone, E. (2003). The children's treatment of animals questionnaire (CTAQ): A psychometric investigation. *Society and Animals, 11*(1), 1–15.

From Virtual to Real

Video Games in the
Treatment of Boys

GEORGE ENFIELD

INTRODUCTION

How often does it happen to a therapist? He walks into the waiting room to meet his next client and all he sees as he enters are the tops of people's heads. They are all sitting with rapt attention, in near silence, staring at a screen of one sort or another. It is not uncommon for a family to enter the waiting area and the boys sit down with a Gameboy™ or Nintendo DS™ while Mom settles in and starts to play solitaire or *Bejeweled* on her phone. Recently, a new addition has arrived in the waiting room in the form of a netbook. With the increased societal drive toward wireless connectivity, there is a strong possibility that we will only continue to see more and more of this curious phenomenon in waiting rooms across the country.

Interactive electronic devices have been around for many years, as far back as 1952. That year, Alexander Douglas (1955) produced a PhD dissertation entitled "Some Computations in Theoretical Physics," which is widely recognized as one of the first, if not the first, academic writings about video games. However, this media really started to take shape in the 1970s with the introduction of games like *Computer Space*, the first coin-operated, stand-up console game. *Pong, Pac-Man,* and *Donkey*

Kong soon followed, attaining great popularity, and the video game generation was born.

Presently, the video game industry is marking a growing presence in the multimedia business, with dozens of ways for consumers to be impacted by their products. People have access to video games for use on televisions, telephones, and the home/office computer, while they also come in the form of handheld game systems and game decks. Children of all demographics are playing these games. They could be using computer-based educational programs, dedicated education systems like Leap Frog™, handheld systems like Nintendo DS, sports games, or racing games, or playing Sudoku on one of the various types of smart phones.

All of these games represent potential interfaces with the child; they can and often do serve as a conduit for connection. For therapists, this media can be a single-sided event that excludes them or a true opportunity for mutual interaction. With an understanding of the subject matter and some creativity, clinicians will be able to expand these opportunities for meeting boys where they are and fostering a meaningful dialogue in service of therapeutic progress.

VIDEO GAMES AND BOYS

According to the most recent demographic and usage data compiled by the Entertainment Software Association (ESA, 2010), 67% of American households play video games. Of these players, 60% are male and 25% are under 18 years of age. Anecdotally, we are more likely to see boys than girls arriving in our offices with their face pressed in a handheld device or hear them speak enthusiastically about the world of one game or another.

Gaming magazines are also extremely popular. *Game Informer Magazine* (*GIM*) has a circulation of nearly 2 million people, making it more widely distributed than well-known titles like *Seventeen* and *Entertainment Weekly*. These magazines are particularly popular with boys and are often rated at the top of their list of favorite magazine genres (Harrison & Bond, 2007). African American children, according to research, play video games more often than White or Latino kids, despite the fact that the characters presented in these games are more likely to be White (Harrison & Bond, 2007).

Clinicians who work with children don't need industry demographics or massive marketing studies to tell them that boys are highly attracted to video games. As a grown-up boy myself, I can tell you that video games are captivating, engaging, and at times frustrating. They hold elements of daily life, yet allow players to have superhuman abilities. They offer opportunities for smaller, less powerful boys to transcend their limitations. Video games let boys fly through the air, lift cars, and wield guns and swords in ways that would not be possible in reality (or at least might get them suspended from school). They allow boys to become heroes and sports stars, and to triumph over digital universes.

Working from a client-centered perspective, therapists will find themselves asking the following fundamental questions in the first moments of treatment: How does this boy explore his world? What is his individual style of communication? What have his experiences of interacting with others been like? What methods does he use to engage with his environment? There is often a disconnection between the client and the clinician in understanding these important areas. As such, the two are not communicating in the same language, or at the least not perceiving the boy's world in the same fashion.

Mental health counseling is often experienced by boys as foreign and bizarre at best. Other times, my male clients have referred to it as "boring" or "torture," especially when being asked to describe their feelings or look at how their emotions influence their behaviors. Clinicians have learned, often through hard knocks, that young boys frequently do not perform well within the traditional framework of the therapy office as a place in which they must sit in chairs with their hands and feet crossed patiently waiting for the grand revelation to arrive.

On many occasions, when working with preadolescent males, I have found that traditional therapeutic questions have resulted in blank stares, shrugs, and the infamous "I don't know." However, when I changed focus and discussed the most recent video game on the market or inquired about the boy's favorite video game, there was often an almost immediate affective shift. Body posture changed and the slouching client shifted forward, looked me in the eyes, and there was at times a visible brightening of affect. Occasionally I would hear surprised comments like, "You know what that is?" This initial spark becomes the beginning of the relationship, as Gardner (1991) suggested.

With the preceding information in mind, it is easy to see why computer/video games should be considered a potential tool for enhancing treatment. The prominence and broad spectrum of people playing games has grown and will most likely continue to grow as the systems and interfaces become more sophisticated and integrated into our daily lives. As clinicians, we are taught to connect with the client so we can begin to address the presenting issues as quickly and efficiently as possible following best-practice rules.

A best-practice focus can be difficult for the therapist interested in using this approach because there have been very limited studies of the uses of video games in therapy. Many of these studies are anecdotal and definitely not conclusive (see Enfield & Grosser, 2008; Favelle, 1995; Skigen, 2008); however, this approach should not be immediately dismissed. There are several organizations developing computer games for communication and educational purposes. The Global Social Venture Competition and the University of Auckland in New Zealand are a couple of the groups currently doing work in this area. Video games are beginning to appear in the professional literature across disciplines, especially in the field of education (Nastasi & Clements, 1993; National Association for the Education of Young Children, 1996), where video elements have been identified as possible means with which to jump-start the expressive process.

WHAT CLINICIANS NEED TO KNOW

With the vast quantity of video games and a fairly broad spectrum of game interfaces, it is possible to tailor a system that has a positive impact on the client and allows the therapist to work to create change through the dialogue that occurs while the game is being played. For those therapists for whom video game culture is foreign, this section seeks to provide an introduction to the types of games available and some of the relevant terminology. Knowing the "basics" is a prerequisite to beginning to incorporate this modality into treatment. However, allowing the client to educate the therapist is another helpful means of acquiring this knowledge.

There are some fundamental elements the therapist will need to understand in order to function with a degree of comfort while using video games in treatment with boys. The first is the method of game delivery, or the game system itself. The most common formats at present are the computer, game deck, and handheld systems. Computer games are those the player installs from software or downloads off the Internet for play on a laptop or desktop computer with the method of interface usually being a keyboard or mouse. These games have the most out-of-game potential and rarely require a proprietary interface.

Game decks are specialized computers with fewer applications, usually just game related. A key element to this type of delivery is that the user interface almost never contains a physical keyboard. Interactions with the system are almost always via a proprietary controller or game console. Some of the most popular trademarked systems include Nintendo's Wii™, Microsoft's Xbox®, and Sony's PlayStation®. These game decks are fairly sophisticated and are taking advantage of the capacity of the Internet to become a complex entertainment system. This ability to exchange vast amounts of information includes downloading games, uploading to social networking sites, streaming video, and Live Chat.

The Live Chat feature allows gamers to talk to each other online while playing a game together virtually. An example of this type of play can be seen in several of the *Medal of Honor* or *Rainbow Six* games where players work together to achieve objectives. Some of the online adventure games also offer the potential for this type of interaction, which allows for the development of new levels of social reciprocity and relationship development in the gaming world. The therapeutic potential exists in the client practicing and receiving immediate feedback on interactions with others in a safe, relatively insulated way. This method can also allow the therapist the opportunity to work with the client to develop methods of interaction and potentially coach the client or provide in-the-moment options for interactions taking place within the game.

The final type of system is the handheld. While handheld games are presently the least complex, and processing speed is limited relative to larger systems, they tend to represent a larger section of the gaming market. The most popular handheld systems include the Nintendo DS™, Sony PSP™, Apple's iPod Touch™, and many of the growing market of "smart phones." As previously stated, the primary advantages of this type of system are the portability of the game, the multiple applications available for use, and increasing multisystem interface (or game play between multiple players). These are the devices that are most likely to make their way into the therapy office.

Inherent to each of these systems is the type of user interface, a term that relates to the type and complexity of controls available. These range from a simple joystick/mouse to more complicated controllers with multiple buttons, or keyboards. When choosing video games for treatment purposes, the therapist should take into account the motor skill level of the client and how the complexity of the game influences the boy's ability to experience success during sessions.

Another factor for consideration is the content of the game being introduced. There is a strong potential that the game itself could have direct or metaphorical impact value for the client. Games may be sports (*NBA Live*) or action-adventure (*Tomb Raider*) oriented, or they may involve the solving of puzzles (*Tetris*) or trivia (*Family Feud*). In role-playing games (RPGs), the player controls one or more characters, each with its own icon, or avatar. These games often contain large, interactive environments in which these characters roam and exist. An example of this type of game is *Final Fantasy*.

The RPG game can cross genres from fantasy to, more commonly, horror and western. Many contain complex puzzles and can require significant problem-solving skills, while others have less complex problem solving and more closely resemble FPS games, described below. These types of games, like *Champions of Norath* or *Baldur's Gate*, are third-person games. Players see and manipulate a character from above or behind. A few games allow for players to shift between first- and third-person perspectives; *World of Warcraft* and several race and flight simulation games are examples.

If players can wander freely about the video game environment at their own pace with no linear pathway, as in *Grand Theft Auto*, the game is referred to as a "sandbox" or "free roam" game. In simulation games, such as *The Sims* (which will be discussed in greater detail later in the chapter), players simulate activities based on the real world and may be involved in the construction of elements of that world. Finally, in first-person shooter (FPS) games, such as *Halo* and *Medal of Honor*, the player's vantage point is through the eyes of the character and often over the barrel of a gun as he wanders and shoots at enemies in a combat, urban, fantasy, or horror-like environment.

In order for the clinician to understand the potential impact and make appropriate selections of video games, an understanding of the game rating system is also important. In an effort to avoid having unnecessary and overly restrictive guidelines, the video game industry adopted a rating system to guide parents in understanding the content of the games. This system, as it was adopted by the Media Awareness Network (2007), is as follows:

EC—Early Childhood (ages 3+): Generally no objectionable behaviors or activities.

E—Everyone (ages 6+): Minimal violence, potentially some comic mischief.

E10+—Everyone 10+ (ages 10+): More violence, mild language, and mildly suggestive themes.

T—Teen (ages 13+): Violent content, mild to strong language, or suggestive themes.

M—Mature (ages 17+): Mature sexual content, increased violence or strong language.

AO—Adults Only (ages 18+): Strong sexual content, themes, or violence.

RP—Rating Pending.

THEORY

Some theorists, like Jones (2002), postulate that children need to feel more powerful in order to describe and develop understanding of the world in which they exist. This power is often symbolic in nature and is developed through play and imagination. It is possible that many of the video games that boys are playing today also possess these same symbolic potentialities. For example, some of the boys who present in my office enjoy "fighting" games. Their engagement in these games could represent an attempt to gain mastery over a disempowering situation, such as being bullied or witnessing violence.

Or perhaps the client is using the gaming environment to vicariously live out or vent personal frustrations without having to express those feelings in the real world. I have heard from boys that without playing video games they might be tempted to violence, and that this outlet allows for a release that helps them to avoid this type of outburst. This seeking of containment for aggressive impulses may be misguided, as many studies report an increase in violence following the playing of video games (American Psychological Association, n.d.; Anderson, 2003; Anderson, Gentile, & Buckley, 2007). In contrast, though, Olson, Kutner, and Warner (2008), in researching the perceptions of early adolescent boys about these games, concluded:

Boys use violent video games (a) as a means to express fantasies of power and glory, (b) to explore and master what they perceived as exciting and realistic environments, and (c) as a tool to work out their feelings of anger and stress. Games—especially violent or sports games—are also social tools that allow boys to compete with and/or work cooperatively with peers. Boys gain status among peers by owning or mastering these popular games. This supports the idea that video game play with violent content may serve a function similar to rough-and-tumble play for young adolescent boys. (p. 69)

Other boys use social networking games like *World of Warcraft*® (*WOW*) as a means to creatively represent themselves. Through a symbolic depiction of what they would like to be more like, the boys are expressing an idealized version of self or traits that they possess but perceive as undeveloped. Examples include a socially withdrawn boy taking on a character who is more aggressive in nature or a boy of small stature choosing a toon with large muscles. It is not unheard of for male players to select a female avatar. In the *WOW* world, it is possible for players to act in ways that might lead to embarrassment in the real world, or to try out alternative ways to engage people in conversation. It is doubtful that players choose characters that do not have symbolic significance to them in some way.

APPLICATIONS

There are a few games on the market specifically designed for the therapeutic environment, which will be discussed in greater detail later in the chapter. However, most video games that capture boys' imagination are not specific to treatment. Like other tools, though, they can be creatively adapted to meet a variety of needs. In this section the discussion will focus more narrowly on the elements of electronic media and how they can be applied to the therapy session. Attention will be given to the establishment of treatment goals, considerations when applying this media within the clinical setting, and a sampling of a few treatment-specific games.

Treatment Goals

In an electronic media session the therapist may have a variety of potential objectives. To determine these, several questions need evaluation: What levels of social interaction are happening? At what level and how can a client support another person? What is the expectation of the client regarding games? Is this an area of perceived strength? If so, how?

The clinician could develop goals with clients about understanding feelings and methods to vent frustration. A treatment goal might use the game as a gauge. For example: "Tyrell will develop three friends outside the game environment." Or a discussion might be initiated about what makes the electronic environment a safer venue than the real world in which to interact with people. In some social gaming, players will run characters with an alter ego to their own; for example, they may be a quiet person and when entering the social chat section of the game become disinhibited and loud, or the passive person may choose characters that are highly aggressive in nature.

For boys, video games are a nice buffer that can offset the intimacy of the therapy relationship or the affect that may be under the surface. They often can, for example, provide the visual distraction that some teens require to feel safe enough to explore painful topics like relationships or past abuse. Still other boys struggle with issues of depression or self-esteem. Their deficits could reflect a mastery issue or be connected to a lack of confidence related to an inability to interact with others. Many video games focus on the development and mastery of a given objective. Video games in which clients are challenged with puzzles of either skill or thought can provide concepts that are directly in conflict with the client's belief structure. The resulting cognitive dissonance offers the clinician an opportunity to begin to explore notions related to depression, impaired self-esteem, or rigidity of behavior.

I have had the most therapeutic success using video games with boys 9 to 15 years of age who present with poor social skills and often with academic deficits. Typically, these clients carry a diagnosis of a mood or developmental disorder. The therapist may implement video games in the context of individual treatment or may determine that a small group would allow the client to practice and develop skills as a safe entry point into treatment. While this approach has been used selectively with trauma victims, it is not recommended at present. There are very few games on the market that address the areas of concern found in the victim. In the trauma situation, other methods may be more effective as a treatment intervention until such time that games with more survival and coping themes are developed.

Considerations

Based on market research and developmental ability, it can be safely assumed that children under the age of about five years rarely play video games independently. Therefore, the population of boys that most clinicians will be using this technique with will be in the age range of 5 to 18. Therapists will likely gather some clues as to the likes and dislikes of the client during the intake process that will inform which games to use during treatment, as well as the targeted issues.

As previously discussed, most video games follow similar patterns with themes of good versus evil or, more simply, player versus opponent. This dichotomy provides many opportunities for possible engagement and discussion, as well as rapport development and the introduction and modeling of alternative thinking processes. The clinician can explore the game mechanics or can play with or against the client (being good at the game is definitely not a prerequisite), allowing the client to demonstrate how the game is played. Competition provides a forum for the clinician to model alternative reactions to losing and a means for clients to feel that they have some control in treatment.

The challenge that the therapist will face outside the availability of the materials has to do with implementation. This type of intervention should not be conducted so that the client is left to play the game in solitude. The nature of the game session is to open the communication and to increase the free exchange of ideas. This intervention is a very dynamic one and is best implemented with a very clear direction for treatment and a thorough understanding of how a specific game may benefit or promote the type of movement that therapist and client have agreed they are trying to accomplish.

The therapist should maintain an almost continuous flow of dialogue related to the principal concern while the client is playing the game. For this reason, this type of intervention is not recommended for the student of counseling, but instead a more seasoned therapist. It requires that the clinician is able to view and work with the client's concerns from multiple levels and perspectives simultaneously. The therapist will need to ask clients about their perceptions of the real-world problem, reactions to the game environment, reflections on the character's interactions, and internal experience while playing the game. While these discussions are occurring, the therapist is also aware of the game, its stages, and how this progression allows for problem solving as well as emotional growth (Olson et al., 2008).

Effective Games

What I have observed when working with boys and men is that often the sources of their distress can be traced to a sense of inadequacy, anxiety, depression, a history of abuse, or impulsive behaviors. When these factors are taken into account, there are several games available that can be used to address and open the avenue for discussion and introspection. Some games the author has found advantageous include the *Sonic* series, *Justice League Heroes*, *Spider-Man: Friend or Foe*, *The Sims* series, and the *Lego* series.

The *Sonic* series of games are an example of a race or pick-up game in which the player's major objective is to collect as many rings as possible. More recently this type of game has grown with the introduction of the *Lego* series, which also involves the collection of items, but the player does not have a life count. Instead, the goal is to unlock new characters and locations inside the game. Video games in which the player does not die or have a limited number of lives provide a sense of accomplishment and skill, especially for boys who cannot easily access feelings of mastery. *Justice League* and *Spider-Man* are games more oriented to mastery and motor control. They can be played with either one or two players, with the latter option serving to help improve interpersonal communication. Players tend to perform better when they talk to each other and develop cooperative approaches that can benefit both of them within the game environment.

The Sims™ is a series of video games in which the player or players have control of a virtual person in the form of a character/toon that they manipulate through their daily activities. Players begin with simple home dwellings that can be modified and decorated to their preferences. They then direct their virtual self through a simulated life—purchasing clothing, developing career lines, working, and eating—and they are encouraged to develop relationships with others and explore the animated environment. *The Sims* is available in multiple versions and formats, with extension packs that expand the capabilities of the game. There are currently versions available for game decks, handheld systems, computers, and iPods.

Using *The Sims* and other simulation games, the therapist has the potential to dialogue with a client about the process of making choices within the virtual environment and how or why the client decided to select or lose a friend. There are also avenues of discussion about how the client perceives the necessity of some of the behaviors programmed into the game. For example, the game often becomes more difficult as the network of friends grows and the player must balance activities like working, sleeping, eating, and bathing with the increased time and energy required to develop and maintain relationships. Tension can be generated in the game, from having to juggle multiple relationships and personality types at the same time. For some clients, the balancing of daily life demands can be similarly overwhelming. Parallels can easily be drawn to the real world, and therapeutic dialogue can be expanded to address clients who struggle with activities of daily living (ADLs), as well as high-achieving boys who take on too much and are stressed as a result.

In the book *Popular Culture in Counseling, Psychotherapy, and Play-Based Interventions* Deidre Skigen (2008) proposed *The Sims* as a possible alternative in play therapy to the use of sand play. While I do not feel that computers and the sand tray share the same experiential qualities, I do believe that there is ample space for both, as they allow boys to engage and interact in the context of an imagined world over which they have influence.

There are limitations to *The Sims* series. The primary one is that the player has a finite number and type of interactions available to him, such that the more subtle complexities of daily activities are often lost. For example, toons in *The Sims* will go to work and return home. There is little to no interaction depicted at the work setting, and there is little ramification for daily behavior impacting the mood/affect of the toon as there is in the real world. Another limitation is in the dialogue and depth of interactions between the toons. There are a very limited number of potential responses to given situations. These limitations impact the directions that the clinician can follow and do impose some form of more regimented structure in the session. The clinician will need to determine for his or her client whether or not this imposition is significant enough to rule out the game as a form of intervention.

A hybrid that exists between *The Sims* and the next set of games would be an RPG like *Second Life*. In this online game, players generate an avatar to represent themselves in the gaming environment. Unlike *The Sims*, however, everything in *Second Life* is player generated. This means that the players create everything from the avatar and its wardrobe to the domicile in which it resides. The list of potential opportunities is almost limitless. The major downside to *Second Life* is that the player interface can be difficult to learn, and it is a relatively slow game to become engaged in until you have passed a very extensive tutorial.

Beyond *Second Life* exists a vast array of online social networking games, including *Cartoon Network Universe: FusionFall, World of Warcraft, City of Villains, City of Heroes*, and *Champions Online*, to name just a few. There are several areas in which this type of game will allow for potential benefits. There is the possibility for clients to socialize with others in a more anonymous fashion through a fantasy alter ego. The characters alone can provide a wealth of information to the clinician about boys' desired methods of communication and possible motives for behavior. In addition, there is the internal benefit for the client of being able to see his character grow and develop through the course of the game. This growth can again become the entry point for metaphorical discussion about skill development and the importance of mastery in many different environments. The degree of flexibility varies by game, and the amount of interaction with the environment is also highly variable. The exchange for this freedom is in potential for loss of confidentiality related to the client interacting with other people. There is much less control because all the interaction takes place inside the gaming environment. With this in mind, therapists utilizing these games should weigh the possible concerns against the potential benefits carefully. Additionally, there is often a financial element involved, as these games are usually subscription based and require some monthly fee to maintain.

Another strong caution about social networking games is that it is quite possible for people to become too immersed in this type of game. It is not uncommon to hear from a gamer that he played for several hours at a time and has even sacrificed a meal or two in order to play or to pay for online service. There are times when my child clients will make comments like "Mom doesn't play with us. She is constantly on the computer" or "I don't fight with my dad. He's always playing video games." I had one client say in session, "If I want to make Dad mad, I just turn off the computer." Another client told me that the best time to talk with his father was when he's playing a game because "I can always get what I want then."

Webkinz, Build-a-Bear, and *Toontown Online* are generally free social networking games that target a younger population and can be used in a productive way with some clients. The method of interaction has to do with providing a framework for the boy outside the game environment. Clinicians have used this tool to allow boys to utilize some of the therapeutic stories readily available to help bring the characters to life. Examples include Webkinz Seal, who follows a story line related to safety, and Webkinz Cats, who have a story of loss and abandonment but, with a therapist and a boy working together, can find a home with beautiful furnishings and people who care. In the *Build-a-Bear* world, a child could also develop a story of abandonment or loss and start to process these feelings through the avatar and stuffed animal of their choosing.

Treatment-Specific Games

Cognitive behavioral therapy, one of the most widely studied and research-supported treatment models, has influenced the development of games specifically geared toward treatment goals. One example is *MyFriendsQuest*, a social emotional awareness game recently released through the BrightMind LABS in New Zealand, which is designed to train young people on identifying affect. *MyFriendsQuest* has two separate levels of interaction. At the easy level, the player reads a fictional situation, for example, "Sally's dog was hit by a car." The player is asked to make the face of the toon character reflect the emotion appropriate to the situation. To accomplish this task, the player matches eyebrows, eyes, and a mouth from groups of three to construct the emotion. While this is generally a fairly easy task for most boys, the challenges can be high because the differences between the various elements can be quite subtle.

When the task is complete, the player has the opportunity to write a note to reflect on the process and to print this reflection and a certificate for completing the task. In the advanced level, the play is initially identical to that of the easy level, but following the completion of the face the player is asked a simple multiple choice question to illustrate an event that the player might experience in daily activities. Again, the player has the opportunity to write notes; additionally, there is a metronome that can provide the player with the opportunity to have another multisensory experience with emotions using different tempos to reflect the emotion in yet another fashion.

Other games that are showing promise include *Healing Rhythms*, which uses a biofeedback process to teach players about relaxation and body awareness. Through a specialized interface with the computer that measures skin conductance and heart rate, players are taught to use breath control and self-awareness to increase relaxation and remain calm during different activities. The program includes direct instruction by leaders in guided imagery and meditation like Deepak Chopra. In addition to the lessons, there are experiential activities that allow players to develop and master skills related to breathing, self-awareness, and self-regulation. Many are simple in appearance but quite diverse in application.

Clinical Vignettes

The following are examples of how video games have been used with boys in a clinic setting to open doors to engagement, serve as a springboard for future discussion, and create a context for therapeutic intervention.

Example 1

Two boys were brought in for treatment separately. One of the boys, Tim, had an extensive history of neglect that led to the development of self-esteem issues. Tim was eight years old at the time, frequently sullen, and had few friends. He reported being happiest when he was playing video games and was not really interested in engaging or developing relationships with others. Another boy, Joey, who was seven years old, was recently diagnosed with Asperger's Syndrome by a leading authority in the field. Joey reported being good at video games and being proud of his success as a player. It was observed that Tim was evasive when offered help while Joey never asked for assistance. The two boys were placed in dyadic therapy together with an approach that specifically allowed for playing video games as a part of the treatment.

The boys played Sega's *Sonic the Hedgehog*. In this game, the goal is to collect rings and defeat the evil Professor Robotnik. The game can be played in either single- or two-player mode. During the treatment period, the boys played in both formats. There was a focus on developing interaction and promoting both self-esteem and interpersonal connection. When the boys played the game in two-player mode, they worked together to increase the distance in the game that they advanced. They also developed shared strategies to accomplish tasks, like beating the boss, through open discussion and trials. This activity also had some reported collateral benefit in that there was an increased tolerance for previously unwanted situations outside of session, according to both sets of parents. In the single-player mode, the boys took turns and would each play one round. This interaction promoted patience, delayed gratification, communication, and positive social interactions.

Tim was very skilled at this particular game, while Joey struggled in some areas. The result after five weeks using this approach was that Tim's family reported increased social interactions with peers and a marked decline in negative behaviors at home and school. Joey demonstrated similar results, with an increase in his willingness to accept change and ask for assistance rather than resorting to his previous tantrum behaviors.

The reader should not assume that this was a situation in which the clients simply played the video game and were left to their own devices. Instead, the therapist was constantly engaged in the interactions—prompting, deescalating when tension developed, modeling, providing coaching through breathing and relaxation techniques, and facilitating a continuous dialogue regarding how the process was working for the boys, reflecting the perceived feelings and confirming accuracy of those feelings. These sessions were very active and dynamic in nature with little downtime for the facilitator. In this case, the video game became the draw that lessened the "heat" of social interaction and allowed for an emotional dialogue to develop.

Example 2

Jayden was a 14-year-old who was refusing to talk with either his family or his therapist. He was virtually nonresponsive to traditional verbal prompts and questions, and had no interest in directive or nondirective uses of play and art. Therefore, it was determined that an alternative approach would be needed to engage him. One thing he was willing to talk about was his ability to play video games, so these games were welcomed into session. When he started playing video games, he was open to exploring and discussing almost any topic. For example, while playing video games he was more willing to discuss the relationship between his parents and the frustration he felt regarding their conflictual relationship and the tension each expressed about the other. Jayden was able to articulate that he felt like the pawn that was shuffled between them, and that his parents rarely listened to his perception of the issues.

It was also during game play that he was able to begin to look at the metaphors in his life. His favorite game was *Naruto*, a player versus player fighting game with a spiritual element. He took great pride in beating me during the game, which was not at all surprising. But when he began to select opponents for me, the tone of the game changed. The theme of the discussion about each parent would match the qualities of the opponent he selected. He would describe situations that were frustrating and then more mindfully explore alternative reactions to the situation. This insight was not initially apparent but was actually identified by Jayden during one session in the form of an unanswered question: "I wonder why fighting video games are fun, but I don't really like to witness fights."

Example 3

In contrast to the previous two examples, in this one, video games were never incorporated into sessions. Instead, Jared, a 15-year-old, talked about the online elements of the games he frequently played as if the players in the game were his best friends. In his everyday life, Jared kept people at a distance, believing this position to be the safest and only possible course of action. Furthermore, it was his firm belief that the interaction he had with people over the Internet and through other computer games had no personal impact on him. This was erroneous thinking, as Jared was prone to still be discussing happenings from the game during session up to a month after they had occurred.

The focus of treatment was on developing Jared's drive to engage with others outside the virtual realm and improve his interactional skills so that he could connect with his peers in both developmentally and socially appropriate ways. To achieve these aims, we utilized the world of the game as a metaphor for the social setting (Alessi & Alessi, 2008). By depersonalizing real-life events and discussing them as occurring inside the game world, Jared was able to achieve enough distance from situations to be able to access insight and thoughtfulness.

During the course of treatment several games were discussed, including *Diablo, Halo, Rainbow Six, Command & Conquer,* and *Stronghold.* By focusing on his interests, Jared was able to demonstrate expertise in a topic and feel more in control than I was. He clearly relished this position of mastery. Several times Jared made comments about the importance of being understood and noted that few truly did understand him.

After Jared felt confident that he had demonstrated some mastery in the area of experience and interaction, we began to discuss how he went about engaging his peers in the games. We reviewed some of the online discussions he had with them, including his leadership in opening groups or guilds in the games. We noted how these interactions were both similar to and different from the interactions he had with peers at school. There were also several discussions about how he could more readily misinterpret the interactions he was having with others online than those he had in person because of the plethora of sensory data available in the real world. We worked for several weeks to improve interpersonal skills and recognize strengths and assets from different perspectives.

Initially Jared was reclusive and avoidant of others. His early life experiences taught him to be cautious around people because they were going to hurt or laugh at him. At the end of treatment, Jared's social network had doubled and he reported having his first girlfriend.

CONCLUSION

While multiple studies conclude that the repeated playing of violent video games can lead to an increase in violent behavior, these games remain a much-loved part of many boys' lives. It is important for clinicians to remember that many games that capture boys' interest are not violent in nature, and most of the studies related to the harmful effects of video games are restricted to those with violent content (Gentile, 2010). Like anything, these games are a tool. If used in excess, they have the potential to be destructive and lead to significant problems. But when used with forethought and careful monitoring, they can assist the therapist in drawing in those boys who initially appear guarded, closed, and reluctant to engage in the treatment process. Video games can provide not only a powerful relationship development tool but also a mechanism for experiential learning and metaphorical discussion.

Clinicians can learn a great deal from their clients about video games, if they lack experience with them. This reversal of the power differential inherent to the treatment relationship allows the client to instead be the expert while the therapist models openness in the face of not having all the answers. Entering into these games with curiosity and openness may help us assist boys in building relationships, skills, and insight in the virtual world that can become the catalyst for the development of these same positive benefits in the real world.

REFERENCES

Alessi, N. E., & Alessi, V. A. (2008). New media and an ethics analysis model for child and adolescent psychiatry. *Child and Adolescent Psychiatric Clinics of North America, 17*, 67–92.

American Psychological Association. (n.d.). *Resolution on violence in video games and interactive media.* Retrieved from http://www.apa.org/about/governance/council/policy/interactive-media.pdf

Anderson, C. A. (2003). *Violent video games: Myths, facts and unanswered questions.* Retrieved from http://www.apa.org/science/about/psa/2003/10/anderson.aspx

Anderson C. A., Gentile, D. A., & Buckley, K. E. (2007). *Violent video game effects on children and adolescents: Theory, research, and public policy.* New York: Oxford University Press.

Douglas, A. S. (1955). *Some computations in theoretical physics.* Doctoral dissertation, University of Cambridge.

Enfield, G., & Grosser, M. (2008). Picking up coins: The use of video games in the treatment of adolescent social problems. In L. C. Rubin (Ed.), *Popular culture in counseling, psychotherapy, and play-based interventions* (pp. 181–193). New York: Springer.

Entertainment Software Association (2010). *Essential facts about the computer and video game industry: 2010 sales, demographic, and usage data.* http://www.theesa.com/facts/pdfs/ESA.Essential_Facts_2010.PDF

Favelle, G. (1995). Therapeutic applications of commercially available computer software. *Computers in Human Services, 11*(1/2), 151–158.

Gardner, J. (1991). Can the Mario Bros. help? Nintendo games as an adjunct in psychotherapy with children. *Psychotherapy: Theory, Research, Practice, Training, 28*(4), 667–670.

Gentile, D. A. (2010). Video games affect the brain—for better *and* worse. In D. Gordon (Ed.), *Cerebrum 2010: Emerging ideas in brain science* (pp. 71–80). New York: Dana Press.

Harrison, K., & Bond, B. J. (2007). Gaming magazines and the drive for muscularity in preadolescent boys: A longitudinal examination. *Body Image, 4*(3), 269–277.

Jones, G. (2002). *Killing monsters: Why children need fantasy, super heroes, and make-believe violence.* New York: Basic Books.

Media Awareness Network (2007). *Understanding the rating system.* Retrieved from http://www.media-awareness.ca/english/parents/video_games/ratings _videogames.cfm

Nastasi, B. K., & Clements, D. H. (1993). Motivational and social outcomes of cooperative computer education environments. *Journal of Computing in Childhood Education, 4*(1), 15–43.

National Association for the Education of Young Children. (1996). *Technology and young children—Ages 3 through 8.* Washington, DC: Author.

Olson, C. K., Kutner, L. A., & Warner, D. E. (2008). The role of violent video game content in adolescent development: Boys' perspectives. *Journal of Adolescent Research, 23*(1), 55–75.

Skigen, D. (2008). Taking the sand tray high tech: Using *The Sims* as a therapeutic tool in the treatment of adolescents. In L. C. Rubin (Ed.), *Popular culture in counseling, psychotherapy, and play-based interventions* (pp. 165–179). New York: Springer.

7

The Therapeutic Use of Superheroes in the Treatment of Boys*

CRAIG HAEN

In a therapy group held in a New York City homeless shelter with five- and six-year-old children, the group members divided themselves into two subgroups following a warm-up game. Throughout the life of the group these youngsters had repeatedly expressed either an inner sense of badness because of being homeless or an ardent need to be "good" so as not to cause their mothers more stress. One session, my co-leader and I invited the kids to role-play a scene in which they either enacted the role of the "good child" or the "bad child." The subgroup of children who chose the latter was comprised exclusively of boys. When we gathered to discuss their reasons for choosing one group over the other, the boys communicated feelings of intense anger directed at someone specific in each of their lives—most often an absent father figure.

When I asked the group what would help them feel less angry, one boy said that he wished he could be Superman. I recalled that the puppet he created several sessions before was in the image of this superhero. All the boys concurred that they, too, would like to be superheroes, and each identified a character that he liked best. Their choices ran

---

* This chapter is a revised and expanded version of Haen, C. (2002). The dramatherapeutic use of the superhero role with male clients. *Dramatherapy, 24*(1), 16–22.

the gamut of television cartoon heroes, and the boys appeared to be empowered by merely invoking the names of these characters.

This scenario is a familiar one. Time and again, the male clients whom I see in treatment have gravitated to hero roles, from more ancient and archetypal warriors and knights in shining armor to the popular culture superheroes featured in movies and cartoons. Groups of resistant boys almost always excitedly engage when I ask them the question, "If you could have any superpower, what would it be?" Younger boys, when given the freedom to create their own stories, often pretend to be superheroes from cartoons and the movies. Adult males in the men's group I facilitated in a day treatment program repeatedly referred to the character of Superman as the ego ideal against which they felt they must compare their lives.

Superheroes have experienced a renewed surge of popularity in the last decade, largely due to several successful film franchises that have become summer blockbusters and a rapidly expanding video game market. This interest has led to the curious recent cultural phenomenon of adults who create an alternative identity for themselves, dress in costume, sometimes carry out good deeds, and purport to be real-life superheroes. An online registry was even created to list these heroes (Bearman, 2008/2009).

With the presence of female superheroes such as Kim Possible, the Powerpuff Girls, Femforce, Wonder Woman, and members of the X-Men and the Incredibles, young girls have shown a degree of interest in superhero roles; however, superhero play remains far more common for boys (Baron-Cohen, 2003; Paley, 1984). Adolescent males are still the largest demographic consumers of comic books, and the superhero genre (including its presentation in comics, on television, and in films) remains dominated by male characters (Baker & Raney, 2007; Paechter, 2007; Pecora, 1992). It is important to note that superhero stories remain ethnically unbalanced as well, with the vast majority of superheroes portrayed as Caucasian (Baker & Raney, 2007). Though space does not permit a fuller discussion of this trend, therapists should consider its ramifications when working with clients of *all* ethnicities.

Previous studies noted a tendency in superhero narratives to reinforce traditional gender stereotypes. For example, male superheroes were portrayed as more intelligent, dominant, task-oriented, technically proficient, and brave, whereas female superheroes were presented as more jealous, romantically focused, passive, dependent, sensitive, domestic, and in need of rescue (Aubrey & Harrison, 2004; Thompson & Zerbinos, 1995). A more recent study did not find these differences and, in fact, found male and female superheroes virtually equivalent in their use of aggression (Baker & Raney, 2007). Some gender differences remained, however, with the study finding male superheroes portrayed as more tough and threatening, and females being shown as more emotional, concerned about personal appearance, and superficial. Males were more often depicted in leadership roles.

Central to the superhero story are qualities that continue to resonate with the male experience across the life span: both those aspects that boys and men find appealing about their gender and those that represent a challenge. Understanding these qualities can inform the therapist's work with male clients and provide a vantage point from which to view the issues with which boys and men grapple. This chapter will focus specifically on the therapeutic use of the superhero with boys, examining the qualities of these characters that may connect with this population as well as presenting clinical applications of superhero stories.

MALE DEVELOPMENT

By one year of age babies are able to differentiate adult men from women, and by the age of three years most children have an established sex identity (Aydt & Corsaro, 2003), readily able to categorize themselves as either male or female. The process of gender role formation quickly follows. Bem (1987) theorized that a child's notions about gender are organized by a gender schema, a cognitive structure based on social experiences and messages that the child receives from society about what is acceptable for his gender. This schema is ever-evolving and develops through observation and acquisition of gender roles. Bem emphasized that the child is an active participant in structuring his gender schema, which serves to inform further development. Chu (2004) reiterated the notion of boys as active participants in the gender socialization process, writing, "It is important to consider how boys draw on their continually evolving self-knowledge and conceptions of reality as they develop an understanding of who they are and what they are like" (p. 79). Gender identity, when viewed in this manner, is akin to an acquired brain concept, those ideas that are formulated in the brain and continually open to shifting and alteration with new experiences and new role models (Zeki, 2009).

The male child's original role models are his primary attachment figures, and their patterns of engagement serve to inform development and relationships throughout the life span. Winnicott (1971) focused on the central importance of play and interaction with the mother in shaping the child's sense of self. As the child ages, he begins a gradual process of separation and individuation. Chodorow (1978) defined what she viewed as the gender differences in this phase, asserting how the female child's development of femininity is marked by affiliation with the mother, while the development of masculinity is dependent upon separation from her. Many authors (Betcher & Pollack, 1993; Krugman, 1998; Lisak, 1995; Pollack, 1998) followed suit in characterizing this normative separation as a premature rupture of the attachment bond, which they suggested was experienced by the male child as shaming and led to interpersonal disconnection and trauma.

This theory initially appealed to many writers and clinicians who were concerned about the emotional needs of boys, including the present author. However, the idea that there is something necessarily traumatogenic about boys' development has failed to find research support (Brooks, 2010) and has instead been utilized to promulgate a "boys are victims" mentality, pathologizing the male pattern of identity formation while upholding female development as ideal and healthy. Such a comparison does a disservice to both boys and girls while also unfairly implicating mothers in perpetrating a rupture of the holding environment instead of recognizing their important role in assisting their sons in the identity development process.

Research suggests that a secure attachment relationship is one in which the child internalizes his attachment figure(s) in the form of mental representations so that his experiences of available, responsive, and protective parenting can be summoned in times of distress (Cassidy, 2008). It is the very security of the relationship—both the actual and the internalized safe haven—that *allows* the child to venture out and face the world. Internalization of the mother, therefore, may be as essential a component of healthy male development as affiliation with the father (Diamond, 2009), and the boys' separation and individuation may be more appropriately viewed as an active, exploratory turn toward male role models rather than a premature push away from femininity and connection. Diamond (2009) wrote:

> A mother's recognition and affirmation of her son's maleness help him to progressively differentiate from her rather than to establish his sense of masculinity in violent opposition to her femaleness. By recognition and affirmation of his maleness, I am referring to the mother's capacity to support her son's journey toward the world of his father—the world of males. (p. 37)

While the father was largely a sideline player in early attachment research, greater attempts have been made in recent years to understand his unique contribution to the parenting process (Lamb & Lewis, 2004; Pruett, 2000). Just as children learn from their mothers through the process of play, so too do they engage with their fathers in a playful way. However, the way that fathers play with their children can be qualitatively different, a difference that can lead to the child showing a preference for paternal over maternal play (Lamb & Lewis, 2004). Fathers are more likely to engage in physically stimulating their children: by bouncing them, swinging them around, and holding them over their shoulder so that they can view the environment surrounding them (Pruett, 2000). As the child ages, the paternal play, particularly with sons, often takes on a physical, rough and tumble quality, mirroring the father's own play style as a child (Maccoby, 1990).

The paternal mode of play, according to researchers, teaches children self-regulation and emotional mastery skills, as well as fostering a sense of excitement and wonder about the world around them (Diamond, 2007; Pruett, 2000). As boys wrestle with their fathers, they learn to gauge the effect of their actions on another person. Dad communicates when the child has gotten too rough, or when he is not in the mood for playing, through his facial expressions and body language. This teaching process is often one not of words but of action. At the same time, an attuned father reads his son's affect, modulating the play based on the boy's needs and tolerance for engagement (Diamond, 2007). As such, from paternal play the child ideally begins to learn to read emotional cues and to self-regulate, as well as developing a template for the containment of violence and aggression (Karr-Morse & Wiley, 1998; Schore, 1994).

The ability to regulate affect is essential to one's capacity to navigate frustration, sustain relationships, and develop a sense of self-efficacy (Schore, 2009). Many of the male clients with whom I work experience their affect as sudden and overwhelming, and many admit to finding their strong feelings frightening. When a father is not able to gauge and control his own emotions, he is unable to teach his child to regulate impulses. One longitudinal study found that boys whose fathers lacked self-control had gross difficulties in later life, including impaired academic performance, poor peer relations, symptoms of depression, and an increase in risk-taking behaviors (D'Angelo, Weinberger, & Feldman, 1995).

As children reach school age, they tend to segregate into groups by gender at recess, according to researchers who have observed them on the playground. This division into same-sex groups, or what Maccoby (1990, 2002) refers to as "two cultures," is remarkably consistent in countries around the world. Boys' desire to be with other boys continues to intensify throughout the early school years (Eliot, 2009; Maccoby, 2002). Gender differences in toy preferences are also reliably robust across cultures at this age, and boys tend to play in exuberantly physical and active ways, demonstrating themes of danger, competition, and heroics (Baron-Cohen, 2003; Maccoby, 2002).

Same-sex peer groups become both the site of gender expression and a source of reinforcement for specific play preferences and interaction styles (Eliot, 2009; Paechter, 2007). As such, when observed within the context of these groups, boys often demonstrate a heightened focus on rules and hierarchy, competing with male peers for ascendancy (Maccoby, 1990; Pinker, 2008). At home, during this period, parents are noted in some studies to talk less (and with a narrower spectrum of language) to their sons about feelings than they do their daughters, particularly feelings of sadness. Instead, they are observed to foster in them a greater pressure to achieve, to be independent, to take on responsibility, and to conform to societal norms (Paechter, 2007; Wexler, 2009).

As boys age, they develop greater awareness of social messages about which emotions are acceptable in order to be masculine (anger being foremost among these) and what qualities are necessary in order to be successful (those of ambition and competitiveness). Relationally, males are more often expected to demonstrate helping behavior that is public and heroic in nature, whereas feminine helping behavior is generally more intimate, nurturing, and interpersonal in quality (Hyde, 1994). The result is that many men formulate a gendered ego ideal against which they frequently try to compare themselves. The discrepancy between this idealized self and who they are in reality can be a source of shame for some males (Krugman, 1998), many of whom strive to fulfill a protector role (Goldberg, 1991). For others, the ego ideal may provide buffering and a source of strength as they begin to identify with the positive aspects of this construct (Diamond, 2009).

SUPERHEROES

Most stories, myths, plays, and films contain some form of a hero character. Superheroes, though, are a breed apart and have specific characteristics that are well known. Rovin (1985) summarized the qualities of the superhero, but points out that some of the most popular characters represent exceptions to these rules:

> In the realm of superheroes, these factors are usually true: superheroes have at least one superpower, whether physical or attributable to a weapon, instrument or conveyance; they work actively and magnanimously for the common good; their values are neither vindictive nor selfish; they tend to operate on earth, though they may not be from this world; they achieve anonymity by assuming a mortal identity or alter ego; and they wear a distinctive costume. (p. xi)

The superhero character has its roots in mythology and ancient drama, and like the tragic hero, many early superheroes had a noble birth and then were cast out by their families or set out to pursue a quest (Haen & Brannon, 2002). Just as modern drama evolved from focusing on the tragic figure with noble origins to focusing on the common man, most modern superhero stories focus on ordinary men who become extraordinary heroes. However, as Rubin (2007) pointed out, "Unlike the classical hero, the modern superhero never fully integrates back into society and is continually confronted with irreconcilable tensions both within him or herself or the society" (p. 8).

At the most basic level, superhero roles appeal to boys because they are empowering. These roles can be effective in the beginning stages of the therapeutic process by providing "an opening into the landscape of alternative perceptions, directly challenging a subscribed view of passivity and fearfulness" (Archer, 1997, p. 77). By invoking the superhero role in fantasy play, the child begins to gain ideals and inspiration for future development (Pecora, 1992).

This was certainly true for one nine-year-old client of mine. Matt had spent his life coping with a host of challenges, including a degenerative muscle disorder that ensured he walked with braces and spent much of his time in physical therapy. He had several co-occurring medical conditions that impaired his cognitive functioning, memory, and academic performance. Not surprisingly, Matt was enamored with superhero stories, and had a particular fascination with Cartoon Network's Ben 10 character. In this series, a boy named Ben Tennyson discovers an alien pod while on a camping trip with his family. Inside it is a watch called the Omnitrix that permanently fuses to his wrist, giving him the ability to change into a variety of alien life forms, each with particular powers. For Matt, a character who has an ability to morph into different body types in order to be competent in situations had an obvious appeal and provided a framework for our treatment, as we began to work on his frustrations about his limitations and on bolstering his self-esteem.

Child therapists have found that, regardless of disability, social standing, or circumstance, clients can feel empowered within the space of dramatic and fantasy play (Bouzoukis, 2001; Crenshaw & Mordock, 2005; Haen, 2008). Pretend play, as Paley (1984) wrote, "disarms and enchants; it suggests heroic possibilities for making changes, just as in the fairy tales" (p. 87). Citing Bettleheim, Erikson, Piaget, and Vygotsky, Rubin (2005) concluded:

> The consensus of the interdisciplinary chorus is that fantasy provides the child with a means of both deepening their understanding of and experimenting with reality, working through feelings related to both positive and negative experiences, and gaining a sense of mastery that is inaccessible to them because of their tender years. (pp. 243–244)

The central goal of an approach to treatment that accesses the child's imagination is that, in playing roles of strength, the client will begin to internalize these qualities or draw upon internal resources that remain untapped. In this sense, the therapist can use superhero play as a form of role modeling and an entrée to helping a boy find heroic qualities to access during times in which he currently makes self-defeating choices. Selekman (1997) supported this sentiment: "If individuals imagine something vividly enough and with their heart bring their senses and emotion into play, their deep mind cannot know the difference between the imagined event and an actual one. The more of themselves they engage in the imagining process, the stronger the desired effect will be" (p. 127). Beyond fantasy play, the superhero story can become a natural attraction for boys who might otherwise be resistant to change, providing a drive toward treatment compliance. One treatment team creatively refashioned the milieu culture of their residential program for adolescents with sexual behavior problems around superhero themes and found exciting results in this difficult-to-treat population (Robertie, Weidenbenner, Barrett, & Poole, 2007).

CASE ILLUSTRATION: INDIVIDUAL TREATMENT
IN A PRIVATE PRACTICE SETTING

Jacob was a nine-year-old Asian American boy who was brought for treatment because of excessive fears he was displaying in the home that were limiting his functioning. His parents reported that he had an active imagination and was particularly reactive to movies that had a supernatural element in them. While he was attracted to films with action and enjoyed acting out "fight" scenes, he quickly became overwhelmed and fearful. He was most afraid of witches and would report that he was scared that they would come harm him when he was alone. While his parents limited his access to these movies, Jacob would perseveratively focus on them after merely seeing a commercial or spying a DVD cover at the video store.

Because of his fears, Jacob refused to be in specific rooms in his home by himself, could not sleep over at friends' houses, and occasionally wet the bed at night. These fears had also gotten in the way of his meeting developmental milestones, as he had been overly dependent on his parents for assistance with dressing, tying his shoes, and completing other age-appropriate tasks. During initial sessions with the parents, it became clear that Jacob's fears were causing stress in the marriage and had led to increased arguments between them about child rearing. Jacob's father wished for him to be more independent, while his mother seemed less certain that it was necessary for Jacob to separate from them. They had brought him to see a therapist six months prior, but Jacob had actively resisted attempts to help him conquer his fears and to implement a behavioral plan in the home.

Jacob was an active boy who engaged readily in sessions. He enjoyed creating stories in the dollhouse in my office, using the family figures to depict his fantasies that witches would sneak in the family home at night to kill them all. As he played, it became clear that some of his fears originated in real-life incidents that had subsequently been metaphorized as he grappled to make sense of them. In one such event, a portion of the roof above his bedroom caved in at night. He had tried to communicate to his parents that he was hearing noises, but they had reportedly reassured him that "everything is all right" and urged him to go back to sleep. When the roof collapsed, Jacob remembered being frightened and later speculated that he possessed a unique ability to detect danger that others did not have.

In one of his play episodes, as he was creating a story about a witch sneaking into a home to capture the family, I paused the action and suggested that perhaps he should give the little boy in the story some superpowers that might allow him to defeat the witch. Jacob was delighted with the suggestion and played with greater energy, "trying on" different superpowers for his character before settling on the ability to become invisible. I asked him to demonstrate how the story might be different with the addition of this power, and he showed his character becoming invisible and then capturing the witch. We decided the build a jail for her from which she could not escape, and Jacob was amenable to leaving the witch in my office so that she would no longer bother him at home.

While this engagement in magical thinking served him well (he reported that no witches bothered him during the week between sessions), he continued to struggle with separating from his parents. I asked him to draw a superhero version of himself, which he named Super Jacob. When asked how he might become Super Jacob at home during the week, he became excited, saying that he could demonstrate bravery. The superhero character became the "hook" that motivated him to engage in a new behavioral plan. As part of this plan, the parents were given a Batman notebook and asked to record each time he became Super Jacob during the week so that we could review the list at the subsequent session. This process became the basis for a series of steps toward increasing independence tied to rewards that Jacob chose. Though he enjoyed the small toys he earned, he was most intrinsically motivated by the pride his father showed in his newfound bravery. When our treatment ended suddenly because his family was relocating out of town due to a job change, Jacob was excited about going to a new house and expressed candidly to me in our last session that he doubted if witches "are really real anyway."

THE THERAPEUTIC POTENTIAL OF SUPERHERO METAPHORS

Because the superhero role is one that represents power and control, it can be an effective tool in working with clients who lack a sense of empowerment in their lives, from boys with low self-esteem to those with problems related to anger and aggression. Like Gallo-Lopez (2005), I have engaged many of my clients in drawing themselves as a superhero, including identifying the unique superpowers they would have, designing a costume for themselves, and identifying a weakness. I have encouraged older and more developmentally advanced clients to explore their superhero's story further, including aspects related to how they obtained their powers, whom they protect, and whom they fight against.

Further examination of the superhero story reveals layers beyond simple empowerment. Jones (2002) attempted to understand how the character of Superman (the first, and most popular, of modern superheroes) could appeal to audiences from youth to adulthood. He concluded that preschoolers are interested in Superman being above pain, while school-aged children admire the character because he is strong. Preadolescents, according to Jones, value Superman's secret identity, while teenagers resonate with his position as protector of a community and take an interest in his history.

Central to each character's story is what Widzer (1977) referred to as the family romance, "the story of the birth of the hero and the manner in which the superheroes acquire their powers" (p. 568). There are two common superhero origin stories, both of which have significance for male clients. In one version, the superhero gains power as the result of some significant trauma, often a freak accident (Bongco, 2000). For example, Spider-Man acquired his powers after being bitten by a radioactive spider. The Hulk, originally a scientist, was exposed to gamma rays as he attempted to save a boy from a detonating bomb at a test site. The second means of power acquisition usually occurs when the character is born as a mutant (like the X-Men) or as an alien outsider who is sent to earth (like Superman or Wonder Woman). In this instance, the character's bonds to family or community of origin are severed, and future relationships are marked by the echoes of early trauma.

As such, many superheroes are first victims who transcend their circumstances to become protectors of other victims. Their power serves to make them popular but also isolates them from others, who are afraid of them. Superheroes often are rendered freaks or outcasts by the mortal characters in the story (Haen & Brannon, 2002). Their powers present a double bind in that they simultaneously connect them to and distance them from society. One recent study of television superheroes found that female superheroes outnumbered their male counterparts in having a mentor available for guidance, and more females than males were portrayed as being part of a team as opposed to working in isolation (Baker & Raney, 2007).

Many boys experience the same juxtaposition of connection and disconnection, or intimacy and distancing, in their own lives. Baron-Cohen (2003) noted that boys tend, in both their make-believe stories and fantasy play, to create superheroes who operate in solitary and are in conflict with others. Girls' stories and play are instead more likely to focus on family and sociality. When taken to the extreme, the power of boys can become a mixed blessing—a force that alienates them from others—and they can struggle to develop the skills required for a mirroring relationship. As such, some boys grow up to be men who have a fuzzy sense of self, unsure of what they feel, or at least how to articulate it to others. As one of my adolescent clients reflected after playing Superman in a group, "I liked being in charge, but there was something about it that still didn't feel quite right."

The metaphor of being excluded because of one's abilities has served well in helping to reframe incidents of prejudice, bullying, and teasing some of my male clients have had to endure. Adam, a 15-year-old Caucasian with Asperger's syndrome, had been seeing me for several months and engaging in co-created stories that we role-played together. This incredibly socially impaired young man was able to present himself as remarkably functional—maintaining eye contact, humor, reciprocity, and spontaneity—when he was in role. After a period of time in which he played stereotypically villainous characters, deriving pleasure from the idea of engaging in misdeeds and causing others harm, he began to shift his characters to more complex superhero roles. In particular, he often made them aliens who were sent to the planet Earth and did not understand the ways and emotions of humans. This theme had an obvious relevance for Adam, who was in mainstream classes and struggling to make it through the day at his present high school.

In one story, he created two aliens from the planet Schmillkop. They were both part fish and had the power to breathe underwater, but were able to survive indefinitely outside of water because of tanks on their body that drew water from the air. All the inhabitants of their planet looked the same. The hero Xong came to Earth after the villain Xing took over the planet. Xing was a tyrannical ruler who forced his people to work and killed them if they did not comply with his orders. He was plotting to take over Earth in a similar fashion. As Adam, in the role of Xong, attempted to warn the Earthlings and save them, he faced the challenge of trying to befriend humans despite their fears of him. He found Earthlings strange and struggled to understand their human emotions. Our mutual engagement in this role play was touchingly emblematic of Adams's real-life struggles in comprehending the fast-paced adolescent social exchanges in his school. Though he never talked about these problems directly, Adam used the superhero metaphor as a means of expressing how distant he felt from his peers. In future scenes, we began to practice basic social engagement skills.

The duality of power and impotence captured in Adam's story is a common facet of the superhero role, as most superheroes also have a weakness. This weakness has an Aristotelian link to the heroes of classic drama who were tragically flawed by excesses of bravery, hubris, and jealousy. Superhero weaknesses often take symbolic and tangible forms, such as Superman's vulnerability to the substance kryptonite. The avoidance of that weakness guides the action of the story and the emotional arc of the character. Likewise, it ensures that the superhero operates in solitude.

In discussing Superman's distance from others, Mamet (1989) wrote:

> Kryptonite is all that remains of his childhood home. It is the remnants of that destroyed childhood home, and the fear of those remnants, which rule Superman's life. The possibility that the shards of that destroyed home might surface prevents him from being intimate—they prevent him from sharing the knowledge that the wimp and the hero are one. The fear of his childhood home prevents him from having pleasure. (p. 178)

Superhero metaphors provide the opportunity to work with boys on issues related to power, self-control, affect management, and aggression. These problems are particularly relevant to boys, who are more likely to engage in overt violence than girls (Feder, Levant, & Dean, 2008) and more likely to derive pleasure from physically aggressive play (Benenson, Carder, & Geib-Cole, 2008). By contrast, the aggression utilized by superheroes is primarily instrumental aggression, that is, aggression used in service of the greater good (Tate, 2008). Some super-heroes are even models of redemption, having been villains initially and then renouncing their past choices by becoming superheroes instead (Robertie et al., 2007).

I have found that my adolescent male clients in particular resonate with the familiar dictum that evolved from the Spider-Man comics and was featured in the first film (Raimi, 2002): "With great power comes great responsibility." I have invoked this phrase during especially challenging family sessions in which my clients are stuck in the typi-cally adolescent stance of wanting more privileges from parents with-out demonstrating sufficient accountability or maturity. Even boys who have grown up amid inner city violence and have engaged in delinquent behaviors connect with the idea of a moral code. As these boys long for male role models (Haen, 2007), superhero characters can provide them with guiding figures who make moral choices, yet are also as exciting as some of the celebrities from gang culture to whom they are attracted.

A more modern trend in superhero stories has been a shift toward exploring the real-world stresses and complications of being a hero (such as in the *Identity* series, which depicts a teenager struggling with the challenges of his superpowers while he negotiates a complex relationship with his alcoholic mother and superhero father, who are separated), as well as the real-life implications of their actions (as was demonstrated in recent films like *Hancock*). Similarly, superheroes have become more morally complex with a rise in antiheroes such as the Punisher, V, and Wolverine, who are motivated by revenge, struggle to regulate their rage, and can enjoy causing harm to others (Clark, 2010; Spivey & Knowlton, 2008). These characters provide interesting fodder for exploration with boys who often can't decide whether to identify with "good guys" or "bad guys" in their own lives. In addition, superhero play can become a means of addressing affect modulation and assist-ing angry and aggressive clients in more accurately assessing threat and determining the appropriate level of response in conflictual interactions (Crenshaw & Mordock, 2005).

THE ABSENT FATHER

Andronico (1996) wrote, "Whether fathers were absent, abusive, pres-ent, pathetic or wonderful, men's feelings and attitudes about them may be the single most important issue that men struggle with in their lives" (p. 217). Currently, only 61% of American children live with both their biological mother and father (Corbett, 2009), and one in three male children lives without his birth father (Tyre, 2008). For these children, the superhero role can be especially powerful.

It is important to note that many single mothers have successfully raised mentally healthy boys, particularly those whose homes are marked by a sense of stability and a lack of conflict (Jones, 2008), and that many boys have nonresidential fathers who are still quite involved in their lives (Perry, 2008). In other instances, male mentors such as coaches, teachers, and members of the extended family may serve as effective role models. However, if the boy has no significant male adults who can serve this role, particularly in the separation and individuation phase (or during its recapitulation in adolescence), the construct of how to be a man may become synonymous with how not to be a woman (Betcher & Pollack, 1993). Boys who formulate their schema in this fashion are more likely to conform to traditional gender roles than to experience a more congruous and integrated masculinity (Wineburgh, 2000).

Another painful and confusing consequence of having an unavailable father is that the eldest, or only, male child often takes on or may get cast in the role of "man of the house." This expectation places a large burden on the child to be a man when he is yet a boy, to be a container for the family rather than being contained by it (Scharff, 1992). He is attracted to the role because it allows him to play out fantasies of power and importance, but ultimately it leaves him feeling inadequate and overwhelmed. Male children also gravitate toward fulfilling the gap created by the absent father because they recognize their mother's needs and long to protect her.

The father, because of his absence, maintains a significant place in the male child's psyche. According to Wineburgh (2000), "a fatherless child creates a fantasized father who is often idealized and maintained as a myth, largely unaffected by the reality of the situation" (p. 257). For the son of an absent father, the superhero role can serve as a metaphor for his quest to fulfill the idealized father image he has created in his mind. Likewise, the deaths of parents are common plot elements in the superhero stories. Superman, Batman, Daredevil, and Spider-Man were all the children of parents who died tragically. Superhero play can represent a connection to that which the boy has lost.

THE USE OF THE SUPERHERO WITH TRAUMATIZED AND ATTACHMENT DISORDERED BOYS

Many of the boys for whom I provide treatment have been exposed to some significant form of trauma in their lives, whether borne of abuse, neglect, or abandonment. Children and adolescents who have been traumatized may experience disempowerment, an invasion of bodily integrity, a feeling that they themselves are worthless or freakish, pervasive fears about safety, and an inability to connect with others (Nader, 2007). Similarly, many superheroes have undergone some form of tragedy, and their stories address many of the aspects of trauma.

Psychoanalyst Bloch (1978) theorized that children incorporate superheroes as part of a compensatory fantasy to cope with unconscious fears of infanticide from their parents. In the present world, in which violence is a part of the everyday lives of children—from the home to the larger canvas of international politics—children's fears live in the consciousness of everyday events. Following the terrorist attacks in New York City on September 11, 2001, there was an even greater proliferation of superhero play among my clients as they attempted to organize and master their shattered perception of the United States as a safe haven and a superpower unto itself (Haen, 2008). In one client's drawings, the World Trade Center was depicted as newly constructed with Superman and Batman standing watch at the top to protect against further attacks.

The roles children use in fantasy play serve as containers for their fears and confusion. By externalizing and symbolizing their problems in a therapeutic space, children can organize and reintegrate fragmented and overwhelming affect and experience (Cattanach, 2008). The act of projecting onto a role provides the safety and distance necessary to face the trauma again. Many of my clients have reframed real-life incidents of abuse and victimization, particularly those occurring in early childhood when events seem larger in scale and depth, in terms of epic battles between superheroes and supervillains. In some sense, this reframing helps to counteract the isolation of the abuse experience, transforming their personal story into one that is more connected to collective society. As Rubin (2007) pointed out, the epic battles of superheroes and villains are symbolic of the internal battles within everyone.

The aforementioned World Trade Center example illustrates one child's intervention fantasy. Such fantasies, in which the traumatized individual wishes he had been powerful, knowledgeable, or heroic enough to stop what had happened, are an "integral part of traumatic memory" (Pynoos, Steinberg, & Goenjian, 1996, p. 349). Secondarily, he may wish that the events had been prevented by a powerful outside force or person. Also common are revenge fantasies (Haen & Weber, 2009), as expressed by an 11-year-old witness of domestic violence who addressed his abuser in one drama therapy group's role play by saying, "Someday I'll be big enough and strong enough to make guys like you sorry."

Spider-Man, Batman, and Robin all became superheroes to avenge the murder of their parental figures, and indeed, there is a proliferation of superheroes who were victims of early abuse or neglect (Mattson & Park, 2008). For example, Bruce Banner, who is the human side of the Hulk, is haunted by memories of his father murdering his mother. Perry (1997) delineated differential gendered responses to trauma, finding that boys in situations of abuse and neglect tended more often to experience hyperarousal symptoms (as opposed to hypoarousal or dissociation) in the aftermath. Hyperarousal symptoms include pronounced fight-or-flight responses and the activation of the sympathetic nervous system in situations of perceived threat, which can in turn lead to an elevated heart rate, hypervigilance, increased startle responses, irritability, and locomotion—all amplified extensions of the body's readiness to locate danger and defend itself through action (Levine, 1997).

Like many boys, superheroes are action-oriented, and their battles with evil villains can provide the client an outlet for his aggression by channeling it into fantasy and metaphor (Jones, 2002). As Sobel (1980) wrote, "The superhero provides an acceptable way for the youngsters to indirectly obtain retribution and initiate a process of self-reparation" (p. 48). The therapy process described here is not, as mistakenly characterized by Smith, Fischer, and Watson (2009), one in which the therapist gives "relatively free rein to aggressive fantasies" (p. 10). As their research demonstrates, such an approach has the potential to further aggression in children who have witnessed violence. Instead, the treatment process is a structured one that utilizes the natural language of children's play as a container for affect, an opportunity to shift rigid and nonrelational fantasy violence toward a narrative that considers the impact of actions upon others, and a catalyst for developing empathy, distress tolerance, affect regulation, and impulse control.

Clients who have been victimized early in life learn that the world is unsafe and unpredictable. Those who were supposed to protect them did not, and often were the same people who victimized them. Bongco (2000) pointed out how the very presence of the superhero in stories emphasizes the inability of the establishment to protect its citizens. In addition, superhero stories have a consistent internal logic that can be organizing when invoked in fantasy play (Jones, 2002). The stories have a clear good guy and a clear enemy, the plot elements are generally predictable, and there is almost always a happy ending (Bongco, 2000). As will be illustrated, therapists can capitalize on these elements in order to help traumatized clients organize their internal worlds.

The split/secret identity, or alter ego, of many superheroes is appealing to traumatized and attachment disordered clients, many of whom had to hide their trauma experiences from the rest of the world by developing a more competent social persona. Those boys whose childhoods have been characterized by victimization have often not had the opportunity to develop an integrated sense of self. They readily understand the secret identity of the superhero as they are intimately familiar with adults who are not what they appear to be (Wegner, 2007).

Many boys, traumatized or not, resonate with having a powerful façade and a secret, more vulnerable interior (Walker, 2004). For clients who have difficulties with self-regulation, a character like the Hulk—who turns into a powerful, green monster when angered—can embody their experience of having strong feelings that seem unmanageable. In fact, many boys report feeling like another person when they are enraged, or reflect that they feel disconnected from themselves in the face of strong affect.

Often, severely traumatized or disturbed clients have not just split, but have fragmented internally, experiencing their core as a collection of unintegrated pieces. The following case study illustrates how superhero roles became significant in individual therapy with a traumatized boy in a hospital setting. For this child, superheroes provided an avenue for affective expression, exploration of a complex history of abuse and neglect, and organization of the self.

CASE ILLUSTRATION: TREATMENT
IN A HOSPITAL SETTING

Seth was a six-year-old African American boy who lived with his biological mother and five siblings in a homeless shelter prior to being admitted for his second hospitalization. There was a strong history of mental illness in his family, and his mother was a substance abuser. Seth had been the victim of severe and chronic physical abuse that included having a broomstick broken over his back and being beaten repeatedly with belts. He also witnessed his father's violence toward his mother. His father no longer maintained a connection to the family.

Seth had many of the same externalizing symptoms as other child victims of abuse. He was hyperactive, impulsive, and emotionally labile. He cried frequently, fought with his siblings, and would often hit himself and bang his head. Seth's crying episodes would last for extreme lengths of time because he was unable to self-regulate. His sleep was reported to be erratic and punctuated by nocturnal enuresis. Two days prior to his admission to the child psychiatric unit on which I worked, Seth had been picked up by the police after being found throwing objects at cars. The following day, he brought a lighter into the home and attempted to burn his toys.

Seth reported having command auditory hallucinations that told him to kill himself. Further examination revealed a complex psychotic system consisting of four auditory and visual hallucinations that he believed were real monsters/ghosts, all characters in horror movies he had seen. Two of the figures were benevolent and two were evil. The latter two were known as Little O'Doul and Gates of Hell.

Seth had several strengths that were readily apparent. He was cute, with a winning smile that attracted the attention of adults. He was strong and athletic, and he had a boundless imagination. I first encountered Seth in the group therapy program that I coordinated on the unit. He initially had great difficulties in the group sessions, as he would often flood the other children by telling them elaborate and inaccurate stories of his mother cutting off his head and his sibling's extremities. When attempts were made to ground him in the here and now of the group, Seth would become oppositional, shouting racial slurs at peers or running around the room flapping his arms. In these moments he often needed to be removed from the group so staff could help him regulate his behavior.

I began to see Seth individually in the playroom on the unit for weekly sessions to target his sequelae of posttraumatic stress disorder (PTSD) symptoms. Our first few sessions were spent in fairly nondirective play in order to gain trust, though I took active steps to help him de-role the toys and find soothing behaviors for the closure of each session. It was in our third session that Seth began to develop two characters that he would often use during our work together: Superman and Spike the dinosaur.

In his stories, which he enacted by using small figures in a sand tray and in the sink, Superman could fly, swim, and spin with finesse, and he owned a magic boat. Seth played out epic battles between Superman and Spike that contained elements of some of the battles he had witnessed in his own family. The scenes were contained by the boundaries of the sand tray and the sink. Seth was able to speak from the perspectives of both roles, as well as distance himself and engage his observing ego, skills that were challenging for him to access in real-life situations. Both characters were externalizations of Seth's inner world and represented two conflicting emotional responses to his traumatic experiences. Spike was rage embodied; he wanted to "kill all the people and rule the world," and he killed his mother "because she hit him." Superman represented family loyalty and guilt, stating that it was okay for kids to love their parents even if their parents had abused them, and declaring that Spike was bad "because he doesn't love his mommy."

It was after our fourth individual session that Seth's behavior in group therapy began to improve. He brought a Barney doll to the group, which he used as a transitional object. Through this doll he began to talk and connect with his peers. Though his processing in the group contained some psychotic content, he was able to talk about real-life events in a more clear and organized fashion. He began to tell the kids about his actual memories of being abused but, without active structuring from the leader, continued to quickly become flooded and psychotic.

As we continued to work individually with Superman, and as Seth began to internalize the qualities of that role, he expressed a desire to create a Superman cape for himself. He wore the cape in sessions and began fully embodied role play as the Superman character. He invited me into his play, casting me as Batman, and together we began to fight the imaginary monsters in the playroom. In doing so, Seth was able to gain mastery over these monsters. Our relationship as crime-fighting partners allowed him to reexperience the frightening ghosts of his past without slipping into psychosis. The metaphorical work was interspersed with cognitive-behavioral techniques that addressed Seth's distortions about the abuse, his negative self-perception, and his struggles to self-regulate.

In our seventh session, Seth came to the playroom and announced that he did not want to play Superman that day and instead wanted to talk about Little O'Doul and Gates of Hell, the two psychotic manifestations he was seeing in his room at night. According to Seth, these two ghosts would torment him, but he felt unable to seek help from the staff and would remain in his room frightened. I asked Seth to draw the two figures on the dry erase board in the playroom. Together, we directly addressed the ghosts in his drawing, telling them how frightening they were and how difficult they made things for Seth. I then encouraged

Seth to use the water bottle in the playroom to squirt the figures. Seth was delighted as the "ghosts" melted away and their remnants ran down the board.

As Seth continued to bring his nighttime episodes into the playroom, we began an active process, through ritual and dramatic play, of enrolling him in the Ghostbusters Club. We watched a scene from this film, which is about a crew of men in New York City who fight ghosts using laser-like guns. We talked about the attributes necessary to be a Ghostbuster, and Seth agreed that he had some of these traits inside: bravery, strength, and the ability to face his fears. We played out scenarios in which the Ghostbusters (Seth and I) let the ghosts know who was in control and made them go away by shooting them with the spray bottle. This ritual of drawing, addressing, and eradicating the ghosts helped him to practice gaining mastery over his fears independently.

Finally, Seth was given a smaller version of the spray bottle in the playroom (this one without water) that he kept under his pillow at night. He was encouraged to use the same tactics outside of the playroom that he was practicing in sessions: "shooting" the ghosts and commanding them to go away. At the end of his admission, Seth reported full nights of sleep, and he brought the spray bottle with him when he left the hospital. His mother was engaged in supporting Seth's management of his psychotic process as he transitioned back into the community.

Seth did return for one more admission to the unit. He continued the superheroes work in the playroom. However, this time he brought a peer with similar issues into sessions. His connection with this boy marked the first friendship in Seth's life. In their dyadic work, Seth invoked his role as Superman and cast his peer in my previously held role of Batman; together they continued to fight monsters. Outside of the playroom, they began to help one another, lending ego support when the other was in crisis.

CONCLUSION

The case examples in this chapter provide illustrations of how superhero roles can be used as tools in individual therapy to address treatment goals that researchers have identified as being salient for boys. I have also applied these roles in a group context with male clients of all ages. In one session, adolescent boys memorably created the character of Bipolar Man. This unique superhero, played by a rotating cast, surfaced periodically to use his power in altering people's moods to positive effect in this group of depressed and socially isolated young men.

In Sam Raimi's (2002) film version of *Spider-Man*, there is a moment in which our hero fights the Green Goblin high above Manhattan's East River. At the point at which the superhero is most vulnerable, a group of people who have gathered on the bridge above unite to throw refuse at the villain. One character utters, "An attack against one is an attack against us all!" Even now, I have vivid memories of watching this film on opening night in New York City, eight months after the 2001 terrorist attacks. At the moment that the crowd in the movie banded together, the audience around me, who had experienced their city being terrorized, unanimously and cathartically burst into applause and cheered. Like the characters in the film, we became united, as a community. More than a few of us, perhaps, left the theater that night empowered, thinking that all the world needed to be saved from itself was a few more superheroes.

REFERENCES

Andronico, M. P. (1996). Fathering and being fathered. In Author (Ed.), *Men in groups: Insights, interventions, and psychoeducational work* (pp. 217–218). Washington, DC: American Psychological Association.

Archer, R. (1997). Tornadoes, boys, and superheroes: Externalizing conversations in the wake of a natural disaster. *Journal of Systemic Therapies, 16*(1), 73–82.

Aubrey, J. S., & Harrison, K. (2004). The gender-role content of children's favorite television programs and its links to their gender-related perceptions. *Media Psychology, 6*(2), 111–146.

Aydt, H., & Corsaro, W. A. (2003). Differences in children's construction of gender across culture. *American Behavioral Scientist, 46*(10), 1306–1325.

Baker, K., & Raney, A. A. (2007). Equally super? Gender-role stereotyping of superheroes in children's animated programs. *Mass Communication and Society, 10*(1), 25–41.

Baron-Cohen, S. (2003). *The essential difference: Male and female brains and the truth about autism.* New York: Basic Books.

Bearman, J. (2008/2009, December 25–January 8). The legend of Master Legend. *Rolling Stone, 1068/1069,* 70–77, 122.

Bem, S. L. (1987). Gender schema theory and its implications for child development: Raising gender-aschematic children in a gender-schematic society. In M. R. Walsh (Ed.), *The psychology of women: Ongoing debates* (pp. 226–248). New Haven, CT: Yale University Press.

Benenson, J. F., Carder, H. P., & Geib-Cole, S. J. (2008). The development of boys' preferential pleasure in physical aggression. *Aggressive Behavior, 34*(2), 154–166.

Betcher, K. W., & Pollack, W. S. (1993). *In a time of fallen heroes: The re-creation of masculinity.* New York: Guilford.

Bloch, D. (1978). *"So the witch won't eat me": Fantasy and the child's fear of infanticide.* Boston, MA: Houghton Mifflin.

Bongco, M. (2000). *Reading comics: Language, culture, and the concept of the superhero in comic books.* New York: Garland Publishing.

Bouzoukis, C. E. (2001). *Pediatric dramatherapy: They couldn't run, so they learned to fly.* London, UK: Jessica Kingsley.

Brooks, G. R. (2010). *Beyond the crisis of masculinity: A transtheoretical model for male-friendly therapy*. Washington, DC: American Psychological Association.

Cassidy, J. (2008). The nature of the child's ties. In J. Cassidy & P. R. Shaver (Eds.), *Handbook of attachment: Theory, research, and clinical applications* (2nd ed., pp. 3–22). New York: Guilford.

Cattanach, A. (2008). *Play therapy with abused children* (2nd ed.). London, UK: Jessica Kingsley.

Chodorow, N. (1978). *The reproduction of mothering: Psychoanalysis and the sociology of gender*. Berkeley, CA: University of California Press.

Chu, J. (2004). A relational perspective on adolescent boys' identity development. In N. Way & J. Y. Chu (Eds.), *Adolescent boys: Exploring diverse cultures of boyhood* (pp. 78–104). New York: NYU Press.

Clark, H. (2010). Mask of shame, mask of death: Some speculations on the shame of death. In J. Kauffman (Ed.), *The shame of death, grief, and trauma* (pp. 141–153). New York: Routledge.

Corbett, K. (2009). *Boyhoods: Rethinking masculinities*. New Haven, CT: Yale University Press.

Crenshaw, D., & Mordock, J. (2005). *A handbook of play therapy with aggressive children*. Lanham, MD: Jason Aronson.

D'Angelo, L. L., Weinberger, D. A., & Feldman, S. S. (1995). Like father, like son? Predicting male adolescents' adjustment from parents' distress and self-restraint. *Developmental Psychology, 31*(6), 883–896.

Diamond, M. J. (2007). *My father before me: How fathers and sons influence each other throughout their lives*. New York: Norton.

Diamond, M. J. (2009). Masculinity and its discontents: Making room for the "mother" inside the male—An essential achievement for healthy male gender identity. In B. Reis & R. Grossmark (Eds.), *Heterosexual masculinities: Contemporary perspectives from psychoanalytic gender theory* (pp. 23–53). New York: Routledge.

Eliot, L. (2009). *Pink brain, blue brain: How small differences grow into troublesome gaps—and what we can do about it*. New York: Houghton Mifflin Harcourt.

Feder, J., Levant, R. F., & Dean, J. (2008). Boys and violence: A gender-informed analysis. *Professional Psychology: Research and Practice, 38*(4), 385–391.

Gallo-Lopez, L. (2005). Drama therapy in the treatment of children with sexual behavior problems. In A. M. Weber & C. Haen (Eds.), *Clinical applications of drama therapy in child and adolescent treatment* (pp. 137–151). New York: Brunner-Routledge.

Goldberg, C. (1991). *Understanding shame*. Northvale, NJ: Jason Aronson.

Haen, C. (2007). "Make me wanna holler": Dramatic encounters with boys from the inner city. In V. A. Camilleri (Ed.), *Healing the inner city child: Creative arts therapies with at-risk youth* (pp. 212–228). London, UK: Jessica Kingsley.

Haen, C. (2008). Vanquishing monsters: Drama therapy for treating childhood trauma in the group setting. In C. A. Malchiodi (Ed.), *Creative interventions with traumatized children* (pp. 225–246). New York: Guilford.

Haen, C., & Brannon, K. H. (2002). Superheroes, monsters and babies: Roles of strength, destruction and vulnerability for emotionally disturbed boys. *The Arts in Psychotherapy, 29*(1), 31–40.

Haen, C., & Weber, A. M. (2009). Beyond retribution: Working through revenge fantasies with traumatized young people. *The Arts in Psychotherapy, 36*(2), 84–93.

Hyde, J. S. (1994). Can meta-analysis make feminist transformations in psychology? *Psychology of Women Quarterly, 18*(4), 451–462.

Jones, G. (2002). *Killing monsters: Why children need fantasy, super heroes, and make-believe violence.* New York: Basic Books.

Jones, K. A. (2008). Reconsidering psychoanalytic notions of paternal and maternal roles in situations of father-absence. *Journal of Contemporary Psychotherapy, 38*(4), 205–213.

Karr-Morse, R., & Wiley, M. S. (1998). *Ghosts from the nursery: Tracing the roots of violence.* New York: Atlantic Monthly Press.

Krugman, S. (1998). Men's shame and trauma in therapy. In W. S. Pollack & R. F. Levant (Eds.), *New psychotherapy for men* (pp. 167–190). New York: Wiley.

Lamb, M. E., & Lewis, C. (2004). The development and significance of father-child relationships in two-parent families. In M. E. Lamb (Ed.), *The role of the father in child development* (4th ed., pp. 272–306). New York: Wiley.

Levine, S. (1997). *Waking the tiger: Healing trauma.* Berkeley, CA: North Atlantic Books.

Lisak, D. (1995). Integrating a critique of gender in the treatment of male survivors of childhood abuse. *Psychotherapy, 32*(2), 258–269.

Maccoby, E. E. (1990). Gender and relationships: A developmental account. *American Psychologist, 45*(4), 513–520.

Maccoby, E. E. (2002). Gender and group process: A developmental perspective. *Current Directions in Psychological Science, 11*(2), 54–58.

Mamet, D. (1989). Kryptonite: A psychological appreciation. In D. Mamet, *Some freaks* (pp. 175–180). New York: Penguin Books.

Mattson, C., & Park, N. (2008). The positive psychology of superheroes. In R. B. Rosenberg (Ed.), *The psychology of superheroes: An unauthorized exploration* (pp. 5–18). Dallas: Benbella Books.

Nader, K. (2007). *Understanding and assessing trauma in children and adolescents: Measures, methods, and youth in context.* New York: Routledge.

Paechter, C. (2007). *Being boys, being girls: Learning masculinities and femininities.* New York: Open University Press.

Paley, V. G. (1984). *Boys & girls: Superheroes in the doll corner.* Chicago, IL: University of Chicago Press.

Pecora, N. (1992). Superman/superboys/supermen: The comic book hero as socializing agent. In S. Craig (Ed.), *Men, masculinity, and the media* (pp. 61–77). Newbury Park, CA: Sage.

Perry, B. (1997). Incubated in terror: Neurodevelopmental factors in the "cycle of violence." In J. D. Osofsky (Ed.), *Children in a violent society* (pp. 124–149). New York: Guilford.

Perry, I. (2008). "Tell us how it feels to be a problem": Hip hop longings and poor young black men. In E. Anderson (Ed.), *Against the wall: Poor, young, black, and male* (pp. 165–177). Philadelphia, PA: University of Pennsylvania Press.

Pinker, S. (2008). *The sexual paradox: Men, women, and the real gender gap.* New York: Scribner.

Pollack, W. S. (1998). *Real boys: Rescuing our sons from the myths of boyhood.* New York: Random House.

Pruett, K. D. (2000). *Fatherneed: Why father care is as essential as mother care for your child.* New York: Warner Books.

Pynoos, R. S., Steinberg, A. M., & Goenjian, A. (1996). Traumatic stress in child-hood and adolescence: Recent developments and current controversies. In B. van der Kolk, A. C. McFarlane, & L. Weisaeth (Eds.), *Traumatic stress: The effects of overwhelming experience on mind, body and society* (pp. 331–358). New York: Guilford.

Raimi, S. (Director). (2002). *Spider-Man* [DVD]. Available from Columbia Pictures.

Robertie, K., Weidenbenner, R., Barrett, L., & Poole, R. (2007). A super milieu: Using superheroes in the residential treatment of adolescents with sexual behavior problems. In L. C. Rubin (Ed.), *Using superheroes in counseling and play therapy* (pp. 143–168). New York: Springer.

Rovin, J. (1985). *The encyclopedia of superheroes.* New York: Facts on File Publications.

Rubin, L. C. (2005). Superheroes and heroic journeys: Re-claiming loss in adop-tion. *Journal of Creativity in Mental Health, 1*(3/4), 237–252.

Rubin, L. C. (2007). Introduction: Look, up in the sky! An introduction to the use of superheroes in psychotherapy. In Author (Ed.), *Using superheroes in counseling and play therapy* (pp. 3–21). New York: Springer.

Scharff, D. E. (1992). *Refinding the object and reclaiming the self.* Northvale, NJ: Jason Aronson.

Schore, A. N. (1994). *Affect regulation and the origin of the self: The neurobiology of emotional development.* Hillsdale, NJ: Lawrence Erlbaum.

Schore, A. N. (2009). Right brain affect regulation: An essential mechanism of development, trauma, dissociation, and psychotherapy. In D. Fosha, D. J. Siegel, & M. F. Solomon (Eds.), *The healing power of emotion: Affective neuroscience, development & clinical practice* (pp. 112–144). New York: Norton.

Selekman, M. D. (1997). *Solution-focused therapy with children: Harnessing family strengths for systemic change.* New York: Guilford.

Smith, C. E., Fischer, K. W., & Watson, M. W. (2009). Toward a refined view of aggressive fantasy as a risk factor for aggression: Interaction effects involv-ing cognitive and situational variables. *Aggressive Behavior, 35*(4), 1–11.

Sobel, C. B. (1980). The use of the superhero with a group of latency-aged boys in a school setting. *Pratt Institute Creative Arts Therapy Review, 1*(1), 44–49.

Spivey, M., & Knowlton, S. (2008). Anti-heroism in the continuum of good and evil. In R. B. Rosenberg (Ed.), *The psychology of superheroes: An unauthorized exploration* (pp. 51–63). Dallas: Benbella Books.

Tate, C. (2008). An appetite for destruction: Aggression and the Batman. In R. B. Rosenberg (Ed.), *The psychology of superheroes: An unauthorized exploration* (pp. 135–145). Dallas: Benbella Books.

Thompson, T. L., & Zerbinos, E. (1995). Gender roles in animated cartoons: Has the picture changed in 20 years? *Sex Roles, 32*(9–10), 651–673.

Tyre, P. (2008). *The trouble with boys: A surprising report card on our sons, their problems at school, and what parents and educators must do.* New York: Crown Publishers.

Walker, B. M. (2004). Frames of self: Capturing working-class British boys' identities through photographs. In N. Way & J. Y. Chu (Eds.), *Adolescent boys: Exploring diverse cultures of boyhood* (pp. 31–58). New York: New York University Press.

Wegner, C. (2007). Superheroes in play therapy with an attachment disordered child. In L. C. Rubin (Ed.), *Using superheroes in counseling and play therapy* (pp. 193–211). New York: Springer.

Wexler, D. B. (2009). *Men in therapy: New approaches for effective treatment.* New York: Norton.

Widzer, M. E. (1977). The comic-book superhero: A study of the family romance fantasy. *The Psychoanalytic Study of the Child, 32,* 565–603.

Wineburgh, A. L. (2000). Treatment of children with absent fathers. *Child and Adolescent Social Work Journal, 1*(4), 255–273.

Winnicott, D. W. (1971). *Playing and reality.* London, UK: Tavistock.

Zeki, S. (2009). *Splendors and miseries of the brain: Love, creativity, and the quest for human happiness.* Chichester, West Sussex, UK: Wiley-Blackwell.

Breaking Through With Art

Art Therapy Approaches for Working With At-Risk Boys

JASON CRUZ

Founded in 1988, Raw Art Works (RAW) is a community arts organization with the mission to ignite the desire to create and the confidence to succeed in underserved youth. RAW offers 38 free arts
groups, including a film school, for youth ages 6–19. RAW is located
in Lynn, Massachusetts, an economically disadvantaged city nine miles
north of Boston where many children lack the basic resources, security, and support to enable their healthy development. In Lynn, all
of the challenges of growing up are compounded by the difficulties
of life in an inner city area with few resources. Out of 351 cities and
towns in Massachusetts, Lynn is currently fifth most dangerous and
consistently ranks in the top 10 (Morgan, Morgan, & Boba, 2009).
Police say that there are over 30 gangs in Lynn, and nearly half of all
violent crime in the city is gang related (Shannon Community Safety
Initiative, 2009). Only 70.7% of Lynn public school students graduate
within four years of entering high school (Massachusetts Department
of Elementary and Secondary Education, 2009). The teen birth rate in
Lynn is more than twice the state average (Massachusetts Department
of Public Health, 2010).

Since 1994, I have worked at RAW with boys and young men ages 6 to 21 who come from all cultural, socioeconomic, and ethnic backgrounds and walks of life. While the majority of the work I do at RAW is group based, I have also worked individually with court-mandated boys as well as males who are active gang members. I work with boys in the eighth and ninth grades who are experimenting with drugs and some who, by late middle school, are already addicted to drugs and alcohol. I work with boys who are homeless, have learning disabilities, are immigrants (both legal and illegal) or children of immigrants, and who are young fathers.

Some of my more challenging work has been done in lock-ups and homeless shelters. When I started work in lock-ups, the stereotype was that art therapists typically approached their clients with the belief that "expressing yourself" was the only goal. I challenge boys to take ownership of their past, present, and future lives, and to do the hard work associated with self-reflection and growth. I focus on what is happening now and help boys create a positive orientation to their futures.

RAW offers three boys' groups that meet weekly for two hours during the school year and occasionally on weekends. These groups are free and boys attend voluntarily (i.e., they are not court mandated). Last year, RAW's boys' groups served 68 of our most at-risk youth: 85% were youth of color, 78% qualified for free or reduced lunch, and over 60% were from single-parent homes. A significant number of the boys had absent or incarcerated parents and lacked strong male role models in their lives.

Boyz Lync serves middle-school-aged boys and Men 2 Be serves high school boys. The Good 2 Go crew spends up to eight additional hours working in the community on public art projects. Men 2 Be and Good 2 Go meet during the summer months as well. RAW's three boys' programs provide boys with a safe place to belong and a community of peers that offers an alternative to gangs, drugs, violence, and street life. At RAW boys find creative and constructive ways to express their feelings, tell their life stories, take appropriate risks, deal with stress, and gain recognition for their art. They receive the sustained attention of caring adults who set higher expectations than the boys typically encounter in school and the community. RAW also provides opportunities for older boys to learn to mentor younger boys and to lead community projects. Many boys spend several years at RAW, gaining skills and responsibility as they mature.

This chapter will explore the therapeutic process used in art therapy groups for boys, including strategies for initial engagement in the art-making process, the selection and use of art materials, and the group dynamics within an art therapy group. I will address the developmental differences between preteen and teen boys and offer different art therapy approaches for each age group. I will explore the use of art to externalize painful experiences, to reframe conflict, and to gain insight and self-discovery. I will then present case studies detailing practical examples of therapeutic approaches that were most effective in helping boys to transcend their limitations, diagnoses, and criminal records.

WHAT IS ART THERAPY?

Art therapy uses the act of creating art to positively affect the physical, mental, and emotional states of participants. It has been used successfully with children, adolescents, adults, and the elderly and can benefit individuals, groups, and families. Art therapists use prompts and discussions so that unskilled participants feel comfortable creating art and revealing the meanings behind their work (Liebmann, 1986). They make sure that participants understand that the goal is not to create beautiful art but to explore ideas (Liebmann, 1986). A key belief is that the process of creating art helps people learn about themselves, solve problems, improve their interpersonal skills and self-image, deal with stress, and manage their behavior. The processes, results, and reflections that follow allow people to come to terms with traumatic events and stress, enhance their previous ways of thinking, and gain pleasure from self-actualization.

Art therapy incorporates practices from the fields of psychotherapy, counseling, and human development into its foundation of visual art of various forms (including drawings, paintings, collages, and sculptures) and the creative processes that give birth to this art. Art therapy can be used to treat mental disorders, anxiety, and depression. It also helps people come to terms with violence and abuse, as well as issues concerning relationships and family, disabilities, illnesses, social problems, trauma, and loss (American Art Therapy Association, n.d.).

BOYS AND ART THERAPY

The boys I work with often lack well-developed ways to effectively express themselves. This may be attributed to gender differences associated with language facility and emotive processing. Unlike the female brain, which appears to enable the verbalization of emotional information more quickly than the male brain, the brains of boys who experience pain or conflict often create the stress hormone cortisol but do not adequately process the related stress-inducing emotional content. This puts them at risk of devolving to fight-or-flight responses, of becoming either aggressive or withdrawn (Gurian & Henley, 2001).

Boys' underdeveloped self-expressive ability can be linked as well to the cultural norms and emotional challenges associated with their environments. Many of the at-risk boys I work with receive mixed messages in their homes, often single-parent homes: "You are the man of the house, but *do as I say*." They do not feel empowered but instead pressured. They feel pressure to join gangs and pressure to live more successful lives than their fathers have. They have extremely limited outlets for expressing their feelings. Boys get the message that real men don't have feelings and don't cry. Many boys, lacking male role models, turn to the media (cable TV, MTV, and video games) to understand how a man should express himself. They see anger and aggression, unhealthy relationships, and domestic violence.

I work with boys to create art to help them acknowledge and make sense of feelings, beliefs, events, and trauma, and to help them choose life-affirming futures. I offer them permission to have feelings and to ask why. Success for me is evidenced in moments such as an 8-year-old boy saying, "Wait, I need time to write down my feelings," or in having a 15-year-old boy write in his year-end evaluation, "Before I came to RAW, I felt shy and nervous and angry. Now I feel creative and like I have a future and like I belong somewhere. I don't want to leave because RAW makes me feel better about myself." Young men in their twenties come back to share both good and bad news and to ask advice on relationships, fathering, legal issues, education, and careers. Through an extended period of making art, trust is built and connections are formed.

Creating art together in a safe environment can help the art therapist and the boy understand the concerns that boys can't express verbally. Many boys, especially those who are struggling academically, socially, and emotionally, seem to respond well to experiential learning (Gurian & Henley, 2001). I observe that they work best by "making stuff."

Through the vehicle of art I can help the child to discover and externalize those cognitions and affect that may be hidden or repressed. An image or a three-dimensional piece can represent a feeling or a thought, and the act of bringing it into creation can make it more tangible. The artwork can then become a catalyst for discussion, which reinforces the externalization process and helps to deepen and clarify the expression. Through art, fear or trauma can be addressed and resolved (Malchiodi, 2007). The arts can heal.

The key role of the art therapist in working with boys is to convey these messages:

- I see and hear you.
- I want to understand you.
- I value you and what you have to say.

Far beyond what is being created—the end product—I pay attention to the process a boy is undergoing to create art. His choices regarding materials, size, color, and intensity of stroke are all part of the expressive process and represent aspects of the boy. The uses of imagery and metaphor are important, indirect ways to confront feelings, conflicts, hopes, and dreams.

Working with young men is really about the potential of an issue or theme. Where can it go? How can I help them take it there so that they find answers, or at least wake up to other perspectives or reasons to keep going? Society often doesn't allow males to say that they hurt or wonder. At a very young age, many of the young men I work with stop being kids who openly dream and hope. Often I wonder if they have the words and voice to share what they feel and think.

Initial Engagement Strategies

Through initial engagement strategies I aim to gain trust by being non-judgmental and genuinely interested in getting to know what makes each boy tick. I try to never impose my belief system on the kids; instead, I try to understand their background stories. I begin by getting to know and then tapping into each boy's interest. One common interest of many at-risk boys is tagging, or graffiti, which I have used as an entry point for discussion. Boys love to make their mark. I begin by teaching them a few simple techniques for lettering. Once they have basic skill with the lettering technique, I have them write their name in graffiti-style letters. After they outline the letters for their name, I ask them to introduce their favorite color and then, within their name, to add representations of other things that are important to them, such as foods, hobbies, and music.

When they share their finished product, I often ask them to describe what motivated them to choose certain images or colors. This can be a nonthreatening way to get a boy to begin to open up about himself. This is also an initial way for me, the art therapist, to become acquainted with the boy and to gather some data and insight about him through what he has chosen to express in his art.

A follow-up activity can introduce the concept that there are many layers to a person, many facets, and many representations. In a common art therapy exercise, I ask the boys to create three concentric circles. The inner circle represents *how I really am*. The next circle represents *how I see myself* and the outside circle represents *how the world sees me*. This exercise can be profound as boys recognize the many dimensions of themselves and the choices they make in how they present themselves to others.

An effective approach I have used to engage gang-related or incarcerated boys is to ask them to create a timeline of their lives. I keep the assignment open-ended and let them interpret it as they will. They use pens and paper, and markers for color. Some make a chart like an EKG with sharply rising and falling lines. I ask what is below the line. Some create a series of points on a line. Often they are able to identify the exact point at which they stopped feeling safe, when a traumatic event happened, or when they felt they needed, often prematurely, to leave their childhood behind. Sometimes I ask the boys to draw their parents' or siblings' timelines. We discuss whether and how these timelines differ from their own and I validate that the boys' timelines (and lives) can be different from their parents'. In a related project, which works well for all boys, I ask them to create a road map as a way to look ahead, visualize a future path, and begin to set goals.

When asking the boys to show me their work, I am never judging. I always point out that there is no good art or bad art; it is just art. These kids have frequently been told that they are not capable of achievement. I try to never project my thoughts about the art onto the boy; I always seek to draw him out and let him lead the discussion. I try to keep things open-ended. I frequently "play dumb" and ask questions to clarify what his message may be: "What is that dude doing?" or "Why is he so small compared with the other guys?"

Materials: Use and Selection

Boys love to work with a wide range of materials. Variety is key, with safety as the only (and critical) consideration. Be aware, however, that based on a boy's history, some materials can cause him to regress due to either their textures, his lack of control, or his inability to perfect the medium. Boys tend to like to see how things work, like to use tools, and enjoy a challenge. Successful boy themes have included animals, vehicles, sports, robots, and aliens.

You don't need a lot of money for supplies; I challenge boys to make something out of what is available—found objects, stones, wood, and things from their city, neighborhood, or from nature. We have made people from paper clips and erasers and shared their unique life stories. I have challenged boys to create a home out of chicken wire, twist ties, and dowels. In doing so, they learn to innovate, and that is empowering for them.

Boys like to be given supplies and a mission, and the freedom to create. In discussing the value of art as an exploratory process and the conditions that result in successful outcomes, art therapist Rubin (1984) wrote, "The conditions essential for such a 'framework for freedom' include sufficient, organized, predictable space and time, as well as a trusting, interested, accepting, supportive attitude on the part of the clinician" (p. 17).

Supplies/materials have included clay for sculpting, papier-mâché, pencils, pens, markers, chalk, paint, paper, fabric, found materials for collage, metal, stone, and wire. Tools have included glue guns, hammers, RotoZips, metal shears, drills, electric saws, nail guns, and staple guns. I invite boys to break out of stereotypic behavior and employ sewing in their artwork. Boys ages 11 to 14 created multilayered self-portraits representing their inner and outer selves that were then stitched together. They learned that sewing is hard, but it made them slow down and think. One 13-year-old boy said, "The needle is my action and the stitch is the result of my action."

Using a variety of materials enables me to frame the discussion in terms of metaphor. When they are using the glue gun, I ask, "Who is it that holds things together for you?" Or, when hammering: "Hey, that nail isn't going in straight but you keep banging it. What's that about? Looks like you have to start over and get it straight." I find those times allow for teachable moments where I don't directly confront the kid or give the impression that he isn't doing a good job.

WORKING WITH BOYS IN GROUPS

According to Yalom and Leszcz (2005), several beneficial outcomes often accompany group work. These curative factors include social interaction, which is especially valuable for boys who feel isolated; universality, or the feeling that one is not alone in his troubles; catharsis through sharing painful experiences with supportive group members; and the instilling of hope when group members share their stories of overcoming difficulties and positive outcomes. Liebmann (1986) stated that group work fosters social learning, and that some individuals who would feel uncomfortable with one-on-one therapy can benefit from group therapy. In art therapy groups, these curative factors become actualized in a process that intertwines art making with verbal processing and dialogue.

"Checking in" is an important ritual at the beginning of my groups. The mood of group members when they arrive is an important factor that is influenced by where they have just come from and what they were doing immediately prior to the session (Liebmann, 1986). I often ask the boys to rate their day on a scale of 1 to 10. During check-in they respond to each other's ups and downs. Issues raised during check-in provide a valuable opening to expand upon during art making. Topics we have explored through group art making have included anger, fear, stereotypes, homophobia, teasing and joking around versus disrespecting, what it means to have a girlfriend, sex/sexuality, choices, gangs, drugs and alcohol, parents, incarcerated parents or siblings, what "being cool" means, and the "isms" (e.g., racism, sexism). Check-in is also an opportunity to remind the group of any new or established rules or time limits.

The initial engagement period within the group provides a way for boys to gain insight about what characteristics and experiences they share in common. Making art can provide both a distraction and a catalyst for engagement and meaningful discussion. As they open up and discuss their art, one by one the boys in the room individually and collectively relax. They realize that they are not so different from one another; they are not alone in their struggles and fears. Many of the artists have similar backgrounds and needs, and they can benefit from one another's feedback. As the group achieves cohesion, the boys learn to cooperate and share their ideas while appreciating and recognizing others. They begin to imitate the positive behaviors of other members and improve their social skills. Some boys exhibit aggressive and antisocial behaviors when they first arrive at RAW but learn to treat each other with respect and recognize similarities. Positive emotion tends to be infectious; it is not uncommon to see a lot of giggling or a group of middle school boys dancing in their places as they work on their art. When a boy comes to group with negative emotions, the group can provide valuable support in talking it out, with other boys expressing how they have worked through similar situations.

Groups provide the opportunity to engage with boys from different backgrounds. One group integrated at-risk, low-income boys with boys from a neighboring middle-class town. In one session, I gave the kids ordinary cardboard shipping tags and asked them to write how they are labeled by others on the front and who they really are on the back. It was valuable insight for all the kids to see that even between diverse economic groups there were significant commonalities. In this way, art served as a bridge between diverse groups, giving them permission to be vulnerable and an opportunity to influence one another.

One downside of group art therapy is the challenge of protecting confidentiality. We have a rule: "What happens in group stays in group." In my experience this norm has been largely respected and upheld. If a young man has an issue that needs one-to-one attention, I make sure to find time to address it after group.

> Since coming to RAW I have been able to talk to people nicely and be more understanding. I want to improve in my art and being loving. RAW can make you a better man.

> —Miguel

DIFFERENT APPROACHES FOR DIFFERENT AGES

Many developmental models have been integrated into art therapy theory. I have found Erickson's (1995) developmental stages as most germane to the work I do with boys. According to Erickson, the school-aged boy (6 to 12 years) in his latency phase is capable of and open to learning new skills and gaining knowledge at a rapid pace. This is also a very social stage of development. Feelings of inadequacy and inferiority among peers can create difficulties in terms of competence and self-esteem. Although parents are still very important, as their world expands the boys' relationship within the school and neighborhood becomes more significant.

The youngest boys I work with are learning to work and play with their peers. They are striving to gain competence and are at risk of feeling inferior as they compare themselves to others. One encouraging adult can make an enormous difference in their lives. In working with this age group it is important to be clear, concise, and consistent. Boys at this age are still not too cool to try new things and are more willing to try less than macho ways of handling issues that may arise.

Middle school boys are mastering cognitive and social skills. They are eager to make friends, learn new things, know themselves, and explore where they fit in with the world. They have gained a better ability to focus and are more patient and willing to experiment with more controllable materials. As they enter the teenage years, if they are being forced into a "man of the house" role at home, they start to lose hope, in some cases becoming quite susceptible to outside influences.

In the adolescent stage (12 to 18 years), developing an identity is a key focus, along with a desire to "make a mark" (Riley, 2001). Up to this stage, according to Erikson (1950), development mostly depends upon what is done to us. From here on out, development depends primarily upon *what we do*. Adolescence is a stage at which a boy is neither a child nor an adult, and life definitely gets more complex as he attempts to establish his own identity, struggles with social interactions, and grapples with moral issues. High school boys are further down the road with the primary adolescent task of forming ego identity. They are determining who they are and where they fit in the larger social order. Their anxiety to fit in makes them increasingly at risk for gang involvement.

In discussing this age group, Linesch (1988) wrote, "Many of the struggles experienced by the adolescent involve conflicts of identity and self-expression. These conflicts can be made accessible for exploration through art productions in a way that they cannot through verbal expression" (p. ix). Peer group relationships become central, and as they approach the young adulthood stage (ages 18 to 35) boys need to have a solid foundation for succeeding in affiliation and love.

This year I learned a lot of things about what I do and how I do it. I learned what type of person I am. Things that I wasn't capable of before, I am capable of now. I am also part of the community now since I am committed.

—Tony

Representative Projects

Younger children are comfortable with storytelling and readily integrate stories with their artwork. Projects for the youngest boys (ages 6 to 10) might include asking the boys what they would look and sound like if they were trees, animals, cars, or songs. I ask them to draw or paint a representation of themselves in this way. Sometimes I have them create a sculpture from clay. When they are finished, I ask, "Why did you choose what you did? What about you makes you like a tiger, or a drum, that song, or a truck?" In one project, children created an identity of another child to whom they ascribed feelings, preferences, and fears. They created a face from scrap pieces of cardboard and paint and, on the reverse side, listed the child's likes, dislikes, and fears. When the child presented his friend to the group, we learned a lot about the child himself: "This is Drake. Drake likes to rap about his life. He likes to help his sister. He doesn't like it when his father yells at his mom." In another group, the members were engaged in collaboratively planning, designing, and building a city using scrap wood and found objects. In order to learn what they were thinking, I asked questions such as "What are the rules of your city? Why?"

As boys mature, they develop the increasing abilities to understand abstract concepts and engage with challenging art techniques and materials that may include wood carving, etching, and metal work. Projects for middle school boys have included:

Armor. Middle school boys made armor out of scrap tin and rivets, embossed it with hammered nails, and used Sharpies to draw a design or crest on it that represented who they are. In presenting their artwork to the rest of the group, they talked about what their designs symbolized, the battles they faced, and what their armor protected them from (e.g., bullies, gang members, family abuse). One young boy, who did not exude any confidence prior to the project, stood proud wearing his armor. He put his helmet on and said, "If someone calls me names it just bounces off my shield."

Robots. More ambitious art projects can span a few sessions. Boys began by creating a blueprint, then a design, and then construction of their own unique robot from a variety of traditional and found materials. The boys addressed the following: "What is your robot's name? What does he like to do? What does he need from you?" The process and skills gained from reflection, planning, design, and execution can be transferred to other areas of a boy's life.

High school boys are ready for more varied and abstract concepts and media. Identity and self-reflection are key themes. Some examples include:

Portraiture. The question "Who are you?" is a meaningful one for boys of this age group. Portraiture projects involve creating realistic or abstract self-images through photography, drawing, sculpture, and painting. Many of the art projects we do begin with a self-portrait. It helps to honor the boy, to give him an opportunity to see himself more clearly and with greater understanding and compassion. In one project, older boys created a self-portrait starting with a simple line drawing of their face. They filled in the face with torn images and "found poetry" from magazines.

Lyrically speaking Using photocopies of a CD, the boys were asked to tell their story or respond to a question using only the song titles. Then they created a new album cover based on their story. Projection of their stories onto these song titles was a key way to get to understand what was going through their minds. One poignant example is Tupac Shakur's (2000) song "The Rose That Grew From Concrete," which describes overcoming the circumstances of one's home and environment using the rose as a metaphor for a young man, with the concrete representing his inner city upbringing. The speaker in Tupac's song says that he appreciates the rose in spite of its blemishes because these are the inevitable consequences of its difficult existence.

This song resonated with all the boys, even as their individual interpretations differed. Using this idea of projection can help a young man start finding his words and not be so afraid to share them. Young men with learning differences seem to be particularly inclined to identify with music. Perhaps, in taking the pressure of writing off them, they are better able to look at themselves and what they really want to say instead of wondering if they wrote it correctly.

Use of Metaphor and Imagery

Imagery and metaphor provide vehicles for discussing important issues in an indirect, nonconfrontational way. Boys experience powerful insight, an "aha moment," when they discover something rather than being told it directly. Artistic metaphors are indirect expressions, and therefore less psychologically threatening than direct statements. The process of making something external that represents internal feelings can help to reframe experiences. The visual image makes the feeling concrete, enabling the artist to examine it from a different perspective, to gain a sense of control and ownership, and to unblock emotions (Moon, 2007).

Exploring perspective is one valuable exercise. The use of perspective in art can start a discussion about different ways of looking at things in life and recognizing different points of view. Boxes or telescopes with photographs pasted inside and lit by flashlights reveal new perspective to the boys. Sources of light and shadow can be discussed in relation to a boy's life.

In one commonly used project on perspective, each boy, while listening to music, with eyes closed or covered, draws a random design. This technique of using "squiggles" as a way to communicate with children was introduced in 1958 by pediatrician and psychoanalyst D. W. Winnicott for both diagnostic and therapeutic purposes (Rubin, 2001). When the music stops, each boy searches for a hidden design in his squiggle. He can turn the drawing 45, 90, 180, and 360 degrees. A partner helps him by giving his perspective on what he finds in the drawing, thus validating or expanding the perspective of the design. The found design is then colored with markers to bring it out of the scribbles and final lines are added for emphasis. Each boy then presents his findings to the group.

Through this process a boy discovers, acknowledges, and shares with others an insight into himself. Art is a valuable vehicle for making the internal more visible for both the boy and for others. Rubin (2001) wrote,

"Art can greatly enhance the analytic experience of insight ('seeing in'). This is probably so because art is concrete and visual, in addition to its value in *uncovering* unconscious imagery and *discovering* unconscious fantasies and impulses" (p. 25).

> Sometimes it's hard to look at my artwork because I have to look at me.
>
> —John

Another metaphor that can be explored is that of black and white and shades of gray. In color theory, there are three attributes in every color: hue (where it is on the color wheel), intensity (how bright or dull it is), and value (where it exists on the continuum from darkness to lightness). Boys experiment with making shades from lightest to darkest and experience the process of creating gradation. Teaching about black and white can provide a foundation for all kinds of valuable discussion, such as: "Do you know the statement that something is black and white ... meaning clear? What are you clear about? What gray areas exist for you?" It also can provide a vehicle for discussing racial difference.

The use of pattern can be another metaphor that boys can relate to. They can design a pattern using colors, stamps, or objects and then identify and consider patterns in their own lives that may be positive or destructive. In our art therapy sessions we often use the metaphor of layering to discuss the multiple layers found in a human. Through projects that include making triptychs from found wood and creating boxes, boys explore: "Who am I on the inside? What do I reveal to others? How do other people perceive me?" These projects can also involve objects or words that are hidden, buried, or obscured that represent feelings that are buried, hurts that live deep inside, or hidden strengths that a child is hoping to tap into.

My a-maze-ing life. In this project boys drew a large maze with the endpoint representing the person they truly are inside or who they want to be (their true or idealized self). They explored: "How do you find the 'real you' through the external difficulties you face, peer pressures, and false personalities?" A second version of this project involved making a three-dimensional version of their drawn mazes based on their lives, using only cardboard and glue guns. In this version, the artist created three-dimensional versions of the peer pressures, external stressors, and false personalities they may encounter. They were invited to include the people who help them get to the endpoint or their goals.

Two sides of me. This project addressed the two worlds that at-risk teens inhabit. We took two photos of each teen boy, one of him dressed in neat, professional clothing, and the other of him in urban attire and baggy pants. The boys cut each photo down the middle and integrated them as a single photo. Boys then wrote about their two sides. In a similarly themed project, middle school boys made two t-shirts cut out of MDO board (a lightweight wood panel often used in sign making); one was flat and the other was cut in half to create a door. On the split shirt boys wrote the label they feel community or society puts on them. When they opened up the shirt, on the inside they wrote how they really see themselves and how they want to be labeled. The boys created a stenciled symbol to illustrate either the negative or the positive word.

Imagery, such as collage artwork, can provide a broad range of information. Collage is a commonly employed technique for self-expression and can be used as a way to integrate the pieces of the boys' complex selves. Collages consist of layers. Boys can begin by laying down what may be a "given" in their lives. Working outward from that starting point, they can layer on top what they would like to add to their lives. I use simple materials and current media (e.g., newspaper, magazines) as supplies to address what's really going on in their worlds. I ask them to reach beyond the typical male themes of sports and cars to find more ways to represent themselves. Sometimes I provide only magazines that are more female-oriented or from an environment they are not familiar with in order to force them to think outside the box. In one collage project about the human experience, boys were asked to represent "what society tells you, what you want to do, what needs to be done, and who or what is teaching you." Through this project, boys gained media literacy and confronted the contradictory and often destructive messages they receive from popular culture.

HEALING PROPERTIES OF THE ARTS

Art therapy came into being in the 1940s. It resulted from psychiatrists' interest in the art produced by patients with mental illnesses and educators' observations that children's artwork offered insight into their mental states and levels of development. Realizing that it both aided patients' recoveries and offered clues to their underlying problems, hospitals began to experiment with art therapy as a supplement to traditional therapy. Today it is a recognized and effective tool for treating and assisting participants (American Art Therapy Association, n.d.).

Art is often used to reframe painful experiences, to gain self-discovery, and to foster insight that can help support healing and moving forward. Art therapy emerged from the idea that art can be used not only to alleviate or contain feelings of trauma, fear, or anxiety, but also to repair, restore, and heal (Malchiodi, 2007). Art therapy is considered a mind-body intervention because it evokes the relaxation response. Recent work in neuroscience has provided evidence that traumatic events are stored in the right brain, the nonverbal and emotional hemisphere (Solomon & Heide, 2005). The process of creating a visual and concrete representation of the trauma serves to build the necessary bridge for ascribing meaning and, with time, language to the painful event, making art an effective agent of healing (Lusebrink, 1990). In groups I employ the power of art making in the following ways to help boys deal with loss.

Communicating about loss. Projects can involve passing along a message to a lost loved one, either living or deceased, through visual art and writing. For at-risk boys, whose connection to male figures is often fragmented (more than half the boys I work with are from female-headed homes), this piece of work provides a way to connect tangibly and ritualistically. It can be cathartic to express all the feelings that have not yet been (or can never be) expressed. Boys have created moving tributes to late relatives, absent or incarcerated fathers, and beloved grandparents.

Confronting a loss. Following a drive-by shooting that resulted in the death of a 13-year-old to gang violence, a group of boys ages 11 to 14 explored "13" (what that age is like—the good, the bad, the ugly—and what opportunities and difficulties it brought). Working in teams, they identified their feelings about the young man's death and expressed them with Cray-Pas on recycled canvases, onto which they also integrated newspaper stories of the incident. Through this exercise, we were able to confront the real (and valid) fears that at-risk boys face living in neighborhoods where violence is common. The activity helped the boys identify and name fears and bond through their shared loss.

Broken record. Boys were presented with vinyl LPs and told to give them names representing hurt or loss. They made lists of situations where they got stuck or "skipped." Then they smashed the records into pieces and used hot glue to reshape the pieces into sculptures. They renamed the records to reflect the change that had occurred. This activity represented catharsis and finding new beginnings instead of returning to old habits.

Torn words. Boys were asked to write about painful experiences and the people who caused them pain. Then they tore up the paper they had written on and used the pieces to construct new three-dimensional objects. Some of the boys created flowers or trees. The activity was about naming and recognizing sources of pain and integrating them into something new.

To heal a community in need of lifting up, the boys have written affirming messages and placed them in collaged and painted matchboxes, leaving them randomly throughout the city. A group of young men in my Good 2 Go public art crew works with city organizations to create public art and murals with themes of transformation and potential. Public utility boxes, walls, and benches can also be canvases for inspiring messages and can fulfill boys' needs for making their mark in the community. Old street signs donated by the city can be modified to deliver critical messages such as "STOP: Before You Judge Someone" or "SLOW: Think Before You Fight."

CASE STUDIES

Danny

Danny was a 17-year-old, White, heavily tattooed, court-mandated client who was committed to the Department of Youth Services. He was from a very low-income family that had a long history with the law. His father was in and out of prison, and his mother was a drug user. When I first met Danny, he was into drug and alcohol use. Danny was not in a gang but ran the streets and was a "brawler." He showed signs of attention deficit hyperactivity disorder (ADHD), was very impatient, and had impulse control issues. Danny was very much aware that his family was perceived poorly in the community and expressed a lack of hope about his ability to transcend this history. He was kind-hearted and really wanted to change but felt conflicted on what was really right and wrong in the context of his life and was not supported by his environment to break the cycle of negative living. For the first year, I worked individually with Danny. He always seemed to skate on the surface, never wanting to ask or answer the tough questions. He was quick to blame others. The first noticeable change came when Danny created a tiger from found wood and began to describe with energy the qualities of the tiger that he also possessed. He displayed a spark of life that was previously unseen. Then he made two figures from wood: one was a boy behind jail bars and the other was a boy relaxing and reading a newspaper. He created a concrete representation of the choices his future could hold.

In his second year, Danny attended group instead of individual art therapy. His trust level continued to increase and he was willing to share more of his past and to envision a future. In a project called "Shoes," boys in the group each created a unique shoe ("If you were a shoe, what would you look like? What is your sole like? Where has your shoe traveled?"). Danny said that his beat-up shoe had "seen a lot," and detailed some of the disappointment and pain he had experienced in his life. At the same time, Danny started setting goals for himself and began to model for the other group members a more engaged and forward-thinking presence. Danny most recently created a piece made of several layers of found cardboard. The layers represented his complex history, the fact that he is a product of his past experiences, and the fact that he is not one-dimensional. On the top layer, he fashioned a tree with branches boldly reaching upward. At the top of one branch, he painted a bright, red bird.

Jona

Jona came to RAW at age 13 and has been here for five years. He is diagnosed with ADHD, is Latino, and comes from a single-parent home where he is the oldest of three children from an overly protective mother. He often deals with anger about feeling trapped and frustration at not being academically successful. Early in his time at RAW, Jona seemed so eager to fit in that he "overcommunicated" and was boastful. Because of his disability, he often missed social cues.

Over time, Jona began to relax and realize that he was welcome at RAW and didn't need to push so hard or feel so anxious about fitting in. When he found security he began to develop his voice and grow his talent. He draws as a way to find peace and relax. When his home seems chaotic he goes to the basement to sketch. At RAW, building, sculpting, and using tools to create three-dimensional artworks seem to fully engage his brain and calm him down. He perseveres where he once would quit out of impatience and frustration.

Jona has been able to chart significant development both as an artist and as a leader. He has gained skills in art forms from graffiti to anime. He has developed his own style and characters that have become part of public art installations. Jona has used art to express views on justice and manhood. His "Bill of Rights" artwork was displayed at the Boston Public Library, and his "Child Soldier" piece compellingly depicted the plight of young African boys forced into fighting. He has stayed committed through participation in Boys Lync and Men 2 Be, and now is a Good 2 Go community artist and a paid RAW Chief mentor who assists the therapists in art groups for younger children. For Jona, everything is a canvas.

He is confident and is teaching others how he has learned to use art as a tool for communication, confidence, and stress reduction. Through his successes he feels proud and validated. In his final evaluation, Jona wrote, "Before RAW I could not connect art to the life we live in. Now I can base my life on art."

CONCLUSION

I have had the honor of engaging with over 900 boys and young men since I began work as an art therapist. I have heard their stories and encouraged them to use the power of the arts to make meaning of and to improve their lives. I have witnessed how participation in art therapy groups delivers benefits far beyond the acquisition of art skills; for example, in their 2009 final evaluations, 100% of boys participating in my groups reported that they are better artists and feel proud of their accomplishments, and 100% reported that their family and community have responded positively to their art. Additionally, 100% said that because of RAW, they know more about what they believe in and have the courage to voice it; 89% have learned to work better with others and have been able to make good friends; and 78% feel that their attitude and effort toward school has improved because of their participation in RAW's boys' groups.

> Before I came to RAW, I felt shy and nervous and angry. Now I feel creative and like I have a future and like I belong somewhere. I don't want to leave because RAW makes me feel better about myself.
>
> —Karl

In this new age of information overload, Facebook, and downloadable entertainment, I think art becomes even more precious. Making art in a welcoming and safe environment with relevant, age-appropriate themes and materials gives boys a tactile connection to their world and the emotional tools they need to stay grounded. The most important guideline I can offer is to keep it real. Boys can sense if you are sincerely committed to working with them or if you are just going through the motions. Try to understand and respect what each one is carrying—at home and at school—and how it affects his view of himself and his future. The right word spoken at the right time in the art-making process can begin a healing process or lighten a heavy load.

REFERENCES

American Art Therapy Association. (n.d.). *History and background.* Retrieved from http://www.americanarttherapyassociation.org

Erickson, E. H. (1995). *Childhood and society.* New York: Vintage. (Original work published in 1950.)

Gurian, M., & Henley, P. (2001). *Boys and girls learn differently: A guide for teachers and parents.* New York: Jossey-Bass.

Liebmann, M. (1986). *Art therapy for groups: A handbook of themes, games and exercises.* Cambridge, MA: Brookline Books.

Linesch, D. G. (1988). *Adolescent art therapy.* New York: Brunner/Mazel.

Lusebrink, V. B. (1990). *Imagery and visual expression in therapy (Emotions, personality, and psychotherapy).* New York: Springer.

Malchiodi, C. (2007). *The art therapy sourcebook* (2nd ed.). New York: McGraw-Hill.

Massachusetts Department of Elementary and Secondary Education. (2009). *2009 graduation rate report (DISTRICT) for all students: 4-year graduation rate.* Retrieved from http://profiles.doe.mass.edu/state_report/gradrates.aspx

Massachusetts Department of Public Health. (2009). *Massachusetts Community Health Information Profile: Perinatal trends for Lynn.* Retrieved from http://www.mass.gov/Eeohhs2/docs/dph/masschip/perinatal_trends/perinatal-trendscity_townlynn.rtf

Moon, B. L. (2007). *The role of metaphor in art therapy: Theory, method, and experience.* Springfield, IL: Charles C. Thomas.

Morgan, K. O., Morgan, S., & Boba, R. (2009). *City crime rate rankings 2009–2010.* Retrieved from http://os.cqpress.com/citycrime/2009/CityCrime2009_Rank_Rev.pdf

Riley, S. (2001). Art therapy with adolescents. *Western Journal of Medicine, 175*(1), 54–57.

Rubin, J. A. (1984). *The art of art therapy.* Levittown, PA: Taylor & Francis Publishing.

Rubin, J. A. (2001). *Approaches to art therapy: Theory and technique* (2nd ed.). New York: Brunner-Routledge.

Shakur, T. (2000). The rose that grew from concrete. On *The rose that grew from concrete* [CD]. Santa Monica, CA: Interscope Records.

Shannon Community Safety Initiative. (2009). *Lynn.* Retrieved from http://www.shannoncsi.neu.edu/community_partners/lynn/

Solomon, E. P., & Heide, K. M. (2005). The biology of trauma. *Journal of Interpersonal Violence, 20*(1), 54.

Yalom, I. D., & Leszcz, M. (2005). *The theory and practice of group psychotherapy* (5th ed.). New York: Basic Books.

Special Populations

9

Doing Anger Differently
Working Creatively With Angry and Aggressive Boys

MICHAEL CURRIE

Alan, a 13-year-old boy, is teased by some classmates on the school playground regarding his sexual preferences. He reacts quickly and angrily, pulling a metal ruler from his bag and hacking into the necks of his classmates, wounding them. One of the boys Alan attacks requires admission to the hospital. After Alan has a tearful, remorse-filled encounter with the deputy principal, the school's head of student welfare asks me to talk with Alan about his anger. The principal, clearly the angry one now, says to me, "He's a nice boy but he just won't do what he says he will. This is his last chance. If you can't help him control his anger and this happens again, he is going to be expelled."

My initial meeting with Alan was similarly filled with tears, remorse, and many promises to "not be bad again." I had been told that his remorse was a familiar script to the school authorities. He appeared genuine but, according to the school, his remorse counted for little if he was provoked. Unlike the majority of his peers, even the threat of dire consequences from the principal appeared to have little effect in helping him abide by the school rules of reasonable conduct. There appeared to be a force operating within Alan that was stronger than any of these factors.

At a second meeting, Alan revealed that he could not stand that someone else thought he was "a faggot" and that the classmates who were teasing him seemed so smug and self-satisfied that he felt he had to strike at them. This seemed to be the first mismatch that was involved in Alan's angry outburst. His rules, necessary for maintaining his view of himself, asserted by his ruler, contravened the school's rules.

I AM NOT WRONG ABOUT MYSELF: MIRRORING AND THE FEAR OF DISINTEGRATION

Peers form an important function in late boyhood and early adolescence. For most older boys, peer groups are the primary means of social expression. It is within the peer group that an important "mirroring function" occurs, which assists a boy in maintaining a coherent self-image. In their social environment, boys encounter friends, classmates, and enemies who reflect back a more or less coherent view of themselves as a whole, integrated person. As the move from boyhood to adolescence progresses, the importance of these peers tends to increase, and the importance of the mirroring function of the family tends to decrease, although family, particularly parental figures, maintain an importance throughout life, as they are associated with the origins of the individual.

We all carry with us a more or less conscious idea of a unified image of ourselves, a sense of who we are as individuals. When this sense is attacked or threatened, by someone who seems to be more successful or beautiful than us, or by someone who directly challenges us regarding our competence, authority, and the like, it is likely to destabilize this coherent image of ourselves. This instability of self-image is particularly marked in boyhood and adolescence, where a sense of stable identity is still being formed and is subject to rapid change within the context of the peer group. Peers come to act as a sort of mirror. Boys tend to think negatively about those peers who reflect a negative image. In some cases, boys can think that their own self-image is threatened with disintegration: It seems one might "fall apart" in comparison to stronger or more competent others. Anger (and resulting aggression) can be seen as an assertion of a boy's own self-image over how he thinks someone else is devaluing him. In short, anger is a statement: "I am not wrong about myself."

Alan's aggression can be seen as a protective act, attacking the unity or wholeness of those whose taunts threaten him with disintegration. Within angry individuals, the fundamental psychic tendencies can be very different from the face that is shown to the world. Rather than the aggressive, swaggering tough guy we might expect, we find a boy who is fragile and vulnerable and reliant on the constant affirmations of those around him. However, precisely because this is how things are organized, his fragility cannot be approached directly.

This is a major problem in speaking with such boys about their difficulties with anger. How can problems about their behavior be discussed without triggering the defensive reaction "I am not wrong about myself"? These difficulties are compounded when it appears to the boy

that the aggressive act, such as screaming at his parents, solves the problem and is thus the best way to respond. However, the repetition of
aggressive acts results in marginalization, then suspension, and finally
expulsion from school or ongoing punishments and a negative atmo-
sphere within the family. An "excluded" status is often perceived by
an aggressive boy as victimization, and he considers himself a rightful
avenger of what has been done to him. He may avenge himself until he
has reached the margins of his family or social group, classmates, and
school. Violent, vengeful acts are ultimately self-destructive. The consequences of these acts tend to have a negative effect on the boy's life
opportunities. Boyhood and early adolescence is a time when intervention can occur before these opportunities disappear. The ideas I outline
in this chapter—the use of percussion, the group work setting, and a
model of intervention called the cycle of identity—are effective ways I
have found to intervene in the face of "I'm not wrong about myself."

Anger and Sadness

The fear of disintegration, discussed above, can also appear to be directed
somewhat arbitrarily outward as anger, or inward as sadness or another
attack on the self. The assertion of anger—"I am not wrong about
myself"—and the resulting attack on those perceived as the source of the
accusation are not far from the statement "I am wrong about myself" leading to an attack on the self. Anger refutes the reflected image, whereas an
acceptance of the image gives rise to sadness, depression, and attacks on
the self. This is why boys who are aggressive may show a worrying degree
of somewhat arbitrary self-destructiveness and recklessness. Anger may
have an important protective function against sadness and depression.
Merely making it a boy's task to reduce or manage the expression of
anger may bring about increases in other negative emotions.

What Do I Want?

For Alan, his problem seemed to be that the teasing from classmates
in the school yard easily smashed his ideas about himself. In addition,
his view of himself was influenced by the wrath of his school's deputy
principal. His permeability to others' views of him pushes Alan back
and forth between anger and remorse *with little prospect of being able to
determine what he wants for himself.* Questions such as "Who am I?" and
"What do I want?" are central but difficult questions for boys. They are
central questions because they provide a future for a boy to hang onto
over and against acting destructively and impulsively.

In Alan's case, he has difficulty making progress on these questions
because his permeability to others means that he is always looking to
what others want of him rather than asking himself what he wants.
Central to his treatment was the discussion of these questions. Such a
discussion cannot occur in the shadow of Alan's (or any boy's) guilt and

remorse, tempting though it may be. The guilt and remorse of an angry boy tends to reassure us that he has had the correct moral response to a crisis situation, but Alan's remorse was a response to what the school authorities had expressed to him in clear terms and was Alan's way of accommodating what the school wanted of him. However, the source of Alan's anger is more worthy of investigation than condemnation. His anger brings us closer to his self-perception and its disturbance by the accusation in the school yard. Although focused on the problem caused by the other, the cry of "that's not what I want" inherent in the angry act may be at least a start on the road of helping a boy answer the question of what he wants.

To reiterate, this question is important, because otherwise a boy has no reason for placing a limit on his lashing out. If a boy has nothing to preserve, cannot imagine some sort of future for himself that he could work toward, then he may as well savor the momentary enjoyment of being a victor in an aggressive exchange, of clearly showing his opponent who is boss. If an aggressive stance is all a boy has, it is unlikely that working toward being "pro-social" will meet with success, as he will then be left with nothing.

Aggression as an Existential Act

The case of Alan (discussed above) clarifies that anger is often an emotion that emerges when the stability of one's self-image is threatened from without. Aggression, the act of physically damaging or destroying something or someone in the world, emerges when this threat becomes unbearable. The angered individual can no longer stand the tension created by the threat to his status and strikes as a way to maintain his self-image. In this way *aggression can be seen as an existential act that aims at "psychical homeostasis."*

Aggression is an externalization in action of the physical arousal inside the aggressor's body. What eludes the aggressor is speech. In bypassing speech, the aggressive act bypasses the codes—reasoning, doubt, ability to wonder—that are contained in the act of speaking. Alan's aggression was a response that guaranteed instant results, stopping the provocation and (presumably) relieving his bodily tension. Retorting with insults, going to the deputy principal to complain, or organizing a program of subtle retribution by exclusion among his friends are all less predictable responses, subject to greater doubt and less complete than the response of physical aggression.

At a fundamental level, the task with aggressive boys is to assist them *to use words rather than fists*. It requires a degree of containment (speaking takes time and the results are often not immediately apparent or able to be perceived by the aggressor) and the ability to withstand frustration (the results of speech are less precise, more imperfect than aggression). I move now to discussing three aspects that I have used to assist with this endeavor: the use of percussion, the use of the group, and the use of a framework for analyzing the relationship between a boy's speech and action. I will add that I have found the approach outlined below to be useful in treating boys with both reactive (or impulsive) aggression—aggression fueled by an overwhelming anger in the moment, as was Alan's aggression—and instrumental (or proactive) aggression, which is more planned and covert, as was John's aggression, discussed later in the chapter. See Connor (2002) for a discussion of these categories of aggression.

THERAPY AND ANGRY BOYS: USING PERCUSSION

Angry and aggressive boys tend to avoid focusing on their inner experience: From a viewpoint that legitimizes coercion, there are seemingly few advantages in speaking about inner experience (Streeck-Fischer & van der Kolk, 2000; Wilson, 1999). However, this focus is exactly what is required in the therapeutic encounter. At the center of the Doing Anger Differently (DAD) program is a series of percussion exercises designed to overcome the myriad problems that prevent angry boys from participating in therapy. The program uses Latin and African percussion—congas, djembes and other hand drums, bass, snare and other stick drums, cowbells, whistles, and shakers—and allows each boy his own instrument with which to participate in the exercises (Currie, 2008a).

Percussion assists boys in symbolizing their inner experience, acting as a bridge between the physicality of the experience of anger and the ability to speak and think about this experience (Currie, 2008a). Many conduct disordered and angry boys experience difficulties in speaking about negative emotion (Fonagy, 2000). This symbolization acts as a metaphor for internal experience, assisting boys in understanding the difference between a situation and their internal response to it. The program addresses the characteristic habits of angry boys, which include blaming others for their feelings and actions, and confusing emotions and actions.

An exercise that illustrates these functions is the "mapping anger" game (see Currie, 2008a), in which boys create a simple map depicting the rise and fall of their anger and reactions following a provoking event. This map is then played on the drums, often with help from other boys in the group, giving musical form to components such as, for example, heart rate, buzzing in the head, thinking, or the urge to punch. Music is isomorphic with emotion: It rises and falls over time. This makes it a tool suitable for the symbolization of affect. Depiction of an episode of anger to the group in this manner can create a powerful moment for a boy in which he understands the anger to be his. Commonly, boys take an interest in the nature of their anger and its effects following this exercise.

Percussion also creates group cohesion, bypassing the negative and destructive language of aggressive boys. It offers an invitation to the possibility of play, creation, and enjoyment within a powerful lattice-work of in-group relationships. This enjoyment has led to boys return-ing to the group, despite commonly disliking school and having chronic conflict with their peers and family.

INTERVENING IN GROUPS

I have found group work with angry and aggressive boys to be a pro-foundly effective method of treatment, despite criticism of such an approach from several quarters (Ang & Hughes, 2002; Dishion, McCord, & Poulin, 1999). In my view, this is because those criti-cal of group treatment view clinical group work as an economic asset rather than a clinical asset. To ignore group process is to aban-don boys to the aggresso-genic meanings that inevitably form in the "storming" (Tuckman, 1965) stage of the group. These meanings must be approached, rather than ignored or "swept under the carpet." Otherwise, group processes influence the group formation outside the formal group sessions in a manner that is as corrosive to individual will and identity as membership in a violent youth gang. Group approaches have been shown to be at least as effective as individual therapy with boys (Hoag & Burlingame, 1997; Kastner, 1998). One reason may be that the group forms a context within which young people can remake themselves, or produce an alternative identity. A second reason may be the interactive immediacy of group work that assists boys in under-standing themselves through an initial emphasis on *doing* rather than *talking* (Malekoff, 2007).

Many acknowledge the clinical efficacy of group work with adoles-cents (Malekoff, 2007; Newman & Newman, 2001); however, there has been little writing on the use of group dynamics and group process in the reduction of anger and aggression with this population (American Group Psychotherapy Association, 2002). The DAD program is an in-group approach specifically for angry boys (see Currie, 2008a).

Anger is most often expressed in the context of interpersonal rela-tionships. The group provides an opportunity to capture and work with this type of anger at the moment of its expression. We have found that a relatively simple framework is best for approaching the complex set of relations that boys bring to and develop within the group. Rather than viewing expressions of anger and aggression in the group as inter-fering with the treatment, I see them as valuable clinical material to be worked on in the here and now. In psychoanalytic terms, therapists can interpret the acting out of within-group transferences to assist boys in understanding their characteristically self-destructive responses to anger. There are two core group techniques used to facilitate this working in the here and now with anger: *it's hot* and *time-out* (for further details about these techniques, see Currie, 2008a).

It's Hot

Group leaders may call a break in the group if a conflict emerges during the session. Here the conflict between group members is worked on, with group leaders acting as consultants. Rather than pursuing or enforcing a resolution, therapists focus on eliciting statements of feeling and a position, description, or reason that accompanies the feeling that does not invalidate the experience of the other boy. Over time, this process can increase group members' capacity to tolerate their own negative emotion as it is validated and tolerated within the group. This tolerance can lead to reduced impulsiveness and a search for alternative ways of responding to anger and related emotions. These alternatives are sought after and taken up by therapists for group discussion, as outlined in the discussion of the cycle of identity, which serves as a reference for intervention within this technique.

The exception to consultation is when a young person may be at physical or emotional risk. Given these circumstances, therapists intervene to ensure physical and psychical safety, for example, when a group scapegoats a member. It's hot is not an easy technique to implement, as it tests the creativity of therapists, but it is generally transforming for boys.

Time-Out

Time-out is called to subvert an individual's disruption in the group or for individual discussion of an important point. Time-out is neither a punishment nor an isolation so a boy might think about his actions. Rather, it is intended as a moment in which the therapist can assist a boy in putting words to his internal state rather than continuing to act out the internal state within the group. Time-out is called when the boy's behavior is disruptive to the group and there appears to be little chance that he will be able to speak about, rather than act out, his internal state in the group context.

The first intervention of time-out is validation of the "kernel of truth" in the boy's actions. The therapist's stance is beside the boy, as an ally, strengthening the therapeutic alliance. At first, speaking of the internal state that brought the disruptive act(s) is prioritized over discussing the acts themselves. As a boy may not be able to name his internal experience, a guess by the therapist based on the boy's behavior or statements in the group that day may be necessary. Therapists also may need to assist a boy in soothing himself if there is a high emotive level. Many boys are surprised by this initial stance, as most expect aversive consequences for their disruptive acts, and this surprise means the moment of time-out can be one of profound difference.

In the second stage of time-out a return to the group is negotiated via discussion about the boy's behavior. The nature of the problem is outlined clearly, and possible changes in behavior are discussed. Therapists offer to help with the change. This might be to assist with time-outs in the future, give reminders about agreements made, or assist with monitoring of anger level. Discussing the means by which the boy could repair the damage he has caused, by words or action, may be important. I have found that within my clinical work, this act of repair tends to halt the cycle of anger and remorse that many angry boys are trapped within (Currie, 2008a).

A key aspect of the group work component is the ongoing cycle of assessment, intervention, and reformulation by therapists as they comment on a boy's characteristic patterns of anger and aggression as expressed in the group. For example, a boy's pattern in the group may be to initially laugh and smile at slights, despite becoming angrier internally, and then eventually exploding. Through the mapping anger game (see above), and the use of repeated time-outs and it's hot, a boy can become better at recognizing this affect and speaking in the group about its cause.

Therapists' interventions occur within a fluid dialogue in which boys participate by action, words, or drums. The experience of being held "in mind" by the therapists, who continually return to the boy their reading or interpretation of his deeds and speech in the light of past, can be a powerful aid for boys in altering their nascent sense of who they are and in speaking about this change.

In my work with percussion groups, drums are the initial common expressive modality of the group. As sessions pass and the group develops, the therapeutic group work is focused on assisting boys in understanding their own particular experience of anger. This individualizing aspect of the approach assumes that, while there are commonalities, anger is an experience that can differ as much from individual to individual as different emotions (such as sadness and anxiety) can differ within the same individual.

The Contribution of the Development of the Group to Individual Change

Changes occur within groups that are of use to the aims of therapy (Bion, 1961; Gordon, 1992; Malekoff, 2007). Some of the changes that are specific to groups researched during the development of DAD are worth noting (for a summary of this research see Currie, 2008a). Often, boys start groups hitting the percussion instruments as loudly and as chaotically as possible, competing with each other to be the loudest. This slowly shifts to interaction and play with others, which is a gauge of the group's development. For example, boys often want to write pieces together, allowing different boys to lead the group, or to rap over the top of rhythms. As sessions pass, the drums are used less as boys become more interested in talking about their difficulties. This parallels members' work on discovering a way of being that is not focused on the physical level. The abstraction involved in talking can lead to an ability to think of alternative ways of responding in the face of negative emotion.

As the group progresses, boys stop looking to the therapists to generate activities, instead creating opportunities themselves. This benchmark is often accompanied by an acceptance of "different" members as part of the group and a cessation of excluding and blaming them. This can include celebratory moments, in which boys join together in putting on costumes, an outpouring of group noise on the drums, or simply sharing food to express their uncontested relatedness.

These group changes have a relation to individual participant's changes. A boy's identity-self is not isolated from the social context within which it is articulated. Identity or "view of the self" is socially constructed and permeable to the social world. The group contributes toward the "reproduction" or "rewriting" of self-identity through the provision of a dialectic within which this identity is renegotiated. A group provides a complex, interweaving latticework of events and understanding about the world. This latticework can have a powerful effect on a young person's identity, particularly if he feels part of the group, which becomes stronger and more formed the longer it continues. The fundamental dialectic of the group is between its physicality on the one hand—members, drums, time, place, ritual—and a restless breaking out of roles and older meanings and understandings within the group on the other. The group itself is continually changing. It is through experiencing, accommodating, and tolerating this continual flux that group membership can provide a fluid, responsive mentality within which participants can grasp themselves and their world (see also Gordon, 1992).

Enjoyment and the Group

As the group develops, the experience of in-group relationships may produce in the boy an enjoyment of interpersonal connection that is absent in his relationships outside the group. A boy's group membership can facilitate a change in motivation for action, from momentary gratification to sustained enjoyment. The problem of reactive aggression is one of being unable to tolerate negative emotion, resulting in impulsive aggression. Many boys commence the group with precisely this problem: perpetrating aggression in accordance with how they feel. Other boys come to the group with symptoms more indicative of instrumental aggression (see the case of John, below). While this sort of aggression is common in the school yard, boys with problematic instrumental aggression often come to the group with a sense of themselves as outsiders (Connor, 2002). They don't want to fit in with anyone else's rules and are often focused on bending peers to their whims. However, as the group progresses, both groups of boys commonly find they enjoy the group and wish to return to it and preserve it.

The value of the group lies in the creation of a linguistic culture—boys may say anything they wish to in the group. Boys tend to be attracted by this aspect of the experience. However, alongside this are the continual disruptions and expressions of anger and aggression that the techniques of it's hot and time-out are designed to target. These techniques do not allow the usual group practice of avoiding anger and aggression. The techniques pose a dilemma for participants, highlighting as they do participants' expressions of anger and aggression that threaten to destroy the fabric of the group, one of the first sets of relationships that they may have explicitly valued. The dilemma is stressed further as therapists turn the problem of in-group aggression or threats of aggression over to the group for discussion. It may be necessary for therapists to emphasize the manner in which aggression threatens the group or an individual's group membership. If a boy continues to hit other group members every time he feels like it or wants something, then the other members may not wish to return to be part of the group with him. There will be no group to return to.

The process for many group members is that they exchange aggression (whether impulsive or instrumental) for the sustained enjoyment that the group provides, because they now have an interpersonal space they wish to preserve. The work of each group member, aided by group therapists, is to find their own, individual ways of expressing, using, or assuaging their anger in the name of preservation of the group. This can be seen as a transition of a participant from acting as a pure individual—acting only according to how he feels, not caring about how his actions affect others—to a social orientation, within which he limits the degree of impulsive action for the sake of preserving the enjoyment the group provides. The motivation for boys to place a limit on their aggression is that they are participating in a group where they wish to be and to remain. In this way, the group can be said to provide a limit on the degree to which boys act impulsively out of anger, a limit that functions in a paternal fashion.

THE CYCLE OF IDENTITY

We have conceptualized a cycle of identity (Figure 9.1; after White, 1994; see also Nicholson, 1995), which is a theory of individual change suited to therapy with angry adolescent males. The cycle of identity is useful due to the difficulty of intervening in the here and now in the individual or the group context, particularly in the midst of the angry and aggressive acting out of distress. The cycle of identity assists therapists in guiding boys through various levels of abstraction about their experiences. It involves a movement from the experience of the event

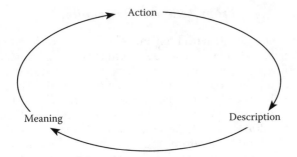

Figure 9.1   The cycle of identity, showing the conceptual progression through stages of description of events in therapy.

to making sense of this experience, to an understanding of how to use this sense outside the group. The aim here is to assist adolescents in gaining a fuller understanding of the implications of anger-fueled impulsivity through speaking about it, thus increasing the capacity for cognitive self-regulation.

This conceptualization assists in therapy by utilizing the incompletely formed cognitive functioning common in late boyhood and early adolescence (Weisz & Hawley, 2002). Although formal operations may be present, this ability is nascent in the young adolescent. Knowledge base, capacity for cognitive self-regulation, memory storage capacity, and organizational efficiency are all capacities that develop in the adolescent years (Moshman, 1999). This means the manner in which knowledge is acquired seems to differ substantially from adults, and this often occurs within an experience-based, acting-out reflection cycle (Gordon, 1989; Hanna & Hunt, 1999; Malekoff, 2007; Winnicott, 1965). This developing cognitive capacity can be seen as a barrier to therapy, particularly with aggressive boys who often appear to lack a developed reflective capacity. However, new and expanding cognitive functions, which often result in a sense of discovery and readiness to experiment, can be helpful in therapy with boys if use can be made of them (Hanna & Hunt, 1999; Malekoff, 2007). The cycle of identity is an attempt to utilize these cognitive changes in aid of the therapy.

Finally, the cycle of identity assists therapists in *working past* the "I'm not wrong about myself": the defensive assertion of anger. The gradual movement from action to performing meaning and its repetition deals with the defensiveness that has shipwrecked many potentially effective therapies with boys and young adolescents (for further discussion see Currie, 2008b). The cycle of identity assists therapists in making use of the experiential material that boys bring to therapy via interventions to guide participants through three levels of cognitive abstraction about their own actions. These three levels are as follows.

From Action to Description

Many young adolescents with high anger levels have difficulties describing past events, instead giving accounts empty of their subjective, emotional response to experience. While there are many individual reasons, childhood trauma is a risk factor for both a reduced ability to articulate emotional experience (Streeck-Fischer & van der Kolk, 2000) and high anger and aggression levels in adolescence (Greenberg, Domitrovich, & Bumbarger, 2001). The experience of anger may become too difficult to speak about. Therefore, the early focus of work is on merely gaining descriptions of experience: The drumming games (in groups) or simple "What happened?" questions are used to further this aim. These descriptions of experience tend to focus on linking external events and actions with thoughts and feelings. This is a necessary first step in changing the manner in which inner experience influences action. Repeated deconstructions of the experience of anger in this manner assist the boy in separating himself from the problematic experience of anger. This separation in turn assists with the use of cognition self-consciously (e.g., "What are my options here?") instead of automatically (as in, for example, the if-then inferential thinking that accompanies anger: "He has hurt me so I have to hurt him!") during the experience of anger (Beck, 1999; White, 1989; White & Epston, 1989).

From Description to Constructing Meaning

Once boys have described several of their experiences of anger, they may be in a position to make sense of these experiences, or to reevaluate the aggression- and coercion-inducing meanings attributed to them. Often, a more considered response gradually emerges in the context of group discussions. They may decide that there were aspects of their actions that were justified and others that were not. Violence ceases to become a necessary response to the experience of anger, and several other possibilities are considered. Essentially, the nature of a boy's response becomes a choice.

Therapists do not focus here on the short-term gains of aggressive acts, but the longer-term consequences, which contribute to a boy's sense of victimhood. This sense is variously apparent in boy's description of their "reputation," their relation with a particularly "hated" teacher, peer, or sibling, or perhaps a sense that they have no friends or peers with whom they have a relationship of trust, often precisely because of their reputation. Therapeutic interest centers on these relationships.

Often latent is a boy's "problem-saturated" (White, 1994) view of himself. This view of self, his view of other's view of him, may need to be brought into awareness and questioned (although not directly) as to whether this is a preferred view of self. The response of many boys is that they do not wish to continue to be dominated by anger, and the image of themselves its expression promotes within the school.

Their work in the group is then to find a way of changing this view of themselves, lying as it does between the self and the other. The effects this search has on the boy are varied and rarely immediately apparent. A boy's attempt to take account of these meanings or understandings about himself could be called performing meaning.

From Constructing Meaning to Performing Meaning

Once the questions have been asked, boys often bring answers to their dilemmas in the recitations of their experience. Boys do not tend to claim to understand something important as a result of the therapist's intervention. Often boys act on their insights, making understandings apparent in the form of actions (Gamsie, 1999; Gordon, 1989; Malekoff, 2007). It is a matter of therapists being able to see and hear these "exceptional outcomes." White (1989) defined exceptional outcomes as events, outcomes, and actions that could not have been predicted by a person's problem-saturated description of himself. Stepping back when stood over by a teacher, leaving his hands in his pockets while negotiating a provocative situation, or giving up on a plan of revenge are all possible examples of exceptional outcomes in which a boy refused to let anger dominate him. These exceptional outcomes largely go unrecognized by a boy or his associates. They are therefore examples of action to be described, discussed, and made meaning of within the therapy. In this way, the participant enters a cycle of meaning that is iterative of identity. Each turn of the cycle, from action to description to meaning to performance (which is a return to action), is an exceptional outcome that creates, or iterates, another cycle of difference in the identity of the young person (for more detail on each of the aspects of the cycle of identity see Currie, 2008b).

CASE EXAMPLE

John found the school system to be oppressive. He disliked the school uniform, the commands from teachers that had to be followed, the regimented turn of the timetable. He was often late for class, dragging his feet down the school's corridors where he was repeatedly found by the deputy principal, or was reprimanded by the class teacher if he eventually made it to his class. John found these reprimands difficult to bear. He would fly into a rage, feeling misrepresented, and perpetrate all kinds of acts that would result in his being given lunchtime and after-school detentions and, occasionally, suspensions. He felt persecuted and victimized by the school staff, who John felt had no idea who he really was outside his reputation as a "troublemaker." This was a mismatch for John: He did not feel he fit into the school system, or that the teachers' ideas about him represented who he really was.

During a therapy group for aggressive boys at his school, John gave the following description of an incident in which he had been involved the previous month: "... that little bastard, we were really getting into him. He got it bad, man! There were four of us getting him. He just started crying, but we were sick of him. We had him on the ground kicking him. There was one time where I had this ring [shows to group] and I had his head and I hit him with my fist and it left this mark on his cheek [group laughs]. It was so good ... he had to go to hospital...."

When I asked John what had provoked the attack, he gave a number of answers, all of which seemed trivial (e.g., the victim's pants were too short) and provoked laughter from the group. Further, it seemed that while there was some generalized anger and discontent directed at the victim, he had done little to provoke the attack, which was planned the day before by John and his friends.

Whatever exaggerations are involved in the retelling of the story, it illustrates one function of anger and aggression: to promote a certain image of a boy's own self to his peers. The image that John was trying to create is one of a man who could do whatever he liked. He seemed to be immune to the consequences of his actions with teachers, police, and parents, as well as to the boy's injuries and the ongoing problems the attack caused for him. In his retelling of the attack, we find in John not a fear of disintegration (as might apply with other boys), but an enjoyment in the telling, as it shored up John's sense of himself as an aggressive, tough, all-conquering individual. In the fantasy that he built about the attack, John painted himself as someone relatively free of the restrictions he had to suffer in his day-to-day life at school. His friends listened admiringly to his account, which hid the unsure and troubled aspects of his encounters with teachers and other authority figures.

In talking about the event, John's fundamental assertion seemed to be: "I am right about myself." Despite all of the difficulties of his life, he is still someone who can do what he likes. Because aggression is necessary to assert that he is right about himself, it makes it clear that there is a degree of doubt in John about whether he is, in fact, right about himself. And while doubt about ourselves is something we all share, John's use of aggression to assuage this doubt causes many problems for him and for others.

John clearly enjoyed retelling the story; his need to enjoy himself as the transgressor of limits others have to obey reveals an absence of enjoyment in other areas of his life. Why should he accept limits when this is his only means of enjoyment?

The problem for John was that this attempt to shore himself up had very real consequences. For example, he was suspended from school following the incident he described in the group. The police were called, although he was not charged. John also managed to pick up a reputation at the school that meant he was the first one blamed for acts of misbehavior and violence there.

The Persecuted Victim

At the same time as playing the "tough guy," John also felt persecuted within school. He told me that he was sick of being angry and sick of being blamed by his teachers for things he had not done. He was repeatedly in conflict with teachers after they accused him. For John, this blame took on a persecutory flavor: It was as if he had turned his own sense of right and wrong onto his teachers and felt persecuted by this sense from without. He told me that the teachers in the school were always ready to tell him off and correct him. They had the wrong view of him.

This persecuted feeling results from another mismatch: "I am not who you say I am." John felt this incorrect view of him was asserted every time he encountered a teacher, which meant he reacted all the more strongly to the accusation. Every attempt to correct him by a school representative, no matter how simple or small—on his uniform, on adhering to the school timetable, on his not bringing his textbooks to class—he heard as if being accused by some ugly, persecutory ogre.

The extraordinary point here is that, while John had clearly been a persecutor in the attack he described to the group, he also thought of himself as the persecuted one. This is a feature of the "one-way" ethics that angry and aggressive boys seem to have. They are often blind to the problems of others, yet hypersensitive to slight criticisms directed to themselves. Perhaps most importantly, this position of being persecuted created a crisis for John. He realized that the reputation he had created for himself at school had real effects, and he was not easily able to "get rid" of his reputation. The crisis was that he realized he would not be able to advance in school as far as he might have liked, as he had been threatened with suspension and expulsion on several occasions. If he was to do something about this, he had to change his view of himself as the persecuted one.

Enhancing Ethics

An aim in intervening with aggression can be to *enhance or widen a boy's already existing ethical and moral views*. Commonly, an aggressive boy acts as if there is an independent moral order that supports his view of the world. Whenever a demand is made on the boy he refers to this "other," inner order. Commonly, the fact that the world does not fit into his way of viewing things causes a great deal of tension that he cannot stand. Aggression is a method of making the world fit. This other order, his view of the way the world "should" be, then justifies his aggression, regardless of the consequences.

There are in fact two laws. One is written in the statutes of the state or country, which enables the policeman, for example, to fine a citizen for jaywalking or running a red light. There is a second law, beyond this written law, which manifests in a different way in each individual. Each person will have his or her own reasons for obeying the law, as well as personal difficulty with doing so. It is this process of an individual finding his or her own law, a law beyond the law of the land, to which we must pay attention in the case of the angry and aggressive boy.

To take the example of jaywalking, the boy impatiently looks at traffic, trying to find a break in the line of cars in order to skip across the road quickly, feeling that the rule of waiting until the lights are green doesn't apply to him. The rules of childhood can become provisional, permeable, trivial even, and subject to the boy's desires. And where is the therapist? The therapist steps back from the curb the boy departs from, is at the other curb as the boy arrives, even talks to the boy as he crosses, saying in the boy's ear: "Why this risk? Why is this haste so important? This is where you have told me you are going. Is it worth risking being knocked down here?"

For boys, it is a matter of crossing, experimenting, pushing, in order to find a law, the law that each individual discovers. Adolescence demonstrates that each individual has to find his own way to his own version of the law, which involves ignoring, or contravening, or dispensing with the law that is laid down in writing. It is this internal law that each individual must find for himself and take up, whether he knows it or not.

The difference between these two laws—the law of the land and the internal law, how what is right or wrong manifests in each individual—is important to keep in mind. This is because the keeping of written law is particularly problematic in the case of an angry boy. Anger is the result of a mismatch between the angered individual's own law and the expectations of others—society's laws, school laws, and family rules. The aggressive boy's attempt to take the law into his own hands causes quite a problem. An adult has to assist an angry boy in the process of finding his own way to keeping the written law. The fundamental aim in helping an aggressive boy is to arrive at a point where—for him—he can act ethically toward what he wants. This principle is useful for boys across the spectrum of anger difficulties, from boys who have extreme problems such as John's to those who have more mild anger disturbances.

John: Beating Victimhood and Taking Action

John's case illustrates how quite extraordinary changes can occur with boys in a short period of time if the right influences and motivations are in place. John's story is a success, despite its grim beginnings. It illustrates some of the ideas I describe in my book that assist in producing such a change (Currie, 2008b).

John came to group for approximately six months. At the end of this time, he had started to think very differently about his aggression and anger. John was a big boy, and many boys in his year were scared of him. After two months of sessions with me, he told me that he had been asked to "sort a guy out" for a friend at school. He said that he had approached the situation cautiously because "you don't really know what's gone on" and that he wanted to discuss the problem with the boy he had been asked to sort out. This was quite different from the attitude he had adopted in his previous encounters. Rather than assuming that people wanted to attack him, he clearly showed signs of wanting to check things out. He told me that he simply kept his hands in his pockets throughout the whole discussion with the boy, and that he managed to resolve the conflict between his friend and the other boy without hitting anyone, asking his friend and the boy to "get along."

It was quite a shift for John. He had begun to use words rather than fists to sort out troubles—contrast this with his earlier behavior. While it is true that he was far from being an angel, I emphasized to him the contrast between his restraint in this incident and his previous, violent attack. I did this to try to help John notice—and understand—the meaning behind his actions. It was his changes in behavior that had led to a better outcome, not chance or external circumstances. Also, he had begun to analyze the social situation, to think about relationships within it, rather than simply overlaying his "paranoid habit of mind" on his social relations. John was able to agree with this, but how had this shift started to occur? John had little difficulty in giving clues, which seemed to lie in his changing attitude toward school.

Three Antidotes to Anger

There is evidence here of what we call the three antidotes to anger. It has recently emerged that three dimensions of mental functioning appear crucial to determine whether "at-risk" youths can recover and make something of their lives (see Hauser, Allen, & Golden, 2006). These dimensions are a focus on relationships, a capacity for reflection and sense making, and a determination to protect one's own ability to act. The three areas are interdependent and are often deficient in chronically angry boys.

Angry people often view their relationships in a defensive way, tending to worry about how others will harm them rather than thinking about how others might be helpful to them. John wanted to change his interactions with teachers, but he had begun to feel the weight of his reputation. He was tired of being the one at whom teachers always looked when there was trouble while their backs were turned to the class, and he hated being wrongly accused. He told me that he really regretted having a heavy reputation that was difficult to throw off. As a result of our reflections, he began to reconsider the value of his relationships, particularly with teachers. This is a *first antidote to anger*; rather than viewing others as malevolent, John began considering the value and usefulness of others and how to preserve relationships.

Anger is by definition made of two cognitive components; First, there is a problem, and second the problem is caused by another. This second component is antithetical to self-reflection, to the idea that one is at least part the author of one's own difficulties. John's ability to analyze the social situations he was confronted with ("You can't just go in without knowing what's going on") showed an ability to reflect on his own part in his troubles. This is the *second antidote to anger*: the ability to reflect.

After quite bit of discussion about his reputation, John decided to leave the school he was attending. He changed to one where his uncle had a minor administrative role and his cousin attended. He told me that he had had long talks with his mother and his uncle about his future, and he had come to several important decisions in consultation with them. He felt his reputation at his original school was so entrenched that he could neither throw it off nor overcome it. However, after several months at the new school he decided he missed his friends too much, and that the original school had suited him better. After more discussions with his mother, he wrote to his original school, requesting they have him back. In the letter, he asked the principal for a fresh start and described how many of his problems had sprung from the fact that he had established a reputation; if the school allowed him to return, he felt that he could do really well. The school agreed to reenroll him.

This is evidence of a *third antidote to anger*, one in which an individual prefers to protect his own means of acting rather than relying on others. Instead of being a passive victim, seeing the solution in others changing their behavior, John changed his stance to a more active one: He did not allow the school to expel him; rather, he took control of the situation and made a move himself.

Reordering the Field of Enjoyment

It also seemed that there had been a substantial reordering in John's mind of the importance of his pursuit of enjoyment, what he wanted for his future, and his faith or belief in rules and conventions that govern civil human interaction. In short, it now seemed to him that there was a point to accepting limitation of his pursuit of enjoyment. Recall John's almost celebratory attitude in the past, as he retold stories of violence toward his peers. John's violence seemed to rest more on enjoyment of the power and dominance inherent in the aggressive act, rather than a reactive, emotional lashing out.

In our meetings, the question that we continually returned to, indirectly, was "Why accept a limit on fun and enjoyment?" We did this in a series of discussions that weaved a complex web of meaning around how John viewed his life and relationships. When John told a story about how he had told another boy that the boy was being "slack" for punching up someone smaller than him, I asked him how this measured against his earlier assault on his fellow student. John had to start considering how he had given himself an exception from his own rules, ones that he thought important.

Interestingly, the story of John being asked to "sort out" someone reveals him in a fatherly position: the one who has the power to decide what is right and wrong, what can and cannot happen—in short, what the rules are. Over the period of our meetings, John shifted from allowing himself an exception from what he thought others should do, to including himself in the rules; he recognized that rules were something that everyone should follow.

He described some of the crazy things his friends did, acting how they pleased, completely outside general rules of society. One had set fire to a dog, another had thrown a chair, breaking the blackboard in class, yet another smoked 10 bowls of dope each night, and another continually asked girls for sex, calling them sluts if they refused. A phrase that John returned to in describing his admiration for these friends was that "they just don't care." We reflected on what the future held for such boys.

John complained that his female math teacher always picked on him, looking first to him whenever there was any trouble in her class. I asked how things had led to this. John replied that there was a time when he didn't care and he just did what he wanted in class and in the school playground. He described a fantasy that there were tunnels linking all the buildings in the school, allowing one to move, unnoticed, between the administration block, the sports hall, classrooms, and the teachers' staff room. This fantasy seemed to represent a dream that John could stay outside the gaze of school authorities, eluding all of the strictures and requirements that were involved in attending school. Over the time of our meetings he seemed to gradually let go of the hold this fantasy had over his life.

It also seemed that his view of the rules changed somewhat during our sessions. His statement "You can't just go in without knowing what's going on" implied a changed stance: John had started to care, had abandoned the "I don't care" status that placed him outside normal rules and conventions that others followed. John now seemed to act as if there was a law worth keeping, and he included himself within this law. He was limiting the degree to which he could simply act on a whim without any regard for the rules. He had mastered the fundamental, paradoxical truth that laid the ground for the passage to adulthood: "You may do anything you please, inside the law."

REFERENCES

American Group Psychotherapy Association. (2002). *The role of group psychotherapeutic interventions in youth violence reduction and primary prevention: A White Paper.* Retrieved January 3, 2003, from www.agpa.org

Ang, R. P., & Hughes, J. N. (2002). Differential effects of skills training with antisocial youth based on group composition: A meta-analytic investigation. *School Psychology Review, 31*(2), 164–185.

Beck, A. T. (1999). *Prisoners of hate: The cognitive basis of anger, hostility, and violence.* New York: Harper Collins.

Bion, W. (1961). *Experiences in groups.* London, UK: Tavistock.

Connor, D. F. (2002). *Aggression and antisocial behavior in children and adolescents: Research and treatment.* New York: Guilford.

Currie, M. (2008a). *The Doing Anger Differently manual: A school group work program for talking about aggression.* Melbourne, Australia: Melbourne University Press.

Currie, M. (2008b). *Doing Anger Differently: Helping teenage boys.* Melbourne, Australia: Melbourne University Press.

Dishion T. J., McCord J., & Poulin F. (1999). When interventions harm: Peer groups and problem behavior. *American Psychologist, 54*(9), 755–764.

Fonagy, P. (2000). *Attachment in infancy and the problem of conduct disorders in adolescence: The role of reflective function.* Address to the International Association of Adolescent Psychiatry, San Francisco, CA. Retrieved March 24, 2002, from http://www.ucl.ac.uk/psychoanalysis/unit-staff/peter.htm

Gamsie, S. (1999). The player of children. In D. Pereira (Ed.), *The psychoanalysis of children: Freud's child and Lacan's* (pp. 25–37). Hawthorn, Australia: The Freudian School of Melbourne.

Gordon, R. (1989). Symbiosis in the group: Group therapy for younger adolescents. In F. J. Cramer Azima & L. H. Richmond (Eds.), *Adolescent group psychotherapy* (pp. 43–51). Madison, CT: American Group Psychotherapy Association, International Universities Press.

Gordon, R. (1992). The group as psychic structure and the locus of the symbolic. In D. Pereira (Ed.), *The Lacanian school: Papers of the Freudian School of Melbourne.* Hawthorne, Australia: The Freudian School of Melbourne.

Greenberg, M. T., Domitrovich, C., & Bumbarger, B. (2001). The prevention of mental disorders in school-aged children: Current state of the field. *Prevention & Treatment, 4,* 58–89.

Hanna, F. J., & Hunt, W. (1999). Techniques for therapy with defiant, aggressive adolescents. *Psychotherapy: Theory, Practice, Research, Training, 36*(1), 56–68.

Hauser, S. T., Allen, J. P., & Golden, E. (2006). *Out of the woods: Tales of resilient teens.* Cambridge, MA: Harvard University Press.

Hoag, M. J., & Burlingame, G. M. (1997). Child and adolescent group psychotherapy: A narrative review of effectiveness and the case for meta-analysis. *Journal of Child and Adolescent Group Therapy, 7*(2), 51–68.

Kastner, J. W. (1998). Clinical change in adolescent aggressive behavior: A group therapy approach. *Journal of Child and Adolescent Group Therapy, 8*(1), 23–33.

Malekoff, A. (2007). *Group work with adolescents: Principles and practice* (2nd ed.). New York: Guilford.

Moshman, D. (1999). *Adolescent psychological development: Rationality, morality, and identity.* Mahwah, NJ: Lawrence Erlbaum.

Newman, B. M., & Newman, P. R. (2001). Group identity and alienation: Giving the we its due. *Journal of Youth and Adolescence, 30*(5), 515–538.

Nicholson, S. (1995). The narrative dance: A practice map for White's therapy. *Australian and New Zealand Journal of Family Therapy, 16*(1), 23–28.

Streeck-Fischer, A., & van der Kolk, B. A. (2000). Down will come baby, cradle and all: Diagnostic and therapeutic implications of chronic trauma on child development. *Australian and New Zealand Journal of Psychiatry, 34*(6), 903–918.

Tuckman, B. W. (1965). Developmental sequence in small groups. *Psychological Bulletin, 63*(6), 384–399.

Weisz, J. R., & Hawley, K. M. (2002). Developmental factors in the treatment of adolescents. *Journal of Consulting and Clinical Psychology, 70*(1), 21–43.

White, M. (1989, Summer). The externalizing of the problem and re-authoring of lives and relationships. *Dulwich Centre Newsletter,* 3–21.

White, M. (1994). Deconstruction and therapy. In D. Epston & M. White (Eds.), *Experience, contradiction, narrative and imagination: Selected papers of David Epston and Michael White 1989–1991* (pp. 109–153). Adelaide, Australia: Dulwich Centre Publications.

White, M., & Epston, D. (1989). *Narrative means to therapeutic ends.* Adelaide, Australia: Dulwich Centre Publications.

Wilson, P. (1999). Delinquency. In M. Lanyado & A. Horne (Eds.), *The handbook of child and adolescent psychotherapy: Psychoanalytic approaches* (pp. 311–328). New York: Routledge.

Winnicott, D. W. (1965). *The maturational processes and the facilitating environment.* London: Hogarth.

CHAPTER

10

Body-Based Treatment Approaches for Young Boys Diagnosed With ADHD

ERNA GRÖNLUND AND BARBRO RENCK

THE FIRST SESSION

Practitioners who treat boys diagnosed with attention deficit hyperactivity disorder (ADHD) are challenged to employ an active approach in therapy that utilizes and channels the boys' high activity levels as they work toward developing better self-control of their behavior. The purpose of this chapter is to describe a special dance movement therapy program developed by the authors to engage boys with ADHD in therapy and teach them methods for self-regulation. We begin our explanation of this therapeutic process by providing the reader with a realistic picture of these clients.

The vignettes that follow describe the first session with three young boys diagnosed with ADHD. Their presentation in the therapy space is illustrated, as are the methods utilized for initial engagement. At the same time, there is a description of how the relationships between the therapist and the boys developed. Pseudonyms are used for each boy in order to preserve his confidentiality.

Eric

Eric, age 6, is wild from the moment he climbs the threshold to the therapy room, a large, open space that allows for movement and play. Without introductions he begins running around the outskirts of the room. Shawls, cushions, and hard balls fly through the air. When the therapist tries to catch him, he throws himself onto the floor and cries out loudly, "Don't touch me! I will kill you if you catch me!"

When the therapist comes close to him and tries to calm him down, he gets angry and attacks her vigorously. The therapist remains calm: "You must not hit me. Do you understand that?" Eric does not answer but he nods affirmatively. "I can see that you are both quick and strong. I wonder how many laps you can do." Eric immediately starts running again. The therapist is now following him. Eric does not protest.

After a while, she shifts the action into a funny "follow the leader" game. Her diverting maneuver succeeds. Eric seems to like challenges because he starts at once. He seems amused when following the instructions, but suddenly stops and wants the therapist to play *his* way and follow *his* rules. She responds positively to his demand, but as soon as she has learned to adhere to his rules, he changes them. Eric's play is destructive. He bounces into the walls and tries to smash all the things in the room. When the therapist tells him not to do so, he answers by screaming loudly, and the destructive behavior escalates.

It seems that when the therapist gives him limits or instructions, he ignores her as if he feels insulted. His temper tantrums are easily triggered, so the therapist senses that she has to be careful when leading him. She is friendly but at the same time firm, determined to limit his aggressive outbursts. When Eric's destructiveness turns into panic, it becomes necessary for the therapist to physically hold him. At the same time she speaks to him in a soothing voice. "You must not be afraid, Eric. It is not dangerous. You and I are just playing together." After a while his tensions are released and she can set him free. By lifting away his panic she has helped him to calm down for the moment. But Eric still wants to be the leader and the whole hour is a long struggle for power. When this first session is over, the therapist is completely exhausted, but Eric's energy is still high and he does not want to end the session. He has to be persuaded to leave the room.

Charles

Charles is seven years old. At the first session he is shy, entering the room with hesitation. He politely presents himself and shakes hands with the therapist. He sits down on a cushion of his choosing and curiously waits for her to start. He takes the therapist's hand and together they run around in the room while music plays. They stop when the music stops. Charles laughs spontaneously: "This was fun. Can we do it again?" And then he wants to repeat the same play over and over again, but now he dares to run without holding the therapist's hand. He is in movement all the time. The tempo is high.

In a slower part of the session, the therapist reads a story to him. He sits down close to her. It is obvious that he has quickly developed confidence in the therapist. When they are sitting together, he is soon climbing in her lap, leaning his head on her shoulder. But he can't concentrate on the story for long and suddenly he is on his feet running again. After a while he throws himself onto the cushions and wants the therapist to do the same. Together, they laugh loudly while roughly tumbling around in the cushions. A big gymnastic ball in the corner of the room catches his attention and he rushes forward to the ball and kicks it hard. "I play that I am hitting my big brother. I do not like him at all. He is not nice to me! He teases me all the time!" And then Charles kicks the ball again and again with all his aggressive strength.

"I can see that you are angry at your brother!"

Charles shakes his head while saying emphatically, "I do not want to speak of him anymore."

Abruptly, Charles changes the subject. Now he wants to play with the big ball and, for a long time, he and the therapist roll the big ball across the floor to one another. The therapist asks Charles if he would like to attempt to stand on top of the big ball. At first he hesitates, saying, "I can't do that. I have no balance!"

"But I can help you." The therapist then helps him to stand in balance on top of the ball. He seems both happy and proud when he succeeds. He sounds astonished when he says, "I can stand on top of the ball. I wish that Daddy had seen that!" When the session is over, Charles is surprised that the time went so quickly. He runs out of the room to meet his father and tell him about how he stood on top of the ball.

Frederic

Fredric is six-and-a-half years old. During the first session, he enters the room happy and lively, jumping up and down. He is eager to start the session. He rapidly understands and follows the therapist's instructions, but quickly gets bored. He interrupts the play and says, "Now I want to be the leader. You shall follow me."

"We can take turns and you and I can be leaders alternately."

"No, I want to be the leader all the time."

Since it is the first session, the therapist lets him be the leader, thereby avoiding a power struggle. Frederic's movements are abrupt and unexpected. Without warning, he suddenly throws himself on the therapist's back and hits her violently. The therapist turns around and catches him. "You may not hit me. Do you understand that?"

He nods. "Yes, I understand."

She takes him in her arms and gives him a hug, shifting the physical language from violence to affection. He then clings to her, kissing and hugging her, and the therapist has to free herself. Frederic has no limits and a great need for touch. The therapist has to balance not rejecting his attempts to connect while also not encouraging boundariless contact. The therapist channels Frederic's contact by allowing him to borrow a stuffed animal, a little kitten. He seems to be happy and, at first, cuddles up with the cat in his arms, but quickly grabs the cat's tail and swings it over his head round and round. Finally, he throws the cat with full strength into the wall. Frederic has a cat at home, and the therapist hopes that he does not treat that cat the same way.

At the end of the session, the therapist asks Frederic to draw a self-portrait. He talks calmly to himself while drawing. On the back of the paper he draws a monster. Seriously, he declares to the therapist, "That is me. I am a very evil, dangerous monster who is sprinkling fire! You should be afraid of me! All the children at school are afraid of me!"

"Yes, you are indeed a dangerous monster, but I am not afraid of you. May I give the monster a hug?" Immediately, he throws himself into the therapist's arms. She gives him a warm hug and the session is over. The therapist follows Frederic out to the waiting room where his mother is waiting.

Commentary

These three boys—Eric, Charles, and Frederic—all started individual treatment in the same year that they started school. They were in many ways very unlike each other, but they also had a lot in common, such as a lack of concentration, a constant bodily anxiety with a high intensity, and above all, an inability to regulate their impulsivity. Many of us recognize boys with those difficulties and problems. We have met them on playgrounds where they frighten other children or in stores where they have temper tantrums if they don't get what they want. They surprise and puzzle us. We have also met their parents, who often express despair and shame about not being able to stop their wild boys.

These children provoke people in their surroundings, both adults and peers. Other children do not understand them and are sometimes frightened of them. They can be bullied by others, or they may themselves become bullies. Therefore, they are excluded from games and play. They have few friends and can often be quite lonely. Since they experience frequent failure, they often have low self-esteem and view themselves as inadequate.

Some grown-ups also turn their backs on the boys and their parents. Boys with ADHD and their parents both need support. The parents frequently experience being misunderstood and disavowed by professionals such as daycare personnel and teachers at school, as well as self-professed experts in medical care. Sometimes, the parents ask themselves if they are to blame for their child's dyscontrol. In these instances, hearing a diagnosis can be a relief: "My boy is not badly brought up. He has ADHD and can't help his behavior. He needs understanding and support."

THE DIAGNOSIS ADHD

Concurrent with the improvement in the physical health of children and adolescents, increasing attention has been paid all over the Western world to factors that threaten their mental health. According to the Swedish National Board of Health and Welfare (2001), between 10 and 15% of all children in Sweden are sent for psychiatric consultation some time during childhood or adolescence. Neuropsychiatric problems are so common and the risks for abnormal mental health development and social maladjustment so great that we may speak of them as a public health problem (Official Reports of the Swedish Government, 1997).

ADHD is the most common neurobehavioral disorder in children and adolescents. Symptoms generally appear to be reduced in adulthood. However, two-thirds (about 66%) of children with ADHD will continue to have problems attributable to the disorder into adulthood (Root & Resnick, 2003), while 36.3% of adults with a history of childhood ADHD continue to meet full diagnostic criteria as adults (Kessler et al., 2005). The prevalence of ADHD has increased over the past two decades (Froelich et al., 2007) and is estimated to afflict 3 to 7% of school-aged children in the United States (American Psychiatric Association, 2000). Worldwide, ADHD impacts 8 to 12% of children (Biederman & Faraone, 2005).

According to the *Diagnostic and Statistical Manual of Mental Disorders*, Fourth Edition-Text Revision (DSM-IV-TR; American Psychiatric Association, 2000), ADHD is a disruptive behavioral disorder with early childhood onset characterized by symptoms of inattention, hyperactivity, and impulsivity. The manual distinguishes three subtypes of ADHD:

1. Predominantly inattentive type
2. Predominantly hyperactive/impulsive type
3. Combined type (which includes significant hyperactivity/impulsivity and inattention symptomatology)

All the boys in our research study and, consequently, all the boys described in this chapter were diagnosed with the combined type of ADHD.

According to Barkley (1997), the deficit in response inhibition present in children with ADHD leads to impairment in four executive functions, which influences the motor system in service of goal-directed behavior labeled motor control, fluency, and syntax.

1. Working memory (the ability to mentally manipulate information)
2. Internalization of speech (verbal working memory)
3. Self-regulation of affect/motivation/arousal
4. Reconstitution (the ability to effectively analyze and synthesize information from the environment to solve problems)

In a review of the literature, Barkley (2003) concluded that research in ADHD is beginning to focus more on poor inhibition and deficient executive functioning as being central to this disorder. ADHD is associated with a variety of cognitive, psychiatric, educational, emotional, and social impairments. Some of these are direct consequences of the disorder, while others may be associated conditions arising from other primary disorders, such as depression or anxiety. Children with ADHD also frequently have low self-esteem (Biederman, 2003) caused primarily by difficulties in school and at home. There is a strong relationship between ADHD and motor perception dysfunction. Piek, Pitcher, and Hay (1999) found that children with predominantly inattentive type ADHD had significantly impaired fine motor skills, whereas children with the combined type of ADHD experienced significantly greater difficulty with gross motor function.

Etiology

Researchers agree that the factors that cause ADHD are still unknown. There is strong evidence that genetic factors have a great influence on the genesis of ADHD, but environmental factors are also central (Swedish National Board of Health and Welfare, 2002). The causal connections are best explained by a stress/vulnerability model, in which psychosocial and biological factors interact (Assarsson & Hofsten, 1997).

The number of boys diagnosed with ADHD is constantly increasing in the Western world, just as it is in the Swedish community. Boys are overrepresented in almost all child neurobehavioral disorder statistics. According to Barkley (2006), ADHD occurs in boys approximately three times as often as in girls in community samples, and five to nine times more often in clinical samples.

However, there is a growing suspicion that the prevalence of ADHD in boys and girls may not be so different. Even if boys with ADHD are greater in numbers than girls with the same diagnosis, the boys are perhaps overdiagnosed. ADHD in girls may be missed for different reasons (Buttross, 2007). Girls seem to be less active than boys, and a girl with ADHD may not stand out as particularly hyperactive, impulsive, or physically aggressive. Pinker (2008) wrote:

> ADD can be seen as what happens when average sex differences in rambunctiousness and self-control—what psychologists call self-regulation—are taken to an extreme. Studies show that from a young age, boys play more high-energy, competitive games than girls, with more chasing and play-fighting and less turn-taking, waiting, and sharing. These behaviors increase when boys are in groups, as they are in school. (p. 34)

Another reason for the discrepancy can be that girls with ADHD manifest more internalizing symptoms, such as depression and anxiety, than boys with ADHD (Gershon, 2002); therefore, the diagnosis may be missed.

In Swedish schools, there are limited resources for helping children who are in need. The available means are given to children who have a clinical diagnosis. Therefore, the ADHD diagnosis can serve as a gateway to obtaining support for the child and relief for the parents (Wrangsjö, 1998). However, the treatment options for these boys remain limited. Doctors prescribe medicine and recommend special education services, but seldom do they recommend psychotherapy (Eresund & Wrangsjö, 2008). Since parents are often afraid their boys might develop side effects from medication, they desire options for alternative treatment. As Panksepp (2007) wrote, "Psychostimulants used to treat ADHD have neurochemical effects comparable to cocaine" (p. 61). It is not surprising, then, that parents are afraid that their children might develop substance abuse disorder later in life from taking these medications to regulate their symptoms.

Boys with ADHD also need help socializing with adults and children their own age, including free play with other children in order to train social ability. This can be a problem since boys with ADHD often also exhibit problems integrating with their peers. "Social-overtures of ADHD-type children have been too rough or primitive—too 'rude'—leading normal kids to avoid play with ADHD-type children" (Panksepp, 2007, p. 62). Getting in contact with, understanding, and expressing their feelings can be a problem for these boys. Managing overwhelming feelings, such as anger and shame, is particularly problematic.

BODY-BASED TREATMENT

Readers may have taken note of the sheer physicality of the sessions described at the beginning of the chapter, both in the use of active movement—play, running, balancing, jumping, and tumbling—and the structured application of physical touch as a means of communication and soothing. No doubt, the sessions described represent a sharp detour from traditional verbal approaches to treatment, in which boys may find themselves sitting in a chair and engaging in verbal processing. However, traditional approaches, by their very nature, start boys with ADHD in a position of failure, for sitting still and talking are the tasks they are least capable of fulfilling.

ADHD is a disorder that manifests itself strongly in the body through hypermotoric and impulsive action. Body-based treatments, therefore, have a potential for working with the disorder at its locus of expression, as well as channeling the strong neurological drive toward social play (Panksepp, 2007). Body or somatic psychotherapies are those treatment methods that integrate practices drawn from yoga, dance, movement, breathwork, and structural integration with psychotherapy theories and approaches. By intervening directly with the body, therapists who utilize these methods work toward the goals of affect and impulse regulation, mindful self-awareness, and mobilization toward effective action (Fisher & Ogden, 2009). The work presented here is specific to the modality of dance movement therapy, which will be described in greater detail later in the chapter.

INTRODUCING TREATMENT

Young boys with ADHD have a strong need to be seen and validated. However, they are used to being viewed as the "naughty boy," troublemakers both at home and in school. Therefore, they are often confronted with suspicion and avoidance. They look at themselves as not being good enough, not worthy of love. If the grown-ups can't establish adequate boundaries for these boys, or show fear of their strength and anger, then the boys will likely develop a sense of omnipotent destructiveness. It is also difficult for parents, whose other children also need attention, to concentrate solely on the boy with ADHD. For this reason, individual treatment can be optimal for these boys, as they then don't have to compete with other children for the attention of the therapist as they do at home with their brothers and sisters.

Research findings show the importance of intervening early in the lives of children with ADHD. The three boys presented at the beginning of the chapter were all tested when they were four to five years old, but none of them were given any kind of treatment before they started school. At school it became obvious that the symptoms of ADHD were a clear obstacle to learning, and the boys were offered therapy with the hopes that it would improve their prognosis in the classroom.

Medication seems to be particularly effective in addressing the core symptoms of ADHD, even if it can be a controversial intervention for families and some educational and mental health professionals (Edwards, 2002). Concerns over the increased prevalence of medication among school-aged children and uncertainty of implications surrounding long-term use have been expressed (Connor, 2006). The nonpharmacologic treatment options for ADHD include cognitive behavioral therapy, support groups, educator/teacher training, parent training, and counseling. The effectiveness of these treatments has been uneven (Greydanus, Pratt, Sloane, & Rappley, 2003). The best approach seems to be a combination of measures in which both child and parent are offered help. Results from the Multimodal Treatment Study of ADHD (MTA) demonstrated that a multimodal approach including parent management training, school interventions, and medication is the current treatment of choice (Edwards, 2002).

In Sweden, psychodynamic treatment models in the context of long-term therapy have been applied to children with mental health problems for nearly a century. However, the circumstances have recently changed. Resources today are primarily restricted to short-term treatment, despite the fact that today's children seem to have more complicated problems. To meet these challenges, treatment models must adapt to individual needs and the conditions in which children live. Child and adolescent psychiatry often uses an eclectic approach, combining medical treatment and a variety of psychotherapy methods in combination or in succession.

Body-based treatments represent a suitable addition to the options mentioned above, as ADHD manifests somatically. Besides having the characteristic symptoms of ADHD—inattention, hyperactivity, and impulsivity—children with this disorder usually have problems with bodily tension, disturbed body image, and fragmented movement patterns, as well as poor coordination and balance. Therefore, it seems logical to address the problems through the body by working with breathing, rhythm, and movement. From a neurological point of view, it is particularly relevant to choose a body-based treatment since, as Barkley (2004) stated in a lecture in Stockholm, "Children with ADHD benefit the most—more than any other disorder—from regular exercise, because movement exercises increase dopamine in the human brain, just like the stimulus does."

THEORETICAL UNDERPINNINGS

Children with ADHD have problems relating to both adults and peers. Since they need help forming relationships, object relations theory provides a logical theoretical base for working with them. Concepts of special importance include Winnicott's (1971) ideas about the "transitional space," the place where the psyche of the therapist and child can play together, and the "holding environment," or the mother's/primary caretaker's ability to provide a secure, containing relationship for the child. Additional concepts include Bowlby's (1988) attachment theory, in which touch is of vital importance; Fonagy and Target's (1994) ideas about the connection between disturbed attachment and impaired ability for reflection; and Stern's (1985) "affect attunement." To foster a sense of security, the therapist acted at times as a substitute mother, allowing touch. When a boy panicked she would hold and thereby soothe him.

For Siegel (1984), it was obvious that children with early disturbances and neurological disorders have strong urges to move, which is exhibited by their hyperactivity. In treatment, the hyperactive boys are allowed to rush as quickly and as long as they can. Since many of these children also have a negative body image, Schilder's theories are well suited to this study. Schilder (1950) noted that body image is in constant flux, especially in movement. He theorized that dance can be an effective way of changing a rigid body posture or a disturbed body image. The dance therapist therefore assisted the boys in establishing a more realistic body image, by both using targeted exercises and having the children draw occasional self-portraits.

Reich's (1972) proposal about a link between personality and posture is useful in body-based treatment. Reich showed that loosening up
the body's armoring and letting go of muscular tensions releases emotions. By using massage, it was possible to help the boys rid themselves
of bodily tension and open up to difficult emotions such as anger and
shame. Chodorow (1991) argued that dance therapy is involved with
both the expression and transformation of emotion. Nathanson's (1987)
theory of shame helps to explain the destructive impulsivity that characterizes the behavior of children struggling with ADHD. Since poor
impulse control is a core symptom, the dance therapist is often working
with anger and shame.

Antonovsky (1987) emphasized the importance of the therapist focusing on the healthy parts of the client. He pointed out that the ability to
resist life stressors depends on one's sense of coherence, which is rooted
in self-esteem. Since children with ADHD often suffer from low self-
esteem, body-based therapy can provide the very avenue they need to
express their strengths and personal resources and to transform underlying emotions such as shame, which can lead to the destructive impulsivity that characterizes their behavior and coping methods. Children with
ADHD are often exposed to high levels of stress because of difficult
demands from parents and teachers. Experiential treatment in which
there is engagement without competition may help to reduce this stress,
and the boy might for once experience himself as good enough.

DANCE MOVEMENT THERAPY

Creative arts therapies such as art, dance, drama, and music therapy are
treatment modalities in which the creative process is used to foster the
power of health. Dance movement therapy (DMT) may be the creative
arts therapy modality of choice for boys with ADHD, as it works most
directly with the body. Dance therapy can therefore also be classified
as a body-based treatment since it is often nonverbal and the dialogue is
primarily based on body language. "How people feel or how they repress
and restrict feelings is visible in the movement. Bodies become sculpted
by life experiences—actions, reactions, and interactions" (Schmais,
1974, p. 10).

Dance and movement loosen muscular tensions and open up hidden
emotions. As Schilder (1950) articulated, "Motion thus influences the
body image and leads from a change in the body image to a change in
the psychic attitude" (p. 208). Dance therapy is about contact on many
levels. In the dancing moment, the patient has contact with his or her
own inner world, with thoughts, feelings, and memories. The dance also
brings the potential to train social abilities. "Dance therapy is founded
upon a fundamental belief that movement expression of the individual is reflective of intra-psychic dynamics, that a change in movement
expression will result in a behavioral change" (Leventhal, 1980, p. 4).

DMT for children is built on the joy of movement and lust for life. In DMT, the play in movement gives the child the possibility of getting in contact with his or her difficult feelings, either in individual therapy or in a group. In individual dance therapy, the anxious child might start by giving form to his or her fear in movement together with the dance therapist. After a while the child will hopefully be able to understand his or her feelings and also know how to put words to them. "Creative dance and movement can enable the children to rebuild a healthier connection with the body, senses and cognitive skills, improving body awareness and body image. It can help to give children a 'sense of wholeness' by connecting body, mind and emotions" (Sherborne, 1990, p. 23).

Dance Therapy for Children With Emotional and Behavioral Disturbances

In a longitudinal study, Grönlund (1994) described and evaluated five years of DMT work with emotionally disturbed and neurologically impaired school children in two special classes. DMT proved successful since, by simultaneously processing both body and emotion, it had a two-pronged effect. The study focused on the turning points that led to a positive change in the treatment and the identification of the curative factors. In another study, Grönlund, Alm, and Hammarlund (1999) demonstrated different ways of using DMT with destructive children who could not modulate their aggression.

At a consensus development conference in the United States, which focused on the diagnosis and treatment of ADHD, dance therapist Dianne Dulicai (1999) stated that the control of motor responses and the multiple biological bases for this disorder have particular implications for dance therapy research. Since research concerning DMT for children with ADHD had so far not been documented in a scientific way, Dulicai encouraged dance therapists to start working with and doing research concerning this particular group of children. She emphasized that studies by dance therapists could greatly contribute to the understanding of ADHD. Her charge inspired us to start the research project concerning DMT for young boys diagnosed with ADHD.

This Swedish study was the first to analyze and document in a scientific way the effects and process of DMT for children with ADHD. In a pilot study, we presented DMT as dyadic treatment for a pair of young boys diagnosed with ADHD. The study was published in an article in the *American Journal of Dance Therapy* (Grönlund, Renck, & Weibull, 2005). The main study was presented in Swedish and published in two reports (Grönlund & Renck, 2004, 2005), focusing on both individual and group therapy.

Two unpublished master's theses from Drexel University in Philadelphia concerning DMT for children with ADHD were documented in 2007 and 2008. Redman (2007) used DMT for students with ADHD in order to reduce the three main symptoms: hyperactivity, impulsivity, and distractibility. DMT was associated with improved behaviors as recorded by classroom teachers. In a recent study, Quesada-Chaverri (2008) designed a site-specific DMT clinical model for addressing the needs of school-aged children with ADHD symptoms and their families. A 10-week model was designed to improve insight, self-control, verbal and nonverbal communication, interpersonal interactions, and parenting skills.

THE DANCE MOVEMENT THERAPY PROGRAM

The DMT approach used in this study was a short-term, supportive, and goal-directed treatment.* The boys in the study had DMT for two or three academic terms. The therapy was adapted to the boys' difficulties and problems and also to the parents' desires. After setting special goals for each child, the dance therapist, together with her supervisor, devised a suitable treatment plan.

It was obvious in this study that a DMT program for young boys with ADHD should address fundamental movement skills before attempting to address the concomitant behavioral and emotional symptoms. Coherence at the body level appears to set the stage for positive prognosis. Establishing trust and creating a safe "transitional space" (Winnicott, 1971) was of utmost importance, because, as research has demonstrated, in all therapies the therapeutic relationship is the most healing. The chance for a treatment to succeed lies in the relationship between therapist and child (Grönlund, 1994).

By design, the tempo of sessions changed all the time, from quick exercises to slower exercises and relaxation pauses. The dance therapist alternately was leading and following the boys. To avoid chaos, she was holding the boundaries firm, an absolute condition for working with boys who are acting out. There were distinct rules, such as not hurting anyone or anything and not leaving the room during sessions. The DMT sessions started and ended each time in the same familiar and secure way, with a rhythmic exercise. Sitting on the floor, the boy and the dance therapist would clap their hands and sing greetings of welcome or goodbye. After the greetings, the DMT sessions continued with running around the room in a very high tempo to satisfy the hyperactive boy's strong urge to move (Siegel, 1984). The sessions also included periods of relaxation and breathing exercises. Then the dance therapist massaged the boy's tense neck and shoulders to help him loosen his muscular tensions (Reich, 1972) and relax enough to speak about his personal problems. Just listening to music could also be a way to relax.

Conversation emerged during these quieter times, covering themes important to the boys, such as longing for a friend, how to handle pets

---

* The Committee of Ethics at Karlstad University approved this study.

and animals without being destructive, the shame of not feeling as clever as the other children in the class, the inability to control aggressive and destructive impulses, and the fear of being abandoned. Siegel's (1984) emphasis on insight and verbalization to make it easier to integrate the nonverbal expression was a vital element of the clinical process. Thus, "small talks" about important topics during each session aimed to help the boys better understand themselves and their problems. Sometimes there was also room for teaching small dances. One boy wanted to learn disco dances, while another was fond of breakdancing, and a third was most interested in learning how to do somersaults. Sometimes the boys lived in a fantasy world, and then the dance therapist tried to help them find a balance between internal and external reality (Winnicott, 1971). She grounded the boys by focusing on the concrete world outside the dance therapy room at the end of each session.

Vignettes From One Boy's Dance Movement Therapy

To give the reader a concrete picture of how a dance therapist can work with a boy diagnosed with ADHD, we have chosen to present a detailed case study of the therapeutic work with one of the three boys, Charles. We have chosen Charles because he had DMT for the longest period, three terms. He was also the only child who was interviewed both immediately after DMT and two years after termination.

Background

Charles lived with his parents, an older brother, and a younger sister. He was an extremely lively baby whose mother got very tired because he seldom slept as other babies do. His sleeping problems increased and, during the second year at school, the problems became so acute that he had to take sleeping pills. At daycare, the staff found Charles unwieldy; either he was hitting the other children or he was hiding under the table. It was very hard to get in contact with him. Therefore, the personnel at the daycare recommended the parents contact the child guidance clinic.

When he was four years old, Charles was tested by a psychologist and diagnosed with ADHD. Despite the diagnosis, he received no treatment. Not until he started school was he offered dance therapy, which was thought to be a relevant treatment because Charles was interested in music and liked singing. He was very rhythmic and especially good at rapping and dancing.

Charles had a pronounced need to control all in his surroundings, especially his mother. He was constantly trying to dominate his brother and sister. He was a strong boy and he furiously used his fists and feet when meeting other children, which led to their avoiding him. He also had periodic urges to attack his mother and father, but had not yet dared to do so. The parents, especially his father, provided him with strict structure.

Charles had pronounced problems with concentration. In school he couldn't sit still or listen for more than five minutes before he began running around and destroying the other children's work or rushed out of the room. Charles was fascinated with fire. If he had matches or a lighter, he set fire to schoolbooks or wastepaper baskets. He was frequently self-destructive, such that when he once set fire to a cabin in the woods near the school, he refused to get out of the burning building. His teacher had to drag him out. After that incident, Charles was offered an aide in school who provided him with additional supervision. Since Charles's fascination with fires was escalating, the parents were afraid that he would develop pyromania. His father kept him under close surveillance, hiding matches and lighters at home. Charles was reluctant to open up and speak about his temptation to set fires. He seemed to be afraid of his own destructiveness and needed help managing his aggressive impulses.

Protective Factors

Eresund and Wrangsjö (2008) identified the following important prerequisites for treatment to succeed:

- The child himself must have experienced the need for help.
- The child needs to have an ability to attach to the therapist.
- The parents must be motivated and believe in the treatment.
- There must be good cooperation with personnel from school.

Those prerequisites were well established in Charles's case:

- Charles was aware of his problem of not being able to control his anger and destructiveness. After a while, he also prepared for asking for help with his fear of what would result from his setting fires.
- Charles established immediate rapport with his dance therapist and relied on her.
- The parents were motivated and believed that dance movement therapy would be an adequate treatment for their boy. Charles's father met with the dance therapist's supervisor continuously throughout Charles's treatment. His parents were interviewed three times.
- The parents mediated news from Charles's teacher on how he was doing at school.

The teachers met the dance therapist, who presented DMT for all the children in Charles's class. After finishing DMT, the teachers were interviewed by the two project leaders, who also were the researchers.

Charles's dance therapy was 40 sessions in length. Charles lived far from the clinic, and his father had to take time off from work in order to be able to bring him to the sessions. Despite these challenges, Charles was present for every session. He attended DMT even when he had a bad cold. His family was indeed motivated to help Charles, and they had good faith in the treatment process.

The Phases of Charles's Dance Therapy Process

The DMT process was divided into three phases: the initial phase, the middle phase, and the final phase. Each will be described in greater detail below.

The *initial phase*, designed to create a "conflict-free sphere" (Hartmann, 1958), emphasized the boy's strengths, countering the potential for revealing weaknesses and shame, feelings that can lead to either aggression or depression (Nathanson, 1987). When Charles eventually dared to try something new, such as balancing on the big ball, the dance therapist gave him positive feedback. This enabled him to become aware of his own resources, increasing his self-esteem (Antonovsky, 1987). During this phase, the dance therapist was directive, trying to maintain boundaries. She was engaged in building trust and a therapeutic relationship. Charles was initially quite shy, but a more secure relationship was quickly established.

The *middle phase*, characterized by Charles's feelings of increased security and familiarity, allowed the dance therapist to be nondirective, following Charles's creative ideas and improvisations, thereby helping him to explore his movement potential and develop his fantasy through play. The focus was on improving Charles's body awareness and body image to give him a better sense of wholeness (Sherborne, 1990). Charles was then occupied with different movement games, and he wanted to learn both steps and whole dances.

In this middle phase, verbal sharing was more frequent (Siegel, 1984). Charles started to talk about his personal problems, above all his fear of not being able to control his fascination with setting fires. He was well aware of the danger in playing with fire and wanted help in stopping himself. In improvised fantasy play, created and led by Charles, he wanted the dance therapist to help him throw spaghetti in a big kettle on the stove. When the spaghetti was boiling, Charles decided that it went all over the kettle and started a big fire. Then he cried, "Look, there's a fire!" The dance therapist then suggested that they together should stop the fire. He agreed to do so. He wanted to play that game for many sessions. At last, he said that he no longer needed to play out this sequence because, in his words, "I am not setting fires anymore."

The *final phase*, the separation, highlighted Charles's growth and development. Then Charles, without shyness, connected to the dance therapist. It was now obvious that he had learned to share his conflicts and fears. He proudly told the dance therapist what he had learned in DMT. He had dared to dance solo in front of his school class. He could now sit still in the classroom, raise his hand, and wait for his turn. His teacher praised him for that progress. He also showed improvement in completing his home-work. He had largely learned to control his aggressive outbursts and was therefore invited into the other children's games. Sometimes he failed, and then the other children became afraid of him again.

When DMT finished, Charles was interviewed by one of the researchers. He then confirmed that he had learned a lot in DMT that he could use at school. He could now articulate why he had attended therapy. Charles said, "In dance therapy I became aware of my problems. I learned how to behave to get friends, and now I try to use words instead of fists when I get angry. I am thankful to my dance therapist."

Two years after dance therapy there was a follow-up interview with Charles's parents. The father then mentioned that Charles had calmed down and did not quarrel so often with his siblings. The mother was content that Charles now often played and had fun with his brother and defended his younger sister if other children bullied her. Charles was also interviewed after two years and when asked what he remembered of the dance therapy, he recalled learning to do somersaults and also to breakdance. He especially pointed out that, in his words, "The most important thing is that I have stopped setting fires!" However, according to his father and the teachers at school, the fascination with setting fires was sometimes still there, even if it had decreased remarkably.

Charles's Results

- Charles's attention showed vast improvement. In DMT he could listen to and follow the therapist's instructions and, according to his teachers, at school he fulfilled his tasks. But he still had prob-lems with doing his homework on time.
- Charles's hyperactivity decreased. In DMT he could change tempo from quick to slow. At school he learned to sit still and wait for his turn, and could stay in the classroom the whole hour.
- Charles could better control his impulsivity, and his temper tan-trums were more seldom. He could play and work with the chil-dren in his class without aggressive conflicts. However, sometimes he failed and then was the troublemaker that he used to be.
- In the physical contact with the dance therapist, Charles achieved rhythmic synchrony with her, which meant that a relationship had established. He demonstrated the ability to lead a dialogue both in movement and in words.
- Charles's motor ability improved, with better coordination and balance. His body awareness strengthened and he had a more posi-tive body image and improved self-esteem.
- Charles was able to use therapy as a safety valve for his anxiety. He could speak openly about his fear of what would become of him if he couldn't stop himself when he got angry or wanted to set fires.

He was aware of the danger in setting fires and asked his father to hide the matches for him.

SUMMARY OF THE RESULTS FOR ALL THREE BOYS

Scientific quantitative and phenomenological qualitative inquiries are needed for a comprehensive view of DMT. Results from the qualitative data were analyzed mostly through observations of videotaped sessions. Furthermore, all the boys' parents were interviewed before, right after, and two years following DMT. Charles's teachers were interviewed right after DMT. Charles was interviewed at this point and two years post-treatment. What follows is a very short summary of the results for Eric, Charles, and Frederic.

For the three boys, the main symptoms of ADHD—inattention, hyperactivity, and impulsivity—decreased somewhat. However, ADHD is a lifelong handicap, and the symptoms might return in stressful situations. Eric and Frederic, who had motor problems, were helped to improve in this area through DMT. Positive results were especially noticeable in regard to better coordination and balance, as well as a more positive self-image. Above all, the boys' progress was marked by improved social functioning. They started to understand their disorder and why their aggressive and destructive behavior prevented them from making friends. They now are trying to control their anger and use words instead of fighting. That new knowledge is of great value for the boys when they get into conflicts, either with grown-ups or with other children.

Results were also presented in quantitative data. Before DMT started, the parents completed a questionnaire with basic demographic characteristics. Two instruments were also used, the Strengths and Difficulties Questionnaire (SDQ) and the Movement ABC Motor Test. Both were administered before and after the full course of treatment.

The SDQ is a behavioral screening instrument that is widely used in epidemiological, developmental, and clinic research. It provides a useful measure of inattention and hyperactivity. The SDQ has five subscales: Hyperactivity, Emotional Symptoms, Conduct Problems, Peer Problems, and Prosocial Behavior. The first four subscales can be aggregated to generate a total difficulty score. The pro-social subscale measures an aspect of social competence and is not incorporated in SDQ Total Difficulties. The SDQ also examines the need for psychiatric intervention, the impact rating (Goodman, 1997).

The results showed rather small differences on SDQ Total Difficulties before and after treatment, and two of the boys (cases 1 and 2) remained at an abnormal level. The Prosocial Behavior subscale scores showed a positive development in that all the boys were at a normal level and demonstrated a greater social competence following DMT. However, the Impact Rating Scale showed that all three boys still needed psychiatric intervention.

TABLE 10.1   Motor Function in Three Cases Measured With the Movement ABC Motor Test Before and After Dance Movement Therapy

	Eric		Charles		Frederic	
Movement ABC Motor Test	Pretest	Posttest	Pretest	Posttest	Pretest	Posttest
Total score	32.5	13.0	13.0	6.5	18.5	7.5
Manual skills	12.5	4.5	2.0	4.0	2.5	3.0
Ball skills	5.0	1.5	8.0	0.5	6.0	0
Static and dynamic balance	15.0	7.0	3.0	2.0	10.0	4.5

Note: Movement ABC Motor Test total score range, 0–40 (manual skills, 0–15; ball skills, 0–10; static and dynamic balance, 0–15). Higher scores (13–40) indicate lower motor competence.

The Movement ABC Motor Test is a screening tool that assesses motor function in children. The instrument can be used as a normative test, for clinical exploration, and as a measure of the capacity for improvement. For a more detailed description of the Movement ABC Motor Test, see Henderson and Sugden (1992).

In Table 10.1, the Movement ABC shows a positive change for all three boys. The improvements include manual skills, ball skills, and dynamic balance. Following dance therapy, all three boys went from having demonstrable motor difficulties to either being within the borderline range (case 1) or having no motor difficulties (cases 2 and 3).

LESSONS LEARNED

Boys who are acting out need a lot of attention from grown-ups. Parents have a hard time in both encouraging their boys' abilities and stopping their impulsivity and destructiveness. It is important that the boys' problems are discovered early so they receive timely intervention. Preventive work can be done in daycare where the boys can get help to satisfy their urges to play freely. Until the boys develop self-regulation skills for engaging with other children, a key intervention is for the personnel to engage in rough and tumble play with them and to create contexts in which boys engaging in exuberant physical play is encouraged (Panksepp, 2007). Laughing together is particularly important.

At school, the groups must be kept small because boys with ADHD have a great need for help and support from the teacher. They are often slow learners, and sometimes a classroom aide is required. The study shows that when working with boys with ADHD, it is important to meet them at their level, and that is on a body level. The boys have difficulties sitting still and concentrating at school since they have a very strong urge to move. One potential way of managing this is for the teachers to start the school day with some movement exercises at a high tempo. Between the teaching of reading and writing, small pauses are recommended in which the children can be engaged in joyful body games, sometimes rough playing and tumbling, sometimes calmer games. However, it is of utmost importance to stress firm boundaries and never allow destructive behavior.

Many boys with ADHD have heightened anxiety. Therefore, therapists working with them must start by establishing trust and security so that a relationship can develop, which is necessary before working with the boy's body and emotions. Boys with ADHD are used to receiving a lot of negative criticism, as grown-ups are often nagging them. The boys often view themselves as failures and need positive feedback. Many teachers may look upon the boys' hyperactivity as undesirable instead of encouraging their high energy. In DMT it is natural to follow each boy's tempo.

Boys with ADHD need help learning how to meet other people, both adults and children their own age, in a friendly, socially acceptable manner. The social training can start, in group therapy or at school, by letting the boys play together in pairs, at first in more structured play under the guidance of the therapist or the teacher, then in free fantasy and pretend play initiated by the boys themselves. This playing may soon start short talks between the boys, with or without the help of the therapist or the teacher, in which they can begin to reflect upon their own behavior and also be empathic toward one another. Hopefully for the first time in the boys' lives they can experience friendship when sharing the various feelings and joy of movement together.

RECOMMENDATIONS FOR THE FUTURE

ADHD is now viewed as a chronic disorder for most children diagnosed with it. The goal of treatment must be to achieve an improvement in the quality of life and to strengthen self-esteem and self-worth. The treatment of boys with ADHD is complex and must in many cases be maintained over long periods of time, starting early in daycare and continuing at school. The families must also get a chance, if the boys have relapses, to receive recurrent treatment. According to Barkley (2006), early intervention, long-term therapy, and multiple treatments in combination are the most effective way to treat ADHD. Dance therapy is one alternative treatment model to combine with other methods or medication. ADHD is not a simple disorder to be solved with two or three terms of DMT, but the results from our study showed positive changes in motor function, improved social competence, and partial reduction of behavioral and emotional symptoms. In this chapter we have focused on individual DMT, but in the study dance therapy in a group was also employed with good results.

REFERENCES

American Psychiatric Association. (2000). *Diagnostic and statistical manual of mental disorders* (4th ed., text rev.). Washington, DC: Author.

Antonovsky, A. (1987). *Unraveling the mystery of health: How people manage stress and stay well.* San Francisco, CA: Jossey-Bass.

Assarson, N., & Hoffsten, G. (1997). *Familjeterapi för barn med neuropsykiatriska handikapp: En utvärdering* [Family therapy in children with neuropsychiatric handicap: An evaluation]. Stockholm, Sweden: Omsorgsnämndens rapport 97:8.

Barkley, R. A. (1997). Behavioral inhibition, sustained attention, and executive functions: Constructing a unifying theory of ADHD. *Psychological Bulletin, 121*(1), 65–94.

Barkley, R. A. (2003). Issues in the diagnosis of attention-deficit/hyperactivity disorder in children. *Brain & Development, 25*(2), 77–83.

Barkley, R. A. (2004, May 5). *ADHD in children and adolescents: Nature diagnosis and management* [Video documentation of a lecture]. Stockholm, Sweden: Sinus AB, Polstjärnan.

Barkley, R. A. (2006). *Attention-deficit hyperactivity disorder: A handbook for diagnosis and treatment* (3rd ed.). New York: Guilford.

Biederman, J. (2003). Overview of ADHD. *Contemporary Pediatrics* (Suppl.), 4–5.

Biederman, J., & Faraone, S. V. (2005). Attention-deficit hyperactivity disorder. *Lancet, 366*(9481), 237–248.

Bowlby, J. (1988). *A secure base: Parent-child attachment and healthy human development.* New York: Basic Books.

Buttross, L. S. (2007). *Understanding attention deficit hyperactivity disorder.* Jackson, MS: University Press of Mississippi.

Chodorow, J. (1991). *Dance therapy and depth psychology.* London, UK: Routledge.

Connor, D. F. (2006). Stimulants. In R. A. Barkley (Ed.), *Attention-deficit hyperactivity disorder: A handbook for diagnosis and treatment* (3rd ed., pp. 608–647). New York: Guilford.

Dulicai, D. (1999). Special report: The National Institutes of Health consensus development conference on diagnosis and treatment of attention deficit hyperactivity disorder, November 16–18, 1998. *American Journal of Dance Therapy, 21*(1), 35–45.

Edwards, J. H. (2002). Evidenced-based treatment for child ADHD: "Real-world" practice implications. *Journal of Mental Health Counseling, 24*(2), 126–139.

Eresund, P., & Wrangsjö, B. (2008). *Att förstå, bemöta och behandla bråkiga barn* [To understand, meet and treat unruly children]. Lund, Sweden: Studentlitteratur.

Fisher, J., & Ogden, P. (2009). Sensorimotor psychotherapy. In C. A. Courtois & J. D. Ford (Eds.), *Treating complex traumatic stress disorders: An evidence-based guide* (pp. 312–328). New York: Guilford.

Fonagy, P., & Target, M. (1994). The efficacy of psychoanalysis for children with disruptive disorders. *Journal of the American Academy of Child & Adolescent Psychiatry, 33*(19), 45–55.

Froelich, T. E., Lanphear, B. P., Epstein, J. N., Barbaresi, W. J., Katusic, S. K., & Kahn, R. S. (2007). Prevalence, recognition, and treatment of attention-deficit/hyperactivity disorder in a national sample of US children. *Archives of Pediatric and Adolescent Medicine, 161*(9), 857–864.

Gershon, J. (2002). A meta-analytic review of gender differences in ADHD. *Journal of Attention Disorders, 5*(3), 143–154.

Goodman, R. (1997). The Strengths and Difficulties Questionnaire: A research note. *Journal of Child Psychology and Psychiatry, 38*(5), 581–586.

Greydanus, D. E., Pratt, H. D., Sloane, M. A., & Rappley, M. D. (2003). Attention-deficit/hyperactivity disorder and adolescents: Interventions for a complex costly clinical conundrum. *Pediatric Clinics of North America, 50*(5), 1–33.

Grönlund, E. (1994). *Barns känslor bearbetade i dans: Dansterapi för barn med tidiga störningar* [Children's emotions processed in dance: Dance therapy for children with early emotional disturbances]. Doktorsavhandling, Stockholms universitet, Pedagogiska institutionen.

Grönlund, E., Alm, A., & Hammarlund, I. (1999). *Konstnärliga terapier: Bild, dans och musik i den läkande processen* [Art therapies: Art, dance, and music in the healing process]. Stockholm, Sweden: Natur och Kultur.

Grönlund, E., & Renck, B. (2004). *Dansterapi—en målinriktad behandling som stöd och hjälp för pojkar med diagnosen ADHD/DAMP* [Dance therapy—A goal directed therapy as support and help for boys with ADHD/DAMP]. Danshögskolan, Nämnden för konstnärligt utvecklingsarbete. Rapportserien Dans-forskning och utveckling, 2004:1.

Grönlund, E., & Renck, B. (2005). *Dansterapi för pojkar med ADHD: Grupp och individuell behandling* [Dance therapy for boys with ADHD: Group and individual therapy]. Danshögskolan, Nämnden för konstnärligt utvecklingsarbete. Rapportserien Dans-forskning och utveckling, 2005:1.

Grönlund, E., Renck, B., & Weibull, J. (2005). Dance/movement therapy as an alternative treatment for young boys diagnosed as ADHD: A pilot study. *American Journal of Dance Therapy, 27*(2), 63–85.

Hartmann, H. (1958). *Ego psychology and the problem of adaptation.* New York: International Universities Press.

Henderson, S. E., & Sugden, D. A. (1992). *The Movement Assessment Battery for Children.* London, UK: The Psychological Corporation.

Kessler, R. C., Adler, L. A., Barkley, R. A., Biederman, J., Conners, C. K., Faraone, S. V., ... Zaslavsky, A. M. (2005). Patterns and predictors of attention-deficit/hyperactivity disorder persistence into adulthood: Results from the national comorbidity survey replication. *Biological Psychiatry, 57*(11), 1442–1451.

Leventhal, M. (1980). *Movement and growth: Dance therapy for the special child.* New York: New York University.

Nathanson, D. L. (1987). *The many faces of shame.* New York: Guilford.

Panksepp, J. (2007). Can play diminish ADHD and facilitate the construction of the social brain? *Journal of the Canadian Academy of Child and Adolescent Psychiatry, 16*(2), 57–66.

Piek, J. P., Pitcher, T. M., & Hay, D. A. (1999). Motor coordination and kinaesthesis in boys with attention deficit-hyperactivity disorder. *Developmental Medicine and Child Neurology, 41*(3), 159–165.

240   *Engaging Boys in Treatment*

Pinker, S. (2008). *The sexual paradox: Men, women, and the real gender gap.* New York: Scribner.

Quesada-Chaverri, I. (2008). *Development of a site specific DMT clinical model for children with ADHD symptoms in Costa Rica: A literature review.* Unpublished master's thesis, Drexel University.

Redman, D. (2007). *The effectiveness of dance/movement therapy as a treatment for students in a public alternative school diagnosed with attention deficit hyperactivity disorder: A pilot study.* Unpublished master's thesis, Drexel University.

Reich, W. (1972). *Character analysis.* New York: Noonday Press.

Root, R., & Resnick, R. (2003). An update on the diagnosis and treatment of attention-deficit/hyperactivity disorder in children. *Professional Psychology: Research and Practice, 34*(1), 34–41.

Schilder, P. (1950). *The image and appearance of the human body.* New York: International Universities Press.

Schmais, C. (1974). Dance therapy in perspective. In K. Mason (Ed.), *Focus on dance VII—Dance therapy.* Reston VA: The American Alliance for Health Physical Education, Recreation, and Dance.

Sherborne, V. (1990). *Developmental movement for children.* Cambridge, UK: University Press.

Siegel, E. (1984). *The mirror of our selves: Dance movement therapy and the psychoanalytical approach* [Dissertation]. New York: Human Sciences Press.

Official Reports of the Swedish Government. (1997). *Röster om barns och ungdomars psykiska hälsa* [Voices about children's and adolescents' mental health]. SOU 1997:8. Delbetänkande av Barnpsykiatrikommittén. Stockholm, Sweden: Fritzes offentliga publikationer.

Stern, D. (1985). *The interpersonal world of the infant: A view from psychoanalysis and developmental psychology.* New York: Basic Books.

Swedish National Board of Health and Welfare—Socialstyrelsen. (2001). *Folkhälsorapport* [Public health report]. Stockholm, Sweden: Socialstyrelsen.

Swedish National Board of Health and Welfare—Socialstyrelsen. (2002). *ADHD hos barn och vuxna* [ADHD in children and adults]. Stockholm, Sweden: Socialstyrelsen.

Winnicott, D. W. (1971). *Playing and reality.* London, UK: Penguin Books.

Wrangsjö, B. (1998). *Barn som märks. Utvecklingspsykologiska möjligheter och svårigheter* [Children who are noticed: Developmental psychological possibilities and difficulties]. Stockholm, Sweden: Natur och Kultur.

CHAPTER

11

Attachment Is a Verb

Experiential Treatment for Addressing Self-Regulation and Relationship Issues in Boys With Sexual Behavior Difficulties

JOHN BERGMAN AND KEVIN CREEDEN

INTRODUCTION: HOW WE GOT HERE

In the late 1980s there was a reemergence of clinical interest in attachment theory and attachment issues (Bowlby, 1969, 1973, 1980), especially in terms of how attachment difficulties influenced problematic behavior in children (Cicchetti & Carlson, 1989; Crittenden, 1988; Greenspan & Lieberman, 1988). This focus on attachment began to appear, at least on the periphery, in some authors' writings regarding the dynamics of sexual behavior problems (Crittenden, 1997; Marshall, 1989; Marshall, Hudson, & Hodkinson, 1993; Ward, Hudson, & McCormack, 1997).

Coinciding with this increased interest in attachment dynamics and problems, researchers in neurodevelopment, with the assistance of increasingly improving technologies, began actively examining the process of brain development and how a variety of interactions with the environment might change or direct that developmental process.

One aspect of this research examined how the experience of trauma in childhood impacts the trajectory of both structural and functional neurodevelopment (Bremner et al., 1997; Perry, 2001; Teicher, Andersen, Polcari, Andersen, & Novalta, 2002). Attachment theory had always posed that early dynamics between the child and caretaker were the organizational basis for later behaviors (Bowlby, 1973; Sroufe, 1979; Sroufe & Waters, 1977), but now we could make a connection between attachment experiences and neurodevelopment (Schore, 2000; Siegel, 1999). In effect, neurodevelopment was influenced and directed by interactions between the child and the environment—and the most important interactions in this process happened between children and their primary caretakers.

In 1999, Daniel Siegel came to the Association for the Treatment of Sexual Abusers conference and, in a brief, elegant presentation, described our brains to us. He described not only how the brain worked, but also how intersubjective attachment influenced the brain's mode of working. As important, Siegel was able to point out how trauma negatively impacts the brain's functionality. For some of us, this was a revelatory moment. It was a moment when we saw that the brain/body was the exquisite physiological center of consciousness. We saw that it could be hurt not only by trauma but also by dangerous attachment experiences that, at their worst, might even lead the brain/body to distort experiences, shut down, and disengage (Siegel, 1999). We saw that the traumatized brain worked differently. It might fall behind nontraumatized brains in its ability to manage development tasks, communicate effectively, and process the vital sensations of "safeness."

For those of us who believed that addressing attachment issues was essential for treating sexual behavior problems, Siegel's presentation opened the possibility of looking at and understanding attachment from a different perspective. We now saw ways to measure the impact of different attachment experiences (Smallbone & Dadds, 2000). We realized that the effects of attachment experiences might be visible with brain measuring equipment such as a functional magnetic resonance imaging (fMRI) or a positron emission tomography (PET) scan (Perry, 2001; Teicher et al., 2002). By looking more specifically at brain functioning, it was also learned that the brain was flexible and adaptive, and that it could be changed if we were thoughtful and creative about our interventions and activities.

For those of us who already believed in promoting change through experiential interventions, we now got a glimpse at how experience itself changed the very structure of the brain. It affirmed Damasio's (2000) observation that the brain processed from the bottom up, not from the top down. We also saw that invariably *experiences* were the channeling strategy for change. Perhaps most importantly, we saw that the brain/body (trauma/attachment) framework for understanding and treating sexual behavior problems allowed us to work with greater clarity and optimism, especially as we addressed those problems in children and adolescents.

Our approach to understanding and treating sexual behavior problems in boys has therefore evolved toward a belief that attachment experiences are part of the very core of the dynamics that precipitate sexual behavior problems. Similarly, we have observed that the fulfillment of attachment needs, primarily for safety, acceptance, and nurturance, has been disrupted in many of the children we treat, by traumatic experiences, inconsistent attachment relationships, or frequently both. We have also learned from the neurodevelopmental research that traumatic experiences, especially for those children with disrupted attachment relationships, can create significant difficulties in the boys' capacity to effectively interact with their environment. These boys experience problems in self-regulation, difficulties in accurately reading social cues, learning problems (notably in language processing and development), and difficulties in flexible and adaptive problem solving (Stien & Kendall, 2004).

Attachment is not a noun, it is a verb. It is not just a theory from which to draw professional validation and acceptance. It is an ongoing, internal test, a relational struggle, a present and future experience of increasing safety that may be the hallmark of all new experiences that clients have after the end of therapy. Attachment is the very essence of the child-parent interpersonal experience from birth. It is an amalgam of experiences, acts of safety making, controlled regard, gentle but fierce containment, and creative play that stimulate synapse growth (Siegel, 2007). Attachment is the creation of the future theory of mind that may well govern all the individual's ideas, concepts, and expectations about relationships. It may be the difference between most of the time feeling safe and most of the time feeling anxious, worried, and unsafe (Bowlby, 1969). At its foundation, attaching, at least in the first year, is active, multimodal, non-language based, and stimulus filled. It is our understanding of attachment from this developmental, interpersonal perspective that directs us to facilitating and repairing attachment relationships through developmentally sequenced, interpersonal experiences.

While the structure, timing, and style of our clinical interventions may vary due to different training backgrounds, different treatment settings, individual differences in the children we treat, and our own idiosyncratic personality quirks, our treatment approach has developed to be remarkably consistent. We both believe that treatment for children and teens with sexual behavior problems:

1. Must be developmental—in that the goal is to facilitate normative, positive development—rather than focus on pathology
2. Must recognize, account for, and address the neurodevelopmental obstacles that trauma can create for our clients
3. Must prioritize secure attachment relationships as the foundation for developmental progress

Finally, we believe that the basis for attachment is attunement, and that attachment is not something one simply discusses, but rather that attachment is built through interpersonal experiences. Therefore, the process of rebuilding or repairing attachment relationships is an experiential process first. An effective cognitive framework can grow from those experiences.

THE FOUR QUADRANTS

The four quadrants refer to the neurodevelopmental, phase-oriented treatment process we developed to work with young people with a variety of dysregulated behaviors, attachment disorders, and problems with sexually abusive actions. The four quadrants are placed within "the cradle." This term refers to a setting that is carefully modulated through controlled environments that create the most secure containment possible for the young client. It is the actively maintained cradle that provides constant support for the quadrant phases.

The quadrants progress from increasing the young person's sensory awareness and practiced self-regulation to the more difficult work of the second quadrant, which focuses on sexual abuse and involves an intensive effort to reduce the impact of dysregulating memories and past experiences of shame. The third quadrant begins the work of dealing directly with the sequelae of trauma symptoms and discovering how to form safe relationships. Finally, in the fourth quadrant we start the return of the young person to his neurodevelopmentally appropriate relational world.

The Cradle: Safety and Containment as the Foundation for Treatment

At the most basic level, the primary goal of attachment is safety. Human beings are biologically predisposed to forming attachment relationships because, especially for the infant, if they cannot find a way to engage an adult in meeting their needs, they will not survive. This issue of safety obviously remains important to all of us throughout our lives. In fact, our brains are hardwired so that cues in the environment that suggest danger (e.g., loud noises, darkness, being alone) are prioritized for rapid processing (LeDoux, 1995). Safety becomes an even more pronounced issue for those individuals with early trauma experiences.

Brain research has indicated that functions in the prefrontal cortex are essential for regulating primary sensory and motor responses and are highly engaged in maintaining homeostasis (Schore, 2000). In addition, the prefrontal cortex plays an important role in attachment functions by processing the information necessary to initiate social activity and by mediating emotional interactions between individuals (Balbernie, 2001;

Schore, 2001). While the brain's limbic system (containing the hypo-thalamus, hippocampus, and amygdala, along with the temporal lobes) is primarily responsible for appraising stimuli, controlling emotions, and processing information in the service of survival, it is the interaction between the limbic system and the prefrontal cortex that allows for the monitoring of physical states, the translation of sensation into recogniz-able emotions, and the evaluation of meaning based upon these interac-tions and previous experience (Balbernie, 2001). Since the prefrontal cortex has only limited development and functioning in infancy, the relationship or *attunement* between the infant and his caretaker in this early developmental period allows the caretaker to serve as the auxiliary prefrontal cortex for the child (Siegel, 1999). Schore (1997) contends that these attunement experiences lay the template, or the foundation, for the processing of emotional information in the prefrontal cortex, and that abuse, neglect, or the chronic lack of attunement between the child and caretaker lead to an impaired ability for the individual to modulate emotions and behavior in response to threat.

Working from a developmental perspective, building or repairing this capacity for effectively recognizing, modulating, and responding to emotional cues necessitates the active modeling, teaching, and creating of opportunities to experience and practice attunement. Through this process, we might thereby stimulate those neural pathways that can lead to developing increased capacities for monitoring physical states, identifying emotions, and evaluating meaning.

Almost all recent treatment models for addressing trauma speak to the need for *phase-oriented* treatment (Allen, 2001; Kinniburgh, Blaustein, Spinazzola, & van der Kolk, 2005; Saxe, Ellis, & Kaplow, 2007; van der Kolk, McFarlane, & Weisaeth, 1996). These models all identify the need for safety and stabilization in the beginning of the treatment pro-cess as the foundation for later progress. This position is consistent with what we know about normative development: that children are more likely to thrive and learn in safe, consistent, supportive, and nurturing environments (Maslow, 1968; Strayhorn, 1988). Bergman talks about this phase of treatment as creating *the cradle*, while Creeden borrows Allen's (2001) use of the term *containment*. Here we will use the notion of creating the cradle to describe those basic but essential issues in treat-ment that need to be addressed before anything else can proceed.

Elements of the Cradle

Young people and their parents/caregivers arrive at treatment and resi-dential centers anxious, angry, shamed, defended, and dissociated. Our emphasis on the cradle is about creating a new and more secure sense of containment for the child and family, a world of safety rather than danger. Some of the elements that make up the cradle, as we shall dis-cuss, include intensive attention to all aspects of the young person's safe environment, calibrating healthy sensory stimulation, reducing shame, assessing the mechanics of secure interaction, creating predictable structures, clarifying mutual expectations, and preeducating caregivers and clients about the basic concepts of the functions of the brain. Perhaps the most crucial element of the cradle is the program's staff members, for they are the ones who play an expanding role in the future healthy attunement of the young people, and therefore must be educated in multimodal communication and basic neurodevelopment.

Safety

One of the first elements for creating stabilization is making sure the environment in which the client is living is as safe as possible. In working with boys with sexual behavior problems, this task is frequently implemented by completing a "risk assessment," or identifying the level of risk the individual has for reengaging in sexually inappropriate or abusive behaviors. However, risk assessments frequently are undertaken without acknowledging two key factors. First, predicting risk for reengaging in problematic sexual behavior has proven quite difficult for professionals to do, especially with regard to adolescent males; second, this "risk" does not reside solely in the child or adolescent but instead in the interaction between the child or adolescent and his environment. Two boys with the same difficulties in self-regulation and similar psychological profiles can present very different levels of risk depending on the level of structure, support, and demands present in the environment in which they function.

Instead of viewing this as a risk assessment, we find that our treatment goals are better served in formulating this as a *safety* assessment. Essentially, the goal is identifying the type of physical environment, daily structure, adult involvement, and level of activity necessary to keep this child and those around him safe. Saxe et al. (2007) have conceived this as an interaction between the level of dysregulation in the child (*regulated, emotionally dysregulated, behaviorally dysregulated*) and the level of stability in the child's social environment (*stable, distressing, threatening*). By assessing the level of dysregulation in the context of social stability, we can then make a determination about the types and intensity of interventions needed to maintain safety. For example, a behaviorally dysregulated teen living in a threatening environment may require a placement outside the home, the removal of an abusive adult from the home, or the intensive involvement of treatment/support services both at home and at school to maintain safety. This same adolescent in a stable environment might merely require the support of a guidance counselor or coach at school and weekly individual and family sessions with a therapist to maintain safety. Structure and safety at this time also relate to the structure and safety of the treatment work itself.

Developing the cradle is sensitive, very active work that can have a profound neurological impact. As we have noted, the heart of the child's early attachment experience with the mother is safety. The mother keeps the child secure and affectively and physically safe. The heart of what we try to create very early on in treatment is exactly the same: secure containment, initiation of attaching activity, and reduction of the level of reactive (frequently subconscious) limbic system arousal.

The imperative is to reduce the wariness, anxiety, or fear that early trauma or disrupted attachment has created in the brain. Hence, we do intentional work at the beginning of treatment to create a nurturing, supportive environment. Because we know that the intimacy of emotional nurturing may be challenging or even frightening to many of these children, this early work is sensitively tuned to the needs of the individual child. Built into our approach is our understanding that the child is concurrently enduring the stress of coming to treatment and, in addition, may be struggling with the ongoing difficulties present in his relationship with parent or caregiver. For many young people, these combined experiences may be greater than the more objective areas of the brain can handle.

This means that we must pay attention to every aspect of the treatment encounter: the treatment space, the use of light and color, sound, scent, and what is drawn on the walls. The words written on the whiteboard as a greeting are carefully calculated. We have used large swathes of color, huge red Chinese symbols, and palm fronds. There are areas of the walls that are reserved for the children's drawings and their other works, which show that they have made huge progress. We use alpha- or theta-centric music that we test beforehand to see that the "energy" created seems right for these young people. They initially react to the music with wariness or criticism, but quickly get used to its "strangeness." Based on the literature, we also began also to use lavender oil mist as a calming agent, given the intense sensitivity that the brain has to odors (Atsumi & Tonosaki, 2007).

The focus of the first session is always to create a peaceful, safe meeting place. We watch the parents and boys connect, looking to gauge the safety or danger of their current interactions. We are also looking to gauge the level of attunement between child and caregiver. Overall, the goal is to reduce as much as possible the intensity of shame and anxiety that the pair is likely to feel as they come into the meeting.

These early meetings are also a chance to watch for the presence of under- or overregulation in individual children. One of the results of trauma, and an indicator of intense anxiety, is the boy's inability to handle stress. The brain's subcortical center has often lost the ability to sustain a low-level response (Stien & Kendall, 2004), so we work quickly to assist the child in reducing the anxiety and increasing the brain's ability to cope.

Within a residential setting, these "early meetings" are parallel to our initial assessment period (generally 30 days), and the goals are essentially the same. We are looking to create a safe and supportive environment, diminish the level of the teen's anxiety and shame, gauge the safety of the teen's style of interaction, and develop a level of attunement between the child and the treatment staff so that we can be proactive in helping the individual youth not get overwhelmed by the demands of the environment or the intensity of the interactions between peers and adults that residential settings create.

An important element of safety and stabilization in any environment will be the presence or establishment of a consistent, predictable structure. Humans generally feel safer when their physical surroundings, emotional and physical demands, level of resources, and level of support are clearly defined and more predictable. Anxiety tends to get heightened as the surroundings are more novel and the demands and resources less predictable. In well-regulated individuals who have a reasonable level of self-esteem, new, demanding tasks or environments can be viewed as opportunities for growth and learning. However, for individuals who have trouble modulating their emotional and behavioral responses, an unpredictable environment and high levels of emotional demands are frequently perceived as threatening. These individuals naturally respond by defending themselves, through fleeing, fighting, freezing, or emotionally withdrawing—all the things that humans normally do when faced with a threatening situation.

Establishing and agreeing to the basics, such as how frequently we will meet, for how long, where, who is expected to be present, how they will get to therapy, and who will take care of the other children (if they're not present) are all important elements of creating a sense of predictability and safety. In addition, agreeing on the priorities and goals of treatment, establishing markers of treatment progress, and broadly clarifying mutual expectations will serve to diminish anxieties. Some of this structure can be managed quite easily and quickly. Other aspects of the treatment structure will need to be negotiated, sometimes for several sessions, before a working agreement can be reached. Different parts of the systems involved with these families and children (schools, probation, social services, churches, and so on) may have quite different priorities and agendas. In addition, we must consider the different priorities or agendas of the teen, the different family members, and the therapist. Identifying the places where these agendas overlap and establishing treatment goals based on these commonalities will at times take considerable effort.

Within families, establishing structure may mean the clarification or development of clear family roles, a daily schedule, routines for doing certain tasks, and some clear guidelines around essential behavioral expectations. Who wakes me up in the morning, who will be around the house during breakfast, who makes breakfast, who is present when I get home from school, what the expectation is around homework, who's making dinner, who is present for meals, when meals happen, when bedtime occurs, what the routine is for going to bed—all of these might be issues to address in helping the family clarify or develop structure. Clearly, there might be numerous struggles between children and parents regarding a number of structure-related issues. In creating the cradle we are looking to *clarify* the structure and expectations, not to resolve every issue. In addition, at this point in treatment we are only looking to prioritize those things necessary for safety and stabilization. Longer-term desires, goals, or conflicts that do not directly affect imme-diate safety concerns can be tabled until later.

Much of defining structure may sound like a process of drawing up schedules and negotiating contracts, and, in fact, there may be some of that taking place with the family. Yet, frequently, we find that these boys and their families are not sure, or can't quite define, what it is they want or need. It is often in creating moments of shared activity, explora-tion, and experience that we'll hear the declarations of "That was great" or "I didn't know that" or "That felt better," which can help children and their families clarify needs and priorities.

The experiential therapies used in the creation of the four quadrants, including drama therapy, movement, and art therapy, are multipurpose tools. They serve as assessment instruments, as mediums of information exchange (especially for those who have trauma-based issues with spon-taneity, or have sensory problems that make more accepted techniques of treatment and learning difficult to achieve), as vital techniques for attaching children and parents, and as a means of making significant bonding markers for therapist and client. Experiential therapies use techniques that emphasize emotional experiencing and "commitment to a phenomenological approach that flows directly from this central interest in experiencing" (Elliott, Greenberg, & Lietaer, 2004).

Preeducation: Brain Function and Development

Educational research has indicated that preexposure to learning mate-rial allows the brain to better organize and assimilate later content. In addition, this preexposure tends to increase motivation for later learn-ing tasks (Luiten, Ames, & Ackerson, 1980; Weil & Murphy, 1982). This has led us to offering the boys in our program and their fami-lies information about brain organization and functioning, as well as information about the impact of trauma on the brain, as an important facet of the initial treatment sessions. We have kept the information in simple language and have incorporated a number of visual presenta-tions to make the information easier to understand. Borrowing from an educational curriculum called *BrainWise* (Gorman-Barry, 2008), we lay out a framework for understanding the connection between sensations, emotions, thinking, and behavior. Although we identify brain areas with their appropriate labels (e.g., amygdala, prefrontal cortex, limbic system, thalamus, and so on), the language that we end up working with in treatment is the BrainWise version, which identifies the limbic areas as the "lizard brain" and the prefrontal cortex as the "wizard brain." The goal of treatment can therefore be defined as always having one's wizard brain working with one's lizard brain in an effort to make thoughtful and effective decisions about behavior.

We then discuss how some past experiences can create obstacles in the way the wizard and lizard brain communicate and work together. We can pull examples from problematic behavior that the families have identified and reframe this behavior in the wizard/lizard dynamic. At this point, the clinician will note how some of the modalities we will use in treatment (e.g., breathing, yoga, movement, drawing, Brain Gym) can help reconnect or improve communication between the wizard and lizard parts of the brain.

We have found that this early exposure to the brain information helps parents/caregivers gain a more comprehensive understanding of their child's behaviors, which allows them to place treatment in a less shameful and more normative context. In addition, this preeducation has offered a rationale and increased motivation for engaging in the active self-regulating experiences (e.g., sensory-based activities, Brain Gym, breathing) that in the beginning many boys and their families might view as being uncomfortable, strange, or "stupid."

Therapists and Staff: An Essential Element of the Cradle

Since we are looking to create a safe, connected environment in which this treatment can take place, the people within that environment become the most important elements in facilitating the cradle's development and maintaining its safety. This includes all staff (clinical, support, residential, administrative, and educational) with whom the boy or his family may have contact. While this is important regardless of the setting, the process becomes more pronounced, and more difficult to achieve, when the work occurs within a residential treatment or other group care setting.

Staff members are educated about neurodevelopment and the types of difficulties that might result from a history of trauma. They are also retrained to examine and understand difficult behavior from attachment-focused and trauma-focused perspectives with an appreciation of how attunement difficulties and processing problems can lead to dysregulation and poor decision making. Staff also need to be made more aware of how the lighting, physical organization, noise level, sounds, colors, and smells of a setting can dramatically affect the dynamics of what occurs in those settings. Additionally, helping staff attend to how their tone of voice, body language, eye contact, and use of touch all impact the client's and family's response on both a conscious and unconscious level requires not only training but persistent modeling, support, and coaching. The clinical staff are also retrained to work in this new way, reading clinical histories for issues ranging from marital discord to early experiences of aphasia, agnosia, and so on. Staff members are taught to look at all activity and to ask themselves, "What could the brain be doing so that this child is acting in this way?"

They are further trained to work in multiple modalities—to be ready to translate all they say into drawing, writing, moving, demonstrating, and creating hands-on techniques. Other teaching techniques include educational kinesiology, play therapy, art therapy, and so on. And, critically, staff are encouraged to keep the therapy speeches to a minimum of words as sensory disturbances in the brain often make it hard for children to work in modalities that conservative treatment finds most comfortable, such as words, logical deduction, memory analysis, or memory as symbolic representation. Again, many of these skills are not highly advanced in *any* child through the age of 15, and trauma is known to affect more typical development capacities in a whole range of neuroprocessing tasks (Teicher et al., 2002). The fundamental message is: Always keep the brain "in mind" and appreciate the fact that the presence of a consistent, supportive, adult relationship in a child's life is the key ingredient to the child's resiliency and competency.

PHASE-ORIENTED TREATMENT

The work of this treatment is broken into four quadrants. The cradle becomes the context into which the work is placed: close connection, strong and real participation from and with caregivers, and genuine therapeutic work to take care of the caregivers and get them through the shock, shame, and anger over what their children have done. We intentionally create a safe, structured, but very connected treatment universe that has some resemblance to the positive, developmental attributes in any generally healthy family. The treatment goals of the four quadrants can be summarized as follows:

Quadrant 1
- Sensing and regulating what is happening inside me
- Learning to become attuned to others (with a focus on attunement between the child and the parent or caregiver)

Quadrant 2
- Increased mindful self-awareness
- Learning the dynamics of my sexually abusive behavior from a strengths-based perspective
- Dealing with the memories and with as little shame as possible

Quadrant 3
- Dealing with my losses
- Addressing my trauma
- Developing the tools to make healthier relationships

Quadrant 4
- Reconnecting to my appropriate developmental world
- Learning about sexuality as a relationship
- Learning about and clarifying my role as a man

Each quadrant builds on the one before. We believe that it is not helpful to begin with sexual abuse issues because these youths' own histories of dysregulation and trauma have so strongly impacted their ability to feel safe containment from another person when they are in distress. They have difficulties regulating their limbic reactivity, not only the shame-filled memories of what they have done, but also the painful memories of what they have personally experienced.

Quadrant 1

The work of the first quadrant is to help boys overcome their dysregulation and be able to become aware of sensations in their bodies that are connected to feelings (what we might call the unheard physical signal). Then they must learn to heed and control, or heed and experience. Early work focuses on helping the young people to understand sensations. Using taste sensations like horseradish or dark chocolate, we ask the young people to describe exactly what they experience when they taste these different foods, and then we use this as a standard for asking about other sensations. Depending on one's clinical style, this would also be the phase of treatment in which one might do a more specific sensory assessment using questionnaires such as the Adolescent/Adult Sensory Profile (Brown & Dunn, 2002) that explore both the boy's perceptions and the caregivers' perceptions of the sensory preferences or needs of the individual youth.

We also look at other triggers for physical sensations, and later in the quadrant we especially look at triggers that are emotionally distressing. Hand in hand with this work are a variety of brain/body-based strategies and techniques, which are taught to the young people to help them regulate some of these different sensations. In particular, Harrison's breath techniques (Harrison, 2005), some yoga, and Brain Gym (Dennison & Dennison, 1994) are used, as well as other mindfulness exercises. In a residential setting, we have found the need to be much more structured and specific in terms of introducing these techniques to young people, and also in terms of defining the times when they practice these techniques. Therefore, within the residential program our clients are first taught a range of breathing or movement techniques by their therapists.

In staff training sessions, educational and residential staff members receive instruction and practice using the same techniques. Following this, the program schedule is structured so that, at set times throughout the day, brief (typically five-minute) periods are set aside for youth to engage in the regular practice of this week's or this month's self-regulation strategies. Individually, therapists will work with a youth to identify those techniques that seem to work best for that particular boy, under different circumstances, at different times of day. These activities or strategies will be incorporated into the child's individual treatment plan and utilized in addition to the program-wide moments of self-regulation learning and practice that are part of the daily schedule.

Fundamental breathing work is particularly important. In the community-based program, when we gave this as a homework assignment with the parent, we often found that the boys and the parents would learn to do the exercises together. In so doing, they began some of the early attunement work so necessary to safe attachment. Of significant effect is a deceptively simple-sounding exercise called the three sighs (Harrison, 2005). This is a series of deep inhalations followed by longer and deeper open-mouthed and sometimes vocalized sighs. This exercise, in itself, seemed to offer the boys less restriction than a more rigid yoga breath, while, over time, increasing the sensations of relaxation. These exercises are gradually replaced with other breath-focused exercises that are designed to intensify hearing and sensation and to slow young people's automatic responses down until they can reach simple mindfulness. Specifically, the aim is for them to use more of their prefrontal cortex (wizard brain) and so be less likely to experience limbic system dysregulation (lizard brain).

Parents are obviously a crucial part of this work. No session within a community-based or outpatient treatment program should be conducted without the parent and child doing work with each other on their intensely complex relationship. In addition, every session practices new attempts at attachment. For instance, the children and their caregiver must sit and face each other, at first for no more than 30 seconds. We collect data from this encounter. Both parent and child, for example, might wear oximeters and take their pulses before they begin their connecting and immediately after the event is done. Or, we take their pulses for them and then record them. Not only do we take pulse rates, but we also count the number of "events" that transpire between them. This might include coughs, facial movements, talking, and so on. Over time, we see the number of events change, and the pulse levels reflect an increased level of comfort. Pulse readings are done as soon as the children and parents enter the treatment space, and then are used as benchmarks to measure arousal. Eventually parents and children become adept at using this as a way to perceive their dysregulation and to use breath interventions to change their response.

Neurodevelopmental research has shown that the capacity of the child and the caregiver, as well as the child and other children, to engage in the imitation of shared motor responses (e.g., body movements, facial movements, vocalizations) plays a key role in the development of a child's sense of agency, self, and self-other differentiation. These characteristics are also the components involved in the development of empathy (Decety & Meyer, 2009). Human imitation is an adaptive way to learn skills and a milestone in the development of intentional communication and social interaction (Decety & Meyer, 2009; Rogers, 1999). Specific to youth with sexual behavior problems, developing a sense of agency (you are responsible for your behavior), disentangling your own experiences from the experiences of others (your behavior impacts other people), and developing an affective response stemming from an understanding of the other person's emotional state (empathy) are frequently identified as key treatment goals. Therefore, this phase of treatment seeks to present numerous opportunities for mirroring or imitation experiences. Parents and children copy each other's breathing, body movements, expressions, and sounds. Group treatment participants, first in dyads but eventually in larger groups, will engage in similar forms of imitation and also in activities such as three-legged races, group jump rope, dancing, or drumming activities, all geared to creating that experience of being "in sync" with the other or others around you. This capacity to mirror has been shown to be fundamental to developing attunement with others, and this attunement is essential to relational attachment. In normal development, it begins with the bottom-up processing of shared motor representations, which are eventually regulated by top-down executive processing in the prefrontal cortex (Decety, 2006). Working from both a developmental and an experiential perspective leads us to start with enriching these capacities for shared experiences before focusing on the top-down processes of understanding and "meaning making."

Toward the end of this phase of treatment, we also utilize simple biofeedback tools to motivate and help boys develop skills in self-regulation and mindfulness. Tools such as the Healing Rhythms program (2006) and computer games such as *Inner Tube* (2004) allow them to transform their computers into biofeedback devices. These tools measure both heart rate variability (HRV) and skin conductance level (SCL) as they guide users through a series of tasks or activities. The goal is to give boys more awareness of the correlation between their mental states and their physical states, and to provide an engaging vehicle that encourages regular practice of mindfulness skills and provides concrete evidence of, as well as positive reinforcement for, progress made in this area.

Quadrant 2

Quadrant 2 is very full, as a number of things are happening concurrently. In this quadrant, we continue mindfulness work, yoga exercises that promote sensory integration, kinesthetic responsivity work, and conjoint homework with parent and child, increasing the attunement skills that each must have. Having boys and parents work together on a task that challenges each side to interpret meaning develops this more focused attunement. These exercises expand on mirroring activities and add active turn-taking exercises. The young people still continue with breath exercises and Brain Gym (educational kinesiology) and, if they are utilizing it, Healing Rhythms. In addition, they do partnered yoga with an underlying focus on such sensory issues as vestibular activity.

It is in this quadrant that we begin and finish the sexual abuse work using the narrative therapy strategy of Ayland and West (2006) called "good way, bad way," a strengths-based approach. They wrote:

Each person has a Good Side and a Bad Side. Usually your Good Side is much bigger than you think. If you listen to your Good Side and learn to act on what it says you will go the Good Way and get the things that you want without getting into trouble. (p. 19)

A clear goal in using this approach is to build a sense of *competency*. The message is that you have skills, you have strengths, and you can make choices. While acknowledging past bad choices and the impact of those choices on others, the focus is on moving forward on a different path and with a different way of viewing yourself in the world.

This strategy works to eliminate the great problem with so many other approaches to treatment of sexual acting out behaviors. This problem is the subtle or unspoken focus on shame, or asking the young person to be ashamed. From a brain perspective, shame is a limbic-based, neurological act that may automatically trigger trauma responses in the young person. We know that young people find it very hard to talk about what they have done without this topic bringing up a variety of profound, anxiety-creating experiences, including their own traumatization (not necessarily sexual), and the traumatization they experienced immediately after they were caught engaging in sexual acting out behavior, or even during the event, when some realized that what they were doing was profoundly wrong.

Ayland and West's approach is one with which a large variety of children seem to be able to work. Everyone can think of the good side of themselves; everyone can clearly see their bad side. In practice, much of the basic work around distorting and distorted beliefs, angry but unrealized sensations, and other triggers is easier and less damaging through the use of narrative work like good way.

Quadrant 3

Quadrant 3 is perhaps one of the most crucial elements of successful work with boys who have sexual behavior difficulties. Again, the theoretical and physical evidence says that when children experience dramatic events in their lives, these events affect the brain most significantly if they have less pronounced resiliency skills. These events scar different parts of the brain, and thus affect the ability of the child to successfully maneuver through the demands of each developmental milestone.

Children with these difficulties run the risk of significantly reduced age-appropriate skills, and therefore are potentially less likely to be able to keep up with their peer group. This can lead to feeling unskilled socially, different from others, lonely and oddly angry, and even feeling inappropriate and unable to judge the cues that everyone else is perceiving and interpreting. One of the other possible behavioral problems can be sexually inappropriate behavior.

This quadrant focuses on loss, grief, and trauma. Children working together in small groups, often with their parents present, focus on losses such as relatives who left, parents who died, being moved from a dangerous home, and so on. In addition, we use eye movement desensitization and reprocessing (EMDR; Shapiro, 1995) and emotional freedom technique (EFT; Craig, 2009) to help reduce flashbacks, freezing, and uncomfortable and dysregulating memories. During this work, we also surface the major blockages for parent and child in terms of dyadic attunement, such as "Mom, what I am afraid of is that you will never love me again, that you will think I am terrible and a freak." Surfacing this allows caregivers and children to speak, cry, be heard, and be loved. Building on the first two quadrants of work, child and parent learn to exchange love and even the beginning of pride. When there are still attachment issues at this point, we intensify the focus of the family group using the supportive strength of all the parents to help the maladaptive parent find a voice that is more in tune with the "family" norm.

The mindfulness work is also intensified. We ask the boys to do the exercises three to five times per week. We include the activity of film making—making a film of their lives—and bringing in photographs of significant people who do elicit feelings from them. This is the quadrant in which we also see the greatest amount of change in that the parents seem more settled, more likely also to support the other children in the group.

We will include a word at this point about our intellectually disabled/developmentally delayed clients. Much of this work is also conducted with these children, though even more work is done to ensure that they have truly understood, and have retained what they have understood. Thus, with these children we have used the concept of "dragon" and "lion," making drawings to create huge pictures of these creatures. Dragon is the fire breather that might get each one of them to go to the bad side/bad way. Lion is the strength inside them that helps them stick to the good side, and therefore go the good way.

In addition, we do some original exercises that focus on developing the nine functions of the middle prefrontal cortex (Siegel, 2007). These functions include body regulation, attuned communication, response flexibility, empathy, insight, fear modulation, intuition, emotional balance, and morality (Siegel, 2007). Our work with body regulation, for example, includes slowing down and speeding up body movement on command, then in relation to sound patterns or with the metronome, and then with the parent.

Quadrant 4

Quadrant 4 is all about relationships: relinking the boy and parent back to their nontherapy world, and linking the child back to what is developmentally appropriate for him as well. The real world of peer relationships is the toughest challenge of all the work. The damage caused to the child has rippling effects throughout the exosystem. Children who have gone through sexual abuse as victims, or profound emotional abuse, may well be fearful of reconnection.

Connecting healthily to therapists is not the same as connecting to people in the free world. In the real world, young peers can be almost brutal in their creation of hierarchy, aloof or cruel about peer inclusion criteria, misguided and lacking empathy about things they know little about, like sexuality, and rigid about trying out new ventures or approaches when they become even slightly fearful. Young people who have gone through treatment are fearful that others will find out, are still ashamed of what they have done, are lacking in self-confidence and in self-esteem, and are filled with psychological insight that very often their peers don't have. Thus, it is not odd that a young man, after nine months of treatment, might still choose to be with younger girls because their developmental levels are so much easier and less confusing for him to fathom.

Hence, the final quadrant is jammed. In this quarter, we do more active work on retrieving old memories from the hippocampus so that the young person can create the fullest autobiography and have a safer portrait of self. The focus is strengths based: The best self operating with the young person's known strengths (sport, fairness, and so on) can make his mother proud. This is reinforced by the parents in the early part of the quadrant, with sessions focused on the boy saying his strengths out loud. We have used scrapbooks as a means for the young person to develop his autobiography, including pictures, drawings, poems, songs, and items that he might have collected during different times in his life. Sometimes these are presented in a "show and tell" type of process in a group or family session; at other times they are merely entered into the scrapbook, much like one would place an entry in a diary.

This process of collecting, organizing, sifting through, and "making sense" not only engages the developmental task of creating a sense of self, but it can also help in placing the youth's trauma experience in the context of his entire life, as opposed to being *the* defining event or events in his life. Finally, the scrapbook also has a section about the future. The boy considers hopes, plans, goals, and obstacles and begins to consider what he is doing currently in his life (including treatment) as an important element of where he is going in the future.

The homework material is all aimed at connecting the boy into active, limbically safe patterns and strengthening the prefrontal cortex to rationalize the fearfulness of the limbic kindling. Thus, in some cases, the trauma work continues. In this quadrant, the major learning foci include maleness, fathers and men as caregivers, and human sexuality as a function of relationship and self-management postpuberty. Especially for parents, it can be a relief to understand how puberty chemically affects the physiology, and thus the reactivity, of the young adolescent. Sexuality for young adolescents, and even older ones, is a complex weave.

For some of the boys, merely talking about sexuality can be enough to frighten them and make them feel far from the sense that surely they know this already. Discussions of sexuality can remind them of the event(s) that got them into trouble. Though they may have drawn up a *cordon sanitaire* around the event, they may not yet have learned, or even wanted to learn, to distinguish between new sexual thinking and old memories. The trauma around being apprehended, loss of faith from family, isolation, and loss of contact with other members of the family may still be with them. So considering a new set of relationships with others, especially with girls, may feel frightening.

We find that boys therefore have a raw reaction to sexuality, tempered by how much sex education is already taught to them. What is surely more difficult to teach is reciprocal sensuality, and how sexuality is a function of caring about someone. Unfortunately, good books for young people about sexuality have not yet been written.

From this place we move to addressing the topics of males, maleness, and relating to adult males, including male caregivers and fathers. The fathers are often not a potent part of the treatment, as they are working during the treatment times. There are times when we have "insisted" that we see them come to pick their child up, and in this time we get to talk with them and learn about their interactions with child and family. Fathers eventually come to trust us to talk about their concerns over how to discipline the dysregulated child. We teach them also how to use pulse regulation, breath regulation, and mindfulness techniques. As is somewhat true for the mothers, though perhaps less so, the fathers utilize the techniques because they give them a way to engage with their sons that is nonconfrontational. Interestingly, when we talked afterward to the fathers about one of the assignments for the boys (talk to your father about sex), the fathers were in the main disappointed at the anxious and shutdown interactions that had occurred. We used this experience to show many of them how young males with trauma and attachment disorders have multiple brain reactions to worry, anxiety, and dread that reduce, restrict, and rigidify their responses. As ever, the heart of some of this type of work is getting others to see past the old paradigm of behavior analysis and into the practice of asking what the behavior indicates the brain is doing and how to treat the brain.

We believe fathers are a frequently underestimated part of the healing equation. The fathers in our program were able to create a safe circle for the young men to sit in, and then began to tell stories about growing up. Eventually we asked them to tell the young boys a healing story. After much discussion among the fathers while the boys were out of the room, the boys were asked back in, and they sat on pillows in the middle of the circle to listen to the metaphoric story that the fathers had prepared. The effect was enormous, especially from fathers who had never realized how much impact their vulnerable selves could have on their connection-hungry sons. The final work is, significantly, a *celebration* of the boys themselves. This is a tribute certainly to their hard work and their accomplishments over the last number of months, but more importantly, it is a public honoring of the courage and the heart that each of these young boys has demonstrated.

MOVING FORWARD

We are learning to listen to the paradigm that creates its own way to approach and work with families and clients. The information we now know about how the brain works and how attachment occurs is mounting steadily. The information is sometimes frustratingly complex and sometimes difficult to explain to other practitioners. Conversely, the appeal of approaching the treatment of problematic behavior in boys from an attachment-focused, brain-based perspective is that it offers a context that is optimistic, sustaining, and consistent with our understanding of healthy human development. Truly engaging in this work means understanding how the brain/body converts various stimuli, and what happens when something goes wrong with this complex human system. It also means appreciating how early life experiences and early life relationships have shaped the brain, and how the brain/body currently processes even the most common daily interactions. Providing treatment then becomes an issue of what will make the brain/body respond more adaptively, more safely, and less dangerously.

Brain-based strategies are sometimes quite simple, and at other times remarkably novel. At their foundation, these interventions are developmental, holistic, relational, and gentle. At its most complex, treatment can involve sophisticated brain mapping and stimulation utilizing expensive computer-based devices; at its most basic, it can involve a parent reading to a child or simply rocking in a chair. The excitement in doing this work is appreciating the profound impact that each of these interventions can have upon the brain and how the child sees himself in relation to others. Merely creating the environment for safely contained, intrarelational interactivity can mean profoundly changing the approach of not just how the family and child relate, but also how staff, educators, administrators, social service systems, and, of course, the therapist relate to the family and each other. What we have come to see is the totality of difference that this way of working really can create.

It is hard to call what we have presented here a *treatment model*; rather, it is a perspective from which we approach treatment and choose interventions to facilitate adaptive, resilient functioning. Mere process will not necessarily replicate what we have done. The quadrants that we discuss, for example, are not really a menu for doing this type of work, but more a signpost to you that you are working within a brain-based paradigm.

Each child, each family, and each caregiver have different problems and different needs. The ultimate goal is holistic and intrapsychic healing. Sexually abusive behaviors, no matter how extensive and repetitive, are not the focus of the work at the beginning. Whether you use educational kinesiology (Dennison & Dennison, 1994), extensive and intensive brain-based learning techniques (Bengis & Cuninggim, 2007), experiential therapy techniques (Bergman & Hewish, 2003), or wilderness and psychodrama (Robson & Lambie, 1995), the work will still demand of the treatment providers a huge leap.

The basic paradigm guides the essence of the work and is not a toolbox approach. What we referred to earlier as being in sync, the experience of attuned relationality, can be arrived at through dozens of pathways. But the issue is first that practitioners recognize why they must create that experience with young people and caregivers/family first, and then create, in the here and now, the experience of being in sync.

Where Might This Work Go?

Dr. Amen, in his very practical book (1998), described work that he does with a range of clients. If he suspects that the client has neurological issues, he does a single photon emission tomagraphy (SPECT), an accurate, nuclear-driven picture that can show linkages between brain structure and behavior on the client and then focuses on what he considers the major brain systems: basal ganglia, prefrontal cortex, temporal lobes, anterior cingulate, and limbic system. His prescriptions for changing these parts of the brain range from medications and neurofeedback to changing schema in much the way that Young, Klosko, and Weishaar (2003) would suggest in their schema-focused therapy.

In time, we may be able to more effectively work with the dysfunctional impulses that show up in the cerebellum and impact cortical motor regions that activate muscles. Sensorimotor therapy (Ogden & Minton, 2000) may well be effective at rebalancing the excitatory and inhibitory activity of the cerebellum. This approach could lead to better treatment of autism, attention deficit hyperactivity disorder (ADHD), and even obsessive-compulsive disorder (OCD).

We hope to see how experiential therapies, with their potent coordinative impact on clients, could nudge the cerebellum's coordination of motion, as well as sharpen the activity of the thalamus as it drives impulses toward the prefrontal cortex. We have learned that approaches such as drama therapy, art therapy, movement, sensorimotor therapy, and mindfulness-based experiential work contain the basic tools for facilitating the brain's achievement of optimal regulatory skills. The modulated brain will subsequently be more accurate in its attempts to synchronize itself with others.

We have learned that the most effective treatment starts with attunement and safe, adaptive experiences, because that is how healthy development starts. Making daily life and daily relationships safe again (or perhaps safe for the first time) is the significant primary foundation to doing effective therapy, just as it is the foundation for healthy development. Once the client is able to regulate brain and body responses, his brain can more accurately process challenges and more effectively make adaptive decisions. The practical work of the four quadrants is a way to consolidate and facilitate developmental tasks that provide steps on the way to neurological regulation and discovery.

REFERENCES

Allen, J. G. (2001). *Traumatic relationships and serious mental disorders.* New York: Wiley.

Amen, D. G. (1998). *Change your brain, change your life: The breakthrough program for conquering anxiety, depression, obsessiveness, anger, and impulsiveness.* New York: Three Rivers Press.

Atsumi, T., & Tonosaki, K. (2007). Smelling lavender and rosemary increases free radical scavenging activity and decreases cortisol levels in saliva. *The Journal of Psychiatry Research, 150*(1), 89–96.

Ayland, L., & West, B. (2006). *The good way model: A strengths based approach for working with young people, especially those with intellectual difficulties, who have sexually abusive behaviour* [Monograph]. Wellington, NZ: Wellington STOP, Inc.

Balbernie, R. (2001). Circuits and circumstances: The neurobiological consequences of early relationship experiences and how they shape later behaviour. *Journal of Child Psychotherapy, 27*(3), 237–255.

Bengis, S. M., & Cuninggim, P. (2007). Beyond psychology: Brain-based approaches that impact behavior, learning and treatment. In R. Longo & D. Prescott (Eds.), *Current perspectives: Working with sexually aggressive youth and youth with sexual behavior problems* (pp. 581–594). Holyoke, MA: NEARI Press.

Bergman, J., & Hewish, S. (2003). *Challenging experience: An experiential approach to the treatment of serious offenders.* Oklahoma City, OK: Wood 'N' Barnes Publishing.

Bowlby, J. (1969). *Attachment and loss: Attachment* (Vol. I). New York: Basic Books.

Bowlby, J. (1973). *Attachment and loss: Separation: Anxiety and Anger* (Vol. II). New York: Basic Books.

Bowlby, J. (1980). *Attachment and loss: Loss: Sadness and depression* (Vol. III). New York: Basic Books.

Bremner, J. D., Randall, P., Vermetten, E. C., Staib, L., Bronen, R. A., Capelli, S., ... Charney, D. C. (1997). MRI based measurement of hippocampal volume in posttraumatic stress disorder related to childhood physical and sexual abuse: A preliminary report. *Biological Psychiatry, 41*(1), 23–32.

Brown, C. E., & Dunn, W. (2002). *Adolescent/Adult Sensory Profile: User's manual.* Antonia, TX: The Psychological Corporation.

Cicchetti, C., & Carlson, V. (1989). (Eds.). *Child maltreatment: Theory and research on the causes and consequences of child abuse and neglect.* New York: Cambridge University Press.

Craig, G. (2009, December 22). *Emotional freedom technique.* Retrieved from www.emofree.com

Crittenden, P. M. (1988). Relationships at risk. In J. Belsky & T. M. Nezworski (Eds.), *Clinical implications of attachment* (pp. 136–174). Hillsdale, NJ: Lawrence Erlbaum.

Crittenden, P. M. (1997). Toward an integrative theory of trauma: A dynamic-maturation approach. In D. Cicchetti & S. Toth (Eds.), *Rochester Symposium on Developmental Psychopathology* (Vol. 8, pp. 33–84). Rochester, NY: University of Rochester Press.

Damasio, A. (2000). *The feeling of what happens: Body and emotion in the making of consciousness.* London, UK: Vintage.

Decety, J. (2006). A cognitive neuroscience view of imitation. In S. J. Rogers & J. H. G. Williams (Eds.), *Imitation and the social mind: Autism and typical development* (pp. 251–274). New York: Guilford.

Decety, J., & Meyer, M. (2009). Imitation as a stepping stone to empathy. In M. de Haan & M. R. Gunnar (Eds.), *Handbook of developmental social neuroscience* (pp. 142–158). New York: Guilford.

Dennison, P. E. & Dennison, G. E. (1994). *Brain Gym* (teacher's ed. rev.). Ventura, CA: Edu-Kinesiology.

Elliott, R., Greenberg, L. S., & Lietaer, G. (2004). Research on experiential psychotherapies. In M. Lambert, A. Bergin, & S. Garfield (Eds.), *Bergin and Garfield's handbook of psychotherapy and behavior change* (5th ed., pp. 493–540). New York: Wiley.

Gorman-Barry, P. (2008). *BrainWise for grades K-5: A guide for building thinking skills in children.* Denver, CO: The BrainWise Program.

Greenspan, S. I., & Lieberman, A. F. (1988). A clinical approach to attachment. In J. Belsky & T. M. Nezworski (Eds.), *Clinical implications of attachment* (pp. 387–424). Hillsdale, NJ: Erlbaum.

Harrison, E. (2005). *The 5-minute meditator: How to relax your body and mind rapidly whenever you want to.* Perth, AU: Perth Meditation Centre.

Healing rhythms. (2006). [Computer software]. Eldorado Springs, CO: The Wild Divine Project.

Inner tube biofeedback game. (2004). [Computer software]. San Diego, CA: Somatic Vision, Inc.

Kinniburgh, K. J., Blaustein, M., Spinazzola, J., & van der Kolk, B. A. (2005). Attachment, self-regulation, and competency. *Psychiatric Annals, 35*(5), 424–430.

LeDoux, J. E. (1995). In search of an emotional system in the brain: Leaping from fear to emotion and consciousness. In M. S. Gazzaniga (Ed.), *The cognitive neurosciences* (pp. 1049–1061). Boston, MA: MIT Press.

Luiten, J., Ames, W., & Ackerson, G. (1980). A meta-analysis of the effects of advanced organizers on learning and retention. *American Educational Research Journal, 17*(2), 211–218.

Marshall, W. L. (1989). Intimacy, loneliness and sexual offenders. *Behaviour Research and Therapy, 27*(5), 491–503.

Marshall, W. L., Hudson, S. M., & Hodkinson, S. (1993). The importance of attachment bonds in the development of juvenile sex offending. In H. E. Barbaree, W. L. Marshall, & S. M. Hudson (Eds.), *The juvenile sex offender* (pp. 164–181). New York: Guilford.

Maslow, A. (1968). *Toward a psychology of being* (2nd ed.). Princton, NJ: Van Nostrand Rheinhold.

Ogden, P., & Minton, K. (2000). Sensorimotor psychotherapy: One method for processing traumatic memory. *Traumatology*, 6(3), 1–20.

Perry, B. (2001). The neurodevelopmental impact of violence in childhood. In D. Schetky & E. P. Benedek (Eds.), *Textbook of child and adolescent forensic psychiatry* (pp. 221–238). Washington, DC: American Psychiatric Press.

Robson, M., & Lambie, I. (1995). Using psychodrama to facilitate victim empathy in adolescent sexual offenders. *Australia and New Zealand Psychodrama Association Journal*, 4, 13–19.

Rogers, S. (1999). An examination of the imitation deficit in autism: The roles of imitation and executive function. In J. Nadel & G. Butterworth (Eds.), *Imitation in infancy* (pp. 254–283). New York: Cambridge University Press.

Saxe, G. N., Ellis, B. H., & Kaplow, J. B. (2007). *Collaborative treatment of traumatized children and teens: The trauma systems therapy approach*. New York: Guilford.

Schore, A. N. (1997). Early organization of the nonlinear right brain and development of a predisposition to psychiatric disorders. *Development and Psychopathology*, 9(4), 595–631.

Schore, A.N. (2000). Attachment and the regulation of the right brain. *Attachment and Human Development*, 2(1), 23–47.

Schore, A. N. (2001). Effects of a secure attachment relationship on right brain development, affect regulation, and infant mental health. *Infant Mental Health Journal*, 22(1–2), 7–66.

Shapiro, F. (1995). *Eye movement desensitization and reprocessing: Basic principles*. New York: Guilford.

Siegel, D. J. (1999). *The developing mind: Toward a neurobiology of interpersonal experience*. New York: Guilford.

Siegel, D. J. (2007). *The mindful brain: Reflection and attunement in the cultivation of well-being*. New York: Norton.

Smallbone, S. W., & Dadds, M. R. (2000). Attachment and coercive sexual behavior. *Sexual Abuse*, 12(1), 3–15.

Sroufe, L. A. (1979). Socioemotional development. In J. D. Osofsky (Ed.), *Handbook of infant development* (pp. 462–516). New York: Wiley.

Sroufe, L. A., & Waters, E. (1977). Attachment as an organizational construct. *Child Development*, 48 (4), 1184–1199.

Stien, P. T., & Kendall, J. (2004). *Psychological trauma and the developing brain: Neurologically based intervention for troubled children*. New York: Haworth Press.

Strayhorn, J. M. (1988). *The competent child: An approach to psychotherapy and preventive mental health*. New York: Guilford.

Teicher, M. H., Andersen, S. L., Polcari, A., Andersen, C. M., & Navalta, C. P. (2002). Developmental neurobiology of childhood stress and trauma. *Psychiatric Clinics of North America*, 25(2), 397–426.

van der Kolk, B. A., McFarlane, A. C., & Weisaeth, L. (1996). *Traumatic stress: The effects of overwhelming experience on mind, body, and society*. New York: Guilford.

Ward, T., Hudson, S. M., & McCormack, J. (1997). Attachment style, intimacy deficits, and sexual offending. In B. Schwartz & H. Cellini (Eds.), *The sex offender: New insights, treatment innovations, and legal developments* (Vol. II, pp. 2-1 to 2-14). Kingston, NJ: Civic Research Institute.

Weil, M., & Murphy, J. (1982). Instructional processes. In H. E. Mitzel (Ed.), *Encyclopedia of educational research* (pp. 892–893). New York: Free Press.

Young, J. E., Klosko, J. S., & Weishaar, M. E. (2003). *Schema therapy: A practitioner's guide*. New York: Guilford.

12

Strengthening Bonds Between Nonresident African American Fathers and Sons as a Way to Reduce or Prevent Youth Risky Behaviors*,†

CLEOPATRA HOWARD CALDWELL,
E. HILL DE LONEY, RONALD B. MINCY,
SERENA KLEMPIN, CASSANDRA L. BROOKS,
AND JANE RAFFERTY

The percentage of youth engaging in high-risk behaviors declined between 1991 and 2005; however, significant numbers of adolescents continue to engage in behaviors that increase the likelihood of negative

* This research was funded by the Centers for Disease Control and Prevention through Grant R06/CCR521580 to the first author. Partial support also was provided through the Community Foundation of Flint, Michigan.
† The authors thank members of the Fathers and Sons Steering Committee for their insightful and dedicated work on this study and the many fathers and sons who participated in this study.

health outcomes such as physical injury, unintended pregnancies, sexually transmitted diseases, and even death (Centers for Disease Control and Prevention (CDC), 2006). Additional cause for concern arises from the disproportionately high prevalence of specific risky behaviors among subgroups of adolescents. For example, while an average of 6.2% of adolescents nationwide initiated sex before the age of 13 in 2005, 26.8% of African American males had done so (CDC, 2006). Additionally, homicide constitutes the leading cause of death for African American males 10 to 24 years old, with a homicide rate of 53.1 per 100,000 compared with 20.1 for Hispanic males and 3.3 for White males (CDC, 2007).

The prevalence of youth risky behaviors and the gravity of their outcomes necessitate a continued focus on prevention efforts to improve the health and well-being of adolescents (CDC, 2006). Interventions designed to reduce, delay, or prevent youth risky behaviors are most effective when implemented prior to the onset of the behaviors (McKay et al., 2004), yet there is little agreement about when to intervene based on age or developmental status. Previous studies have focused on preadolescence, early adolescence, or a combination of the two developmental stages (Paschall & Hubbard, 1998; Stanton et al., 1994). Furthermore, age of initiation varies by race/ethnicity, sex, and type of risky behavior (CDC, 2006). Nevertheless, prevention science advocates for early intervention to be most effective (Flay et al., 2005). Consistent with this approach, we developed and evaluated the effectiveness of a theoretically based, culturally specific health protective intervention for nonresident African American fathers and their 8- to 12-year-old sons.

This chapter describes the development and content of the Flint Fathers and Sons Program. This program is designed to strengthen relationships between nonresident African American fathers and sons as the core strategy for prevention. It focuses on preventing substance use, violent behavior, and early sexual initiation among sons, while enhancing parenting and health behaviors (i.e., help-seeking behaviors) among fathers by actively engaging both fathers and sons in structured interactions to facilitate parent–child communication, cultural awareness, effective parenting skills, and avoidance tactics for risky behaviors (Caldwell, Rafferty, De Loney, Reischl, & Brooks, 2008; Caldwell, Rafferty, Reischl, De Loney, & Brooks, 2010). The significance of the Fathers and Sons Program is that it involves nonresident African American fathers more fully in the lives of their sons who are at risk for experiencing negative health outcomes without guidance and positive role models. Lessons learned in working with nonresident fathers and sons are described, including strategies for engaging African American fathers in interventions intended to benefit their children.

The Fathers and Sons Program was developed using a community-based participatory research (CBPR) approach involving collaboration between several community-based organizations in Flint, Michigan, the Genesee County Health Department, and the Prevention Research Center of Michigan at the University of Michigan's School of Public

Health. Each group was engaged as equal partners in the design, implementation, and evaluation of the intervention program (Caldwell, Zimmerman, & Isichei, 2001). Community residents were trained to implement the program and to collect evaluation data. The program has strong community appeal and addresses concerns relevant to an array of constituencies, including families, communities, and service providers. Therefore, we expect that the Fathers and Sons Program has utility for other communities concerned with preventing youth risky behaviors from a family-centered perspective.

As part of the CBPR process, more than 100 African American nonresident and resident fathers, sons, and mothers participated in eight focus groups and five pilot tests of the intervention curriculum. Approaches for working with nonresident African American families based on examples from the fathers and sons who assisted with curriculum development and the 287 additional families who participated in the program evaluation are used to illustrate challenges and lessons learned about engaging father-son families in intervention research. Suggestions for working with nonresident fathers and sons and policies to support father involvement are offered as they relate to reducing or preventing youth risky behaviors from a social ecological perspective.

BACKGROUND

Nationally, two out of five births are to unmarried mothers; however, this figure is even higher for African American births, with more than two-thirds of these children born to unmarried mothers (Hamilton, Martin, & Ventura, 2006). The high rate of nonmarital births is a cause for concern because poverty and behavioral problems are more common among children and youth in families without a father present (Carlson, 2006; Demuth & Brown, 2004). The high divorce rate also contributes to the growth of single-parent families headed by females. Currently, one in three children in the United States live apart from their fathers (Senator Bayh, 2009). Because African American children and adolescents are less likely than other racial and ethnic groups to live in two-parent families, additional support may be necessary to assist them in avoiding youth risky behaviors. Researchers and governmental officials have argued that ecologically based efforts are needed to prevent youth risky behaviors at multiple levels of influence, including the individual, family, school, community, and policy levels (Thornton, Craft, Dahlberg, Lynch, & Baer, 2002). Research involving mothers in family-centered youth preventive interventions is well established (Dancy, Crittenden, & Talashek, 2006; DiIorio et al., 2006; Lefkowitz, Sigman, & Au, 2000). Far less intervention research has been devoted to father involvement, especially with regard to nonresident African American fathers. The involvement of nonresident fathers in the lives of their children is more prevalent than past father absent research would suggest (Tach, Mincy, & Edin, forthcoming). Empirical findings indicate that the involvement of nonresident African American fathers can have positive influences on child outcomes (Coley & Medeiros, 2007; Zimmerman, Steinman, & Rowe, 1998). Moreover, although African American fathers are less likely than Whites to live with their children at birth, they are more likely to remain involved in their lives once their romantic relationship with the mother ends (Edin, Tach, & Mincy, 2009; Waller, 2002). Thus, efforts to improve the health and well-being of African American children and youth should consider involving nonresident fathers more effectively in the lives of their children (Caldwell et al., 2010; Mincy, 1994; Mincy & Pouncy, 1999).

Over the past 25 years, responsible fatherhood programs have emerged as part of the human service sector to support the involvement of nonresident fathers in the lives of their children (Mincy & Pouncy, 1994, 2002). Perhaps because of the prevalence of nonmarital births among African Americans, these fatherhood programs are widespread in African American communities. Most of these programs began as spontaneous or donor-sponsored collaborations between hospitals, welfare and child support enforcement agencies, and community-based organizations with a goal of reducing teenage or unwed births, increasing employment and child support payments by low-income fathers (Miller & Knox, 2001; Sylvester & Reich, 2002), or encouraging healthy marriages among low-income parents (Sylvester & Reich, 2002; Dion et al., 2003). While much has been learned about the limits of responsible fatherhood programs, evidenced-based practice has played almost no role in their development (Mincy & Pouncy, 2002; Sylvester & Reich, 2002). Further, a focus on parenting or engaging fathers and their children together in programming efforts has been limited.

From a policy perspective, members of Congress have expressed increased interest in responsible fatherhood programs. President Obama has demonstrated support for nonresident fathers through his public statements and through the introduction of the Responsible Fatherhood and Healthy Family Act with Senator Bayh (S. 1626) when he was a U.S. senator (Haskins, 2006; Mincy & Pouncy, 2007). The bill included provisions to fund responsible fatherhood programs throughout the United States. This bill was reintroduced in the House as the Julia Carson Responsible Fatherhood and Healthy Families Act of 2009 (H.R. 2979) by Representative Danny Davis and in the Senate as S. 1309 by Senator Bayh on June 19, 2009, with a focus on increasing nonresident fathers' employment, earnings, and child support payments. These bills do not incorporate parenting behaviors as part of responsible fatherhood programs, which is a missed opportunity for strengthening family relationships through these fatherhood programs. The approach that we have taken in the Fathers and Sons Program offers promise for expanding this policy initiative and for informing clinical practice concerned with working with nonresident African American fathers and sons.

FAMILY INFLUENCES AND ADOLESCENT
RISKY BEHAVIORS

A number of antecedents have been associated with youth substance use, violent behavior, and early sexual debut (for reviews see Kirby & Miller, 2002; Thornton et al., 2002). These include living with a single parent, having an absent father, or permissive attitudes from parents regarding risky behaviors, youth engaging in other risky behaviors or antisocial behaviors, living in neighborhoods without economic resources or job opportunities, youth's permissive attitudes about risky behaviors, a lack of confidence in avoiding risky behaviors, and depression from a lack of family support (Dittus, Jaccard, & Gordon, 1997; Lammers, Ireland, Resnick, & Blum, 2000; Resnick et al., 1997).

Protective factors include school attachment, motivation for academic success, pro-social attitudes and norms about risky behaviors, having high-achieving friends, parental closeness, parental support, parental monitoring, high parental expectations, agreement with parental attitudes about risky behaviors, and parent–child communication about risky behaviors (Carvajal et al., 1999; Dittus et al., 1997; Lammers et al., 2000; Mackey & Immerman, 2004; Meschke, Zweig, Barber, & Eccles, 2000; Resnick et al., 1997; Thornberry, Smith, & Howard, 1997). Most studies of parental influences on sexual debut and substance use have focused on White youth; however, a recent study of 297 African American families with 12- and 14-year-old children conducted by Wills, Gibbons, Gerrard, Murry, and Brody (2003) found that parental supportiveness influenced adolescent sexual behavior indirectly by shaping self-control behaviors and defining the social images of youth who abstained from sex. They recommend increasing communication about risky behaviors between parents and children and improving child self-control skills as useful strategies for prevention programs. They also noted that boys in their study were at greater risk than girls for substance use and early sexual debut because they had less self-control and more unfavorable opinions about abstainers.

Several parenting behaviors have been found to be protective against youth risky behaviors. These are parenting monitoring, parent involvement, parent–child communication generally and specifically about family values/social norms regarding moral sexual issues and violent behaviors, parental supportiveness and closeness, and father's residential status (Dittus et al., 1997; Mackey & Immerman, 2004; Resnick et al., 1997; Thornton et al., 2002). It is important to note that many parenting behaviors were associated with less youth violence and later sexual debut for females, but not for males. This suggests that parents may be less effective in supervising their male children during adolescence. Thus, a gender-specific family intervention may be helpful in addressing youth risky behaviors by allowing program content to be tailored to the needs of male adolescents. We developed an initial framework for the Fathers and Sons Program based on myriad consistent antecedents for youth risky behaviors involving families identified in the literature review. Strengthening family relationships and parenting behaviors are core components of our intervention strategy.

A critical aspect of this work is recognizing that in working with African American families, their life experiences cannot be ignored (Kumpfer, Alvarudo, Smith, & Bellany, 2003). The roles of race, culture, gender, and class have to be considered, including cultural strengths that exist that can protect against youth risky behaviors. Strengths of African American families include commitment to religious beliefs, egalitarian gender roles, collectivist orientation, and connections to extended family systems and their racial group (Harrison, Wilson, Pine, Chan, & Buriel, 1990; Taylor, Chatters, & Levin, 2004). Few preventive interventions incorporate these strengths as significant areas for intervention. The belief in the interconnectedness of people among African Americans, for example, suggests that it is important to engage family members when working with African American youth (Harrison et al., 1990). Previous research highlighted the role of race-related socialization, racial pride, and group affiliation with better mental health and less risky behaviors among African American adolescents (Belgrave et al., 1994); thus, incorporating these issues into preventive interventions is expected to be beneficial.

AN OVERVIEW OF THE FLINT FATHERS AND SONS PROGRAM

In this section we describe the Fathers and Sons Program, including our conceptual model and the program's intervention content. There was limited intervention research available to provide guidance for working with nonresident fathers of preadolescents. We therefore relied on our preliminary qualitative work with nonresident African American families and the knowledge of our community partners who worked with these families to structure the program.

The Flint Fathers and Sons Program is designed to prevent adolescent risky health behaviors by strengthening relationships between nonresident African American fathers and their 8- to 12-year-old sons. It is based on social science evidence suggesting that bonding, authoritative parenting, and feelings of closeness are critical pathways through which nonresident African American fathers can influence the attitudes and behaviors of their children. It is guided by a conceptual model based on the theory of reasoned action (Ajzen & Fishbein, 1980), social cognitive theory (Bandura, 1977), and models of social networks/social support (Israel & Round, 1987) and racial identity development (Sellers, Rowley, Chavous, Shelton, & Smith, 1997). Components of our model target points for intervening at the individual, family, and community levels of influence. The details of this model are provided elsewhere (Caldwell et al.,

2010, 2004). In sum, however, our conceptual model highlights parental behaviors as mediators between environmental factors and behavioral intentions and behaviors (Caldwell et al., 2004). Environmental factors include both challenges, such as poor neighborhood conditions, racial discrimination, and depression among fathers (Davis, Caldwell, Clark, & Davis, 2009), and community assets, such as support from other family members, churches, and community resources. The Fathers and Sons Program is designed to influence fathers' parenting attitudes and behaviors (e.g., monitoring, communication skills, role modeling, and race-related socialization), parent–child relationships, and behavioral intentions about avoiding risky and aggressive behaviors among sons.

We used a quasi-experimental, nonequivalent group, pretest-posttest design to evaluate the effects of the intervention with 158 intervention and 129 comparison group father-son families from Flint and Saginaw, Michigan. Quantitative evaluation findings indicated that the intervention was effective for enhancing several key parenting attitudes and behaviors among fathers thought to be protective against youth risky behaviors (e.g., monitoring, communication about sex, race-related socialization, intentions to communicate, help-seeking behavior). It was also successful for increasing sons' confidence in their relationship with their fathers, including communication about sex, and their intentions to avoid violence (Caldwell et al.,2010). We found that improvements in fathers' attitudes and behaviors were associated with sons' healthy intentions (Caldwell, Rafferty, & De Loney, 2009). Findings from qualitative data showed the need to connect nonresident fathers to community resources that could assist with fulfilling their fathering responsibilities.

The Fathers and Sons Program Curriculum

The Fathers and Sons Program curriculum was designed to be culturally, developmentally, and gender appropriate. It consists of 45 program hours, including 24 hours spent in 12 content-driven sessions, 9 hours of homework assignments, 4 hours participating in cultural events, and 2 hours for data collection. Although the 12 content-driven sessions were 2 hours each, the opening and closing sessions were 3 hours each. The content-driven sessions focused on specific topics, while other sessions reinforced learning. The program took about two months to complete for each group. One booster session was conducted four months after the intervention ended.

The intervention included opportunities for developing mutually beneficial activities to strengthen family relationships, obtain information about parent/child responsibilities and expectations, practice relevant skills, address barriers to achieving goals, and share experiences with nonresident fathers and sons facing similar challenges. Four consistent themes were addressed in the intervention: (1) improving father-son communication, (2) enhancing parenting attitudes and behaviors among fathers and avoidance skills for sons, (3) reinforcing cultural awareness for both, and (4) developing family strategies against youth risky behaviors. Focus groups were used as part of the intervention to assess how well the program was working and why. Comparison group families only completed the pre- and posttest questionnaires.

The intervention was implemented in small groups of up to 12 families per group. The average group size was 8 families across 21 intervention groups. We found that the ideal group size was 8 to 10 families. This number allowed the group to still be large enough to create a safe environment for interacting and accomplishing intervention activities even when a few families were absent. Our practice was to have organizations that assisted with recruitment host the intervention. This made the proximity of the intervention convenient for most participants. Nevertheless, we found that transportation was a problem for many fathers; therefore, we partnered with a local church to rent its van to provide transportation for participants who needed it. Based on the results of the pilot tests, intervention groups typically were scheduled for Mondays and Wednesdays or Tuesdays and Thursdays from 6:00 to 8:00 p.m. most evenings. Financial incentives were provided to both fathers and sons for their participation. We achieved a response rate of 85.4% for the intervention group and 69.4% for the comparison group, for an overall response rate of 77.4%. Seventy-seven percent of fathers and about 80% of sons participated in 11 or more of the 15 intervention sessions.

Two staff members, one facilitator and one observer, were present during each intervention session. It was the facilitator's responsibility to conduct the session, while the observer took field notes on group dynamics and key discussion points that emerged during the session. In most cases, one male and one female worked together as a team to be the facilitator and observer for a group. The same person facilitated all 15 sessions so that families could bond with that person as the group leader. When separate activities were required for fathers and sons, the observer worked with the sons, and both the facilitator and observer provided field notes for the session. Three intervention sessions were audio recorded because they involved detailed group discussions. We wanted to capture the full range of content covered by men, who typically are not the focus of intervention research.

One recorded session, session 6, was specifically designed to engage the fathers and sons in separate dialogue about their experiences in the program, and to focus on directions for their future participation. The two other recorded sessions were built around content in the pre- and posttest questionnaires. We found that answering these questions elicited a range of emotions about past and current family experiences. We linked specific program activities with key constructs in our conceptual model to provide clarity in assessing the effects of the intervention program. Table 12.1 provides the linkages between each theory or model construct and relevant intervention activities as an example of how we translated theory into practice.

TABLE 12.1 From Theory to Practice With the Fathers and Sons Curriculum

Program Session and Goals	Activities	Theoretical/Model Link
Session 1: Program overview Goals: To provide an overview of the program and to begin to build rapport among participants	Discussions: • Expectations • Diversity among families (PowerPoint[a]) • Adolescent development (PowerPoint) Taking family pictures Homework: Let's get acquainted	Social cognitive theory Social environment
Session 2: Information gathering Goals: To gather pretest data and to allow families time to discuss issues that are important to them related to relationship building	Face-to-face interviews Participant focus groups (Separately for fathers and sons) Memory book and journal for sons	Theory of Reasoned Action Attitudes • relationship building • youth risk behaviors Social networks • informal social support Subjective norms • relationship building • youth health risk behaviors
Session 3: People of African heritage Goals: To familiarize participants with cultural practices, values, and beliefs of African people—encourage racial identity development as a health promotion concept	Homework: Letter writing assignment Study the map of Africa Present history of Adinkra symbols Adinkra cloth making Homework: Group naming with Adinkra symbol African American quiz	Racial Socialization Racial Identity Centrality Private regard Public regard

(continued)

TABLE 12.1 From Theory to Practice With the Fathers and Sons Curriculum (Continued)

Program Session and Goals	Activities	Theoretical/Model Link
Session 4: Health enhancement strategies Goals: To discuss physical activity as a way to strengthen father-son bonds, discuss risky behaviors, and engage in recreational activities to show the benefits of physical exercise for a healthier lifestyle	Mentoring through sports and recreational activities Communicating through physical activity Promoting safety Homework: Picture-taking activity: physical activity and teachable moments	Theory of Reasoned Action Attitudes • relationship building • physical activity and safety Subjective norms • relationship building • physical activity and safety Behavioral intentions • relationship building • physical activity and safety
Session 5: General communication Goal: To learn good communication skills as a way to strengthen family relationships	The listening chain Discussion of different communication styles Role play Homework: Communication exercise	Theory of Reasoned Action Subjective norms • relationship building • health risk behaviors Social Networks Informal social support Reciprocity in relationships Racial Socialization
Session 6: Fathers and sons having their say Goal: To have fathers and sons share their feelings about the program, changes and commitments made, and future directions	Sharing family pictures from homework assignment "Rap sessions" • Fathers only • Sons only	Theory of Reasoned Action Behavioral intentions • relationship building • health risk behaviors Racial Socialization

	• Together Homework: Picture-taking activity: family responsibilities	Theory of Reasoned Action Behavioral intentions • relationship building • health risk behaviors Racial Socialization
Session 7: Family functioning and parenting Goals: Enhance awareness of the importance of parenting behaviors, values, and expectations for child behaviors and reinforce the meaning of quality parent-child relationships; parental monitoring for both fathers and sons when they do not live together	Family movie segments of an appropriate popular movie Group discussion Homework: Fathers and sons write a family play showing how each would feel in a role reversal situation: substance use	Social Cognitive Theory Role modeling Theory of reasoned action Subjective norms • relationship building • health risk behaviors Self-efficacy • relationship building • health risk behaviors • parenting behaviors Behavioral capacity • refusal skills • parental monitoring • father–son communication

(continued)

TABLE 12.1 From Theory to Practice With the Fathers and Sons Curriculum (Continued)

Program Session and Goals	Activities	Theoretical/Model Link
Session 8: Parenting behaviors and relationships Goals: Build on what happened in Session 7 and begin discussions about social relationships and community supports; provides an opportunity for fathers to see who their sons' friends are and important family members for both; also allows fathers to discuss knowledge available community resources	Share family pictures Family role reversal activity Social network activities Family tree activity for sons	Social Cognitive Theory Role modeling Theory of Reasoned Action Subjective norms • relationship building Social Networks Informal social support Formal social support
Session 9: Using computers to communicate Goal: To introduce or reinforce the use of computers as communication and information gathering resources; an important part of this session is to provide strategies for parental monitoring in the age of technology	Introduction to the Internet and the World Wide Web Helpful parenting/child websites generally and for risky behaviors Designing a web page	Social Cognitive Theory Self-efficacy • relationship building Behavioral capacity • parental monitoring • refusal skills • father-son communication Social Networks Informal social support Formal social support

Session 10: Communication about risky behaviors I Goals: To provide information about the health effects of substance abuse for fathers and sons and sexual behavior for sons, and to practice refusal skills in these areas	PowerPoint: Substance use prevention Communication exercise about substance use values and expectations for fathers and sons PowerPoint: Sexual behavior Exercises: • Violence prevention • Communication about sex	Social Cognitive Theory Self-efficacy • health risk behaviors • father–son communication Role modeling Behavioral capacity • father–son communication • parental monitoring • refusal skills Social Networks Informal social support Formal social support
Session 11: Communication about risky behaviors II Goals: To build effective communication skills within families for influencing violent behavior decision making and to practice refusal skills in this area.	PowerPoint: Violence Homework: "Your Black Family Pledge Against Violence"	Social Cognitive Theory Self-efficacy • health risk behaviors • father–son communication Role Modeling Behavioral capacity • father–son communication • parental monitoring • refusal skills Social Networks Informal social support Formal social support

(continued)

TABLE 12.1 From Theory to Practice With the Fathers and Sons Curriculum (Continued)

Program Session and Goals	Activities	Theoretical/Model Link
Session 12: Health enhancement strategies II Goals: To reinforce health promotion techniques introduced in session 4 and to develop a family mission statement about strengthening family bonds and pro-social behaviors for the future	Family commitments to physical activity Family mission statement Recreational activity Homework: Letter writing activity part II	Theory of Reasoned Action Attitudes • relationship building • physical activity and safety Subjective norms • relationship building • physical activity and safety Behavioral intentions • relationship building • physical activity and safety
Session 13: Culture and health Goals: To introduce African cultural practices as communication and health-promoting strategies for physical and mental well-being	African drum and dance Group discussion	Racial Socialization Racial Identity Centrality Private regard Social Cognitive Theory Self-efficacy • physical activity • relationship building

Session 14: Information gathering II Goals: To gather posttest data and to allow time for families to discuss issues that are important to them related to relationship building and program content	Face-to-face interviews Focus groups Memory book activity	Theory of Reasoned Action Attitudes • relationship building • youth risk behaviors Subjective norms • relationship building • youth health risk behaviors Racial Socialization Social Networks Informal social support Formal social support
Session 15: Closing ceremony Goals: To congratulate participants for completing the program through a graduation ceremony, and to provide resources in the community to assist them in continuing to strengthen their relationships; family and friends are invited to the celebration	Taking pictures Presentations: • Memory books • Journals • Group poster presentations Open discussion Graduation ceremony with certificates	Theory of Reasoned Action Attitudes Subjective norms Behavioral intentions Racial Socialization Social Networks Social Cognitive Theory Self-efficacy Racial Identity

(continued)

TABLE 12.1 From Theory to Practice With the Fathers and Sons Curriculum (Continued)

Program Session and Goals	Activities	Theoretical/Model Link
Booster session—4 months after the program ends	Second posttest Parenting behaviors Refusal skills Social support	Theory of Reasoned Action Attitudes Subjective norms Behavioral intentions Social Cognitive Theory Self-efficacy Social Networks Cultural factors
Community outreach and alumni activities	Intervention activities: • Kwanzaa • Juneteenth Day • Parents day at school • Community health fair • BUST workshop After intervention ends: Father support group Use of community resources Family newsletter	Social Networks Informal social support Formal social support Racial Identity Race Socialization Reinforcements

[a] PowerPoint presentations used as discussion guides.

Program Content

As indicated in Table 12.1, a number of strategies were used to engage fathers and sons in the intervention program. In addition to disseminating information about parenting strategies and youth risky behaviors and relying on interactive discussions, we engaged fathers and sons in role reversal performances to highlight communication, social network mapping to demonstrate parental monitoring, sharing pictures and recreational activities to strategically emphasize opportunities for communication, and participation in cultural and community service activities as ways to reinforce ethnic identity and family bonding. Adinkra symbols (i.e., African designs from Ghana that illustrate specific moral values) were selected by each group and placed on T-shirts to represent their program group. These T-shirts became outward signs of solidarity among families sharing a common experience and cultural connections.

One activity designed to enhance father-son communication was a letter-writing activity in which fathers and sons were asked to write letters to each other at the beginning and near the end of the program as a homework assignment. Letters were shared within families and artistically prepared to be placed in memory books that the sons maintained throughout the program. A preliminary analysis of the content of letters from sons to fathers showed a shift in emphasis of wanting to spend time with their father to more of an expectation of having more time together. Below is an example of quotes from one pair of these letters that reflects this shift.

LETTER 1

Dear Dad,

I would like to go more places with you and play basketball with you more, Dad. I would like to build our relationship up and it will be fun to do things with you. We can build airplane kits and stuff like that!

Love,

John

Dear Son,

Just because you and I don't live under the same roof doesn't mean that I am not the father your friends have. You can come to me and ask me anything. If I don't know the answer, I will try my best to find the best answer. You can talk to me about anything. John, I can't spend the kind of time with you I really want to, so that's one of the reasons why we are in this program. Now that I'm going to school more, our time will be lost but hold on. John, one of the reasons why I want you to get good grades and get on the honor roll is because I want you to go off to college and see the world.

Love,

Dad

LETTER 2

Dear Father,

When we go fishing I will catch a lot of fish. It would be fun to play basketball too dad. On Friday we can go put my money in the checking account. We can play football too. If you get to go to D-World then I will see you there.

Love,

Your Son John

Dear John,

I'm writing to let you know that since we joined the Fathers and Sons Program I have learned things about you that I should have already known long before we joined the program. I know you're not afraid of talking in front of a crowd, so I know you can talk to me about anything. As long as you get good grades in school you will be rewarded not because of your grades, but because of the hard work and effort you put into it. Remember I will always love you and I will always be there for you. I tell you to save your money, always put some aside and you get mad, but when you get older you'll understand.

Love,

Dad

The shift in tone for several fathers changed from one of explanation as to why they could not always be there for their son to expressing pride in their son and finding that "teachable moment." Finding teachable moments was an important part of the program, and reinforcement of the importance of parent–child communication and role modeling through multiple activities within the intervention program, homework assignments, community service commitments, and recreational activities was a critical strategy for enhancing parent–child relationships.

Fathers Support Group

After several groups of families completed the intervention program, there was interest among fathers and sons in staying connected with others in the program. Consequently, the fathers suggested establishing a fatherhood support group that would operate in the Flint community for "graduates" of the Fathers and Sons Program. The intent was that this group would be operated by the fathers themselves with assistance from the Fathers and Sons Program staff to help with the initial organizational tasks. Our lead community partner organization offered space for group meetings. Meeting reminder notices were sent from the program office. This was done to protect the confidentiality of study participants. With assistance from the Fathers and Sons Program outreach coordinator, the Fathers Support Group was launched with 10 families. It eventually grew to include 45 families meeting once per month. This group operated for almost two years, until several participants in leadership positions became involved with other black male initiatives in the Flint community. Several fathers were so committed to the program that after their participation in the study ended, they were trained to be program interviewers or facilitators for subsequent intervention groups.

LESSONS LEARNED AND
IMPLICATIONS FOR PRACTICE

There were a number of challenges in conducting an intervention program for nonresident African American fathers and sons; however, there were also a number of lessons learned. This section shares a few of those lessons that may be useful for clinical practice with men and boys.

- One criticism of previous interventions targeting men is that they traditionally have relied on feminine methods, such as encouraging men to be extremely verbally expressive, in touch with their emotions, and highly vulnerable (Sinclair & Taylor, 2004). Perhaps because most interventions involve women, the language used to discuss issues can be decidedly feminine. One strategy that we used to attract men to the Fathers and Sons Program, especially those who thought of themselves as traditionally masculine, was to remove the feminine stigma by changing the name of "intervention sessions" to "meetings" or "classes." This was supported by the addition of homework assignments as part of the intervention. Some fathers commented that they had not done homework since high school, if then. However, most actively participated by completing homework assignments and being prepared to discuss their experiences. This same strategy can be useful in clinical practice by changing the name of "counseling" and "psychotherapy services" to "seminars," "coaching," or "classes" (Good & Sherrod, 2001; McCarthy & Holliday, 2004; Robertson & Fitzgerald, 1992).

- Curriculum materials developed for the program were pilot tested with nonresident African American fathers and sons in an effort to ensure that they would be sensitive to generational and gender issues. The role of masculinity in framing discussions about parenting issues, risky behaviors, and help seeking was vital to effective communication and creating a safe intervention environment. What it means to be an African American man trying to fulfill his fathering responsibilities when he is unemployed, for example, was incorporated into intervention content. One example of this is a social networking activity in which fathers supervised their sons as the sons completed a social network diagram of important people in their lives (Antonucci, 1986). The goal of this activity was to reinforce with fathers the significance of knowing who their sons' friends are and who other important people are in their life as part of the father's monitoring responsibilities, regardless of employment status. This activity was useful for allowing fathers to determine how well they were monitoring their sons and for generating ways to improve this parenting behavior in a nonthreatening activity. A lack of knowledge about who was important to their sons was a motivator for fathers to want to provide more supervision to their sons.

• Instead of using didactic methods for disseminating information about the importance of parental monitoring (Sinclair & Taylor, 2004), fathers were asked to be helpers for their sons as they completed the social network exercise. Sons were told that they could rely on their father to help them with spelling the names of people they were including in their network diagram and for identifying family relationships about which they were unsure. Fathers were comfortable in their role as "problem solver" for their son until some realized that they did not know many of the people included in their sons' social network diagram. This realization was the stimulus for learning more about the importance of monitoring in preventing youth risky behaviors. It prompted discussions between fathers and sons about who they were spending time with and why these people were important to them. Fathers completed their social network diagrams by identifying specific people in agencies that had been helpful for solving specific problems they faced. The intent was to share this information with other fathers to encourage help-seeking behavior for things that interfered with achieving their fathering responsibilities.

• It was vital that these fathers and sons had a safe space in which to participate in the program. Safety was defined as both physical and emotional in nature. The act of sharing with other African American men and boys created an environment for them to express themselves in ways that were compatible for males who are often reluctant to self-disclose (Pederson & Vogel, 2007). We learned through our pilot testing that it was not always the most vocal person in the group who benefited the most from the program. This prompted us to develop a participant engagement form for the observer to complete for all participants in each session. We struggled with the definitions of levels of engagement because we knew that some men who did not talk much were often encouraging their sons to talk, and these men did not miss many sessions. Thus, the first indication of engagement was simply being there. As observers got to know the participants, their engagement assessments moved beyond who talked the most to noting body language and nonverbal communication (e.g., leaning forward to be closer to the group during discussions), who completed homework assignments, and how fathers and sons worked together as indicators of effective engagement. It was often the men who spoke least that cried most when they received their certificate of completion for the program. In working with nonresident African American fathers and sons it is important to listen to what they say, but also to observe what they do when assessing engagement.

- If more than one son was eligible for participation in the program, we invited multiple sons to participate. This relieved parents of the responsibility of having to choose between sons or the study design only allowing the oldest or youngest son in the age range to participate. Our concern was to avoid disrupting family harmony by selecting only one son for the program. Sisters and siblings not in the program's age range living in their households had already been excluded. The complexity of family relationships for nonresident families was evident as the fathers and sons completed their family mission statement. This activity required fathers and sons to work together in developing a statement that reflected their family goals around strengthening their relationship. The first challenge was to determine the structure of their family. Some sons included their father as part of their family with their mothers. Others saw themselves as having two separate families—one with mother and one with father—while some sons articulated a blending of the two families, especially when the father had other children. Older (11- to 12-year-old) boys seem to express more divided families when fathers cohabited with other children. These are preliminary qualitative assessments based on data from both the family mission statement and the letter-writing activity, which suggested that some boys had increased expectations for father involvement by the end of the intervention (Caldwell, De Loney, Reischl, & Brooks, 2007). An analysis of the quantitative data in this area will provide more information about these issues, including correlates. However, the meaning of family that the sons expressed in articulating who is part of their family, especially when their father lived with other children, should be examined by researchers and clinicians to determine under what conditions these boys may be at risk for engaging in problem behaviors as adolescents because of feelings of rejection. Age may be an important consideration in this regard, with older boys with unresolved issues with their fathers at more risk than younger boys.

- Fathers in the intervention requested assistance for alcohol abuse more often than fathers in the comparison group (Caldwell et al., 2010). This was an important finding because role modeling is a parenting construct in our conceptual model. To address the issue of role modeling, fathers and sons engaged in a role reversal activity around substance use behavior. Fathers acted out peer pressure scenarios, while sons acted out fathers' behaviors when drinking. Again, this was an eye-opening experience for some fathers because they were not aware of how accurately sons could mimic their behaviors. This often led to these fathers becoming emotional. They thought that they were hiding the undesirable drinking behaviors that sons were able to accurately re-create. It is not clear what prompted intervention fathers to ask for help with their drinking, but some fathers expressed sadness about disappointing their sons. This recognition could be a powerful motivator for fathers to change their own risky health behaviors.

• Mothers were frequently interested in what was happening during the intervention sessions, some even offering to bring food to be involved. (Each intervention session began with dinner.) But we restricted the intervention to fathers and sons so that they could have dedicated time together to work on their relationship. Mothers did have an opportunity to participate in the initial program orientation meeting and in the closing ceremony. Mothers were informed about their sons' activities in the program through a monthly calendar of events. This method of engaging mothers was critical to avoiding conflicts with family activities. Because many of the children looked forward to this time with their fathers, some mothers used the threat of not allowing them to participate as leverage for getting the sons to do their chores or as a form of punishment. We were not able to address this issue in the intervention because mothers were not consented to participate in the study. Future programs will include a role for mothers. We currently include the issue of co-parenting for the benefit of the child from the fathers' perspective. Obtaining input from both parents on this issue would be useful. Our goal would be to have a separate supplemental program for mothers. Conflict between mothers and fathers was evident for some families. The current program is not designed to address this issue. Future programs should include both parents when possible to obtain a better account of these dynamics for nonresident families.

• Mothers were crucial to the success of the program because we recruited nonresident fathers through the mothers. Mothers had to want the fathers to be actively involved in their son's life. When confronted with the question of whether or not the father may be harmful to the child, our strategy of recruiting through mothers provided some measure of protection. Most mothers would not want fathers involved with their child if they thought fathers would be a harmful influence. Even in families where there was a stepfather present in the home, many mothers wanted their sons connected to their biological father. Mothers' preference is a bias that is built into the current Fathers and Sons Program that we believe is helpful. We will conduct analysis to examine the fathers' risky behaviors as moderators of intervention effects to partially address this issue. Co-parenting and relationship quality among nonresident parents are areas to understand, especially for boys who view their fathers as role models.

CONCLUSION

Fathers are important in their children's lives, especially for helping them to develop a healthy sense of who they are and what they can become. This study was conducted to evaluate a family-centered preventive intervention program that could benefit African American fathers and sons who did not live together. Evaluation results for the Fathers and Sons Program suggest that nonresident African American fathers can improve their parenting skills in an effort to prepare their sons to make decisions for themselves related to some of the biggest challenges that youth of today face. This speaks to the need to recognize the role of nonresident fathers not only as providers, but also as nurturers and socializing agents for their children.

Promising aspects of the intervention program include monitoring, communication about sex, intentions to communicate more effectively with their son, and race-related socialization for fathers (Caldwell et al., 2010). If fathers are to be health educators for their children, they need information and skills to effectively assume this role. Acquiring effective communication skills is critical. Support services must be provided that can assist fathers in dealing with their own emotional traumas so that they can better assume their fathering responsibilities. Attempts to teach fathers to be health educators for their children require special attention to programming efforts that are appropriate for males and that speak to the idea that fathers matter in the lives of their children.

Finding ways to reinforce connections between nonresident African American biological fathers and sons may be a promising additional layer of protection against youth risky behaviors. A popular violence prevention strategy is mentoring programs involving adult males and male youth. Mentoring programs that invite the involvement of nonresident biological fathers of boys as mentors may be beneficial. Further, expanding responsible fatherhood programs to include parenting behaviors and opportunities for fathers and their children to be together in program activities would be important for influencing a broader range of family dynamics. Finally, clinicians working with nonresident African American fathers and sons must consider going beyond the individuals to better understand the meanings they assign to their complex family relationships and the social context in which these relationships can thrive.

REFERENCES

Ajzen, I., & Fishbein, M. (1980). *Understanding attitudes and predicting social behavior.* Englewood Cliffs, NJ: Prentice Hall.

Antonucci, T. C. (1986). Social support networks: A hierarchical mapping technique. *Generations: Journal of the American Society on Aging, 10*(4), 10–12.

Bandura, A. (1977). Self-efficacy: Toward a unifying theory of behavior change. *Psychological Review, 84*(2), 191–215.

Belgrave, F., Cherry, V., Cunningham, D., Walwyn, S., Latlaka-Rennert, K., & Phillips, F. (1994). The influence of Africentric values, self-esteem, and Black identity on drug attitudes among African American fifth graders: A preliminary study. *Journal of Black Psychology, 20*(2), 143–156.

Caldwell, C. H., De Loney, E. H., Reischl, T., & Brooks, C. L. (2007). *The Flint Fathers and Sons Evaluation Project: Final progress report.* Centers for Disease Control and Prevention. Funded by Grant R06/CCR521580.

Caldwell, C. H., Rafferty, J., & De Loney, E. H. (2009, January 21). *Love does not get lost on the way home: Strengthening bonds between nonresident African American fathers and sons as a strategy for preventing youth risk behaviors.* Invited address for Grand Rounds at the Department of Psychiatry, University of Michigan, Ann Arbor, MI.

Caldwell, C. H., Rafferty, J., De Loney, E. H., Reischl, T., & Brooks, C. L. (2008). The Flint Fathers and Sons Program. *Practice Notes: Strategies in Health Education & Behavior, 35*(2), 155–157.

Caldwell, C. H., Rafferty, J., Reischl, T., De Loney, E. H., & Brooks, C. L. (2010). Enhancing parenting skills among nonresident African American fathers as a strategy for preventing youth risky behaviors. *American Journal of Community Psychology, 45,* 17–35.

Caldwell, C. H., Wright, J. C., Zimmerman, M. A., Walsemann, K. M., Williams, D., & Isichei, P. A. C. (2004). Enhancing adolescent health behaviors through strengthening nonresident father-son relationships: A model for intervention with African American families. *Health Education Research: Theory and Practice, 19*(6), 644–656.

Caldwell, C. H., Zimmerman, M. A., & Isichei, A. C. (2001). Forging collaborative partnerships to enhance family health: An assessment of strengths and challenges in conducting community-based research. *Journal of Public Health Management and Practice, 7*(2), 1–9.

Carlson, M. J. (2006). Family structure, father involvement, and adolescent behavioral outcomes. *Journal of Marriage and Family, 68*(1), 137–154.

Carvajal, S. C., Parcel, G. S., Basen-Engquist, K., Banspach, S. W., Coyle, K. K., Kirby, D., & Chan, W. (1999). Psychological predictors of delay of first sexual intercourse by adolescents. *Health Psychology, 18*(5), 443–452.

Centers for Disease Control and Prevention. (2006, June 9). Surveillance summaries: Youth risk behavior surveillance—United States, 2005. *Morbidity and Mortality Weekly Report, 55*(No. SS-5). Retrieved from http://www.cdc.gov/HealthyYouth/yrbs/index.htm

Centers for Disease Control and Prevention. (2007, Summer). *Youth violence: Facts at a glance.* Retrieved from http://www.cdc.gov/ncipc/dvp/YVP/default.htm

Coley, R. L., & Medeiros, B. L. (2007). Reciprocal longitudinal relations between nonresident father involvement and adolescent delinquency. *Child Development, 78*(1), 132–147.

Dancy, B. L., Crittenden, K. S., & Talashek, M. (2006). Mothers' effectiveness as HIV risk reduction educators for adolescent daughters. *Journal of Health Care for the Poor and Underserved, 17*(1), 218–239.

Davis, R. N., Caldwell, C. H., Clark, S. J., & Davis, M. (2009). Depressive symptoms in nonresident African American fathers and involvement with their sons. *Pediatrics, 124*, 1611–1618.

Demuth, S., & Brown, S. L. (2004). Family structure, family processes, and adolescent delinquency: The significance of parental absence versus parental gender. *Journal of Research in Crime and Delinquency, 41*(1), 58–81.

DiIorio, C., Resnicow, K., Thomas, S., Wang, D. T., Dudley, W. N., Van Marter, D. F., … Denzmore, P. (2006). Keepin' it R.E.A.L.! Results of a mother-adolescent HIV prevention program. *Nursing Research, 55*(1), 43–51.

Dion, R., Devaney, B., McConnell, S., Ford, M., Hill, H., & Winston, P. (2003). *Helping unwed parents build strong and healthy marriages: A conceptual framework for interventions.* Washington, DC: Mathematica Policy Research, Inc.

Dittus, P. J., Jaccard, J., & Gordon, V. (1997). The impact of African American fathers on adolescent sexual behavior. *Journal of Youth and Adolescence, 26*(4), 445–465.

Edin, K., Tach, L., & Mincy, R. B. (2009). Claiming fatherhood: Race and the dynamics of paternal involvement among unmarried men. *Annals of the American Academy of Political and Social Science, 621*, 149–177.

Flay, B., Biglan, A., Boruch, R. F., Castro, F. G., Gottfredson, D., Kellam, S., … Ji, P. (2005). Standards of evidence: Criteria for efficacy, effectiveness and dissemination. *Prevention Science, 6*(3), 151–175.

Good, G. E., & Sherrod, N. B. (2001). Men's problems and effective treatments: Theory and empirical support. In G. R. Brooks & G. E. Good (Eds.), *The new handbook of psychotherapy and counseling with men* (pp. 22–40). San Francisco, CA: Jossey-Bass.

Hamilton, B. E., Martin, J. A., &Ventura, S. J. (2006). Births: Preliminary data for 2005. In *National Vital Statistics Reports, 55* (Tables 1, 3). Hyattsville, MD: National Center for Health Statistics. Retrieved from http://www.cdc.gov/nchs/products/pubs/pubd/hestats/prelimbirths05/prelimbirths05.htm#ref02

Harrison, A. O., Wilson, M. N., Pine, C. J., Chan, S. Q., & Buriel, R. (1990). Family ecologies of ethnic minority children. *Child Development, 61*(2), 347–362.

Haskins, R. (2006). Poor fathers and public policy: What is to be done? In R. B. Mincy (Ed.), *Black males left behind* (pp. 249–292). Washington, DC: The Urban Institute Press.

Israel, B. A., & Round, K. A. (1987). Social networks and social support: A synthesis for health educators. *Advances in Health Education and Promotion: A Research Annual, 2*, 311–351.

Kirby, D., & Miller, B. C. (2002). Interventions designed to promote parent-teen communication about sexuality. *New Directions for Child & Adolescent Development, 97*, 93–110.

Kumpfer, K. L., Alvarudo, R., Smith, P., & Bellany, N. (2002). Cultural sensitivity and adaptation in family-based prevention interventions. *Prevention Science, 3*(3), 241–246.

Lammers, C., Ireland, M., Resnick, M., & Blum, R. (2000). Influences on adolescents' decision to postpone onset of sexual intercourse: A survival analysis of virginity among youths aged 13 to 18 years. *Journal of Adolescent Health, 26*(1), 42–48.

Lefkowitz, E. S., Sigman, M., & Au, T. K. (2000). Helping mothers discuss sexuality and AIDS with adolescents. *Child Development, 71*(5), 1383–1394.

Mackey, W. C., & Immerman, R. S. (2004). The presence of the social father in inhibiting young men's violence. *Mankind Quarterly, 44*, 339–366.

McCarthy, J., & Holliday, E. L. (2004). Help-seeking and counseling within a traditional male gender role: An examination from a multicultural perspective. *Journal of Counseling and Development, 82*(1), 25–30.

McKay, M. M., Chasse, K. T., Paikoff, R., McKinney, L. D., Baptiste, D., Coleman, ... Bell, C. C. (2004). Family-level impact of the CHAMP family program: A community collaborative effort to support urban families and reduce youth HIV risk exposure. *Family Process, 43*(1), 79–93.

Meschke, L. L., Zweig, J. M., Barber, B. L., & Eccles, J. S. (2000). Demographic, biological, psychological, and social predictors of the timing of first intercourse. *Journal of Research on Adolescence, 10*(3), 315–338.

Mincy, R. B. (Ed.). (1994). *Nurturing young black males: Challenges to agencies, programs, and social policy.* Washington, DC: The Urban Institute Press.

Mincy, R. B., & Pouncy, H. (1994). Out-of-welfare strategies for welfare-bound youth. In D. S. Nightingale & R. H. Haveman (Eds.), *The work alternative: Welfare reform and the realities of the job market* (pp. 157–182). Washington, DC: The Urban Institute Press.

Mincy, R. B., & Pouncy, H. (1999). There must be fifty ways to start a family. In W. F. Horn, D. Blankenhorn, & M. B. Pearlstein (Eds.), *The fatherhood movement: A call to action* (pp. 169–176). Lanham, MD: Lexington Books.

Mincy, R. B., & Pouncy, H. (2002). The responsible fatherhood field: Evolutions and goals. In C. Tamis-LeMonda & N. Cabrera (Eds.), *The handbook of father involvement: Multidisciplinary perspectives* (pp. 555–597). Mahwah, NJ: Lawrence Erlbaum Associates.

Mincy, R. B., & Pouncy, H. (2007). Why we should be concerned about young, less educated black men. In J. Edwards, M. Crain, & A. L. Kalleberg (Eds.), *Ending poverty in America: How to restore the American dream* (pp. 191–204). New York: The New Press.

Paschall, M. J., & Hubbard, M. L. (1998). Effects of neighborhood and family stressors on African American male adolescents' self-worth and propensity for violent behavior. *Journal of Consulting and Clinical Psychology, 66*(5), 825–831.

Pederson, E. L., & Vogel, D. L. (2007). Male gender role conflict and willingness to seek counseling: Testing a mediation model on college-aged men. *Journal of Counseling Psychology, 54*(4), 373–384.

Resnick, M. D., Bearman, P. S., Blum, R. W., Bauman, K. E., Harris, K. M., Jones, J., ... Udry, J. R. (1997). Protecting adolescents from harm: Findings from the National Longitudinal Study on Adolescent Health. *JAMA, 278*(10), 823–832.

Robertson, J. M., & Fitzgerald, L. F. (1992). Overcoming the masculine mystique: Preferences for alternative forms of therapy among men who avoid counseling. *Journal of Counseling Psychology, 39*(2), 240–246.

S. 1626. Responsible Fatherhood and Healthy Families Act of 2007. Retrieved from http://thomas.loc.gov/cgi-bin/query/F?c110:1:./temp/~c110ZUQve8: e906:

Sellers, R. M., Rowley, S. A. J., Chavous, T. M., Shelton, J. N., & Smith, M. A. (1997). Multidimensional inventory of black identity: A preliminary investigation of reliability and construct validity. *Journal of Personality & Social Psychology, 73*(4), 805–815.

Sinclair, S. L., & Taylor B. A. (2004). Unpacking the tough guise: Toward a discursive approach for working with men in family therapy. *Contemporary Family Therapy, 26*(4), 389–408.

Stanton, B., Li, X., Black, M., Ricardo, I., Galbraith, J., Kaljee, L., & Feigelman, S. (1994). Sexual practices and intentions among preadolescent and early adolescent low-income urban African-Americans. *Pediatrics, 93*(6), 966–973.

Sylvester, K., & Reich, K. (2002). *Making fathers count: Assessing the progress of responsible fatherhood efforts.* Annie E. Casey Foundation.

Tach, L., Mincy, R., & Edin, K. (Forthcoming). Parenting as a package deal: Relationships, fertility, and nonresident father involvement among unmarried parents. *Demography.*

Taylor, R. J., Chatters, R. M., & Levin, J. (2004). *Religion in the lives of African Americans: Social, psychological, and health perspectives.* Thousand Oaks, CA: Sage Publications.

Thornberry, T. P., Smith, C. A., & Howard, G. J. (1997). Risk factors for teenage fatherhood. *Journal of Marriage and the Family, 59*(3), 505–522.

Thornton, T. N., Craft, C. A., Dahlberg, L. L., Lynch, B. S., & Baer, K. (2002). *Best practices of youth violence prevention: A sourcebook for community action.* Division of Violence Prevention, National Center for Injury Prevention and Control, Centers for Disease Control and Prevention.

Waller, M. (2002). *My baby's father: Unmarried parents and paternal responsibility.* Ithaca, NY: Cornell University Press.

Wills, T. A., Gibbons, F. X., Gerrard, M., Murry, V. M., & Brody, G. H. (2003). Family communication and religiosity related to substance use and sexual behavior in early adolescence: A test for pathways through self-control and prototype perceptions. *Psychology of Addictive Behaviors, 17*(4), 312–323.

Zimmerman, M. A., Steinman, K., & Rowe, K. (1998). Violence among urban African American adolescents: The protective effects of parent support. In S. Oskamp & B. Arriaga (Eds.), *Addressing community problems: Research and intervention* (pp. 78–103). Newbury Park, CA: Sage Publications.

13

Creative Approaches to Working With Gender Variant and Sexual Minority Boys

MARK BEAUREGARD AND DARBY MOORE

INTRODUCTION

This chapter is dedicated to boys who struggle with issues of sexual identity and gender variance, boys who need educated and compassionate clinicians to help them when other sectors of their life seem disconnected or unavailable. We will identify important clinical issues related to the experience of sexual minority and gender variant boys to better help clinicians understand and reach youth in need of help, particularly urban youth of color. By presenting two case studies and five principles of working with gender variant and sexual minority boys, we will illustrate how creative interventions both in and out of the therapist's office help provide these boys with tools to find self-acceptance and satisfaction. We will explore treatment from a dual perspective, recognizing that while sexual minority and gender variant boys may indeed face potential stressors in their lives, they are also resilient, strong, and as full of promise as any child regardless of sexual or gender expression.

For the purposes of this chapter we define sexual minority and gender variant boys as follows: boys who identify as gay, bisexual, or are questioning their sexual orientation, as well as boys for whom sexual orientation is not necessarily the issue, but who display gender expressions that do not "fit in" with social gender expectations. These could be boys who display what might be considered cross-gender behaviors, or who are labeled effeminate. They identify themselves as boys, but struggle with issues of somehow not feeling like the *right kind* of boys, or not quite matching up to gender expectations.

Transgender and gender dysphoric youth (youth whose gender identity does not match that of their biological sex) require specific care that is beyond the scope of this chapter. For information on this, we refer you to other resources of care and information (Brill & Pepper, 2008; Di Ceglie, 2000; Ettner, 1999; Greytak, Kosciw, & Diaz, 2009; Lev, 2004; Mallon & DeCrescenzo, 2006; Menvielle & Tuerk, 2002).

To treat sexual minority and gender variant boys effectively and compassionately, it is necessary to first ascertain what life is really like for them, particularly as they navigate their way to becoming young adults. It is also imperative to understand the particulars of each boy and to not lump individuals into a categorical mass. Given the unique problems this subset of young males face, how can clinicians adapt traditional treatment approaches to maximize therapeutic gains in working with these boys? Lastly, clinicians must examine their own history or influences in regard to sexuality and identity to better understand how their own possible preconceived notions impact the therapy process.

STRESSORS AND EXPERIENCES OF SEXUAL MINORITY AND GENDER VARIANT BOYS

Research indicates boys who identify as a sexual minority or who express their gender differently than other male counterparts have unique struggles and challenges if not provided the proper support (Goodenow, Szalacha, & Westheimer, 2006; Greytak et al., 2009; Hansen, 2007; Kayler, Lewis, & Davidson, 2008; Kiselica, Mulé, & Haldeman, 2008; Kosciw, Diaz, & Greytak, 2008; Mallon & DeCrescenzo, 2006; Peters, 2003; Poteat, Aragon, Espelage, & Koenig, 2009; Sandfort, Melendez, & Diaz, 2007). Most lesbian, gay, bisexual, and transgender (LGBT) adults report that from an early age they experienced feeling profoundly different from their peers and adult role models, and subsequently felt that they did not fit in (Kayler et al., 2008; Robertson & Monsen, 2001). Sexual minority and gender variant boys are made aware of this difference frequently, significantly impacting the potential for negative self and social development. These boys can potentially begin to withdraw from the very social supports that might have the ability to bolster them, such as family, school, church, and community. They may consequently look for support in outside circles of potential risk and danger in order to fulfill needs for relationship and connection (Kiselica et al., 2008). It is therefore important for clinicians to be cognizant of positively reframing circumstances in order to shift focus to ways in which these boys do fit in, emphasizing communities of acceptance, and to foster and maintain connections to positive resources.

Children and adolescents spend most of their time in school. It is a fundamental place for all levels of learning and character development. But for boys who are openly gay, or who have been labeled as a "fag," or those whose gender expression does not fit typical standards of masculinity, school can be difficult to cope with. In a survey conducted on behalf of the Gay Lesbian and Straight Education Network, Kosciw and colleagues (2008) interviewed 6,209 middle and high school students across America on their experiences in school. They found that 86.2% of LGBT students reported being verbally harassed, 44.1% reported being physically harassed, and 22.1% reported being physically assaulted as a result of their real or perceived sexual orientation (Kosciw et al., 2008). Furthermore, 73.6% reported hearing derogatory remarks frequently or often in their schools; 60.8% of the students surveyed reported they felt unsafe in school because of their sexual orientation, and 38.4% felt unsafe because of their gender expression, causing students to frequently miss class and school days.

It is natural to assume that when youth face turmoil at school, they then seek comfort at home with family for support and encouragement. This may be true for some boys lucky enough to have supportive families. For those that do not, it is common to fear parental disappointment, abuse or physical punishment, being kicked out of their home, or being forced to see a therapist to change who they are (Kiselica et al., 2008). Peters (2003) found that 56% of the students surveyed in his research heard antigay comments frequently made by family members. Such findings highlight the fragility of the homes of many sexual minority and gender variant boys. Without solid supports, how is it that these boys cope with life? Where do they turn if they feel they cannot get what they need at home or in school?

It is widely documented that lesbian, gay, bisexual, transgender, and questioning (LGBTQ) youth are at risk for elevated negative emotional consequences such as intense distress, isolation, internalized homophobia, depression, substance use/abuse, suicide, violence and victimization, family conflict, poor school performance, sexually transmitted diseases, and homelessness (Greytak et al., 2009; Hansen, 2007; Kayler et al., 2008; Kiselica et al., 2008; Kosciw et al., 2008; Lev, 2004; Pearson, 2003; Peters, 2003; Poteat et al., 2009). Research also suggests that gay and lesbian teenagers may be three times more likely to attempt suicide than their heterosexual counterparts, and that gay teens may account for 30 to 40% of all teen suicide attempts (Hansen, 2007; Savin-Williams & Ream, 2003). In a recent, large-scale study of 14,439 adolescents, Poteat and colleagues (2009) found markedly consistent results in regard to the experiences of individuals across lines of gender, sexual orientation, and race. The study found that, in general, youth who identified them-selves as questioning reported higher rates of perceived victimization, substance abuse, and depression and suicidal thoughts. This was fol-lowed by youth who identified as lesbian, gay, or bisexual, with the low-est numbers reported by the identified heterosexual contingent.

On all scales, questioning boys reported significantly higher scores in relation to perceived victimization, depression, and sui-cidality than either LGB identified or heterosexual peers (Poteat et al., 2009). This finding speaks to the specific needs and emotional vulnerabilities of boys who may go unnoticed, who have not come to terms with their sexuality, and who are living with a constant struggle of identity formation. It also speaks to the importance of clinicians not only focusing on the issues of youth who have estab-lished an LGBT identity for themselves, but also in helping those who are confused or questioning find greater support in their strug-gle to define their sexual orientation and come to a greater sense of peace within themselves.

RESILIENCE: ANOTHER PERSPECTIVE

These statistics paint a harsh and frightening picture of many realities of life for gender variant and sexual minority youth. However, we also hold the notion that there is a faction of boys who are gender variant or identify as GBQ who are well adjusted and may never see a therapist's office. To depict all gender variant and sexual minority boys as inevita-bly growing up with mental illness, committing suicide, or being dam-aged is misleading and incorrect.

Gender variance and minority sexual orientation are not inherently pathological. It is now more commonly understood that if gender vari-ant and sexual minority boys do indeed suffer from greater stressors than their peers, the source of these stressors is most often homopho-bia and stigmatization. All major mental health organizations denounce the treatment of homosexuality as pathological. Attempts to change, "repair," or convert someone's sexual identity are unethical, ineffec-tive, and damaging (Lev, 2004; Mallon & DeCrescenzo, 2006; Savin-Williams & Cohen, 2004).

Regarding the large numbers of high-risk statistics specific to LGBTQ youth, there are researchers who argue these findings are skewed as a result of data being collected from participants who already define themselves as LGBTQ individuals, as well as those who are seeking supportive services, thereby inaccurately reflecting the larger number of unidentified sexual minority individuals. They insist that there is a more resilient population of individuals that are not reflected in the data, and that a more strengths-based look at LGBTQ youth should be used (Cohler & Hammack, 2007; Savin-Williams & Cohen, 2004; Savin-Williams & Ream, 2003). Savin-Williams stated:

The field has so pathologized gay youth, claiming that they're depressed, suicidal, radicals, leftists, anything and everything … and the reality is extraordinarily different. Like anybody else, there are some gay teens who are depressed and some who are unhealthy and some who are confused. But most are just ordinary adolescents and they just want to live their lives. They are not any more outlandish than other teens, and they want the same kinds of things that *all* kids want. (Saval, 2009, p. 120)

It is reassuring that such kids are depicted in current American media. One can turn on the television and watch any number of prime-time television shows depicting queer characters, many of whom are male teenagers living with supportive families and friends. This means a great deal not only for those kids who these television shows represent but also for the larger society who desperately need images that counter the stereotypes and negative assumptions that exist about queer youth.

As media is displaying a broader and more positive queer visibility, so must research. There is a lack of research available to the public that emphasizes strengths-based perspectives and identity affirmation, and more quantitative research is needed to accurately reflect positive outcomes of interventions and support for LGBTQ youth. Some research does point to the strength and importance of interventions made in both the home and school system. Ryan, Heubner, Diaz, and Sanchez (2009) emphasized in their research the detrimental effects that family rejection can have on LGB youth's future risk behaviors and mental health. Young people with families with no or low levels of rejection, or whose families make adjustments in their level of acceptance, have significantly less risks related to depression, suicidality, substance use, or risky sexual behavior. This finding emphasizes the need of the therapist to understand fully the client's family context, as well as engaging the family whenever possible.

Promising research also has been done in looking at the implementation of school support. In a recent school survey by GLSEN, only 36.3% of the students reported having a Gay-Straight Alliance in their schools, and sadly, only 18.7% attended a school with a school safety policy toward sexual orientation and gender expression (Kosciw et al., 2008). However, research shows that the establishment of Gay-Straight Alliances in schools, in addition to the implementation of school policies in regard to safety for sexual orientation and gender identity/expression, significantly reduces reports of victimization, as well as resulting suicidality. These measures also have been proven to increase academic attendance, achievement, and motivation in this population (Goodenow et al., 2006; Hansen, 2007; Kayler et al., 2008; Kosciw et al., 2008; Peters, 2003).

Identity-Affirming Models and Guidelines

Lastly, when considering providing affirmative treatment for gender variant and sexual minority boys, therapists are wise to consult and utilize
models and guidelines that help contextualize clients' experiences and
needs. The American Psychological Association (2000) has created the
"Guidelines for Psychotherapy With Lesbian, Gay, and Bisexual Clients,"
which provides clear and concise guidelines for appropriate and affirmative care. Similar clinical books exist regarding guidelines for treating
gender variant populations with appropriate sensitivity (Brill & Pepper,
2008; Ettner, 1999; Lev, 2004).

Gender and sexuality theorists have created models to capture the
experience and coming-out process of many LGBT individuals (Cass,
1979; Devor, 2004; Troiden, 1989). These models do have limitations,
but can nonetheless be useful for the clinician in assessing a boy's place
in the process of identity development. Each model consists of sequen-
tial stages, moving progressively from a point of identity confusion and
questioning to an eventual acceptance and integration of one's sexual/
gender identity into a fully out lifestyle.

There is value in using these models as assessment tools in helping
to appropriately design interventions that support a boy's positive identity formation. However, some issues are worth noting. First, as with
any stage model, the clinician should not assume that sexual and gender identity will progress so linearly. Also, of greater importance, many
models stress an out and visible lifestyle as the pinnacle or end stage,
underestimating the difficulties and potential dangers that might exist
for individuals in certain life circumstances to be out publicly (Kiselica
et al., 2008). Individuals choose, for various reasons, the contexts in
their lives in which to be out (e.g., work, school). To suggest that not
being out in all aspects of one's life is less evolved does not take into
account the everyday realities of queer people. Nonetheless, these models are a valuable resource for therapists to utilize.

CARLO AND JAMES: TWO CASE STUDIES

The following case studies serve to personify the research and issues
described previously and show the overlap of identity struggle, culture,
family, and systems interventions within a range of settings and age
levels. Each case involves a Latino boy from an underserved neighborhood in New York City. Carlo's story is one of the gender variance of a
7-year-old, while the story of James focuses on a 17-year-old struggling
with family conflict and coming out. In each case the authors sought
to address treatment with the goals of being culturally sensitive as well
as fostering a positive and affirming process of identity development
rooted in creativity and the arts.

Cultural Considerations

Before elaborating on the two cases, it is important to examine some of the research related to ethnicity and culture in the context of gender variant and sexual minority boys. Both authors' work has predominantly been in communities of low socioeconomic status in New York City. In our work with Latino, Caribbean, West Indian, and African American youth, issues of gender and sexuality, particularly in the way they are stereotyped and perceived, are easily demonstrated in the youth's daily interactions and comments. Boys are called "fags" for almost any social mistake. Derogatory terms are used frequently and consistently to keep boys aligned with a traditional vision of masculinity. Boys must be "masculine," and being bisexual or gay means they are not manly. For adolescents in particular, the task of identity formation alone can be daunting. Adding to this tension are the requirements of adapting to socioeconomic conditions less favorable for supporting vocational, educational, and long-term economic success.

For minority boys who are out, the difficulties faced can outweigh those of their Caucasian counterparts. Diaz and Kosciw (2009) reported that, out of a sample of 2,000 minority students who identified as LGBT students of color, 4 out of 5 in each major group reported verbal harassment because of sexual orientation and gender expression. But, combined with that, almost half of these students also reported verbal taunting due to their ethnicity or race. Less than half of the students of color who reported having been victimized stated they would inform a parent or another school official (Diaz & Kosciw, 2009).

In a study exploring rates of mental distress in Latino gay and bisexual men, Sandfort and colleagues (2007) found that gay and bisexual Latino men who considered themselves to be more effeminate had higher levels of mental distress, and more frequently reported histories of victimization and harassment, than gay and bisexual Latino men who did not identify as effeminate. Their research speaks to the difficulty of those who cannot easily "blend in" with traditional gender norms. It is clear that issues of homophobia and stigma around gender nonconformity can be highly damaging for boys struggling to navigate both cultural and sexuality/gender identifications. Specifically, Latino men have been found to show higher numbers of negative family reactions to their sexuality in adolescence, and consequently higher rates of negative outcomes for mental health and HIV risk (Ryan et al., 2009).

Carlo

I (MB) met Carlo when he was admitted to the child psychiatric inpatient unit that I was working on at the time as a creative arts therapist and primary therapist. Carlo, a 7-year-old Latino boy, was hospitalized due to dangerous behaviors that included threatening to kill his brother, running into the streets, and attempting to set a fire in a department store. He was diagnosed with mood disorder, not otherwise specified, and gender identity disorder.

This was Carlo's first hospitalization. Very little was known about him and his history other than the fact that his biological parents were reported to be drug addicts who abandoned him and his older brother during early childhood. Carlo was raised by his adopted mother since the age of 18 months. He was placed into foster care two months prior to hospitalization due to reported physical abuse by the adopted mother.

On the unit, Carlo was impulsive, aggressive at times, hyperactive, and labile, with extreme tantrums and poor boundaries. He displayed many attachment issues, and his presentation could shift rapidly, one minute sweet and the next provocative. The clinical team created several behavior plans designed to address his hitting and oppositional behaviors, as well as to promote the staff's consistency of interaction and behavior management with Carlo.

Though not the reason for his hospitalization, Carlo's many gender variant behaviors quickly became a focus of the staff and peers around him. Carlo frequently drew pictures of girls. He loved to wear feminine clothing and would become very excited, asking to wear the staff's high heels and "have dress-up time." He was highly resourceful in his desire to dress up, using large Lego blocks from the playroom to make his own high heels and creating long, beautiful fingernails with scotch tape and markers, culminating in walking imaginary fashion runways and calling himself supermodel "Marissa."

Comprised of diverse cultural backgrounds, the unit staff became quickly divided about how to "deal with" Carlo. Many nurses became uncomfortable with his gender nonconformity and would verbally scold him, telling him to "act like a boy." He was frequently teased by his peers on the unit as well, often called derogatory names by the other boys. Carlo was clearly affected by these interactions. At times, he responded by increasing his provocative and aggressive behaviors. Other times he became quite sullen and sad. On some level, Carlo was aware he was "different." It was clear he struggled with the ambivalence of loving his feminine traits while hating being ostracized because of them.

It became necessary to utilize clinical meetings to educate staff about issues of gender expression diversity in young children in an effort to remove the stigma he was facing in a place he was supposed to be receiving treatment. It was eventually decided that, because Carlo's gender variance was not ego dystonic and not the reason he was hospitalized per se, it did not require staff intervention. However, what became clear was that this boy needed safe spaces where he was allowed flexibility of gender expression and, ultimately, freedom of emotional expression. This safe space was provided in the context of individual and group therapy. Establishing his gender identity, future sexuality, or a label for either was not the prime clinical need; after all, he was only seven years old, too young for the establishment of a consistent identity. For his short stay, the most important goals were allowing safety of expression, improving self-esteem, fostering positive social interaction, and increasing coping skills for peer ostracism, thereby helping Carlo obtain an improved emotional stability.

Most interventions that were utilized with Carlo centered on play therapy approaches and the use of creative arts therapy, namely, drama therapy, in both individual and group therapy sessions. For more information about drama therapy, readers are encouraged to see related references (Emunah, 1994; Landy, 1994; Johnson & Emunah, 2009; Weber & Haen, 2005). Carlo was informed that therapy sessions would provide a space where he could "act" and "be anything" he wanted to be. The sessions quickly became a container for his ambivalent feelings about his gender expression, a place in which he was able to express both love and frustration toward being different.

Individually, we began with mostly unstructured play sessions, giving Carlo the lead to set the tone and tempo of our work together. Carlo immediately took to the pretty, long gloves and tiara in the office, playing out extended dramas in which the princess (Carlo) would order the servant (therapist) around the room to do various errands and tasks. We played like this for a few sessions until he suddenly shifted the roles, turning me into a "mean princess," and hiding from me. Carlo, through the use of a magic wand and powers, then beat the mean princess up and turned me into a "good princess." In role, I asked him to help join me in finding friends who would love me for who I was and who would not make fun of me. We proceeded to go around the room collecting friends to treat us nicely. Puppet friend interviews commenced; however, only the ones who treated us with respect were selected for the friends pile.

It is important that Carlo was able to project the princess role onto the therapist, and equally important that the therapist take on that feminine role. Carlo could see another male figure not threatened by "feminine play." Therapists taking on and playing out projections of sexuality and gender can not only be validating but also serve as a means for clients to externalize and interact with their issues in a more distanced and less threatening form. In this case, it allowed Carlo the space to take the role off of himself and play with his own ambivalence of love and hate toward the feminine role. This work also encompassed the critical skill of choosing friends and more clearly identifying positive social behaviors.

In subsequent sessions I began to incorporate more clear direction and structure, focusing on assessing and improving Carlo's sense of self-image. He was asked to create several different masks that represented things he wanted to be. He created many paper masks of various characters, representing duplicities of good and bad, pretty and ugly. He was asked to use these masks by speaking as the character while I interviewed each of them. Some of the more shadowy and aggressive figures he simply chose to banish, perhaps elements of himself that he was not ready to explore given his age. At the same time, he enjoyed using characters he named "Pretty" and "Bunny," representing his more feminine qualities. Pretty and Bunny were taken home with him when he left the unit a week or so later, providing him with transitional objects that hopefully would continue to serve as positive sources of identity.

Group sessions were primarily drama therapy groups focusing on social skill building through the creation of role play and drama scenes. Carlo's participation in these sessions occurred once his aggression and impulsivity had decreased substantially. Carlo was provided support to express his feelings when hurt by other peers' derogatory comments, as well as given opportunities in group exercises to make positive connections to peers and to hear their feedback regarding his impulsivity. One group became specifically significant as it focused on the theme of difference, due to the fact that many of the group members were "different" on various physical and social levels. Group members were asked to create stories of characters that were different from others. After developing and playing out each character individually, the group members were then asked to create a group drama scene utilizing these characters. Carlo had great difficulty developing a character initially and kept himself on the periphery. When the group created their scene, they decided they wanted a superhero to help them and asked Carlo to play that role. He decided he wanted to be Super Girl, something the other group members tolerated well. Super Girl then completed the scene by flying in to grant each character a wish. This was a powerful moment for Carlo. He was so excited to be accepted into the play in the form he knew best. What was truly touching was how this integration began to generalize to the group's play outside the sessions as well. Carlo was more frequently accepted by his peers on the unit and incorporated into the free play group activities, rather than spending most of his time in his room alone. He was becoming a more confident, social child.

There are facets of Carlo's treatment that have not been addressed here as they are beyond the scope of this chapter. What is important is the concept of developing a safe space, a laboratory if you will, in which youth can explore gender in its various forms, and a space that will help the child in coping with social stigma and prejudice. Carlo did, in fact, demonstrate a significant decrease in his aggression, not solely because of—but certainly due in part to—experiencing a sense of acceptance of his gender expression. It was important in considering his next phase of treatment that his outpatient therapist be informed of Carlo's gender dynamics in order to help maintain a therapeutic relationship that was gender sensitive and allowed Carlo the ability to continue to explore his gender expressions and developing identity.

James

The case of James exemplifies some of the cultural and familial difficulties for young men who are struggling with their sexual identity.

At a milieu day treatment program in New York City based on psycho-dynamic principles, a 17-year-old male was admitted from an inpatient program where he was treated for having taken 11 hits of acid. The opinion of the intake worker was that he was suffering from residual psychosis, which may or may not dissipate. The case was transferred to me (DM), and it became apparent that the young man was not psychotic, but emotionally conflicted. In our first meetings, he showed signs of apathy, anxiety, avoidance, and a seeming disconnect from his present situation.

James was the third sibling in a middle-class, Puerto Rican family of divorced parents. He disliked his father, whom he rarely saw, but was close to his mother, whom he respected as a parent. His older sister was in the army and out of the country. His oldest sibling, a brother, was married and lived out of state. The family was nominally Roman Catholic, but not excessively religious. The extended family, however, was more religious and conservative, and there were seasonal family get-togethers.

James had attended a small, elite public high school on the upper west side of Manhattan before having his "break." His attire was that of a young downtown Goth, with bright dyed hair. He did not identify with the kids from the "hood," and listened to alternative music rather than the hip-hop of the majority of his peers. He also didn't clearly identify as Latino, as he preferred to be called by an anglicized version of his name. At the day treatment program, he connected to the strongest, largest female, who, like himself, was artistic, poetic, and expressive. The relationship remained platonic.

After his first therapist left the program to go on maternity leave, this writer was assigned as his primary therapist. At this point staff thought James was mostly drifting aimlessly, not particularly engaged or connected in his treatment. James would meet with me once weekly for individual therapy. He was also in the various creative arts therapy and other groups I facilitated during the week. The initial task was to develop the therapeutic relationship (Shirk & Saiz, 1992). This progressed easily, though slowly, with the young man mostly interested in recounting his relationships with friends and aspects of their "partying." In receiving neither judgment nor admonishment, James was encouraged to shift from relaying information to expressing affect and assessing the wisdom of his actions and behavior. While this movement toward reflection was a sign of progress, there was an element of showing off how cool he was in order to impress me. I still had to jump through hoops to prove my trustworthiness. One day I agreed to go outdoors and walk during our session. Since I often took groups outside, this was not difficult until he raised the ante and requested that he be allowed to smoke on these walks. The decision to allow James to smoke was not taken lightly, though most likely more easily than if it had been now, fifteen years later. While James's mother knew that he smoked, she didn't approve, and he said he knew I wouldn't approve either. My response was that I was not in the "approving or disapproving business, but the mental health business."

Consequently, during the warm weather, we walked or sat on park benches and talked. The quality and tone of our sessions changed accordingly. James appeared more relaxed in his body language and facial muscles. He laughed more when talking and started allowing me to see his personal art and his journal, which he hadn't indoors. His journal contained similar material to his weekly stories about friends and parties, clothes and music. The artwork, however, was figurative, and provided an opening into James's inner world. This came about by asking basic questions such as: "Where did this idea come from?" or "Are these images related to anything specific in your life?" Once asked, James would initially minimize any significance to himself in his drawings with responses such as "Oh, that's just something I made up." Eventually, he connected the pictures to an affective component with comments such as "I really, really like this look, and wish I looked like this." We were then able to segue into talking about his low self-esteem regarding his looks.

Teenagers in general experience discontent and anxiety around their appearance, and James was no exception. In self-description he used words such as hideous, atrocious, and ugly. Once again, while it's not unusual for teens to be self-deprecating about their looks, James had overdosed on hallucinogens and had been failing at school. So while it was clear that James was artistically talented and created agreeable images for himself on paper, he did not have a positive vocabulary or narrative. I suggested, therefore, that he try writing poetry as well as journaling, and he agreed. Subsequently, however, he didn't bring in his journal or sketchbook for weeks and reverted to talking about movies, music, and friends. I asked whether he was having trouble with identifying positive words about himself, and he replied that he was and that his drawings had nothing to do with him, that they were "just pictures." It was clear that I had pushed beyond his comfort zone. I then suggested he write down every single negative thought, as well as words he uttered that were self-deprecatory, and bring them to our next session. When he returned he had several notebook pages filled with insulting and negative thoughts. We looked at them together and he reported that he was shocked at the number and frequency of the negative self-talk, and that if he really thought other people thought those things about him, he would kill himself. I asked if he believed people thought those things about him, and he replied that he didn't think so, that they just thought he was "kinda weird," but that's what he wanted them to think. If he thought those things about himself, I asked, but others didn't, how did he explain that dichotomy? He didn't know, except perhaps that he was good at hiding things from others.

The next week, James reported that he had had a dream about the governor. I asked, "Mario Cuomo?" He replied, "No, just the governor," and that the dream was frightening because in it he had been kidnapped and brought to the governor, who he believed was trying to kill him. This dream became the basis for the understanding that led to James being able to identify himself openly as gay and ultimately disclose to his mother and family members. We explored the various elements in the dream from a loosely Jungian (Jung, 1964) perspective in that I encouraged James to recognize that he produced the dream and that he could own all of its aspects. He came to adopt the idea that he was the governor and, because he did not conform to the world around him, he should die.

The prevailing emotions in the dream were shame and anger: shame that he did not conform and anger at his sister, whom he felt had delivered him to the governor as a sex slave. When asked what part of his sister in the dream was himself, he replied that, indeed, he had engaged in an incestuous relationship with his older sister at age 7, and therefore was old enough to know that it was wrong. Nevertheless, he had blamed her for being the instigator and felt guilty for blaming her. He also, apparently, felt guilty for "turning his sister into a lesbian." I reminded James that, in the dream, he had escaped the governor without being harmed, and asked what he made of that. He replied that he actually knew that he didn't turn his sister into a lesbian any more than she had turned him into a "fag."

While the term *fag* was pejorative, this was also the first time James had brought up his own sexuality in these terms. Prior to this, he had made mild references to heterosexual behaviors in descriptions of his social life, but not in a style or manner I had come to expect from male teens, even in interaction with a middle-aged, female therapist. I responded by asking James what he meant, and he replied that it was pretty clear that while all his best friends were girls, he really, *really* liked boys, and his girlfriends all said he was gay. I remarked that *gay* was a kinder word than *fag*, which is how he had referred to himself and asked him if he had noticed that. He replied that being gay was a problem because he believed that his father had instinctively rejected and abandoned him as a result, and had even killed his dog. His mother, on the other hand, didn't know because she worked too hard to be able to notice, but if she did, she would be horrified. I responded that I was confused, since his father had left the family when James was around five. I suggested that perhaps this conclusion was instead one the "governor" had made that James had subsequently adopted. He replied, "Yeah, that probably couldn't really be the cause." I suggested at this point that he might wish to speak to the governor and remind him that he, James, was in charge of his life. He replied that he knew that, and that being a sex slave to the governor was just being a sex slave to himself. When asked in what sense, he answered that by not allowing himself to be who he really was, he was trapped like a slave.

I worked with James for another year until he graduated from high school. He gradually made the decision to come out to his mother. She did not reject him, and while it took many months to work through the feelings with them both, she was a proud mother when he graduated. On the strength of this, James decided to come out to the rest of his family. Many members of his extended family remained censorious. Others, while not embracing his homosexuality, did not reject James as a person, while still others tried to evangelize him. His relationships with his sister and brother required significant attention. Ultimately, however, James had made peace with himself to the degree that these challenges were possible. James did not refrain from some recreational drug use, but showed no further clinical markers of self-injurious behaviors, nor anxiety, depression, or psychosis. His self-esteem was good. The etiology of James's identity coalescence had numerous important elements: First and foremost was the safe environment of a milieu day treatment program with a 2:1 student-to-staff ratio; second was the therapeutic alliance created by the (probably unprofessional) walking/smoking sessions; third, the attention to his artistic expression as projective material; finally, the dream work.

Five Principles for Working With Gender Variant and Sexual Minority Boys

The cases of Carlo and James, as well as many other boys we have worked with, highlight five common principles that guide our approach. These principles emphasize the use of creativity, play, and empowerment in moving clients toward a stronger and more defined sense of self. The principles are: (1) establishing space for playful permissive exploration, (2) building intimacy and relationships, (3) mitigating the victim role, (4) developing coping skills for the outside world, and (5) making the therapist an agent of change.

Under each principle we offer creative interventions utilized within our own practices. The intervention examples are meant to provide the reader with possible inspiration for developing interventions appropriate for the particular clients and settings in which you practice. Creative approaches must fit individuals and circumstances. Avoid the temptation to impose directives that do not emerge organically. This population in particular has had the imposition of expectations placed on them more intensely than most. Therapists may become enamored by various techniques and interventions and may inadvertently hinder a positive therapeutic relationship by trying to fit square pegs into round holes. Clinicians can access creative ideas simply by listening and taking the lead from the client(s).

A Word About Trust, Safety, and Neutrality

All therapy should be based in the principle of establishing a safe therapeutic space that allows for a trusting relationship to emerge. Before one can explore potentially anxiety-producing issues of sexual and gender identity openly, a level of comfort must exist between therapist and client(s). Though we encourage the therapist and client(s) to explore and play with identity issues, it is assumed that before this process begins, cohesion and safety has been established.

Neutrality on the part of the therapist is important as well. Therapists must not steer LGBTQ youth down paths they are not ready to pursue, and should avoid letting countertransference take over their therapeutic interventions. Youth may want the therapist to take their side against people (family, peers, etc.) who don't accept their differences. Obviously, no matter how we feel, we need neutrality in helping guide clients toward defining their own solutions to these dilemmas. The obvious exception to this is in the case of abuse and neglect that meets the reportable criteria. Likewise, when dealing with families and caregivers, we must maintain a strictly neutral stance in order to maintain the possibility of cooperation and collaboration when and if the primary client so indicates he may be ready to work directly with this cohort.

Establishing Space for Playful Permissive Exploration: Gender/Sexuality Lab

As child and adolescent therapists, we find the use of humor and playfulness to be motivating and engaging for our clients, bringing in a needed sense of security and distance when exploring otherwise stressful issues. We encourage therapists to use the therapeutic space as a laboratory for identity exploration (Emunah, 1994). Develop a "play space" that allows issues of gender and sexuality to be more easily introduced and "playable," so that clients feel a permission to explore them from various perspectives. As Fontaine and Hammond (1996) wrote, it is important to "encourage the young person in their exploration of sexual identity issues. Throughout this process, it is important to allow the teen to 'try' on labels, rather than adopt them" (p. 828). Clients can explore and counter stereotypes, try on roles, discard roles, and literally play around with identity, all in a safe space without consequence. From a humorous and playful perspective the therapist and client(s) alike can introduce material that has personal or collective meaning and gain a new or different perspective.

Intervention Examples

- **Therapist in role.** The therapist takes the role of a gay/gender variant character and begins to interact with client(s). The choice on how to play the role can depend upon the clients you are working with. It has been helpful in our practice to use this as a tool to discuss and offer perspectives that counter stereotypes, and to explore questions such as "What are gay people like?" or "What are boys supposed to act like?" This technique takes the pressure off the client and allows the therapist to play out and take on client projections and assumptions that can later be processed.

- **Play with it.** When encountered by clients who are playfully presenting with sexual or gender dynamics, engage with it. A 16-year-old boy in an outpatient psychiatric program insisted on wearing female attire and jewelry, creating a drag persona named "Coco-butter," and attending girls groups in the program. The author did not shut it down and instead played along, interviewing Coco-butter about her hopes, dreams, and aspirations. This led spontaneously to other group members doing the same, allowing the whole group a sense of freedom to express and play with gender roles.

- **Popular media as a reflection of identity.** Youth respond enthusiastically to popular media, particularly music and videos. Bringing in clips from movies, television series, or music and lyrics is a powerful way to connect with youth and explore identifications. For sexual minority and gender variant boys, LGBTQ-specific plays, films, poetry, and music can be particularly effective in providing a reference to validate their own perspectives and self-image. The boys can also be asked to bring into sessions media that they feel best represents themselves or an issue close to them, empowering self-evaluation and freedom of choice.

- **Stories and storytelling.** Societal and group story making and storytelling have long functioned to help define group identity and forge a common narrative (Emunah, 1994; Lahad, 1992; Landy, 1994). Groups can use stories from various cultures and act them out, followed by processing the identification and differences with the characters and situations. Groups may also choose to act out something from pop culture, as years ago one group of mixed youth recreated Star Wars, and an emerging gay male requested the role of Princess Leia. In creating their own stories, group members experience the added benefit of accomplishment and ownership of material that has been generated intrinsically.

- **Boxed in.** Using any type of box, such as a shoebox, invite the client(s) to create a "masculinity box" with various art supplies and collage materials. On the outside the boy(s) depict messages they feel society sends them regarding expectations of how they should be as a male. The inside of the box is used to depict their internal feelings, personal experiences and beliefs about what being male means to them. Process as a group or individually in session at whatever pace the client needs to reveal the inside. This can be a useful way to assess a boy's sense of self and feelings related to gender and sexuality. It also makes concrete the process of verbalizing and sharing internally held gender- and sexuality-related issues. This same process can be used to explore issues related to sexual orientation and prevalent heterosexism in society at large.

Building Intimacy and Relationships

As a result of the isolation that exists for some sexual minority and gender variant boys, and the challenges that may arise from not finding a truly accepting peer group, therapists must concentrate on improving skills for building intimacy and relationship. Youth need a space where they can reveal and experience themselves in the presence of others they trust, thereby improving self-concept. Therapists who see clients individually should strongly consider group therapy. Support groups have been found to significantly improve quality of life for queer youth (Kayler et al., 2008; Lemoire & Chen, 2005). Group-based intervention can serve to help move clients from "as if" fantasized social relationships to an actual, reality-based experience where they can find and identify positive peers and community supports (Lock, 1998). Therapists can also assist boys in developing their "family of choice," composed of their strongest allies in both their biological family and social circle (Sanders & Kroll, 2000).

Intervention Examples

- **Find your community.** Have the group or individual research activities and centers that are available and accessible in their community, as well as online. Potentially have liaisons attend group to present their agency/club and explain social options available to the youth. The Gay-Straight Alliance group one author facilitated at a high school in the South Bronx was not comfortable with traveling to Manhattan to check out some of the well-established community resources for youth. Through an Internet search they discovered an LGBT youth center not far from the school and made contact with someone there who encouraged the group to make use of the offerings. This same group invited someone from Parents, Families, and Friends of Lesbians and Gays (PFLAG) to come and speak with the group and, when a supercilious looking Westchester matron appeared, it seemed as if the contact might be ineffectual. However, when she spoke of her son and his coming out and eventual illness and death due to AIDS, she had them. She related her experience with simplicity and sincerity, and it transcended the difference in ethnicity and socioeconomics. Several group members were brought to tears. They talked together and were mutually inspired and supported by this interface.
- **Hopes, fears, and expectations** (Sternberg & Garcia, 2000). Each member writes something about his hopes, fears, and expectations on a piece of paper. The leader collects them and passes them back out randomly. Each person acts out the aspect of the paper they receive. The group then guesses what was on the paper, as well as which group member wrote the example. The group explores identifications and differences as they relate to their identity and future

projections. This is a distanced method to enable the expression of material that young people often have difficulty revealing. This process can be followed by a sociometric exercise whereby group members place a hand on the shoulder of the person whose hopes, fears, and expectations they find most compelling. The leader may then point out where the group's "energy" is generally directed by indicating where there are clusters and clumping of connections.

- **Affirmations.** Write the name of each group member on a sheet of paper and place the pages around the room. Each group member is invited to write/draw something positive on each other's sheets. Discuss their experience of the process with the group members. This is a simple, effective relationship-building exercise that emphasizes the giving and receiving of praise.

Mitigating the Victim Role

Mitigating the effects of victimization is an important part of therapeutic support for gender variant and sexual minority boys. The victim role will turn up within the context of this population and should not be avoided, as many of these boys may have been verbally, physically, or even sexually abused or battered. Carefully steering individuals and groups toward seeing how the victim is not the only role they play in life, and that there is room for an expansive role repertoire, can attenuate the negative aspects of living in the victim role. The therapeutic work thus begins to focus on moving forward, identifying strengths and positive qualities, and exploring new roles of identity.

Intervention Examples

- **Three-chair monologue.** Set up three empty chairs. Each chair can represent a specific time in the boy's life (i.e., past, present, future), or related roles (i.e., victim, survivor, hero). Have the client(s) sit in each chair and speak an improvised monologue from the perspective of that role. This was used with an openly gay, 14-year-old Latino boy who was admitted to an outpatient, short-term day program due to extreme bullying at school that led to an emotional breakdown. At the time of his discharge, we created three chairs representing "my first day," "today," and "tomorrow when I go back to school" in order to emphasize and concretize his growth and strength.
- **TV news interview.** The therapist takes on the role of a TV news reporter who then interviews client(s). The therapist begins with an improvised introduction, such as "Coming to you live with Channel 7 News, we are here meeting some very important boys who have overcome immense hurdles in their lives and are here to share with us how they did it...." The therapist interviews each

client. Discussion and processing around personal strengths then occurs.

- **Letter to myself.** This is a future projection technique in which the client writes a letter to himself that is meant to be read in the future. Clients can use the letter to express hopes, dreams, accomplishments, advice on looking back, comments on the person they've become, and so on. The client may choose to keep it as a daily reminder for himself, or seal it and open it in the future.
- **Victim and survivor body tracings.** On mural paper, have the client(s) create two body tracings, in the roles of "victim" and "survivor." Inside of the tracings have the client(s) write or draw messages they've received, incidents that have occurred, and significant feelings and thoughts in relation to the role. Verbally process the experience and outcome. If in a group setting, members should be encouraged to view everyone's tracings and identify connections. This can also be helpful in providing therapists insight into the ability of the client(s) to access qualities of resiliency.

Building Coping Skills for the Outside World

Gender variant and sexual minority boys must be given tools and coping strategies to effectively handle stressors. Exploring feelings within the therapeutic space is essential. Equally important is giving boys tangible coping skills for when they walk out of the therapist's office and encounter the world. Therapists must explore with boys options and choices on how to handle situations such as coming out, having relationships, gender expression in public, teasing and bullying, and so on.

Intervention Examples

- **Six-part story making with BASIC Ph** (Lahad, 1992). This exercise utilizes either a drawn storyline in boxes, or just the written elements. The six parts consist of: "Who is your main character?" "What is your character's mission?" "Who or what can help your main character (if anything)?" "What stands in the way of your character completing his or her mission?" "How does he/she cope with this obstacle?" and "What happens next?" This process is often coupled with a model for understanding an individual's capacity for resilience under stress called BASIC PH, standing for belief and attitudes (B), affect (A), social (S), imagination (I), cognition (C), and physical (Ph). Both the story and the BASIC Ph model highlight areas of focus for specific interventions and can target developing coping skills for various future projections and scenarios when the story is couched in sexuality and gender themes.

- **The bully, the bullied, and the bystander** (Coloroso, 2003). This technique is appropriate for group and community settings to empower change in bystander reluctance. Have group members record actual instances of bullying they witness during a specific time period. They should identify the roles of bully, bullied, and bystander, not necessarily by name but by categorical identification within the setting or school. Group members should take on the role of bystanders to an enactment of the incident and do an inner monologue from that point of view. Subsequent to the monologue, group members can interview the bystanders in more detail as to what they think about the incident. Brainstorm and then role-play ways to do interventions with actual bystanders. Bullies need bystanders who support them, and unmaking supportive bystanders begins to even the playing field.
- **Family role plays.** The possibilities for role-playing and problem-solving issues of family dynamics for sexual minority and gender variant boys are limitless. Deciding when and how to come out to family, exploring ways to improve positive interactions with family members, or simply expressing strong emotion that the client has been unable to do in reality can easily be accomplished within the safety of the dramatic space. Group members can also provide one another with valuable feedback and suggestions on how to handle stressful situations, and then use role play to rehearse these strategies. Role plays can be applied to many other scenarios that are not family related as well.
- **Strength cards** (Cossa, 2006). Members are asked to think of personal strengths boys might have—such as assertiveness, confidence, and loyalty—and to write them on index cards. The cards are passed around, and group members illustrate examples on the cards. Cards can be spread out on the floor, and members can be asked to stand next to words they relate to and also qualities they aspire to achieve. This experience can be verbally processed or moved into role plays for added emphasis.

Making the Therapist an Agent of Change

With the considerable social, cultural, and political issues that queer individuals face, it is simply not enough to attempt to try to effect change only in one's clients. We argue that it is necessary for therapists to look beyond the walls of their offices and begin to effect change in the larger community. Therapists must consider the effect of working to instill change in the person's environment, and thereby positively affecting their functioning and mental health. By addressing concrete problems within a particular setting (school, hospital, community organization, and so on) and brainstorming ideas to ameliorate conditions, clinicians empower clients to advocate for themselves by example. Therapists should not shy away from taking on the roles of advocate and activist.

Intervention Examples

- **Start a Gay–Straight Alliance (GSA).** Establishing a GSA in a school, community, or organization can create dramatic changes for the better. A helpful resource in this effort is www.GSAforSafeSchools.org. One of the authors was asked by her clients to facilitate a GSA in a public high school in the South Bronx. It was a powerful experience that helped the students to find a safe space to explore their feelings and form their identities, and empowered them to make personal growth decisions. One 15-year-old Latino boy in particular was able to utilize the group to process and gather support around intense school bullying issues, familial conflict, and a sense of isolation. He was able to make supportive connections at a local LGBT teen center, and to find support from peers in dealing with whether or not to come out to his family.
- **Create a visible safe zone/safe space.** Make yourself a visible advocate and ally for LGBTQ youth by putting up a safe zone sticker in your office (http://safezonefoundation.tripod.com) or learning about making your office or organization a safer space with GLSEN's Safe Space Kit (www.glsen.org/cgi-bin/iowa/all/library/record/1641.html). The organization Advocates for Youth (www.advocatesforyouth.org) also has an excellent tool kit for creating safe spaces for LGBTQ youth that readers may find useful.
- **Raise awareness in the broader community.** Increase awareness and visibility to LGBTQ issues in the community by facilitating workshops and trainings both within the mental health field and outside of it, presenting at conferences, publishing articles, and so on.
- **Action research as community intervention.** "Action research involves empowering a group of people affected by a social problem to conduct their own research and address the problem themselves" (Peters, 2003, p. 331). Peters (2003) provided an example of how to incorporate the arts into community change and activism efforts for LGBTQ youth. A network of youth workers created a project to evaluate school-based homophobia within their community. Interviews, artwork, and anecdotes were collected from area students and presented at a one-day conference where the findings were used as a catalyst to brainstorming how the community would respond. In addition, the anecdotes of students were also created into a theatre piece that was performed by a group of LGBTQ peer educators. This work and other examples of advocacy and activist work are compelling instruments of change that therapists might consider in broadening how they support their queer clients.

CONCLUSION

Clinicians should not underestimate the power they have in providing an accepting, affirmative, and safe relationship for sexual minority and gender variant boys, subsequently altering the course of their lives for the better. It is imperative that clinicians remain knowledgeable about issues that pertain specifically to LGBTQ youth and provide clear messages to clients about their ability to provide a safe space where issues of identity, sexuality, and gender can be addressed.

We have outlined specific challenges and obstacles faced by sexual minority and gender variant boys. At the same time, we have presented an approach to working with these boys that emphasizes their resilience, strength, and creativity—significant gifts they offer us as therapists and the world at large. Sexual minority and gender variant boys are an important subgroup of boys who are unfortunately not always acknowledged in the male experience. By virtue of writing this chapter, we have chosen to include sexual minority and gender variant boys in the mainstream discussion on how clinicians treat boys and young men, realizing that while they are unique, they also simply need caring adults to provide acceptance and positive role models, as does any young man.

Furthermore, part of being a positive role model is broadening the discussion of the male experience through educating others and making LGBTQ issues more visible. Clinicians must always remember that work done outside the office, whether in the community, local church, LGBT center, or other public sector, can be just as important as work done behind a closed door. By making efforts in the community and within sessions, we have an invaluable opportunity to make a significant impact in the lives of young men.

REFERENCES

American Psychological Association, Division 44, Committee on Lesbian, Gay, and Bisexual Concerns Task Force. (2000). Guidelines for psychotherapy with lesbian, gay, and bisexual clients. *American Psychologist, 55*(12), 1440–1451.

Brill, S., & Pepper, R. (2008). *The transgender child: A handbook for families and professionals.* San Francisco, CA: Cleis Press, Inc.

Cass, V. C. (1979). Homosexual identity formation: A theoretical model. *Journal of Homosexuality, 4*(3), 219–235.

Cohler, B. J., & Hammack, P. L. (2007). The psychological world of the gay teenager: Social change, narrative, and "normality." *Journal of Youth and Adolescence, 36*(1), 47–59.

Coloroso, B. (2003). *The bully, the bullied and the bystander.* New York: Harper Resources.

Cossa, M. (2006). *Rebels with a cause: Working with adolescents using action techniques.* London, UK: Jessica Kingsley.

Devor, A. H. (2004). Witnessing and mirroring: A fourteen stage model of trans-sexual identity formation. *Journal of Gay and Lesbian Psychotherapy, 8*(1/2), 41–67.

Diaz, E. M., & Kosciw, J. G. (2009). *Shared differences: The experiences of lesbian, gay, bisexual, and transgender students of color in our nation's schools.* New York: GLSEN.

Di Ceglie, D. (2000). Gender identity disorder in young people. *Advances in Psychiatric Treatment, 6*(6), 458–466.

Emunah, R. (1994). *Acting for real: Drama therapy process, technique, and performance.* New York: Brunner/Mazel.

Ettner, R. (1999). *Gender loving care: A guide to counseling gender-variant clients.* New York: Norton.

Fontaine, J. H., & Hammond, N. L. (1996). Counseling issues with gay and lesbian adolescents. *Adolescence, 31*(124), 817–830.

Goodenow, C., Szalacha, L., & Westheimer, K. (2006). School support groups, other school factors, and the safety of sexual minority adolescents. *Psychology in the Schools, 43*(5), 573–589.

Greytak, E. A., Kosciw, J. G., & Diaz, E. M. (2009). *Harsh realities: The experiences of transgender youth in our nation's schools.* New York: GLSEN.

Hansen, A. L. (2007). School-based support for GLBT students: A review of three levels of research. *Psychology in the Schools, 44*(8), 839–848.

Jung, C. G. (1964). *Man and his symbols.* New York: Anchor.

Kayler, H., Lewis, T. F., & Davidson, E. (2008, January 31). Designing developmentally appropriate school counseling interventions for LGBQ students. *Journal of School Counseling, 6*(6). Retrieved March 8, 2009, from http://www.jsc.montana.edu/articles/v6n6.pdf

Kiselica, M. S., Mulé, M., & Haldeman D. C. (2008). Finding inner peace in a homophobic world: Counseling gay boys and boys who are questioning their sexual identity. In M. S. Kiselica, M. Englar-Carlson, & A. M. Horne (Eds.), *Counseling troubled boys* (pp. 243–271). New York: Routledge.

Kosciw, J. G., Diaz, E. M., & Greytak, E. A. (2008). *2007 National School Climate Survey: The experiences of lesbian, gay, bisexual and transgender youth in our nation's schools.* New York: GLSEN.

Lahad, M. (1992). Storymaking: An assessment method for coping with stress. In S. Jennings (Ed.), *Dramatherapy: Theory and practice 2* (pp. 150–163). London, UK: Routledge.

Landy, R. J. (1994). *Drama therapy: Concepts, theories and practices* (2nd ed.). Springfield, IL: Charles C. Thomas.

Lemoire, S. J., & Chen, C. P. (2005). Applying person-centered counseling to sexual minority adolescents. *Journal of Counseling and Development, 83*(2), 146–154.

Lev, A. I. (2004). *Transgender emergence: Therapeutic guidelines for working with gender-variant people and their families.* Binghamton, NY: Haworth Press.

Johnson, D. R., & Emunah, R. (Eds.). (2009). *Current approaches in drama therapy* (2nd ed.). Springfield, IL: Charles C. Thomas.

Lock, J. (1998). Treatment of homophobia in a gay male adolescent. *American Journal of Psychotherapy, 52*(2), 202–214.

Mallon, G. P., & DeCrescenzo, T. (2006). Transgender children and youth: A child welfare practice perspective. *Child Welfare, 82*(2), 215–241.

Menvielle, E., & Tuerk, C. (2002). A support group for parents of gender-non-conforming boys. *Journal of the American Academy of Child and Adolescent Psychiatry, 41*(8), 1010–1013.

Pearson, Q. M. (2003). Breaking the silence in the counselor education classroom: A training seminar on counseling sexual minority clients. *Journal of Counseling and Development, 81*(3), 292–300.

Peters, A. J. (2003). Isolation or inclusion: Creating safe spaces for lesbian and gay youth. *Families in Society, 84*(3), 331–337.

Poteat, P. V., Aragon, S. R., Espelage, D. L., & Koenig, B. W. (2009). Psychosocial concerns of sexual minority youth: Complexity and caution in group differences. *Journal of Consulting and Clinical Psychology, 77*(1), 196–201.

Robertson, L., & Monsen, J. (2001). Issues in the development of a gay or lesbian identity: Practice implications for educational psychologists. *Educational and Child Psychology, 18*(1), 13–31.

Ryan, C., Heubner, D., Diaz, R. M., & Sanchez, J. (2009). Family rejection as a predictor of negative health outcomes in White and Latino lesbian, gay, and bisexual young adults. *Pediatrics, 123*(1), 346–352.

Sanders, G. L., & Kroll, I. T. (2000). Generating stories of resilience: Helping gay and lesbian youth and their families. *Journal of Marital and Family Therapy, 26*(4), 433–442.

Sandfort, T. G. M., Melendez, R. M., & Diaz, R. M. (2007). Gender nonconformity, homophobia, and mental distress in Latino gay and bisexual men. *Journal of Sex Research, 44*(2), 181–189.

Saval, M. (2009). *The secret lives of boys: Inside the raw emotional world of male teens.* New York: Basic Books.

Savin-Williams, R. C., & Cohen, K. M. (2004). Homoerotic development during childhood and adolescence. *Child and Adolescent Psychiatric Clinics of North America, 13,* 529–549.

Savin-Williams, R. C., & Ream, G. L. (2003). Suicide attempts among sexual-minority male youth. *Journal of Clinical Child and Adolescent Psychology, 32*(4), 509–522.

Shirk, S. R., & Saiz, C. C. (1992). Clinical, empirical, and developmental perspectives on the therapeutic relationship in child psychotherapy. *Development and Psychopathology, 4,* 713–728.

Sternberg, P., & Garcia, A. (2000). *Sociodrama: Who's in your shoes?* (2nd ed.). Westport, CT: Praeger.

Troiden, R. R. (1989). The formation of homosexual identities. *Journal of Homosexuality, 17*(1–2), 43–73.

Weber, A. M., & Haen, C. (Eds.). (2005). *Clinical applications of drama therapy in child and adolescent treatment.* New York: Brunner-Routledge.

INDEX

A

Accommodation, 13
Affect attunement, 227
Affect, regulation of, 157
Affect, suppression of, 16, 43, 44
African American fathers (nonresident)
    and sons; strengthening bonds
    alcohol abuse assistance, 285–286
    challenges, 283
    content of program, 281–283
    criticisms of program, 283
    curriculum of fathers/sons program,
        271–272, 283–284
    demographics, 267
    fatherhood programs, 268
    help-seeking behavior, encouraging,
        284
    high-risk behaviors, links, 265–266
    interventions, 266
    mothers, role of, 286–287
    multiple sons, involvement of, 285
    overview, 270–271
    parent–child communication, 266
    risky behavior demographics, 267
    safe space, creating, 284–285
Aggression, male, 8, 11
    Alex, case study of, 91–93
    anger, antidotes to, 213–214
    case study, John (aggressive boy in
        school, labeled troublemaker),
        209–210, 211, 212–213, 214–215
    cycle of identity, use of with (see
        Cycle of identity)
    existential act, as, 201
    genetics elements, 20
    group work with, 202–203

intergroup conflict, 21
percussion therapy, 201–202
problematic, 205
time-out, declaring, 203–204
Aggression, relational, 21
Alcohol abuse, 285–286. *See also* High-
    risk behaviors
Alexithymia, 16, 71
Alpha males, 18, 20
Alternative schools, 82–83
Altruism, 65–66
Animal-assisted interventions with
    at-risk boys
    adjuncts to clinicians, animals as,
        125–127
    animal abuse, 118–119
    animal care, 128
    animal-children bond, 116–119
    animal-human bond, 116
    anthropomorphic attitudes toward
        animals, 116
    catalyst for discussion, animal as, 125
    conceptualizing, 120
    confidantes, pets as, 117
    emotional catalyst, animals as, 123
    Green Chimneys case, 115
    guidelines, 128
    intervention types and terminology,
        119–120
    pets, importance of to children,
        117–118
    social lubricant, animals as, 121–123
    stress buffer, animals as, 118
    teachers, animals as, 124–125
    therapist training in, 127

D

Dance movement therapy
  adapting to ADHD boys, 230–231
  case study, 231–235
  longitudinal study on use with
    emotionally and behaviorally
    disturbed children, 229–230
  movement skills, 230
  overview, 229
Dance therapy, 96–97
Delta Society's Pet Partner Program, 127
Devaluation of boys, 42
Development, male. *See* Male
  development
Developmentally delayed clients, 256
Dirty Harry image, 64
Disintegration
  aggressiveness as result of fears of,
    199
  anger as result of fears of, 198, 199
  overview, 198–199
  sadness as result of fears of, 199
Diversity in therapy, 80–81
Doing Anger Differently, 201
Domestic violence, 21
Dynamic play therapy
  adolescents, with, 103, 110–111
  attuned play, 100
  balloon games, 110
  description, 98
  directive *versus* nondirective
    activities, 101
  form/energy, 100–101
  hide-and-seek, 105
  infant games, 104
  monster, 106
  Mr. Opposite Man, 108–109
  older school-aged boys (8-12 years),
    with, 108–110
  parental involvement, 102, 103
  pillow games, 105
  play materials, 102, 103
  play room setup, 102
  principles of, 98–99
  school-aged boys (5-7 years), with,
    105–108
  screaming without making a noise,
    109

slow motion races, 109
therapist facilitation, 99, 101–102, 103
toddler games, 104–105
tug-of-war, 107
verbalization, use of, 101–102
volcano, 109
wrestling play, 106–107
younger children (0 to 4 years), with,
  103–105
younger children, with, 103

E

Educated Canines Assisting with
  Disabilities, 124
Educational kinesiology, 251, 260
Efficacy, treatment, 6
  defining, 24
  strengths, recognizing, 25
  tailoring treatment, 25
Emotional constriction, 41
Emotional expression, range of, 49
Empathy, 21–22
  developing, through use of dogs,
    122 (*see also* Animal-assisted
    interventions with at-risk
    boys)
Engagement in therapy, 43–44, 44
Entry, portals of, 46
Environment, therapy, 27
Erikson, Erik, 184
Ethics, enhancing in cases of aggressive
  boys, 211–212
Expression of emotions, Western
  constraints on, 44

F

Family relationships, fostering, 31
Fathers
  absent, 31, 164–165
  African American nonresident (*see*
    African American fathers
    (nonresident) and sons)
  male development, influence on,
    156–157
  physical play, involving in (*see*
    Physical play as part of
    therapy)